What Critics and P...
About the "Imp...

What Seasoned Travelers Say

THE TREASURES AND
PLEASURES OF INDIA

Books & CD-ROMs by Drs. Ron and Caryl Krannich

101 Dynamite Answers to Interview Questions
101 Secrets of Highly Effective Speakers
201 Dynamite Job Search Letters
Best Jobs For the 21st Century
Change Your Job, Change Your Life
The Complete Guide to International Jobs and Careers
The Complete Guide to Public Employment
The Directory of Federal Jobs and Employers
Discover the Best Jobs for You!
Dynamite Cover Letters
Dynamite Networking For Dynamite Jobs
Dynamite Resumes
Dynamite Salary Negotiations
Dynamite Tele-Search
The Educator's Guide to Alternative Jobs and Careers
Find a Federal Job Fast!
From Air Force Blue to Corporate Gray
From Army Green to Corporate Gray
From Navy Blue to Corporate Gray
Get a Raise in Seven Days
High Impact Resumes and Letters
International Jobs Directory
Interview For Success
Job-Power Source CD-ROM
Jobs and Careers With Nonprofit Organizations
Jobs For People Who Love to Travel
Mayors and Managers
Moving Out of Education
Moving Out of Government
The Politics of Family Planning Policy
Re-Careering in Turbulent Times
Resumes & Job Search Letters For Transitioning Military Personnel
Savvy Interviewing
Savvy Resume Writer
Shopping and Traveling in Exotic Asia
Shopping in Exotic Places
Shopping the Exotic South Pacific
Treasures and Pleasures of Australia
Treasures and Pleasures of China
Treasures and Pleasures of Hong Kong
Treasures and Pleasures of India
Treasures and Pleasures of Indonesia
Treasures and Pleasures of Italy
Treasures and Pleasures of Paris and the French Riviera
Treasures and Pleasures of Singapore and Bali
Treasures and Pleasures of Singapore and Malaysia
Treasures and Pleasures of Thailand
Ultimate Job Source CD-ROM

IMPACT GUIDES

THE TREASURES
AND PLEASURES OF

India

BEST OF THE BEST

RON AND CARYL KRANNICH, PH.DS

IMPACT PUBLICATIONS
MANASSAS PARK, VA

THE TREASURES AND PLEASURES OF INDIA: BEST OF THE BEST

Cover Art: Courtesy of the Government of India Tourist Office.

Library of Congress Cataloging-in-Publication Data

Krannich, Ronald L.
　　The treasures and pleasures of India: best of the best /
Ronald L. Krannich, Caryl Rae Krannich.
　　　　p.　cm.—(Impact guides)
　　Includes bibliographical references and index.
　　ISBN 1-57023-056-0 (alk. paper)
　　I. Shopping—India—Guidebooks.　2. India—
Description and travel. 3. India—Guidebooks.
I. Krannich, Caryl Rae. II. Series.
TX337.I4 K73　　2000
380.1'45'9992554—dc21　　　　　　　　　　99-052152

Publisher: For information, including current and forthcoming publications, authors, press kits, and submission guidelines, visit Impact's web site: *www.impactpublications.com*

Publicity/Rights: For information on publicity, author interviews, and subsidiary rights, contact the Public Relations and Marketing Department: Tel. 703/361-7300 or Fax 703/335-9486.

Sales/Distribution: For information on distribution or quantity discount rates, call (703/361-7300), fax (703/335-9486), e-mail (*india@impactpublications.com*) or write: Sales Department, Impact Publications, 9104-N Manassas Drive, Manassas Park, VA 20111-5211. Bookstore sales are handled through Impact's trade distributor: National Book Network, 15200 NBN Way, Blue Ridge Summit, PA 17214, Tel. 1-800-462-6420.

Contents

PART I
Traveling Smart

PART III
Nine Indias For Treasures and Pleasures

Liabilities and Warranties

While the authors have attempted to provide accurate and up-to-date information in this book, please be advised that names, addresses, and phone numbers do change and shops, restaurants, and hotels do move, go out of business, or change ownership and management. Such changes are a constant fact of life in India. We regret any inconvenience such changes may cause to your travel plans.

Inclusion of shops, restaurants, hotels, and other hospitality providers in this book in no way implies guarantees nor endorsements by either the authors or publisher. The information and recommendations appearing in this book are provided solely for your reference. The honesty and reliability of shops is best ensured by **you**—always ask the right questions and request proper receipts and documents. Chapter 5, as well as individual city chapters, provide useful tips on how to best do this in India.

The Treasures and Pleasures of India provides numerous tips on how you can best experience a trouble-free adventure. As in any unfamiliar place or situation, or regardless of how trusting strangers may appear, the watch-words are always the same—*"watch your wallet!"* If it's too good to be true, it probably is. Any *"unbelievable deals"* should be treated as such. In India, as well as in the rest of the world, there simply is no such thing as a free lunch. Everything has a cost.

Preface

Welcome to another Impact Guide on the treasures and pleasures of shopping and traveling to a very special place—India. Join us as we explore this fascinating country from a very different perspective than what is normally found in other travel guidebooks or, for that matter, in any other book written on India.

India is big, it's challenging, and it's incredibly seductive. Like others who have gone before us, you'll quickly discover there is never a dull moment in India. And you may or may not be prepared for the "India experience" that seems to come at you from so many different directions. In the end, you won't be indifferent to this place. It touches you in so many ways, both positive and negative.

If you are familiar with our other Impact Guides, you know our books are very different from most guidebooks. We operate from a particular perspective and we frequently show our attitude rather than just present you with "the travel facts." We're not budget travelers who are interested in taking you along the low road to India; we don't find that to be an attractive road nor particularly enlightening. We've been there, done that. If that's the way you want to do India, you'll find lots of great guidebooks on budget travel to India. At the same time, we're not big on immersing ourselves in local history and taking in lots of sightseeing. We get just enough history and sightseeing to make our travels interesting rather than obsessive. And we're not preoccupied with hotels, restaurants, cultural shows, and other forms of entertainment.

What we really enjoy doing, and think we do it well, is shop. Indeed, we're street people who love "the chase" and the serendipity that comes with our style of travel. We especially enjoy discovering quality products; meeting local artists and craftspeople; unraveling new travel and shopping rules; making new friendships with local business people; staying in fine places; and dining in the best restaurants where we often meet the talented chefs and visit their fascinating kitchens.

Like Winston Churchill and many other focused travelers, our travel philosophy is very simple:

My needs are very simple—I simply want the best of everything.

When we travel, we seek out the best of the best—just like we often do back home. In the case of India, we want to discover the works of the best artists, craftspeople, and jewelers. In so doing, we learn a great deal about India and its talented people. For us, shopping makes for great travel adventure.

Exotic India offers wonderful treasures and pleasures for those who know what to look for, where to go, and how to best enjoy this fascinating country.

The chapters that follow represent a particular perspective on travel to India. We purposefully decided to write more than just another travel guide with a few pages on shopping. While other books briefly examine the "whats" and "wheres" of shopping, we saw a need to also explain the "how-tos" of shopping in India. Such a book would both educate and guide you through India's slippery shopping maze as well as put you in contact with the best of the best in accommodations, restaurants, and sightseeing. Accordingly, this book focuses primarily on the shopping **process** as well as provides the necessary details for making excellent shopping **choices** in specific shopping areas, arcades, shops, and markets.

Rather than just describe the "what" and "where" of travel and shopping, we include the critical "how"—what to do before you depart on your trip and when you are in India. We believe you are best served with a book which leads to both **understanding and action**. Therefore, you'll find little in these pages about the history, culture, economics, and politics of India; these topics are covered well in other types of books. Instead, we focus on the whole shopping process in reference to India's major shopping strengths.

The perspective we develop throughout this book is based on our belief that traveling should be more than just another adventure in eating, sleeping, sightseeing, and taking pictures of unfamiliar places. Whenever possible, we attempt to bring to life the fact that India has real people and interesting products that you, the visitor, will find exciting. This is a country of talented designers, craftspeople, traders, and entrepreneurs who offer you some wonderful opportunities to participate in their society through their shopping process. When you leave India, you will take with you not only some unique experiences and memories but also quality products that you will certainly appreciate for years to come.

Our focus on **the shopping process** is important for several reasons. The most important one is the fact that few travelers are prepared for India's shopping culture. Shops may be filled with familiar looking goods, but when there are no price tags on items, the process of acquiring them can be difficult if you do not understand such basic processes as bargaining, communicating, and shipping. What, for example, should you do when you find a lovely painting, antique, or piece of jewelry but no price tag is displayed? How do you know you are paying a "fair" price? More importantly, how do you know you are getting exactly what you bargained for in terms of quality and authenticity? And if you buy large items, how will you get them back home? These "how" questions go beyond the basic "what" and "where" of shopping to ensure that you have a successful and rewarding trip to India.

We have not hesitated to make qualitative judgments about the best of the best in India. If we just presented you with shopping and traveling information, we would do you a disservice by not sharing our discoveries, both good and bad. While we know that our judgments may not be valid for everyone, we offer them as **reference points** from which you can make your own decisions. Our major emphasis is on quality shopping, accommodations, dining, and sightseeing, and in that order. We look for shops which offer excellent quality and styles. If you share our concern for quality shopping, as well as fine restaurants and hotels, you will find many of our recommendations useful to your India adventure.

Buying items of quality does not mean you must spend a great deal of money on shopping. It means that you have taste, you are selective, you buy what fits into your wardrobe and home. If you shop in the right places, you will find quality products. If you understand the shopping process, you will get good value for your money. Shopping for quality may not be cheap but neither need it be expensive. But most important, shopping for quality in India is fun and it results in lovely items which can be enjoyed for years to come!

Throughout this book we have included "tried and tested" shopping information. We make judgments based upon our experience—not on judgments or sales pitches from others. Our research was quite simple: we did a great deal of shopping and we looked for quality products. We acquired some fabulous items, and gained valuable knowledge in the process. However, we could not make purchases in every shop nor do we have any guarantee that your experiences will be the same as ours. Shops close, ownership or management changes, and the shop you visit may not be the same as the one we shopped. So use this information as a starting point, but ask questions and make your own judgments before you buy.

We wish to thank the Government of India Tourist Office for their assistance with this project in both 1992 and 1998. They are justly proud and enthusiastic about what India has to offer visitors who still know so little about their country. We also want to thank the many public relations managers and concierges who shared their insights into travel and shopping in India as well as Northwest Airlines who took us safely to and from India in exceptional comfort and with excellent service.

We wish you well with your India adventure. The book is designed to be used prior to and during your stay in India. If you **plan your journey** according to the first three chapters, **handle the shopping process** according to the next two chapters, and **navigate the streets** of India based on the nine city destination chapters, you should have a marvelous time. You'll discover some exciting places, acquire some choice items, and return home with many fond memories. In the end, the shopping side of India may also become seductive as you decide to return again to explore India's many other treasures and pleasures. You definitely will not be indifferent to India. If you put this book to use, it should become one of your best travel friends—the ultimate passport to the unique treasures and pleasures of exotic India!

Ron and Caryl Krannich

The Treasures And
Pleasures Of India

INDIA

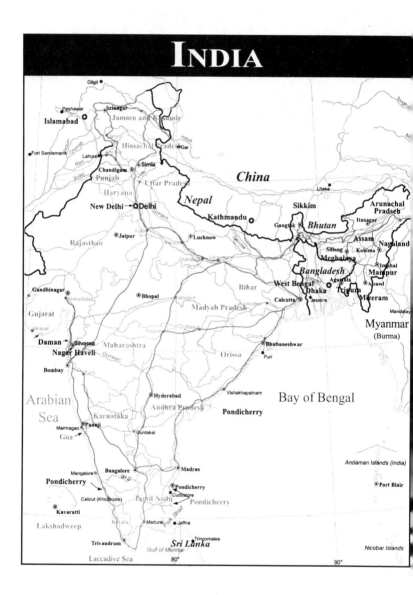

Gilgit

Peshawar
Islamabad
Srinagar
Jammu and Kashmir

Fort Sandeman
Lahore
Chandigarh
Simla
Punjab
Himachal Pradesh
Gar

Indus

New Delhi → Delhi
Haryana
Uttar Pradesh
Nepal
China
Lhasa

Sikkim
Arunachal Pradseh
Itanagar

Jaipur
Lucknow
Kathmandu
Gangtok
Bhutan

Rajasthan

Assam
Nagaland
Sillong
Kohima
Meghalaya

Gandhinagar
Ahmadabad
Bhopal
Bihar
Bangladesh
West Bengal
Agartala
Dhaka
Tripura
Manipur
Imphal
Aizawl
Mizeram

Gujarat
Madyah Pradesh
Calcutta
Jessore

Veraval
Mandalay

Daman
Silvassa
Nagar Haveli
Maharashtra
Orissa
Bhubaneshwar
Puri

Myanmar
(Burma)

Bombay

Arabian
Sea
Hyderabad
Andhra Pradesh
Vishakhapatnam
Pondicherry
Bay of Bengal

Karnataka

Marmagao
Panaji
Goa
Guntakal

Andaman Islands (India)

Mangalore
Bangalore
Madras
Port Blair

Pondicherry
Calicut (Khozikode)
Pondicherry
Cuddalore
Pondicherry
Tamil Nadu

Kavaratti

Kerala
Madurai
Jaffna

Lakshadweep

Trivandrum
Trincomalee
Sri Lanka
Gulf of Mannar
Nicobar Islands

Laccadive Sea
80°
90°

Welcome to
Surprising India

Welcome to the wonderful treasures and pleasures of fascinating, colorful, and compelling India. You're in for an unforgettable adventure, one that you will probably relive with amazement for many years to come. If this is your first trip to India, you're in for a real treat. You are about to discover a country and people unlike any you have ever encountered. It may overwhelm you, and then seduce you. If this is a return trip, much of what you learned about India will quickly come back to you. Indeed, many things never seem to change in India, especially its complexity, chaos, and exotic embrace. India remains intoxicating. At the same time, you'll recognize a "New India," one that has undergone rapid economic development during the past decade, especially in major metropolitan areas where new hotels, restaurants, shops, factories, and roads continue to proliferate in the midst of the "Old India."

A TYPE OF WORLDLINESS

Steeped in a rich history, exhibiting numerous traditions, yet operating in a thoroughly modern world, India exudes a certain

1

worldliness that at times seems to encompass centuries in a single moment. Bustling and intoxicating, India is all about tolerating and managing heady chaos. The living chaos throbs everywhere. Overcrowded buses, trucks, and cars honk their horns in the midst of a steady stream of oxen carts, camels, goats, and cows that meander down the streets seemingly unaffected by the surging masses of humanity that appear to come at you from all directions. You instantly recognize 200 years of transportation modes converging on you. This is street theater without a director; crowded, contentious, and often confused, everyone seems to be doing their own thing, coming and going in a riotous parade of color and striking composures.

> ❑ India is an unforgettable adventure–one you'll relive for many years to come.
>
> ❑ India is all about tolerating and managing heady chaos.
>
> ❑ There's never a dull moment in India.
>
> ❑ India is both a physical and spiritual adventure.

Then take to the highway by car and you may think you've been taken on a suicidal ride as you dodge speeding trucks and buses, abandoned wrecks, and all types of potential road kill. You'll instantly understand what is meant when your speeding driver tries to calm your nerves by explaining India's fateful rule of the road: *"To drive in India, you need three things: good horn, good brakes, good luck."* Hopefully, you also have a good driver!

There's never a dull moment in India. With eyes wide open, or shut, you somehow survive this colorful, noisy, and often steamy chaos. India is a world unto its own.

Welcome to India. It's both a physical and spiritual adventure. From the moment you arrive until the day you leave, India will continually test your concepts of comfort, convenience, efficiency, and common sense as its charming and not-so-charming chaos assaults your senses and sensibilities like no other place you've ever visited. If you are in search of the real India, you have a long and challenging road ahead. It's a big and diverse country with lots of people and many interesting things to see and do, including shopping for unique treasures produced by India's many talented artists and craftspeople.

THE ULTIMATE TRAVEL CHALLENGE

This is definitely an exotic place that seems to engage all of your senses simultaneously. Offering a visual and sometimes bewildering feast of sights, sounds, and smells, India is many things to many different people. Some people fall in love with

India; they return again and again to pursue its many fascinating treasures and pleasures. To them, India is addictive; each trip yields another exciting adventure in one of the world's most interesting cultures. Others, who expect a certain level of basic orderliness, cleanliness, and service, find India at best challenging and at worst appalling and forgettable; they can't wait to return to their own world of orderliness, predictability, and cleanliness. Many have difficulty understanding why anyone would want to go to India. And still others both love and hate it, depending on the time of day, place, and people they encounter. This is not neat and tidy Europe, orderly North America and Australia, nor structured and sanitary East Asia. As you will quickly discover, India beats to its own drummer, who is loud but never quite clear, nor in time, nor in tune.

> ❑ India beats to its own drummer, who is loud but never quite clear, nor in time, nor in tune.
>
> ❑ India touches the whole range of emotions.
>
> ❑ India's uniqueness is what makes it such an interesting and special place to visit.

Whether you come to love it or hate it, chances are you won't be indifferent to India. It's not that type of travel experience. India is a very special place, a complex society that tends to generate strong emotions. You'll most definitely have strong feelings toward this country, its people, and its amalgam of cultures. India has a reality and logic of its own that often defy description or explanation. Like many other Third World countries, there is a certain worn, broken, makeshift, confusing, and sometimes mystical quality about this place; "yes" often means "no" and vice versa; maintenance seems to be a foreign concept; and vehicles do seem to mysteriously get up and running after breaking down. You simply have to be in India to understand its reality and logic, or lack thereof.

Above all, India touches the whole range of emotions. For most people, it all begins when they apply for a visa and next pass through India's chaotic immigration lines and airports; these initial "India experiences" immediately draw strong reactions. It challenges your senses and sensibilities as well as questions your real tolerance levels for the downside of travel—lines (or the lack thereof), crowds, chaos, bureaucratic inertia, miscommunication, and stupid mistakes people make. You'll see and do things in India that you never imagined or thought were possible. Your stories of travel and encounters in India will perhaps be the most interesting and humorous of any trip. India most likely will linger with you for many years.

Regardless of your predispositions for India, we believe you'll have a wonderful time exploring this fascinating place; it may well become one of your favorite travel destinations. At least that's our wish—that you have an absolutely marvelous travel and shopping adventure, indeed, one of the best trips you've ever taken anywhere. India's sites, smells, sounds, and colors are truly unique, and it's this uniqueness that makes India such an interesting and special place to visit. May it embrace you in a very special way.

Best of all, you'll discover numerous treasures and pleasures and learn that not all are material in nature. India is as much an Eastern spiritual experience (reputed to be the home of 330 million gods and goddesses and thousands of temples, mosques and churches!) as it is a Western material experience. Like many other travelers who have preceded you to this fabled and flawed land, you'll forever wonder what India, and life, is all about. When you return home, you'll have pictures and purchases that only tell part of your "India story." And you may surprise yourself with having unwittingly compiled so many interesting travel stories you can tell about your "India experience." And it's in your story-telling that both spiritual and material India come to life.

A LAND OF MANY UNIQUE MOMENTS

India is the world's second largest country and the world's largest democracy with nearly 1 billion people. Unless you've been living there too long to notice anymore, India really is big, crowded, worn, and often hot, steamy, and dirty. It is people everywhere. Indeed, it's often difficult to escape from people, unless you are on a special meditation track. If it had a background color, it would be a combination of dusty green, fading brown, and ochre. For most outsiders, India looks and feels intimidating. It's about suffering the pains of excess population scrambling to make a living in what was once considered the world's most impoverished place.

❑ India is the world's largest democracy with nearly 1 billion people.

❑ For most outsiders, India looks and feels intimidating.

❑ India boasts the world's largest middle class of 375 million.

❑ It's best to approach India with a very laid-back, "no problem" attitude.

Today, many people talk about a "New India," one that is only 50 years old as a nation, one boasting the world's largest middle class of 375 million people whose highly educated and talented classes harbor the world's second largest number of high-tech workers who turn out an impressive array of innovative software (exporting nearly $3 billion each year). It's a huge and diverse country undergoing a massive transformation as it enters the 21st century global economy in competition with its giant northern neighbor, China. Foreign investors and exporters look upon India with a very different set of eyes than they did ten or twenty years ago. Perhaps lots of money can be made from this so-called new middle class, even though this class makes less than US$1,000 a year!

For many uninitiated outsiders looking in, India seems to have tremendous potential, especially given its huge population which in the past was seen as a major impediment to development. If only it could shed much of its inert Byzantine government bureaucracy, India could soon have its day in the sun as it emerges as the world's largest consumer market, out-pacing the much hyped China market. As you will quickly discover, India is just full of interesting surprises, even for people who feel they really know her. If there is any good time to visit India, it is now. It will never be the same.

NOTHING COMES EASY IN INDIA

Some things are never meant to be. It's true what they say about India—nothing comes easy here, including your initial application for a visa. It's a place that often complicates even the simple things in life. For travelers on a tight schedule, such complications can disrupt plans and force one into revising schedules. If you're in a hurry, India will most likely slow you down to its own muddling pace.

Travel can become very painful if you don't approach it with the right understanding and attitude. Whatever you do, please expect to encounter difficulties when traveling and shopping in India. While nothing seems to work right, at least things do function tolerably well, although usually at the last moment as they muddle through in an ad hoc, makeshift, crisis management manner. If you want to best enjoy India, you must approach it with a very laid-back, "no problem" attitude; a sense of humor; and a tolerance for the unusual and unexpected. Take it easy and expect to encounter frustrations at every stage of your trip. In the end, many of your so-called problems will become humorous stories about the challenges of traveling in India. There is always another tomorrow.

A TRIP WELL WORTH TAKING

Similar to traveling in China, we and many others have long been ambivalent about traveling to India—a kind of love-hate relationship we develop with a country we know so little about yet find so alluring as well as expect to be difficult navigating on our own. India has always been one of those places we wanted to visit but really never got around to because of other priorities, commitments, and perhaps a reluctance to take on such a formidable challenge. India has long been a budget and adventure destination, not particularly noted for great travel amenities, such as quality hotels, restaurants, and tours, or quality shopping. When we wanted to visit India and include Kashmir, it always seemed the military shut Kashmir down because of armed conflicts with Pakistan which continue to this very day.

Despite the glossy travel brochures of the beautiful and romantic Taj Mahal, colorful Hindu temples, exotic ruins, lush tropical jungles, and intriguing wildlife, India remains a special challenge for many travelers. But it's a trip well worth taking today. India is still the perfect place for adventuresome budget travelers who find the cost of traveling and living within India to be extremely inexpensive. Indeed, many such travelers, with lots of time on their hands, decide to settle down in India for several months to absorb the spiritual side of this vast country which can be a truly inexpensive place; many also include a trekking adventure to neighboring Nepal. For history and religious buffs familiar with this subcontinent's history and the world's great religions, it doesn't get much better than India. This is one of the world's oldest civilizations with a large collection of stone monuments, carved figures, majestic fortresses, and intriguing palaces still standing to prove that this was once the home to great empires, opulent rulers, and important religious forces.

❏ India is one of the world's oldest civilizations.

❏ For history and religious buffs, it doesn't get much better than India.

❏ India is all about diversity and complexity.

❏ The 26 states that make up modern India in many respects represent 26 different Indias.

From the snowcapped mountains and foothill valleys in the north to the plateaus, tropical rain forests, and sandy deserts in the east, west, and center to the stone temples, ruins, and palm fringed beaches in the south, India is all about diversity and complexity. The 26 states that make up modern India in many respects represent 26 different Indias. To see it all would take several grueling months, and even then you might not feel you've seen the real India.

Whatever you do, decide to visit India soon. It's an extremely interesting and diverse country in great transition. It's both a very modern and traditional place. On the one hand, it boasts a thoroughly hip Indian-style MTV generation with steamy movies, videos, television shows, music, dance, and beauty pageants centered in Mumbai (Bombay). On the other hand, visit other cities, such as Varanasi and Chennai, and you'll step back into traditional, religious India that seems to be centuries apart from Westernized and material Mumbai and New Delhi. As you will quickly discover, much of the old and new coexist simultaneously in India. The vast panorama that makes up India will both fascinate and entertain you in many ways. It may well enrich your life forever.

DISCOVERING NINE INDIAS

Depending on where you visit, each region and city in India has it own distinctive character. Our selection of destinations is somewhat arbitrary, although centered around our concept of the best of the best in traveling and shopping in India. We had neither the time nor desire to cover all of India. We leave that task to more general and comprehensive guide books that take "travel" as their central theme. Our focus is on quality travel and shopping in India. We chose destinations that offer excellent quality travel amenities, interesting sites, and good shopping opportunities. In addition, we selected popular areas that could be covered in a fast-paced two- to four-week trip. This inevitably led to selecting such major cities and well traveled destinations as Mumbai (Bombay), Delhi, Varanasi, Agra, and Jaipur. We also selected the fascinating cities of Jodhpur and Udaipur in colorful Rajasthan because of their unique arts and crafts; the pearl city of Hyderabad in south central India because of its unique shopping emphasis; and Chennai (Madras) because of its strategic southeastern coastal location. In each of these cities, we sought out the best of the best in traveling and shopping. The remainder of this book outlines our discoveries in these nine destinations. For us, these are our nine Indias.

MUMBAI (BOMBAY)

The name has been changed to Mumbai, but most people still know it as Bombay. Home to over 15 million people, Mumbai is a city of great wealth and poverty, a place where India's rich and famous settle and where Asia's largest slum, the Dharvani, houses over 1 million people. Mumbai also is home to India's largest middle class. Whether you are rich or poor, Mumbai is an entrepreneurial city of great economic and social promise.

Located along the west coast and facing the Arabian Sea,

Mumbai is India's most cosmopolitan commercial and industrial center; some might say it's also India's most decadent city that tends to set controversial Western trends in India. Unlike any other city in India, bustling Mumbai exudes an image of India's future. Its high-rise commercial buildings, five-star hotels, night clubs, trendy restaurants and pubs, chic boutiques, nuclear power plant, factories, banks, stock market, movie studios, stately Victorian buildings, busy harbor, and growing suburbs seem to rise above the slums that surround this vibrant city. Mumbai is also a city of young entrepreneurs and highly educated professionals who are largely responsible for moving India into the global economy. Much of Mumbai is all about making and spending money. Just hang around the lobbies of the Taj Mahal and Oberoi Hotels and you'll see a steady stream of local and foreign businesspeople doing what they do best —business.

Mumbai also is a great place to shop for arts, antiques, silk, jewelry, furniture, home decorative items, and crafts. You can easily spend three days in Mumbai just exploring its many shops, shopping arcades, markets, and factories.

While Mumbai may not represent the "real" India, it does have its own character, and it represents a thoroughly Western image of India's future that has little to do with religion but a lot to do with economics and consumerism. Whatever you do, make sure you include Mumbai in your travel plans. In fact, you may want to start your India adventure in Mumbai. If you begin in Mumbai, you may find this is the easiest place to begin making the transition to a more traditional and religious India which you will soon discover in other parts of the country.

DELHI

All roads and air routes seem to converge on New Delhi, India's rapidly developing capital of nearly 10 million people. Consisting of two contiguous cities—Delhi (old) and New Delhi—separated by a street and different settlement patterns, this is a sprawling metropolitan area that is relatively easy to get around in, except for the traffic and people which have a tendency to disrupt the best laid travel and shopping plans! Chances are you will begin your India adventure here simply because of the convenience of direct international flights into New Delhi. While not as large as Mumbai or Calcutta, New Delhi is not far behind. It's the city of government, industry, commerce, and many historical monuments. Some people dislike New Delhi because it doesn't look or feel like the "Old

India." It's largely a creation of a great Muslim dynasty, 20th century British colonial rule, a post-independence government, and an expanding business community involved in banking, transportation, manufacturing, and technology. You'll find lots of architecture and monuments reflecting each of these key forces that have shaped Delhi's diverse and expanding urban landscape during the past 400 years. But the last 20 years of development have significantly transformed this city.

While Mumbai is to India what New York is to the U.S., Delhi is to India what Washington, DC is to the U.S.—it is a low-rise capital with tree-lined streets, gardens, and parks as well as numerous traffic jams. It's also a relatively clean city, especially in the areas with wide boulevards, government offices, and diplomatic quarters. The fastest growing metropolis in India, New Delhi is filled with unique treasures and pleasures that deserve at least a four-day visit. In fact, some of India's best shopping will be found in New Delhi. If you love shopping and only have time to visit one city, make sure it's New Delhi. It may not be India, but it's certainly close enough for us to spend several days here! You should have a wonderful time discovering many of India's unique treasures and pleasures in New Delhi. It may well become your favorite shopping destination and central shipping point in India, and you'll most likely indulge yourself in many of New Delhi's fine restaurants and hotels. After awhile, you'll wonder why some people still dislike New Delhi. They really miss out on some of India's great buys and delightful sightseeing.

- ❑ Mumbai is an entrepreneurial city of great economic and social promise.

- ❑ Delhi is a city of government, industry, commerce, and many historical monuments.

- ❑ Varanasi is India's most sacred city, the religious center of Hinduism. It's also one big hospice.

- ❑ The "Golden Triangle" consists of Delhi, Agra, and Jaipur, three of India's best cities for shopping.

VARANASI

The crumbling and clanging ancient city of Varanasi, also known by the locals as Banaras, is one of the most unique, exotic, and fascinating urban experiences you'll find anywhere in the world. If you're interested in traditional Hindu India, great photographic opportunities, and purchasing religious paraphernalia, make sure you include Varanasi on your itinerary. It's India's most sacred city, the religious center of Hinduism, a major learning center, and one of the world's oldest and most holy cities. It's also a colorful and noisy city of over 2,000 temples and shrines and hundreds of minarets, domes, pinnacles, and towers. It's the only place we have ever encountered in which traffic becomes so completely ensnared that it's literally impossible for anyone to move for at least a half hour, despite the presence and heroic efforts of traffic police! Simply amazing. For tourists, Varanasi is also a photographer's dream come true where the old saying that *"a picture is worth a thousand words"* really is true. Get ready to experience a very different India in Varanasi. Some people mistakenly think this may be the "real" India. It's not. It's merely one of the most interesting of many Indias you will encounter.

Located nearly 800 kilometers southeast of Delhi on the road to Calcutta, Varanasi is a city of nearly 1.3 million residents as well as thousands of uncounted religious pilgrims and tourists who come here and to the nearby city of Sarnath, one of Buddhism's most sacred cities. Located along the Ganges River, this is one of India's most crowded, congested, and polluted cities. It's also one of the great visual feasts and time warps of travel—people, traffic, markets, architecture, temples, transportation modes, dress, and a wide range of fascinating street activities. It could be the 18th, 19th, or 20th century or perhaps the 12th, 13th, and 14th centuries. Except for the erratic electricity and motorized vehicles, you could easily imagine yourself being in one of these other centuries. No wonder so many pilgrims come here to meditate!

Narrow streets and lanes packed with people and the rhythmic sounds of clanging temple gongs lead to the river's edge where pilgrims from all over India and abroad come to be blessed by the holy waters of the Ganges. Varanasi also is one big outdoor hospice—many come here to die, to be cremated along the banks of the river, and to have their ashes cast on the water. For some visitors, this can be a disturbing city with all its people, many deformed and struggling for survival—oppressive crowds—and poor sanitation. For others, Varanasi is simply a fascinating city, a "must see" when visiting India. Indeed, it may well become one of the major highlights of visiting India.

There's never a dull moment here. Bodies burn; beggars and touts abound; religious followers bathe and drink from the polluted river; holy men meditate and wander; colorful religious sects congregate; and brides and grooms joined by large entourages of relatives and guests congregate to complete their marriage ritual along the banks of the Ganges River. In the midst of all this, tourists roll their cameras, rent boats to get a different view of the river drama, and try to make sense of what is one of the most amazing and spontaneous outdoor theaters. Behind the concrete staircase (ghats) and buildings fronting the river lies a labyrinth of narrow lanes, small shops, and Hindu temples catering to the material and spiritual needs of the thousands of new pilgrims the descend on this ancient and worn city each day.

People watching may well become your favorite pastime in Varanasi. No other city in India has such interesting and fascinating people-watching opportunities. After awhile you may unwittingly find yourself staring at people who make up this theater.

Because of potential cultural shock, it's best to visit Varanasi after transitioning from Mumbai, Delhi, or some other less extreme city. Plan to spend at least two days in Varanasi. After that, the place becomes redundant, and you'll begin suffering the pains of traffic, pollution, and crowds. Varanasi is one of those places where you'll be glad you came and you'll probably be glad you're leaving. This is heady stuff. Once you leave Varanasi, you'll enter into a very different India and perhaps a very different century!

AGRA

Agra is home to India's most enduring symbol—the Taj Mahal —the sprawling Agra Fort (Red Fort), and a few other noted monuments that date to the 16th and 17th centuries when Agra was the capital of the Mughal rulers. Going to India without visiting the "Taj" is like visiting France without seeing the Eiffel Tower. It's a "must see" attraction that, despite the sometimes awesome crowds, does not disappoint the visitor. Despite its slow deterioration due to air pollution, the Taj is still beautiful, romantic, and inspiring, more so than in many photographs.

Located 200 kilometers south of Delhi (four hours by car or two hours by train) in the state of Uttar Pradesh and situated along the right bank of the heavily polluted Yamuna River, Agra is part of the popular "Golden Triangle" that includes Delhi, Jaipur, and Agra. Once a great medieval Mughal city noted for its distinctive and grand Muslim art, architecture, and culture, today Agra is a crowded, bustling, dusty, and polluted tourist and industrial city of nearly 1 million people. It's a primary destination for most first-time visitors to India who come here to see the fabled Taj Mahal. They often plan a long full-day trip or an overnight in Agra.

But Agra is much more than just the Taj Mahal, crumbling fortresses, and tales of Mughal history. It's also a shopper's paradise for gems, marble, leather, and a large variety of arts and crafts. Indeed, unknown to most visitors, much of India's gem cutting is done in Agra which partly explains why prices tend to be better here than in other places, such as Jaipur, which are reputed to be India's inexpensive gem centers.

If you decide to include Agra in your travel plans, we recommend staying overnight so you will have enough time to see the major sites and shop. A one-day trip to Agra will only permit enough time to see the Taj Mahal, Agra Fort, and a few other sites. You may be disappointed to later learn that you missed out on some of India's best shopping by not allotting enough time in Agra.

JAIPUR

Jaipur exudes the image of Maharajas who controlled great wealth and operated forts, country estates, and other symbols of this city's once powerful and wealthy Rajput rulers. Founded in 1727, Jaipur is the capital and gateway city to the legendary state of Rajasthan. Surrounded by the dry and barren Aravalli Hills, Jaipur boasts a population of nearly 1.8 million. The third city in the "Golden Triangle," Jaipur is located 261 kilometers southwest of Delhi. It takes about four hours by car to reach Jaipur from either Delhi or Agra.

Colorful and crowded, Jaipur has its own distinctive character that makes it such an interesting place to visit. It's a city of color, from pink walls and colorful textiles to red turbaned residents. Also known as the "Pink City," because of the pink walls of the old city, Jaipur's bustling bazaars, street shops, palaces, museums, and nearby fort (Amber Fort) delight most who visit this exotic and energetic city. For many visitors, Jaipur is a shopper's paradise for jewelry, textiles, miniature paintings, and puppets. Shop its many bazaars and jewelry shops and you'll leave Jaipur with a treasure trove of memorable purchases.

Given Jaipur's many attractions, it's best to stay one or two nights in or around the city. Its many quality hotels and restaurants, along with attractive palace hotels and resorts, make Jaipur one of the most pleasant places to stay in India. It will not disappoint you.

JODHPUR

The gateway city to the Desert Triangle of Jaisalmer and Bikaner, Jodhpur is a pleasant surprise for many visitors who find this friendly and attractive city a shopper's paradise. A city of nearly 800,000 people, it's a city with a magnificent towering fort, marble palaces, distinctive temples, narrow streets, and bustling markets. It's also a favorite destination for many foreign dealers who come here to buy container-loads of distinctive handicrafts and furniture for resale in Europe and North America. In contrast to many other cities, Jodhpur is a relatively tout- and beggar-free city where you can leisurely shop without being hassled by many entrepreneurial strangers.

This also is the city of the opulent Umaid Bahawan Palace Hotel, one of India's most impressive palace hotels. Just staying here may make the trip to Jodhpur well worth while!

UDAIPUR

Located in southern Rajasthan, this city of nearly 350,000 people is a surprise to many visitors who are used to encountering the many desert-bound cities that dot the State of Rajasthan. Udaipur's three attractive lakes, forested hills, and lush gardens give this city a special ambience unlike most other places in India. A favorite destination for many travelers, Udaipur also is a city of attractive palaces and museums. But Udaipur is a shopper's paradise for many unique items produced in and around the city, especially miniature paintings, furniture, and batik textiles. Stroll the hilly, narrow, and winding streets and lanes and you'll discover numerous artists and craftsmen demonstrating their skills in the old city's many quaint shops. Stay in one of the regal palace hotels, especially the Taj Lake Palace Hotel on Lake Pichola or Shivniwas Palace Hotel, and you're be enveloped in a fascinating by-gone era of Maharajas and their opulent lifestyles. Relax in Udaipur's pleasant lakeside ambience and recharge your batteries before hitting the road for more challenging destinations in India.

HYDERABAD

Welcome to India's intriguing South with its wealth of treasures and pleasures. Lakeside Hyderabad, the capital of the southeastern state of Andhra Pradesh and India's fifth largest city, is a pleasant surprise for many visitors. Boasting a population of 5 million, sprawling Hyderabad and its less interesting twin city of Secunderabad are relatively clean cities. But like many other large bustling Indian cities, at times it becomes extremely crowded; indeed, on a hot day, of which there are many, Hyderabad's notorious traffic jams, noxious fumes, and sea of people can be horrendous.

Above all, this is a very interesting and exotic city with lots of things to see and do. While still somewhat off the well beaten tourist map, Hyderabad remains a popular center for business and commerce with emphasis on high-tech industries (telecommunications and software development), textiles, pearls, and handicrafts. Its many hotels are primarily filled with businessmen, although more and more tourists are now discovering Hyderabad's charms. The city has much to offer visitors who are interested in unique history, sightseeing, cuisine, and shopping.

Founded in 1591 by the Qutub Shahi dynasty on the banks of the Musi River and subsequently ruled by the Moghuls and Nizams, the city remains rich in Muslim inspired architecture. Indeed, it remained under Muslim rule until 1948. Numerous mosques, minarets, monuments, museums, and markets testify to the fact that Hyderabad has a long and indelible Muslim history. It still remains an important center for Muslim culture.

❑ Jodhpur is a favorite destination for many foreign dealers for buying distinctive handicrafts and furniture.

❑ Udaipur is a surprising city of attractive palaces, museums, and shopping.

❑ Hyderabad is India's most important pearl center.

❑ Chennai offers a wealth of opportunities for art, jewelry, textiles, furniture, handicrafts, and home decorative items.

If you decide to explore southern India, you should seriously consider including surprising Hyderabad on your itinerary. A two- to three-day visit here should be sufficient for sightseeing and shopping. The city offers excellent shopping opportunities for pearls, textiles, and handicrafts. In fact, Hyderabad is India's most important pearl center. Pearls from Southeast Asia are shipped here for sorting and stringing. If you love pearls and jewelry, you'll thoroughly enjoy your visit to Hyderabad.

CHENNAI (MADRAS)

Chennai, until recently (1996) known as Madras, is the capital of India's southernmost state of Tamil Nadu. It's also India's fourth largest city with a population of over 4 million. Stretching along the coast of the Bay of Bengal, this is a city rich in colonial history as well as Hindu tradition. It was originally established in 1639 by the British East India Company as a fort and trading post. Today the old Fort St. George still stands along with the Christian churches of missionaries and expatriates. But the city is much better known for its colorful Hindu temples and as a gateway city to variety of interesting attractions in the state of Tamil Nadu, such as the cave temples at Mamallapuram and the temple and silk town of Kanchipuram. As you will quickly discover, this is temple territory. Rich in religious architecture and old ruins, the whole area is a sight-seer's dream.

Like so many other large Indian cities, Chennai also is choked by traffic, people, and pollution and deafened by loud vehicles. It's also a very dynamic city which is undergoing rapid development in part stimulated by multinational corporations that have recently settled in Chennai. Building and road construction add to the city's exciting traffic problems.

Being a hot and steamy southern city (pick your seasons carefully!), like Hyderabad, Chennai is off the beaten tourist path. This is good news for shoppers who will find a wealth of shopping opportunities in Chennai for art, jewelry, textiles, furniture, handicrafts, and home decorative items.

Plan to stay in Chennai for at least three days. You'll need that much time to enjoy the many treasures and pleasures of Chennai and the surrounding area.

RICH HISTORY, EXTREME EXPERIENCES

India is an ancient land that oozes with history and an extreme human experience that often defines the fabric of daily life. It's a history of great religions; of conquests; of being ruled by for-eigners; of a new nation-state forged from many diverse peoples and cultures. It's a history of adaptation and survival; of extreme wealth and poverty; of fascinating heros and villains; of great comfort and convenience as well as great discomfort and inconvenience; of terrific and lousy weather; of hard living and hardly staying alive; of death and rebirth; and of remarkable artistic, cultural, and technological achievements. In India, religion is a way of life—the "rules" so to speak—rather than a one-day-a-week celebration.

As someone remarked to us years ago in contrasting India with their country, India is all about the extremes of human experience: *"It may get hot in our country, but it really gets hot in India; we may have poverty in our country, but they really have poverty in India; and it may rain and flood in our country, but it really rains and floods in India!"* The same might be said for crowds, traffic, accidents, pollution, sanitation, epidemics, violence, and other aspects of life in this big and intriguing country. Train wrecks don't just kill three people and injure 25; in India they may kill 300 and injure 700! Traffic doesn't just get jammed; in India it often gets completely immobilized and entangled in the biggest mess you'll ever see anywhere in the world. You may have seen or experienced it elsewhere, but in India you will *really* experi-ence such aspects of life. You also may experience an extreme range of emotions in India—that love/hate thing that often affects first time visitors as well as seasoned travelers to India.

While nothing may come easy in India, at the same time, few things are neutral in India. There are many faces to India, none of which are completely satisfying nor accurate. In many respects, India pushes everything to the nth degree. It embodies the human experience like no other country we have visited. So much of traveling in India is all about experiencing the extremes of travel and life itself.

If you've studied the rich fabric of Indian history and understand its many diverse cultures, you'll be enthralled by visiting its plethora of ancient monuments, temples, fortresses, palaces, and museums. You'll see the scars of conquest and the symbols of religion as well as marvel at India's many living traditions that continue to survive in a so-called modern world. You'll sometimes find yourself in a time warp but you'll eventually get your time right.

If you're not well versed in Indian history, much of what you see may be overwhelming, appear interesting, or seem boring. Without a historical frame of reference, all the ancient monuments, temples, fortresses, palaces, and museums will seem like a blur after awhile. At best, such historical places may tweak your interest in learning more about India's fascinating history and returning again to explore her further.

Whatever your perspective on Indian history, you will surely find it compelling and leave India with a better understanding of what India is all about. Hopefully, you'll want to soon revisit India to further appreciate its many rich treasures and pleasures and explore other areas of this fascinating country.

PURPOSE AND PLACE

Perspectives on India tend to center on two distinct views of travel. First, there's almost an anthropological bias of many travelers and writers on India to focus on understanding and enlightenment. Since the place is so exotic, complex, paradoxical, and permeated with religion, culture, and philosophy, many people want to better *understand* India as if it were a single entity that could be defined and explained. Many of these same people seek *enlightenment* through India's many religious sects. In fact, there is probably no better place in the world to contemplate the universe than in India!

But if understanding and enlightenment are not your purposes in visiting India, you'll need to take a different approach to the place. If you come to India to experience the

standard treasures and pleasures of travel—shopping, sightseeing, hotels, restaurants, and entertainment—you won't be
disappointed. India offers lots of great opportunities in these
departments. At least in major cities, such as Mumbai and
Delhi, you'll find good quality four- and five-star hotels, excellent restaurants, and terrific shopping. You'll achieve a different
level of understanding and enlightenment that doesn't require
you to go "bush" and experience the daily struggles of living and
traveling in India on a shoestring. In the end, you'll experience
some level of understanding and enlightenment simply because
of your presence in India.

MEET A DIVERSE PEOPLE

You can't avoid people in India, because there are so many of
them around you—in markets, in temples, in hotels, in restaurants, at sites, and along the street. Densely populated, India is
all about the diversity of people. It's a constant parade of
colorful people drawn from different regions, tribes, religions,
and ethnic and language groups. If you are like many other
visitors to India, you'll find the people and their settings
fascinating. As you also lose yourself in time, you may quickly
discover one of your favorite pastimes is simply people watching, as a unique street theater unfolds before your eyes each
day. At times, you may think the many people in traditional
dress are drawn from a different era. The diversity of faces,
expressions, dress, and activities make India a very special place
to visit. Some of your best memories of India may well be your
personal encounters with the people.

ENCOUNTER SURPRISING COMMUNITIES

There's a certain negative Third World quality about Indian
cities—most are more or less crowded, congested, polluted,
dirty, worn, crumbling, and makeshift. Their narrow streets and
lanes tend to be overwhelmed with people, vehicles, and
animals. Basic urban services tend to be rudimentary and
unpredictable. In some communities, electrical outages can be
frequent. At the same time, these communities have their
pockets of beauty which are usually centered around their
temples, monuments, historical sites, museums, and surrounding areas of lakes, rivers, mountains, and deserts.
    Each community tends to have its own unique character
that distinguishes it from other communities in India. Mumbai
and Delhi are modern and cosmopolitan cities whereas Agra,

Jaipur, and Varanasi have their own traditional character centered around palaces, temples, and religion. Hyderabad and Chennai are southern cities less influenced by tourism. When you leave India, you will have experienced several different Indias.

UNIQUE TREASURES, SMART SHOPPING

In many respects India is a shopper's paradise. This is especially true for inexpensive arts and crafts which are produced in abundance throughout the country. In fact, all state governments promote the production of handicrafts for both local consumption and international export. India also is a terrific place to purchase quality art (paintings and sculptures), antiques, furniture, jewelry, and textiles. As you will see in the individual city chapters, India is one of the best places to shop for inexpensive home furnishings and decorative items. And prices here are some of the best you'll find anywhere in the world. India's is a true bargain hunter's paradise.

❑ So much of traveling in India is all about experiencing the extremes of travel and life itself.

❑ In many respects India is a shopper's paradise. It's a great place for bargain hunters.

❑ Many drivers and guides receive 30-40 percent commissions from shops.

But there are lots of perils and pitfalls of shopping in India. If, for example, you are not familiar with the quality of gems and pearls, you can easily make mistakes by purchasing inferior quality jewelry. If you are taken by a guide or driver to their favorite shop, you are probably being taken to a mediocre place that gives them a 30-40 percent commission which you end up paying in the price of your purchases. If you don't compare prices, you can easily pay too much for the same item that is found in many other shops. If you don't bargain right, you may end up of paying twice as much as you should for items. And if you don't learn how to firmly and often say "no," you can easily be persuaded to buy something you don't want from very savvy and tenacious Kashmiri merchants who disproportionately operate, and monopolize, handicraft and rug emporiums throughout India.

One of our purposes in writing this book is to make sure you become a savvy and happy shopper in India. Not only do we recommend rules for avoiding the perils and pitfalls of shopping in India, we also deal with such important issues as shipping your purchases home with the least amount of hassle and disappointment. Shopping to us is one of the great pleasures of traveling in India. You'll discover some wonderful treasures as well as meet many interesting people, from the artists and craftspeople whose work you may purchase directly, to the dealers, merchants, and shippers who offer quality products and reliable services. If you know how to shop India right—the who, what, where, and how—you should have an absolutely marvelous time there. You'll acquire some wonderful products that you will appreciate for years to come. You're also likely to meet some very interesting people who will continue to be your link to India in the years ahead.

SURPRISING PLEASURES

While we are especially interested in uncovering India's shopping treasures, we also recognize its many travel pleasures. Above all, India is one of the world's most exotic places with all the sights, sounds, and smells associated with being exotic. From the colorful street, river, and desert scenes that often transcend centuries to the majestic symbols of previous rulers (fortresses, palaces, monuments, and ruins), a rich religious tradition (temples, shrines, mosques, churches, and festivals), and indigenous and colonial histories (museums), India displays a treasure trove of history and culture that should not be missed. At the same time, India is experiencing a major transition from the old to the new. Teenagers are into music, movies, and MTV. Young professionals and the wealthy are increasingly label conscious when shopping for Western imported goods. Western cartoons, soap operas, and satellite news are increasingly popular in India. In large cities nightlife includes bars, discos, and clubs. As India increasingly participates in the global economy and enlarges its middle class, businesses continue to expand with new commercial buildings and hotels going up to meet the increased demand for office space and accommodations.

In each of our cities and surrounding areas, you'll find plenty of interesting things to see and do. In addition, you'll find many excellent hotels and restaurants that represent some of the India's best hospitality and cuisine. Within the past five years, India's hotel and restaurant scene has increasingly gone international. Major hotel chains have now moved into India and helped raise the standard of service to an international level. You'll even find excellent French, Continental, and Italian restaurants in Mumbai and Delhi, staffed with noted European chefs, that offer top cuisine at bargain basement prices.

Approach It Right

Try as we may, there's no one best way to approach India. Few first-time visitors are really prepared for this place. They read about it, view videos and movies on the country, and talk to others who have been to India. They know it's a very exotic, challenging, and often bizarre place. Then they arrive in India. Within a day or two their expectations and first impressions quickly give way to a host of experiences that can be disorienting and frustrating. India is such a multifaceted place that it defies simple explanation and stereotyping. As soon at you think you know her, a new experience contradicts your impressions. After a while, you discover this is a very complex place where you are constantly peeling layer after layer of India, each of which appears different from the previous layer. You'll never find its core—only its many different layers.

Do your pre-trip research and planning on India, but chances are you won't be fully prepared for your "India experience." Our best advice is to pack well and be sensitive to your attitude. For your attitude may soon show in India as you experience its incredible street-level theater that draws you in as both spectator and player. You can easily develop an attitude problem in a country that evokes such strong emotions as India.

India requires some serious attitude adjustments. Indeed, your attitude toward this place may change within the space of a few hours—you may hate it in the morning but love it in the evening, and vice versa. You'll probably hate it if you expect everything to run properly and on schedule; efficiency is not a well developed Indian trait. That's not the Indian way.

Don't make too many assumptions about this place. In India, things don't work well; getting from point A to point B can be frustrating; communication can be maddening; and at times you may be exasperated with the place. Don't worry; this too will pass. Just sit back, take it in, and go with the flow. You're not about to change this place. It will most likely change you, instead.

After a week or two in India, time has a way of disappearing. It's best to go with the chaotic flow. Be forgiving of their errors. Best of all, build in a few extra days in India—just in case you need them for everything from illness to serendipity and inefficiencies that alter your best laid plans. Remember, you'll be home soon and getting upset really doesn't make a difference at this time and place.

EXPECT A REWARDING ADVENTURE

Whatever you do, enjoy your shopping and travel adventure to India. This is a very special country that offers many unique treasures and pleasures for discerning travelers.

So arrange your flights and accommodations, pack your credit cards and traveler's checks, take your sense of humor, wear a smile, and head for one of the world's most interesting shopping and travel destinations. You should return home with much more than a set of photos and travel brochures and a weight gain attendant with new eating habits. You will acquire some wonderful products and accumulate many interesting travel tales that can be enjoyed and relived for a lifetime.

Experiencing the treasures and pleasures of India only takes time, money, and a sense of adventure. Take the time, be willing to part with some of your money, and open yourself to a whole new world of treasures and pleasures. If you are like us, your shopping adventure will introduce you to an exciting world of quality products, friendly people, and interesting places that you might have otherwise missed had you passed through India only to eat, sleep, see sites, take pictures, and keep up with a tour group's hectic schedule. When you travel and shop in India, you learn about some exciting places by way of the people, products, and places that define this country's many treasures and pleasures. You'll understand a very different aspect of India that is largely absent in other guide books on this fascinating country.

Enjoy! May your Indian treasures and pleasures last a lifetime and forever enrich your life.

PART I

Traveling Smart

2

Know Before You Go

I f you are a first-time visitor to India, you should be aware of certain basic facts about this place before you arrive. This information should help you better plan how, when, and where you will arrive so you can literally hit the ground running!

POPULATION AND AREA

Anyway you look at it, India is big and diverse. Home to nearly 1 billion inhabitants, India is the world's second largest country in terms of population. As a subcontinent with a total land mass of 3.3 million square kilometers, India lies between Pakistan, China, and Nepal. It's the world's sixth largest country in terms of land area—about the size of Europe.

Geographically India is a very diverse country. Jutting like an arrowhead into the Indian Ocean, with the Arabian Sea on the west and the Bay of Bengal on the East, India has three distinct physical regions each with its own internal diversity. The north is bordered by the world's highest mountains, the Himalayans, which separate India from China. Further south lies the Gangetic Plains and the holy Ganges River (the Ganges) which cuts through the heartland of northern India. Here you find plateaus in the center, tropical rain forests to the east, and sandy deserts to the west with palm fringed beaches along the Arabian Sea and the Bay of Bengal. Further south lies the Indian Peninsula with it tropical humid climate along the coasts and dry inland plateaus. Visitors can go mountain climbing, skiing, and trekking in India's far north as well as enjoy the beaches year-round in the hot and steamy south.

India's people also are very diverse. The 26 states that make up the world's largest democracy overlay a great deal of ethnic, linguistic, cultural, and religious diversity. At the very north lies the high altitude desert of Ladakh with its Buddhism traditions. To the northwest are sandy deserts noted for the spartan and colorful lifestyles of its people. The central states of Orissa and Madhya Pradesh and the northeast states of Nagaland, Mizoram, Tripura, and Manipur are the homes to India's many colorful tribes. The southeast peninsula is home to the religious and conservative Tamils who comprise one of India's most important cultural centers for music, dance, and religion.

❑ India is the world's second largest country in terms of population and the world's sixth largest country in terms of area.

❑ India officially recognizes 15 languages amongst the more than 700 dialects spoken.

❑ The best time to visit most of India is between October and March, with November, December, and January being the best months.

Even the cuisines vary greatly, from the rich and meaty Mughal dishes in the North to the spicy vegetarian dishes of rice and coconut milk in the South. While India officially recognizes 15 languages and some 700 dialects are reported to be spoken, the good news for visitors is that English is still widely spoken.

CLIMATE, SEASONS, WHEN TO GO

Much of the Indian subcontinent is hot and humid, but not everywhere nor all of the time. India's climate is affected in large part by the monsoons that sweep across the subcontinent from mid-June to mid-September. In the extreme and mountainous north (near Ladahk, Darjeeling, Kulu, Manali), which experiences significant seasonal changes, the best time to visit is between May to October. However, outside these Himalayan areas, and especially in the South, the best time to visit is between October and March, with November, December, and January being the best months. If you find yourself in the central plains, eastern rain forests, or the steamy south during May, June, and July, you may think you'll die from the heat and humidity.

Whatever you do, try to plan your trip according to India's best seasons. You'll have enough on your hands just coping with the traffic, crowds, touts, beggars, and unusual sights, sounds, and smells than to further complicate your trip with really lousy weather.

GETTING THERE

Most visitors arrive in India by air via Europe or East Asia. For international flights, India's major gateway cities are Mumbai and New Delhi. However, more and more international flights now go into Agra, Calcutta, and Chennai.

We recommend the Mumbai or New Delhi entry points. These are cosmopolitan cities that are relatively easy to adjust to during your first few days in India. As you get further into India, you'll appreciate many of the treasures and pleasures you initially encountered in these cities. These also are cities where you may want to return to do final shopping and to make final shipping arrangements.

On our most recent trip to India, we chose **Northwest Airlines** which also works with its partner, **KLM**, in servicing India. We found their schedules to be the most convenient, the flights very comfortable, the service attentive, and the food well prepared. When we encountered a delayed flight to Mumbai due to ground problems with Indian authorities, Northwest and KLM personnel quickly managed to overnight all passengers in Amsterdam and bring in new equipment from the U.S. for a specially scheduled flight the following day. We have often appreciated the good service we find as we travel in Asia. We found the attentive but not obtrusive service on Northwest compared very favorably with what we have experienced traveling on the most highly rated overseas airlines. The flight attendants went out of their way to make passengers comfortable and well cared for.

Best of all, we found Northwest Airlines' route—especially from East Coast and Midwest cities in the United States—to be very convenient. We flew directly from Detroit to Amtersdam and then changed planes for a final 8 hour and 10 minute direct flight from Amtersdam to Mumbai. We also could have selected their daily flight to New Delhi.

But Northwest offers more than just a great routing to India. We really enjoyed our Northwest flight and were impressed with several innovative programs that should appeal to anyone interested in ecology. Northwest has been cited for the second consecutive year as the most eco-friendly airline.

Indeed, Northwest developed the first in-flight recycling program, and it pioneered a program to allow passengers to choose their food items from an a la carte service which both pleases passengers and has cut food waste by 20 percent.

If you fly frequently, consider membership in Northwest's WorldPerks℠ (frequent flyer) and WorldClubs℠ (airport lounges and special services) programs. For more information on the **WorldPerks℠** frequent flyer program which also is partnered with KLM, contact Northwest by phone (1-800-447-3757) or mail: Northwest Airlines Customer Service Center, 601 Oak Street, Chisholm, MN 55719. For information on the **WorldClubs℠** program, contact Northwest by phone (1-800-692-3788), fax (612-726-0988), or mail: Northwest Airlines, Inc., WorldClubs Service Center, 5101 Northwest Drive, Department A5301, St. Paul, MN 55111-3034. You may want to make these contacts before doing your ticketing.

For most visitors from North America and Europe, the flight to India is a long one. Thus, you may wish to upgrade your ticket to "Business Class" for more room and comfort. You will pay more for this upgrade but the increased comfort may be well worth it.

TOURS AND INDIVIDUAL TRAVEL

Should you travel to India on your own or join a packaged tour? That's up to you, depending on how you normally travel and how much time you have available to organize your own itinerary. India can easily accommodate both styles of travel, although group travel is usually the cheapest and most convenient way to see the country. However, India poses special challenges to individual travelers who may not be prepared for the extreme chaos, disorganization, and bureaucratic inertia frequently encountered in this country. At best, India is a unique challenge for individual travelers.

❑ India poses special challenges to individual travelers.

❑ More than 100 tour groups operate in India from North America and Europe.

❑ Many specialty tour operators offer unique tours of India.

If this is your first trip to India, you may want to join one of the more than 100 tour groups that operate in India from North America and Europe. Since India still remains an inexpensive destination, most of these groups offer good value and convenience. Fourteen-day trips that include stops in Mumbai, New Delhi, Agra, Jaipur, and Varanasi can cost as little at $1,700 per person, including round-trip airfare. It's virtually impossible to match that amount by traveling to India on your own, unless you are an extreme budget traveler who enjoys staying at the low end of the economic spectrum and using the local buses and trains. This may be fun and enlightening, a very special cultural experience that puts you in close contact with locals, but it can also be very time consuming trying to figure out bus and train schedules and off-the-beaten path locations for accommodations. If your time is limited and you're not in search of a low-end cultural experience, you actually may end up paying less by joining an inexpensive first-class packaged tour than if you try to do India on your own as a budget traveler.

We highly recommend shopping around for a packaged tour to India. While many itineraries are similar, you may find some unique features that are well worth comparing, especially specialty tours. Your travel agent should have plenty of brochures on regularly scheduled tours to India and other parts of Asia. While many of these tour cover the basics of sightseeing, such as the Golden Triangle of New Delhi, Agra, and Jaipur, others are more specialized: mountain and desert trekking adventures, wildlife safaris, train trips, tribal visits, palace junkets, and cultural, culinary, photo, ecological, nature, and arts and crafts tours. Some of the major tour operators include:

- **Abercrombie and Kent**: 1520 Kensington Road, Oak Brook, IL 60521-2141, Tel. 1-800-323-7308 or Fax 708/954-3324. Email: *info@abercrombiekent.com*

- **Absolute Asia:** 180 Varick Street, New York, NY 10014, Tel. 1-800-736-8187 or Fax 212/627-4090.

- **Access Adventure Tours:** 2035 Park Street, Atlantic Beach, NY 11509, Tel. 516/371-0067 or Fax 516/371-1352.

- **Adventure Center:** 1311 63rd Street, Emeryville, CA 94608, Tel. 1-800-227-8747. Email: *tripinfo@adventure-Center.com*

- **Adventures Abroad:** 2148 - 20800 Westminster Hwy., Richmond, BC, V6V 2W3, Canada, Tel. 1-800-665-3998 or Fax 604/303-1076. Email: *adabroad@infoserve.net*

- **Adventures Unlimited:** 210 Post Street, #1112, San Francisco, CA 94108, Tel. 1-800-554-4224.

- **Asian Pacific Adventures:** 9010 Reseda Blvd., Suite 227, Northridge, CA 91324, Tel. 1-800-825-1680 or 818/886-5190. Website: *www.asianpacificadventures.com*

- **Amtour Vacations:** 15760 Ventura Blvd., #803, Encino, CA 91436, Tel. 1-800-469-8687 or Fax 818-389-7072. Email: *amtour@ix-netcom.com*

- **Aries Travel Service:** 300 Gateway Street, Suite 800, Gateway Mall, Springfield, OR 97477, Tel. 1-800-746-0979 or Fax 541-746-1218.

- **Azure Travel Bureau:** 309 Fifth Avenue, New York, NY 10016, Tel. 1-800-882-1427 or Fax 212/252-1057. Website: *www.source india.com/azure/*

- **Bestway Tours & Safaris:** 103-3540 West 41st Avenue, Vancouver BC, V6N 3E6, Canada, Tel. 1-800-663-0844. Website: *www.bestway.com*

- **Big Five Tours and Expeditions/Amtour Vacations, Inc.:** 819 South Federal Highway, Suite 103, Stuart, FL 34994, Tel. 1-800-244-3483 or Fax 561/287-5990. Website: *www.bigfive.com*

- **Bryan World Tours:** 1527 Fairlawn Road, Topeka, KS 66604, Tel. 1-800-255-3507 or Fax 913/272-6244.

- **Capricorn Travel 'N' Tours:** 9623 Southwest Freeway, Houston, TX 77074, Tel. 713/270-5519 of Fax 715-270-5868.

- **Ceylon Express International:** 9542 Dumbreck Drive, Huntington, Beach, CA 92646, Tel. 1-800-423-9566 or Fax 714-968-4296. Website: *www.ceylonexpress.com*

- **Classic Journeys Worldwide, Inc.:** 249 N. Brand Blvd., Suite 417, Glendale, CA 91203, Tel. 1-888-746-2599.

- **Close Up Expeditions:** 858 56th Street, Oakland, CA 94608, Tel. 510/654-1548 or Fax 5101/654-3043.

- **Compare Tours, Inc.:** 5 N. Wabash Avenue, Suite 818, Chicago, IL 60602, Tel. 312/853-1144 or Fax 312/853-2446.

- **Cox & Kings Travel:** 25 Davis Blvd., Tampa, FL 33606, Tel. 1-800-999-1758 or Fax 813/258-3852. Website: *www.zenonet.com/cox-kings/*

- **Craft World Tours:** 6776 Warboys, Byron, NY 14422, Tel. 716/548-2667 or Fax 716/548-2821.

- **Cross Cultural Adventures:** P.O. Box 3285, Arlington, VA 22203, Tel. 703/237-1000 or Fax 703/237-2558.

- **Design Travel & Tours:** 340 W. Butterfield Rd., Suite 2A, Elmhurst, IL 60126, Tel. 1-800-543-7164 or Fax 708/530-0059.

- **Destinations and Adventures:** 8489 Crescent Drive, Los Angeles, CA 90046, Tel. 1-800-659-4599. Website: *www.dai travel.com*

- **Destination Himalayas:** 521 North 52nd Street, Omaha, NE 68132, Tel. 402/556-0303 or Fax 402/556-0220.

- **Destination Marketing Group:** Twelve Oaks Center, Suite 1003, 15500 Wayzata Blvd., Minneapolis, MN 55391, Tel. 612/473-9331 or Fax 612/473-9135.

- **Discovery Tours, American Museum of Natural History:** Central Park W. 79th St., New York, NY 10024, Tel. 1-800-462-8687 or Fax 212/769-5755.

- **Eagle Flight Tours:** 9215 Sagebrush Street, Apple Valley, CA 92308. Tel/Fax 619/247-8728.

- **East Quest:** 1 Union Square West, New York, NY 10003, Tel. 1-800-638-3449 or Fax 212-741-1786. Email: *eastquest1@aol.com*

- **Esplanade Tours:** 581 Boylston St., Boston, MA 02116, Tel. 1-800-426-5492 or Fax 617/262-9829.

- **Exotic Journeys, Inc.:** 500 N. Michigan Ave., Suite 1405, Chicago, IL 60611, Tel. 1-800-554-6342 or Fax 312/832-9746. Website: *www.exoticjourneys.com*

- **Far Fung Places, LLC:** 1914 Fell Street, San Francisco, CA 94117, Tel. 1-800-410-9811 or Fax 415/386-8104. Website: *www.farfungplaces.com*

- **Far Horizons:** 795 Franklin Avenue, Franklin Lakes, NJ 07417, Tel. 201/891-1735 or Fax 201/891-1923.

- **Force 10 Expeditions:** P.O. Box 1925, Eagar, AZ 85925, Tel. 1-800-922-1491 or Fax 520/333-4840. Email: *force-10@himalayan.com*

- **Gate 1 Ltd.:** 101 Limekiln Pike, Glenside, PA 19038, Tel. 1-800-682-3333 or Fax 215/886-2228. Website: *www.netaxs.com/people/gate1/*

- **General Tours:** 160 East 38th Street, Suite 34H, New York, NY 10016, Tel. 212/949-6799 or Fax 212/599-5137.

- **Geographic Expeditions:** 2627 Lombard Street, San Francisco, CA 94123, Tel. 1-800-777-8183. Website: *www.geoex.com*

- **Geeta Tours & Travels:** 1245 W. Jarvis Avenue, Chicago, IL 60626, Tel. 312/262-4959 or Fax 312/262-4978.

- **Globus & Cosmos:** 5301 S. Federal Circle, Littleton, CO, Tel. 1-800-221-0090 or Fax 303/347-2080.

- **Glorious Adventures:** 10007 Gaynor Avenue, North Hills, CA 91343, Tel. 818-893-9030 or Fax 818/893-9151.

- **Grand Circle Travel:** 347 Congress Street, Boston, MA 02210, Tel. 617/346-6632 or Fax 617/346-6700.

- **Great Adventure Travel Co. Inc.:** 645 N. Michigan, Suite 800, Chicago, IL 60611, Tel. 1-800-874-2826 or Fax 312/880-5780.

- **Great American Travel:** 1110 East Missouri, #510, Phoenix, AZ 85014, Tel. 1-800-929-8638 or Fax 602/279-9952.

- **Hanns Ebenstein Travel, Inc.:** 513 Fleming Street, Key West, FL 33040, Tel. 305/294-8174 or Fax 305/292-9665.

- **Hari World Travel:** 25W 45th Street, Suite 1003, New York, NY 10036, Tel. 212/997-3300 or Fax 212/997-3320. Website: *www.hariworld.com*

- **Hibiscus Tours:** 885 Third Avenue, Suite 2900, New York, NY 10022, Tel. 1-800-653-0802 or Fax 212/753-6582. Email: *Hibsctours@aol.com*

- **High Adventure Travel:** 353 Sacramento Street, #600, San Francisco, CA 94111, Tel. 1-800-428-8735 or Fax 415/912-5600. Email: *India@highadv.com*

- **Himalayan International Tours:** 286 5th Ave., #705, New York, NY 10001, Tel. 212/564-5164 or Fax 212/564-2188.

- **Himalayan Odyssey:** 307 N. Cedarbrook Dr., Auburn, AL 36830, Tel. 1-800-252-5340 or Fax 334/844-2851. Websitel: *www.webdzyne.com/odyssey*

- **Himalyan Treasures and Travel:** 3596 Ponderosa Trail, Pinole, CA 94564. Tel. 1-800-223-1813 or Fax 1-510-223-5309. Email: *govindsh@himtrek.com*

- **Himalayan Travel Inc.:** 110 Prospect Street, Stamford, CT 06901, Tel. 1-800-225-2380 or Fax 203-359-3669. Email: *worldadv@netaxis.com*

- **International Ventures and Travel Inc.:** 551 Fifth Avenue, #1923, New York, NY 10176-0180, Tel. 1-800-338-2624 or Fax 212/557-5790.

- **Japan & Orient Tours, Inc.:** 3131 Camino Del Rio N. #1080, San Diego, CA 92108, Tel. 1-800-377-1030 or Fax 619/283-3131.

- **Jetset Tours Inc.:** 5120 W. Goldleaf Circle #310, Los Angeles, CA 90056, Tel. 213/290-5800 or Fax 213/294-0432.

- **Journeys:** 1536 NW 23rd Street, Portland, Or 97210, Tel. 503/226-7200 or Fax 503/226-4940.

- **Journeys International, Inc.:** 4011 Jackson Road, Ann Arbor, MI 48103, Tel. 1-800-255-8735 or Fax 313/665-2945. Website: *www.journeys-intl.com*

- **Journeyworld International, Inc.:** 119 W. 57th St. N. Penthouse, New York, NY 10019-2303, Tel. 1-800-635-3900 or Fax 212/956-0487.

- **Kali Travel & Tours:** 169-12 Hillside Ave., Jamaica, NY 11432, Tel. 718/291-9292 or Fax 718/262-0928.

- **Lotus Travels:** 1644 N. Sedgwick Street, Chicago, IL 60614, Tel. 312/951-0031 or Fax 312/951-7313.

- **KLM/Northwest WorldVacations:** Contact your travel agent or call 1-800-800-1504. Website: *www.nwa.com*

- **Maupintour, Inc.:** 1515 St. Andrews Drive, Lawrence, KS 66044, Tel. 1-800-255-4266 or Fax 913/843-8351.

- **McNeil Travel Service:** 152 N. Water Street, Kent, OH 44240, Tel. 216/678-8890.

- **Micato Safaris:** 15 West 26th Street, New York, NY 10010, Tel. 212/545-7111 or Fax 212/545-8297.

- **MTS Tours:** 124 East Main St., 4th Floor, Ephrata, PA 17522, Tel. 717/738-7300 or Fax 717/733-1009. Email: *naomiw@mtstravel.com*

- **Murdock Travel:** 36 South State, #900, Salt Lake City, UT 84111, Tel. 801/521-7850 or Fax 801/328-5490.

- **Myths and Mountains:** 976 Tee Court, Incline Village, NV 89451, Tel. 1-800-670-MYTH or Fax 702/832-4454

- **Nature Expedition Ltd.:** P.O. Box 11496, Eugene, OR 97440, Tel. 1-800-869-0639 or Fax 541-484-6531.

- **Olson Travel World:** 1145 Clark Street, Stevens Point, WI 54481, Tel. 715/345-0505 or Fax 715/345-0525.

- **Orient Flexi Pax Tours:** 630 Third Avenue, New York, NY 10017-6780, Tel. 1-800-545-5540 or Fax 212/661-1618.

- **Orient Lines, Inc.:** 1510 S.E. 17th St., Suite 400, Ft. Lauderdale, FL 33316, Tel. 1-800-333-7300 or Fax 954-527-6657.

- **Orient Odyssey:** 1385 Gulf Road, Suite 203, Point Roberts, WA 98281, Tel. 1-800-637-5778.

- **Our Personal Guest, Inc.:** 20 E. 53rd Street, New York, NY 10022, Tel. 212/319-4521 or Fax 212/319-4526.

- **Photo Adventure Tours:** 2035 Park Street, Atlantic Beach, NY 11509-1256, Tel. 516/371-0067 or Fax 516/371-1352.

- **Pollina Tours & Travel, Inc.:** 143-04 Cherry Ave., Suite 3A, Flushing, NY 11355, Tel. 718/321-7873 or Fax 718/886-9282.

- **Rama Tours:** 6 N. Michigan Avenue, Chicago, IL 60602, Tel. 1-800-TEL-RAMA or Fax 312/853-0225.

- **Rare Earth Explorations:** 10 Waterside Plaza, #4K, New York, NY 10010-2610, Tel. 212/686-7411 or Fax 212/686-2366. Email: *ninarao@wildindia.com*

- **Resch Tours Ltd.:** 738 Kahela STR, #306, Honolulu, HI 96814, Tel. 808/947-3302 or Fax 808/947-3106.

- **Safari Center:** 3201 N. Sepulveda Blvd., Manhattan Beach, CA, Tel/Fax 310/546-3188. Email: *info@safari center. com*

- **Saga Holidays:** 222 Berkeley Street, Boston, MA 02116, Tel. 617/262-2262 or Fax 617/375-5950.

- **S.E.T. Ventures Ltd. (Sky Bird Tours):** 60 East 42nd Street, Suite 1406, New York, NY 10165, Tel. 212/697-0022 or Fax 212/697-0089. Website: *www.setltd.com*

- **Shangri-La Adventures:** 361 Main Street, Suite #3, El Segundo, CA 90245, Tel. 1-800-843-8228 or Fax 310/ 416-9158. Website: *www.shangri-laadventures.com*

- **Silver Wings Holidays Ltd.:** 1516 Butterfield Road, Downers Grove, IL 60515, Tel. 708/495-7101 or Fax 708/495-7165.

- **Sita World Travel, Inc.:** 16250 Ventura Blvd., Suite 300, Encino, CA 91436. Tel. 1-800-421-5643. Website: *www.sitatours. com*; 551 N. Michigan Ave., #210, Chicago, IL 60611, Tel. 312/822-0300 or Fax 312/822-0048; 8125 San Femando Road, Sun Valley, CA 91352, Tel. 1-800-42-5643 or Fax 818/767-4346; 3050 Post Oak Blvd., #1320, Houston, TX 77056, Tel. 713/626-0134 or Fax 713/626-1905; 767 Fifth Avenue, New York, NY 10153, Tel. 212/759-8979 or Fax 212/759-0184.

- **SmarTours Inc.:** 501 Fifth Avenue, Suite 812, New York, NY 10017, Tel. 1-800-337-7773 or Fax 212/297-0965.

- **South India Travel Agency Inc.:** 40-40 79th Street, Suite A-404, Elmhurst, NY 11373, Tel. 1-800-267-3494 or Fax 718/898-8449.

- **Special Interest Tours & Travel:** 10220 N. 27 St., Phoenix, AZ 85028, Tel. 1-800-525-6772 or Fax 602/ 493-3630. Website: *www.GoSafari.com*

- **Spectrum International Tours & Travel Inc.:** 63 Unquowa Road, Fairfield, CT 06430, Tel. 1-800-666-9464 or Fax 203/254-8239.

- **Spirit of India:** Box 446, Mill Valley, CA 94942. Tel. 1-888-367-6147 or Fax 415/381-5861. Website: *www.spirit-of-india.com*

- **T.B.I. Tours:** 787 7th Avenue, Suite 1101, New York, NY 10019, Tel. 1-800-223-0266 or Fax 212/307-0612.

- **Third Eye Travel:** 33220 Sandpiper Place, Fremont, CA 94555, Tel. 1-800-456-3393. Website: *www.thirdeyetravel. com*

- **Tiger Tops International Inc.:** 205 Camino Alto #220, Mill Valley, CA 94941, Tel. 415/383-0384 or Fax 415/383-0793. Email: *Tigertops@aol.com*

- **Timeless Tours:** 501 Fifth Ave., Suite 2110, New York, NY 10017, Tel. 1-800-488-1421 or Fax 212/972-1206.

- **Tour Arrangements, Inc.:** P.O. Box 300, Prides Crossing, MA 01965, Tel. 1-800-343-3487 or Fax 508/524-4120.

- **Tours of Distinction:** 1841 Central Park Avenue, Suite 16N, Yonkers, NY 10710, Tel/Fax 1-800-888-8634.

- **Trade Wind Associates, Inc.:** 420 Lexington Ave., Suite 2616, New York, NY 10170, Tel. 212/286-0667 or Fax 212/687-4421. Email: *twai@baxter.net*

- **Travcoa:** 2350 S.E. Bristol, Newport Beach, CA 92660, Tel. 1-800-992-2003 or Fax 714/476-2538.

- **Travel Interlink:** 1348 Van Nuys Blvd. #206, Sherman Oaks, CA 91403, Tel. 1-800-888-5898 or Fax 1-800-888-0191. Email: *TRAVELINK@aol.com*

- **Trek Sikkim:** P.O. Box 7046, Yorkville Station, New York, NY 10128-0110, Tel. 212/996-1758 or Fax 212/996-8062.

- **Turtle Tours:** Box #1147, Carefree, AZ 85377, Tel. 1-888-299-1439 or Fax 602/488-3406.

- **Uniglobe Travel Center:** 36 S. Wabash Avenue, #620, Chicago, IL 60603, Tel. 1-800-621-5228.

- **Unique Journeys:** 71 Keystone Avenue, Reno, NV 89503, Tel. 1-800-421-1981 or Fax 702/323-6914.

- **United Vacations:** 8907 N. Port Washington Road, Milwaukee, WI 53217, Tel. 1-800-328-6877 or Fax 414/351-5826.

- **Victor Enamual Nature Tours:** P.O. Box 33008, Austin, TX 78744, Tel. 512/328-5221 or Fax 512/328-2919. Email: *VENT BIRT@aol.com*

- **Wilderness Trekkers:** P.O. Box 1363, Lomita, CA 90717, Tel. 1-800-335-8735. Email: *Wldtrk@aol.com*

- **Wonder Bird Tours Inc.:** P.O. Box 2015, New York, NY 10159, Tel.1-800-BIRD-TUR or Fax 212/736-0965.

- **Worldview Tours:** 14041 Prospect Ave., Tustin, CA 92780, Tel. 714/505-0800 or Fax 714/505-1686.

- **Worldview Travel:** 125 Lakewood Centre Mall, Lakewood, CA 90712, Tel. 310/630-3311 or Fax 310/630-5435. Email: *znacorp@ ixnetcon.com*

The "best of the best," which also means going in style with the most expensive, is the venerable **Abercrombie and Kent**: 1520 Kensington Road, Oak Brook, IL 60521-2141, Tel. 1-800-323-7308 or Fax 708/954-3324.

If you are interested in specialty types of tours to India, we highly recommend surveying the many advertisements that appear in *International Travel News*. Each monthly issue of this newsletter runs over 150 pages and is filled with information on exotic travel destinations, including tips from travelers who frequent India. For a free sample, contact: ITN, 2224 Beaumont Street, Suite D, Sacramento, CA 95815. Yearly subscriptions run only $17.95. To subscribe, call 1-800-366-9192.

You should also consult your travel agent and survey the travel sections of the Sunday *New York Times, Washington Post, Los Angeles Times,* and other major city newspapers for special packages to India.

VIRTUAL INDIA—INTERNET RICHES

If you are Internet savvy, you can easily access information on travel to India through one of the major travel sites, such as *www.travelocity.com* and *www.expedia.com*. However, you'll find many excellent India-specific sites that yield a wealth of information on all aspects of India. Try these sites for starters:

All India
www.allindia.com/cities

Destination India
www.destinationindia.com

Discover India
www.indiagov.org

Discover India Magazine
www.pugmarks.com/d-india

Government of India Tourist Office
www.tourindia.com

India Buzz
www.indiabuzz.com

Indiacity
www.indiacity.com

India Insight
www.indiainsight.com

India Travel Network
www.inetindia.com/travel/index.htm

India Travel Promotion Network
http://travel.indiamart.com

India World
www.khoj.com

Ministry of Tourism
www.tourindia.com and *www.tourisminindia.com*

Travel-India
www.travel-india.com

Welcome to India
www.welcometoindia.com

For information on several cities covered in this book, examine the following Web sites:

www.tourindia.com (select "Tourism" and "Major Cities")
www.allindia.com/cities/mumbai/default.asp
www.allindia.com/cities/delhi/default.asp
www.allindia.com/cities/hyderabad/default.asp
www.allindia.com/cities/chennai/default.asp

Also, try searching for a particular city by using one of the major search engines, such as HotBot, Yahoo, Infoseek, or Lycos. If you have the time and patience to search through all the information clutter on the Web, you might find some useful information as well as make contact with a travel group. However, your local travel agent will probably yield better quality results and save you a lot of time.

DOCUMENTS YOU NEED

You will need a valid passport and a visa to enter India. Make sure you give yourself plenty of time to get a visa prior to departure. The Indian bureaucracy operating abroad often manages to operate at the same chaotic, snail's pace as it does in India. Trying to get a visa at the last minute can be an absolute nightmare.

You can obtain a visa through the Indian Embassy, consulates, or travel agencies. Tourist visas for U.S. citizens are issued for 6 months (US$50) and 1 year (US$70). Canadian citizens can get 3 month ($30), 6 month ($55), 1 year ($70), and 5 year ($140) visas. U.K. citizens can get 3 month (£13) and 6 month visas.

Allow a minimum of 15 days for visa approval but plan to apply for your visa at least 60 days in advance of your departure—just to be safe with the slow bureaucracy. If you do not apply in person, it's best to send a self-addressed prepaid Federal Express, UPS, DHL, or Airborne air bill with your application. Apply at an Indian embassy or consulate nearest you. Indian embassies and consulates located in North America can be contacted as follows:

United States

Embassy of India
2107 Massachusetts Ave., NW
Washington, DC 20008
Tel. 202/939-7000
Fax 202/939-7027

Consulate General of India
3 East 64th Street
New York, NY 10021-7097
Tel. 212/879-7800
Fax 212/861-3788

Consulate General of India
150 N. Michigan Avenue
Suite 1100
Chicago, IL 60601
Tel. 312/781-6280
Fax 312/781-6269

Consulate General of India
540 Arguello Boulevard
San Francisco, CA 94118
Tel. 415/668-0662
Fax 415/668-2073

Consulate General of India
1990 Post Oak Blvd, Suite 600
Houston, TX 77056
Tel. 713/626-2149
Fax 713/626-3252

Canada

High Commission of India
10 Springfield Road
Ottawa, Ontario K1M 1C9
Tel. 613/744-3751
Fax 613/244-0913

Consulate General of India
2 Bloor Street West, #500
Toronto, Ontario M4W 3E2
Tel. 416/960-0751
Fax 416/960-9812

Consulate General of India
325 Howe Street, 2nd Floor
Vancouver, BC V6C 1Z7
Tel. 606/662-8811
Fax 604/682-2471

If you are traveling with a tour group, they may take care of the visa for you. But be sure to check with the company before departing to make sure you have a valid passport and visa.

Tourist Offices

Both the national and state governments maintain an extensive network of tourist offices and information desks to assist tourists. They dispense travel literature, give advice, sponsor tours, arrange licensed guides, and assist tourists in many different ways. The national government's tourist organization is called the **Government of India Tourist Office**; it operates under the Department of Tourism. It has offices abroad as well as in most major cities of India. You can access information on these offices and other aspects of tourism in India by visiting two useful Websites:

www.tourindia.com (New York City)
www.tourisminindia.com (Delhi)

Tourist offices in North America are found in New York, Los Angeles, and Toronto:

India Tourist Office
30 Rockefeller Plaza
Suite 15
North Mezzanine
New York, NY 1011
Tel. 212/586-4901
Fax 212/582-3274
Website: *www.tourindia.com*

India Tourist Office
3550 Wilshire Boulevard
Suite 204
Los Angeles, CA 90010
Tel. 213/380-8855
Fax 213/380-6111

India Tourist Office
60 Bloor Street West
Suite 1003
Toronto, Ontario
M4W 3B8, Canada
Tel. 416/962-3787
Fax 416/962-6279

Within India, you'll find tourist offices and information desks at airports, train stations, and in the commercial sections of major cities. You may want to visit these offices for assistance. While many of these offices operate on spartan budgets, we've found most of them eager to assist tourists.

ORDERING YOUR ITINERARY

We prefer beginning and ending our India adventure in one of the two gateway cities—Mumbai or Delhi. We do this for two main reasons. First, it's much easier to adjust to India by easing your way into one of these cosmopolitan cities. Second, these are good places to survey shopping options and arrange for shipping. If, for example, you expect to purchase large items requiring packing and shipping, it may be best to identify a central point in either Mumbai or Delhi and have everything shipped there for final consolidation, packing, and shipping. A two or three-day return visit to one of these cities at the end of your trip may prove useful for finalizing any last minute shopping and shipping plans. You may want to revisit several shops that offered items that initially interested you but you decided against until you finished your tour of India. Our personal preference is to enter and exit India by way of Delhi. Better still, make Mumbai your first stop and then go directly to Delhi. Spend a few days in Delhi. Treat Delhi as your central consolidation point and return there for the last two days of your trip to finalize your shopping odds and ends.

RECOMMENDED READINGS

You'll find lots of good reading on India. You may want to do some background reading on India before leaving on your adventure. Once in India, you'll find many inexpensive books in India's bookstores and hotel kiosks.

If you are a budget traveler or if you seek detailed information on sightseeing, we recommend Lonely Planet's *India*, a 1,200+ page tome written for backpackers and other budget travelers who seek a cultural adventure in India. Since this book is big, heavy, often irreverent, and filled with lots of historical, cultural, and religious information you probably don't need as you travel, it's best to tear out those sections that relate to your destinations and interests.

APA's *Insight Guide India* provides a useful pictorial introduction to India with many interesting historical and cultural observations. It doesn't travel well because of its size and lack of practical information. If you are interested in "understanding" from historical and anthropological perspectives, this is a good starter book with great pictures and excellent writing.

Other good guidebooks on India include *The Insider's Guide to India* (Hunter Publishing), *Frommer's India From $45 a Day* (Macmillan), *India Handbook* (Footprint/NTC Publishing), *Cadogan Guides India* (Globe Pequot), and Fodor's *India*. Most of these guides primarily focus on standard travel guide topics: history, culture, hotels, restaurants, and sightseeing.

You'll find some great reading on Indian history, culture, and contemporary politics. Many of these books make great travel companions for long train trips and airport waits. For starters, try Stanley Wolpert's *An Introduction to India*; M. M. Kaye's *The Far Pavilions*; Kamala Markandaya's *City of Joy*; Kushwant Singh's *Delhi*; A. L. Basham's *The Wonder That Was India*; Bamber Gascoigne's *The Mughals*; Tariq Ali's *The*

Nehrus and the Gandhis; Larry Collins and Dominique La-
pierre's *Freedom At Midnight* and *Mountbatten and Independ-
ent India*; Mark Tully and Zareer Masani's *From Raj to
Rajiv—40 Years of Indian Independence*; George Michell's *The
Royal Palaces of India*; William Dalrymple's *City of Djinns: A
Year in Delhi*; M. G. Vassanji's *The Gunny Sack*; Elisabeth
Bumiller's *May You Be the Mother of One Hundred Sons*; V. S.
Naipaul's three books, *An Area of Darkness, A Million Muti-
nies Now*, and *India—A Wounded Civilization*; Salman Rush-
die's *Midnight's Children* and *The Moor's Last Sigh*; Vikram
Chandra's *Red Earth and Pouring Rain*; Suzanne Slesin and
Stafford Cliff's *Indian Style*; Sunil Khilnani, *The Idea of India*;
William Gerber, *The Mind of India*; Steve Coll's *On the Grand
Trunk Road: A Journey Into South Asia*; Gitanjali Kolanad's
Culture Shock! India; Gita Mehta's *Karma Cola: Marketing the
Mystic East*; Mala Sen's *India's Bandit Queen: The True Story
of Phoolan Devi*; Gary Snyder's *Passage Through India*; and
Norma Lewis's *Goddess in the Stones: Travels in India*. For
entertaining travel writing on India, see Paul William Roberts's
Empire of the Soul; Travelers' Tales Guides *India*; Joe Robert's
Three Quarters of a Footprint; Alexander Frater's *Chasing the
Monsoon*; Eric Newby, *Slowly Down the Ganges*; Norman
Lewis's *A Goddess in the Stones*; and Sarah Lloyd's *An Indian
Attachment*.

NEWSPAPERS, MAGAZINES, TELEVISION

You'll find English-language newspapers in most major cities as
well as several local magazines published in English. However,
you may want to access two of India's major newspapers on the
Internet prior to arriving in India:

>   *www.indiaexpress.com*
>   *www.indiatimes.com*
>   *www.timesofindia.com*

For linkages to many online versions of English-language publications in India, visit this site:

>   *http://indiagov.org/info/links/links.htm#pub*

Most five-star hotels have copies of the *International Herald-
Tribune* and *USA Today*. International magazines, such as *Time*,
Newsweek, and *The Economist*, also are available in these hotels.
    Many of the major hotels will have local English-language

news programs as well as CNN, BBC, and Asian satellite networks.

3

Navigating Your Way Through India

You should now be well prepared to begin your travel and shopping adventure in earnest as soon as you arrive in India. Assuming you will arrive and depart India by air, it's useful to examine how to best orient yourself to the arrival and departure processes so that you can truly enjoy India from the very moment you arrive. There are certain practical aspects of traveling in India that you should know about. Most important of all, there are certain *attitudes* you need to develop to truly enjoy this place.

ARRIVING AND GETTING AROUND

As we noted in Chapter 2, we prefer starting in Mumbai and then traveling to Delhi, Varanasi, Agra, Jaipur, Jodhpur, Udaipur, Hyderabad, and Chennai. We normally return to Delhi for a final two days to do any last minute shopping as well as finalize shipping. Except for the nearby Golden Triangle cities of Delhi, Agra, and Jaipur, which we do by car or train, we fly to all of our destinations. We do this for two main reasons. First, flights between major cities are frequent, convenient, safe, and reasonably priced on India's three major domestic airlines:

Indian Airlines, Jet Airways, and Sahara Airlines. Second, our time is too valuable to spend on long train or bus rides. A one to two-hour flight is much more appealing to us than a 10 to 15 hour train or bus ride which can be uncomfortable.

Both Indian Airlines and Jet Airways offer special domestic "Discover India" and "Visit India" airfares. You can fly to an unlimited number of cities within a 15-day period for US$550; a 21-day pass costs $800. Check with your travel agent on these special rates. They are good values, especially if you plan to travel to several cities within these time periods. The Government of India Tourist Office's Website includes linkages to these airlines and their specials: *www.tourindia.com*

Be sure to book your domestic flights well in advance of your arrival in India. Many flights tend to be fully booked weeks in advance. If you wait until the last minute to book these flights, especially during high season, you are likely to be disappointed and your travel plans for all of India may quickly go awry. Ask your travel agent to book all of your domestic flights at the same time you do your international ticketing. Once in India, be sure to *always* reconfirm your on-going flight as soon as you arrive in a city. If you fail to do so, your reservation is likely to be automatically canceled. You'll arrive at the airport without a reservation. Your hotel concierge will take care of this reconfirmation. In fact, the first thing you should do upon checking into a hotel is to ask the front desk or concierge to reconfirm your onward airline ticket.

❏ Look for special domestic "Discover India" and "Visit India" airfares through Indian Airlines and Jet Airway. Fly to an unlimited number of cities within 15 days for only US$550!

❏ Be sure to always reconfirm your on-going flight as soon as you arrive in a new city.

❏ Given the crowded conditions of airports, plan to arrive 2 hours before departure.

❏ Look for prepaid taxi counters as you exit the baggage retrieval areas of domestic airports.

The airports in India seem to be in different states of organization and maintenance. Some can be extremely chaotic, especially in Mumbai when several international flights arrive around the same time late at night. The major problem tends to be very crowded facilities and long and chaotic lines when waiting to check in for flights to popular destinations. If you are with a tour group, you will be able to avoid many of the hassles involved in handling your own tickets and check-in. If not, ask questions, get in line, and work your way to the front.

Given the crowded conditions of many airports, plan to arrive at least two hours before departure time. While flights are often delayed, some actually leave on time. Expect to occasionally experience delays due to a combination of weather conditions and mechanical problems. Most major airports include restaurants, shops, and business facilities. International airports also include duty-free shopping.

Most domestic airports have both national and state tourist information desks which provide information and advice on hotels, transportation, and tours. They also have prepaid taxi counters, as you exit the baggage retrieval areas, which are convenient for arranging transportation from the airport to your hotel. They may charge a little more than what you might be able to bargain for outside the terminal, but they are very convenient and will save you the headaches of having to deal with so many pushy drivers who want your business.

DEPARTURE TAX

There is a departure tax upon leaving India. The cost is Rs 250 if you are flying to the neighboring countries of Afghanistan, Nepal, Pakistan, Bangladesh, Burma, Sri Lanka, Bhutan, or the Maldives. The departure tax for all other international destinations is Rs 500. Since you must pay this departure tax in local currency, be sure to set aside enough rupees for this final expense.

CUSTOMS

Customs procedures tend to meet most international standards. You need to make an oral declaration of your baggage and foreign currency. You also need to fill out a Disembarkation Card and complete a Currency Declaration Form from Customs. If you are bringing in high value items that could be questioned by Customs, be sure to complete a Tourist Baggage Re-Export Form (TBRE). If not, you may be liable for duties on such items. You should no problem bringing a computer into India, although you may be questioned about it at Customs and you may need to include it on the TBRE form.

INDIA TIME AND SERENDIPITY

All of India is on one time zone which is 5½ hours ahead of GMT and 10½ hours ahead of EST in the United States.

Synchronizing your watch is one thing; operating according to "India Time" is another. In general, time has a way of getting away from you in India. Since so much of the India experience is serendipitous—you're always discovering something new and exciting that distracts your attention—you often find that time seems to get away from you, despite your best efforts to manage your time well. Best laid plans and schedules may need to be revised by mid-day because you encountered heavy traffic; a place you planned to visit was closed; you spent too much time at your last stop; or a shopkeeper invited you to visit his wonderful warehouse and factory on the other side of the city (there goes another unexpected three hours, just like yesterday and the day before!). Punctuality is not a well developed Indian trait. If you are invited to someone's home for dinner, for example, it's best to arrive a half hour late. Dinner will probably start much later than you expected. Appointment times often slip because of unforeseen circumstances. If you are a very time-oriented person, who plans tight schedules and places great value on being and leaving on time, India may frustrate you. It's best to factor in "India time" and keep and approach your travels in India with a new attitude toward time and planning. Better still, automatically build in a few extra "hours for serendipity" each day so you won't be too disappointed when your schedule slips as you experience another fascinating aspect of this alluring country.

INTERCITY TRANSPORTATION

Your transportation options within cities are numerous. In the case of transportation, serendipity is not a good idea. Aside from the horrendous traffic, you should have little difficulty getting around in most cities and outlying areas. Except for Hyderabad and Udaipur, **taxis** are plentiful and relatively inexpensive in most large cities. They can be found at hotels, at taxi stands, or flagged down along the street. While most taxis have meters, many have not been recalibrated in years to reflect current rates. In both Mumbai and Delhi, taxi drivers must add a percentage to what appears on the meter to reflect the official taxi charge. In other cities, taxi drivers prefer negotiating rates rather than using their "broken" meter. In these cases, make sure you negotiate a rate before departing for your destination. An accurate rate may be 25 percent less than the first quoted rate. If a taxi driver asks for Rs 200, counter with Rs 125 and then settle for Rs 150.

The little noisy three-wheeled **auto-rickshaws** are relatively inexpensive and convenient. While some are metered, you will probably have to negotiate the rate in many cases. These vehicles are not comfortable on a hot and rainy day or if you are stuck in traffic for very long. You'll experience the worst effects of air polluting buses, trucks, and cars while waiting in the confines of these ostensibly cute vehicles.

All cities have a **bus** service. While extremely cheap, buses are often overcrowded, dirty, and uncomfortable. Furthermore, it's often difficult to know where a bus is going because signage is not tourist-friendly. Many destination signs at the front of buses are in Hindi. We've been there, done that. Our advice: avoid buses; you don't need another cheap form of aggravation.

We much prefer hiring a **car and driver** in each city we visit. This is one of the best deals you'll find on transportation anywhere in the world! Hiring a car with a driver is cheap, convenient, and relatively comfortable, especially if you get an air-conditioned car on a hot and heavily polluted day. Expect to pay from US$20 to US$30 a day (8 hours) for a car and driver within the city; charges may increase by US$10 for traveling outside the city. It's money well spent since your car and driver will always be available wherever you visit. If you're shopping, the car will come in handy for hauling your goodies throughout the day. Be sure to write down your driver's name and license number, since many taxi cabs look the same and you may forget what your driver looks like in a crowd of other drivers; at hotel stops, you'll need to call your driver (by name) at the front taxi desk. You can normally arrange a car and driver through your hotel tour desk, directly with a taxi driver, or through a tour agent or tourist office. It's best to make arrangements the day before. Prices are usually negotiable, especially if the price quoted seems out of line with the going rate. You should never have to pay more than US$40 a day for a car and driver.

CURRENCY AND EXCHANGE RATES

India's currency units are the *rupee*, which is abbreviated and referred to as Rs, and the *paisa* (100 paisa equals one rupee). Paper bills come in denominations of 1, 2, 5, 10, 20, 50, 100, 500, and 1,000 rupees. Since the bills stay in circulation a long time, many of them are very worn, torn, and dirty. Your hands will be constantly dirty from handling these bills. Try to avoid accepting worn and torn bills which are more trouble than they are worth. Coins are available in denominations of 5, 10, 20, 25, and 50 paises as well as 1, 2, and 5 rupees. The problem with Indian currency is that it's inconvenient to carry because there is so much of it in small denominations. In addition, banks staple piles of bills together which are hard to separate without tearing the banknotes.

The rate of exchange has been relatively stable for the last few years, fluctuating around Rs 38 to Rs 40 to US$1. At the time of this writing, the rupee had fallen to a new low—Rs 43.5 = US$1. Don't waste your time looking for black market rates which are not significantly different from the official exchange rate. You may end up with less than you expected.

Visa and MasterCard are increasingly accepted in India. However, don't expect street vendors and small shops to accept credit cards. Some places accept American Express. And don't expect to use your ATM card much in India. It's best to carry lots of cash, traveler's checks, and a Visa and/or MasterCard.

HOTELS AND RESTAURANTS

India is in the midst of a hotel and restaurant revolution. For years, India's major hotels were dominated by three Indian chains: Oberoi, Taj Group, and ITC. Often competing head to head, the Oberoi and Taj hotels represented India's "best of the best" in accommodations. Hotel prices for these five-star properties ranged from US$200 to US$400 a night, which often seemed high by international standards, although they primarily catered to business travelers. The ITC chain was run by the government; their hotels, such as the Ashok, often had nice facades but their rooms and service leave a lot to be desired. Except for the Oberoi and Taj Group, India's top hotels were largely managed by locals who had little international experience, and especially little experience promoting one of the great strengths of most top international hotels—food and beverage. Consequently, most top Indian hotels were primarily room-oriented; they neglected other important features of the hotel business, from restaurants to business facilities. Indeed, while most of the world's major hotel chains maintain a 50/50 revenue balance between rooms and other facilities, in India the ratio has been closer to 65 percent for rooms and 35 percent for other facilities. As a result, India's top hotels have to charge more for their rooms, and be very room-dependent for revenue, because they never generate enough operating income from their other facilities, especially restaurants.

Major changes have come to the India hotel industry during the past five years. With the lifting of government restrictions on foreign owned and operated hotels, more and more international hotel chains have come to India and created new competition and a new look in the hospitality business by moving closer to the 50/50 ratio. With them have come international standards, expat managers, and increased emphasis on developing attractive food and beverage services. More and

more foreign chefs have been brought in to develop and man
new international restaurants. As a result, India's major hote
chains have followed suit by opening more top quality restaurants and recruiting international talent to become more
competitive in this new environment. Not surprisingly, India's
"best of the best" Oberoi hotel chain has gotten even better as
it has hired top international general managers and opened
many new restaurants under the management of talented
European chefs; its new property in Jaipur, the Rajvillas,
exemplifies these new emphases on international standards and
opulence. One of the real bargains, and best kept secrets, in
India are the top French, Continental, Chinese, and Indian
restaurants at the major five-star hotels. They often offer fine
dining with top chefs and at relatively low prices. Indeed, you
can dine at one of India's top restaurants for US$40 per person,
a restaurant that might cost US$150 or more per person in
another country. The overall trend is to continue to energize
the hospitality industry with more and more hotels and restaurants operated under international standards of management
and service.

At the same time, India offers some intermediate and many
budget accommodations. However, good quality mid-range and
budget hotels have been difficult to find until recently. Recog-
nizing the need for less than luxury accommodations, both the
Oberoi and Taj chains have developed several mid-range hotels
that offer excellent accommodations at reasonable prices aimed
toward budget-minded business people and tourists. Not surprisingly, these hotels have been very successful. They especially
appeal to individual travelers and tour groups. Look for the
Oberoi's **Trident** hotels and the Taj Group's **Gateway** hotels
for good value. More and more of these mid-range hotels will be
built throughout India given the recent success of the Trident
and Gateway chains.

In many respects, India's hotel and restaurant infrastructure
is just beginning to blossom. Many good things are happening
in the hospitality industry that should change the face of
tourism in India in the coming decade as India appeals to more
and more groups that cannot afford five-star hotels but neither
want to rough it in a backpacker's "almost free" no-star hotel.

Locally-operated budget hotels seldom meet international
standards. You basically get what you pay for, which in many
cases, is not a great deal. Nonetheless, if you don't mind the
general lack of service and amenities, these hotels will be a real
budget-saver. As most seasoned backpackers to India will testify, you can live very cheaply in India if you don't mind the
hassles and inconveniences that often come with this style of

et a whole different class of people which
travelers.

ater several taxes added to your hotel and
els that charge Rs 1200 (US$32) a night or
nt expenditure tax to your room, food, and
ddition, individual states add luxury and
ry from state to state. Don't be surprised if
.0 percent higher than what you expected
because of these additional taxes.

WATER AND DRINKS

Tap water in India is not potable even though it is chemically
treated in most cities. Bottled water is readily available and can
be purchased in many shops. Most hotels provide bottled water
in rooms for drinking purposes.

There's plenty to drink in India, from teas, coffees, and local
beers to locally bottled soft drinks and fruit juices.

ELECTRICITY

Electricity throughout India is supplied at 220 volts and 50
cycles AC. Most electrical outlets are configured in three-prong
(round) pins. If you're traveling with appliances, such as a hair
dryer, be sure it converts to 220 volts. Also, take a conversion
plug to handle India's electrical configuration. Otherwise, ask
hotel housekeeping for an adaptor.

We always travel with our handy and much used little 15-
foot extension cord. Invariably we find electrical outlets for
using our computer and hair dryer to be inconveniently located
behind furniture or far from good lighting or a mirror. In many
hotels we would be better off with 25 feet of extension cord or
two 15-foot lengths!

Expect to encounter frequent power shortages in many
cities. While power usually returns within a few minutes, it can
be irritating if you're trying to read, watch television, or dine,
or if you are stuck in an elevator.

BUSINESS HOURS

Most government offices, post offices, banks, and museums
keep similar hours: 10am to 5pm, Monday to Saturday (closed
alternating Saturdays) for **government offices**; 10am to 5pm,
Monday to Friday, for **post offices**; and 10am to 2pm, Monday

to Friday, and 10am to noon on every other Saturday for **banks**; 10am to 5:30pm, Tuesday to Sunday (closed Monday) for **museums**; 10am to 5:30pm, Saturday to Thursday (closed Friday) for **archeological sites**. Many **temples and mosques** are open daily from 6am to 8pm but closed in the afternoons.

Shop hours vary, depending on the city or shop. In general, most shops are open six days a week, from 10am to 7pm. Some shops open at 11am and close at 7pm; others open at 9am and close at 5pm. The particular day of the week they close will depend on the particular shop and neighborhood—various areas close on different days of the week—although many shops routinely close on Sunday as well.

Before venturing out to do early morning sightseeing or shopping, check with your hotel about hours and closing days. Since not much is going on before 10am, you may want to enjoy a nice leisurely breakfast before heading out into India's challenging streets!

LANGUAGE

India officially recognizes 15 languages and boasts nearly 700 other languages and dialects. **Hindi** is the most widely used language (20 percent of population, mainly in the north-central region of India) and it's the official language of government. Other important languages are **Tamil** in the south, **Assamese** in Assam, **Bengali** in West Bengal, **Gujarati** in Gujarat, **Kannada** in Karnataka, **Kashmiri** in Jammu and Kashmir, **Malayalam** in Kerals, **Marathi** in Maharashtra, **Oriya** in Orissa, **Punjabi** in Punjab, **Telugu** in Andhra Pradesh, and **Urdu** in Jammu and Kashmi. **Sanskrit** is India's classical language.

But the good news for travelers is that **English** is widely understood, spoken, and written due to the British legacy in India. Except in remote areas, you should have no problem getting around with English. Taxi drivers and shopkeepers may speak a strange yet charming form of broken English, but after awhile you'll get use to the idioms, structure, and pronunciation to communicate in English.

TOURS AND TRAVEL AGENTS

Despite what you may have read or heard from others, India really is an easy place to travel to these days because it's very accessible for both groups and individuals. However, you must approach it differently from many other countries.

If you arrive on your own, you'll have no problem arranging local tours through a variety of travel agents who offer a wide range of travel services. As outlined in Chapter 2, numerous travel agents operate both inside and outside India. Many of the more than 100 tour agencies based in North America use a variety of ground operators in India for both group tours and customized individual tours. If you don't like traveling with groups, you can easily arrange a customized itinerary for you and your fellow travelers. You, in effect, go as an independent traveler who is met at various destinations with a car, driver, and guide.

❑ English is widely understood, spoken and written. Except in remote areas, you should have no problem getting around with English.

❑ Given the availability of numerous tour companies and cars with drivers for hire, it's very easy to design your own travel itinerary at a very reasonable price once you arrive in India.

❑ At least where tourists can be found, tips are expected and early sought.

❑ Sometimes you don't know if you should be tipping or bribing (*baksheesh*) someone for service.

You also can make local tour arrangements once you arrive in India. Most Government of India Tourist Offices (for contact points, visit *www.tourindia.com*) offer half-day and full-day group tours as well as arrange individualized itineraries involving a licensed guide. Also, check with your hotel tour desk which can offer you many group and individual tour options. In most cities you will find many local tour operators and car rental companies eager to assist you on a one-to-one basis.

The really good news for travelers to India is that you can pretty much design whatever type of travel experience you want at a very reasonable price. Despite all the chaos you see in the streets, it's very easy to cut through this seeming chaos by arranging your travel plans. Best of all, you can quickly make such arrangements once you arrive in India.

TIPPING AND *BAKSHEESH*

You may hear that tipping is not part of India's culture. Don't believe it for a moment. At least where tourists can be found, tips are expected and eagerly sought. The problem is that no one really knows what the "rule" is for tipping. The "situation" often defines when and what to give. While some restaurants add a 10 percent service charge, others put this not-so-subtle statement on the bill: *"No service charge added."* Drivers expect Rs 50-100 per day; restaurant personnel expect 10 percent of the check; porters like to get Rs 10 per bag; room boys would like to be tipped Rs 20-40 for your stay; and a doorman likes Rs 20. When in doubt, give a few rupee (Rs 10-20), keeping in mind that many of these "service personnel" make less than US$100 a month.

Sometimes you really don't know if you should be tipping or bribing (*baksheesh*) someone for service. The easiest way to keep the two separate is to think of *baksheesh* as something you give *before* a service is performed versus a "tip" being something you give *after* a service is performed. In other words, *baksheesh* is up-front money to grease the wheels, whereas a tip expresses your appreciation for a service well done. However, if you make such an academic distinction, you'll quickly find that you're dispensing more *baksheesh* than you are tips!

Unfortunately, the two get confused when you arrive at your hotel with four bags and four porters quickly grab one bag each and take them to your room. They then stand around looking for their "tip." So, instead of tipping a single porter for what should be a one-man job, you get to tip all of them! One way out of this situation is to identify who looks to be the oldest porter and give him one bill (Rs 10 per bag is sufficient) and tell him to share it with "the boys." Now it's their problem as to who gets how much of your group tip. But it's good to tip at this stage of your visit. You may even want to over-tip because you want some extra service from these individuals. But be prepared to meet a parade of these people, from the people who bring your bags to those who offer you tea, two who turn down your bed, another who brings you a flower, another who checks your water, another who pulls your drapes, and another who wants to know if everything is okay. Indeed, you may meet ten people during your first hour who seem concerned about your well being. They often identify themselves: *"I'm your room boy. I clean your room."* He then waits to get his "tip" before he performs his service. This is a form of *baksheesh*. They all want a tip from their new guest.

Similar situations arise at airports, train stations, and sites. Before you know it, you're surrounding by people who want to offer you a service, from carrying your bags to checking you through a line to giving you a tour of a temple compound or archeological site. Many of these "volunteered" services are nuisances; others are very valuable—especially when faced with a very crowded and chaotic airport with long and intimidating lines. In the end, the volunteer may demand exorbitant prices since you failed to agree upon a price before receiving the service. This sometimes becomes a form of extortion or reverse *baksheesh*. Don't be intimidated. Give them a nominal tip (Rs 50), ignore their pleas for more, and walk away without making eye contact. Always be firm and direct your attention elsewhere.

Even your driver will remind you in not-so-subtle ways that it's almost "tip time"—he wants a special tip from you. He might say something to this effect:

> *"When I take Mr. Daryl around last month, he treat me real good. Gave me very nice tip. And Miss Nancy did same thing the week before. Very nice people. Do you know them? They from California. Treat me real good."*

If you have a driver for a five-day period, he'll start working on this subtle "tip message" by the third day and continue repeating it again until you depart for good. You get the message. Hopefully, you will know when it's your "tip time"!

You may find occasions when you want to "tip" someone in order to get things done. Greasing someone's palm with a few rupee can result in getting better service or overcoming obstacles such as long lines and onerous regulations. At train stations, for example, many travelers must "tip" the ticket manager in order to get a ticket. Customs officials also are known for their appetites for *baksheesh*. When someone tells you something is not possible or that you can't do something, think about the role of *baksheesh* in motivating people to overcome seeming obstacles. Money really does talk and walk in India.

Annoyances And Coping Well

From traffic to touts, India has lots of annoyances that can test your patience and affect your attitude toward India as a whole. For many visitors, the annoyance list is very long. For others, India's annoyances are tolerable since they only last for a few weeks and then they will disappear altogether when you return home.

You really need to be forgiving of most annoyances or you will have difficulty with your trip. Above all, this is a country of heat, chaos, and hard living. Expect to encounter many of these annoyances as you travel through India:

- **Chaos:** It's everywhere. If you are a very neat and tidy person who likes visual order and predictability, India can be very disorienting. In India, everyone seems to muddle through the chaos. While things may not work well in India, eventually they do work and you will survive with lots on interesting stories of your "India Adventure." If you ask questions and go with the flow, you'll manage this chaos with little difficulty. After awhile, the chaos may actually be fun! It leads to lots of serendipitous experiences.

- **Service:** Service can be excellent in India, especially where customer service training has taken place in top hotels and restaurants. But service also can be terrible, especially when dealing with government offices, hotels, and shops. Many bureaucrats in India tend to have a sense of entitlement. They seem to have institutional-ized the long line and bureaucratic nonsense.

- **Touts:** Expect to encounter touts wherever tourists congregate. They come in many forms, from shoeshine artists to self-appointed guides and trinket salesmen. Many will pester you to death if you don't deal with them immediately and firmly. These are not nice people who want to become your friend; they are entrepreneurs who only want your money. The best way to deal with them is to (1) be firm, (2) avoid eye contact, and (3) direct your attention elsewhere as if they don't exit. Being firm means immediately telling them, *"No, I'm not interested. Go away."* If they persist, which they will, completely ignore them. They will soon get the message —you are a waste of their time—and go on to someone who is more naive and engages them in a conversation or argument.

- **Power outages and water shortages:** Many cities, such as Delhi, Varanasi, and Agra, have persistent problems with power and water. It's not unusual for power to go out frequently. Be sure to carry a flashlight when you travel in India. It may come in handy on many occa-sions. Some cities, such as Chennai, experience major water shortages during the summer months.

- **Noise:** The noise pollution in India's cities can some-times be deafening. Loud mufflers and honking horns, along with heat, air pollution, and crowds, can ruin your day. It's always good to identify a few oasis you can escape to during the day to get away from such irritants, especially coffee shops and restaurants in top hotels.

- **Pollution:** Air pollution is especially bad in cities due to a combination of pollution-belching vehicles and facto-ries. You may experience headaches because of such pollution. Whenever possible, take air-conditioned taxis or cars to avoid some of the worst effects of such pollution. Water pollution is widespread because raw sewerage and factory wastes are pumped into rivers and lakes.

- **Crowds:** Cities and attractions tend to be very crowded. City streets are especially congested during early morning and late afternoon rush hours. If you value private space, you may find the crowds to be very tiring.

- **Traffic:** Most cities experience frequent traffic jams and congestion throughout the day. Traffic on highways can be very dangerous since vehicles speed a lot and take many risks. Traveling by bus or car can be a very frightening experience.

- **Restrooms:** Public restrooms may shock you. They tend to be dirty and toilet paper may be non-existent. You may want to travel with your own supply of toilet paper or tissues. If you need to use restroom facilities, seek out the restrooms in the public areas of the top hotels.

- **Beggars:** Beggars seem to be everywhere in India, but especially in large cities. Many are very persistent and disturbing. Don't be intimidated by the aggressive ones who seem to practice a form of beggar-*baksheesh*. Many are literally professional beggars (they come from clever villages noted for their excellent begging skills) while others may be genuinely in need. We do not recommend supporting beggars since doing so further encourages this activity—especially professional beggars who are not as poor as they look. India has numerous charitable organizations that work with the poor. Give to them rather than individual beggars.

- **Littered and unsanitary public areas:** This is not a clean and sanitary place. If you are really into public cleanliness and personal hygiene, India may shock you. Many public areas, especially streets, are littered with trash. Lacking a sense of public responsibility, many people freely litter public areas as if they belong to no one. Parts of cities often look filthy with garbage alongside the roads and sidewalks and with open sewerage systems. Animals wander around defecating on sidewalks and streets. Always watch where you step!

PART II

Acquiring Treasures With Ease

4

India's Shopping Treasures

I f you like to shop for jewelry, furniture, textiles, art, and antiques as well as browse for handicrafts, collectibles, carpets, home decorative items, clothes, and accessories, you'll love shopping in India. Few places in the world offer such a profusion of handcrafted goods as India. The range and depth of colorful shopping is at times staggering.

In many respects, India is one great big arts and crafts emporium offering a wide range of locally designed items in a variety of unique shopping environments. You can literally *"shop 'til you drop"* here and still only touch the surface of this vast country of talented craftspeople who produce a dazzling array of products at very reasonable prices. In fact, in addition to India's many historical monuments and expressions of culture, one of the major highlights of visiting India is discovering its many shopping treasures. In so doing, you'll learn a great deal about this country and its people by examining and acquiring what they produce. On numerous occasions, you'll have opportunities to meet artists and craftspeople who demonstrate their work. You'll encounter well established shops known for their quality products and reliable service, including packing and shipping abroad. Best of all, you'll discover great bargains on items that cost only a fraction (five or ten times less) of what they might cost back home.

TALENTED CRAFTSPEOPLE

Similar to China, with its rich history and cultural traditions, India is a country of talented artists and craftspeople who produce a sometimes bewildering array of arts and crafts. Indeed, the sheer volume of such shopping can be overwhelming, especially when visiting the many arts and crafts emporiums sponsored by the federal government, various state governments, and several private entrepreneurs. While much of what you find in emporiums and markets can be classified as tourist kitsch, India also produces fine quality textiles, jewelry, and furniture that appeal to international visitors.

At the same time, acquiring products is often a challenge because of the type of unsavory middlemen you often meet. Like many other visitors to India, you will most likely encounter very aggressive, and frequently annoying, Kashmiri rug merchants who pester you with mountains of carpets and assorted handicrafts you neither need nor want. You'll also encounter numerous drivers, tour guides, and touts who attempt to steer you to shops that offer them 30 to 40 percent commissions on everything you purchase.

In many respects, India is one big workshop producing everything from textiles, jewelry, paintings, sculptures, and pottery to furniture, brassware, carvings, puppets, and toys. The list goes on and on. While much of the jewelry, arts, and crafts have a decided ethnic look, others integrate well with Western homes and wardrobes. Emporiums, shops, and bazaars are packed with goods produced for India's growing number of tourists, both domestic and foreign, as well as for its large Western-oriented export market.

Consider for a moment what you will be encountering on your India adventure: a very diverse country of 1 billion people with a 4,000 year old history centered around numerous cul-

- ❏ You'll learn a great deal about this country and its people by examining and acquiring what they produce.

- ❏ Expect to discover bargains on items that cost only a fraction of what you might pay back home.

- ❏ India produces fine quality textiles, jewelry, and furniture that appeal to international tastes.

- ❏ Don't be surprised to encounter numerous enterprising drivers, guides, and touts who attempt to steer you to shops that offer them 30 to 40 percent commissions on everything you purchase.

- ❏ India may be the ultimate "field of dreams" when it comes to arts and crafts.

tural traditions and royal intervention that supported the profusion of visual arts and crafts; it's a country that continues, through government encouragement, to promote both the production and distribution of arts and crafts. Not surprising, you encounter an incredible number of arts and crafts wherever you visit in India, from government emporiums to hotel shops and bazaars. Indeed, you will on more than one occasion wonder where all of this stuff came from and where it will eventually go since so much of it seems over-produced in relation to market demand. India may be the ultimate "field of dreams" when it comes to arts and crafts. It could become your field of dreams for acquiring many of India's treasures.

FIVE SHOPPING CULTURES

You are likely to encounter at least five different shopping cultures in India, each with its own characteristics and set of shopping rules:

1. Government fixed-priced emporiums.
2. Private emporiums, shopping centers, and shops.
3. Hotel shopping arcades with upscale shops offering quality goods.
4. Factories and warehouses selling both retail and wholesale.
5. Specialty markets and bazaars where everything is negotiable.

India is the land of the **shopping emporium**. Both the federal government and state governments each operate large arts and crafts emporiums that are jam-packed with local products. Expect to find everything from textiles, carvings, and brassware to furniture, carpets, and jewelry in these two to six-level stores. Since prices are fixed, these are good places to start surveying your shopping options before venturing into other types of shops that require bargaining. However, prices are not necessarily the cheapest. You may find similar items in private shops and bazaars at better prices. Expect to find lots of tourist kitsch in these places along with some good quality, tasteful items that should integrate well into your home and wardrobe. Most of these places are experienced in packing and shipping abroad.

Private emporiums, shopping centers, and shops offering a wide variety of shopping options. Most of these places have fixed prices. Some may extend a 10 to 20 percent discount, if you ask. **Private emporiums** often tend to look and feel like government emporiums but they are not as trustworthy, despite their claim to be fixed-price "government approved" shops. They often use names that confuse them with their government counterparts. The largest and best quality such emporiums are the nearly 50 Kashmiri-run C.I.E. (Cottage Industry Emporiums) shops, along with their upscale Saga Department stores, which are found in India's major cities. A few cities have Western-style **shopping centers**, but most tend to approximate open-air strip malls and are primarily popular with local shoppers. These places are one step above the more traditional neighborhood bazaars. A few of them, especially in Delhi, have shops of interest to international visitors. Street **shops** of interest to visitors are usually found in and around the major shopping areas and hotels.

Hotel **shopping arcades** often house some of India's best and most expensive shops for jewelry, arts, crafts, antiques, textiles, and home decorative items. The best shops tend to be found in India's best hotels, especially the Oberoi hotels and the Taj Group's Khazana boutiques. If you have limited shopping time and you're interested in top quality items, a good rule of thumb is to first visit the shopping arcades in a city's top hotels. Prices may be higher in these shops but so is the quality. Most prices are fixed although not necessarily so in Kashmiri carpet and shawl shops. Expect to get at least a 10 percent discount in these places and possibly a lot more, depending on your negotiation skills and their daily cash flow needs.

If your shopping interests include arts, antiques, furniture, and home decorative items, expect to find numerous large **factories and warehouses** that sell both retail and wholesale. Especially in Mumbai and Delhi, you may enter a small shop that also has two or three large warehouses and/or factories on the outskirts of the city. These larger operations tend to cater to international dealers who purchase containers of items for export abroad. Be sure to ask shops if they have other shops, warehouses, or "farms" elsewhere in or outside the city. They may

> ❑ Fixed-price government shopping emporiums are good places to start surveying shopping options *before* venturing to other types of shops.
>
> ❑ Private emporiums often look and feel like government emporiums—but they are not as trustworthy.
>
> ❑ Be sure to ask shops if they have other shops, warehouses or "farms" elsewhere near the city.
>
> ❑ A shop's "catalog" is usually a photo album of their larger inventory.
>
> ❑ Specialty markets and bazaars are basically cultural experiences rather than good places to shop.

say *"Yes, we have three more places"* and then show you their "catalog," which is usually a photo album of their larger inventory. If you're interested in the items, they may take you to their warehouse which may mean an additional two to three hours of unexpected but fascinating shopping. You may be pleasantly surprised at what you discover! The good news is that prices tend to be very reasonable at these warehouses and they are experienced in packing and shipping abroad.

Traditional **specialty markets and bazaars** are found in all cities. Mainly catering to local shoppers, these places tend to specialize in a few items, such as fruits and vegetables, clothes, jewelry, textiles, and household goods. Many are basically cultural experiences for visitors rather than good places to shop. A few of the bazaars are primarily designed for tourists and include lots of arts, crafts, clothes, and tourist kitsch. Be sure to bargain hard in these places, expecting to receive anywhere from 20 to 60 percent on your purchases.

WHAT TO BUY

You won't run out of things to buy in India. This is one big shopping emporium for arts, crafts, furniture, textiles, jewelry, clothes, and accessories. Once you arrive in India and visit a few government emporiums and hotel shopping arcades, you will quickly get a good overview of what lies ahead. The product mix tends to be very similar wherever you go. You'll find some regional variations (marble table tops in Agra, pearls in Hyderabad, and intricate silk embroidery in Varanasi). Indeed, you may become tired of seeing so many of the same things wherever you go, especially the ubiquitous carpets, sandalwood carvings, miniature paintings, inlaid wood boxes, papier mache items, and brassware that flood the emporiums and shops.

While you will encounter lots of shopping in India, chances are you will buy only a few things as you quickly learn to become a discriminating shopper for both quality and designs. It's really not difficult to become a discriminating shopper in India because only certain items will appeal to your sense of taste and design. The reason for this is the fact that much of what appears on the local markets tends to be very ethnic in nature. The fascinating silk embroidery work in Varanasi, inlaid marble work in Agra, carpet and silk weavers, and 22 karat gold jewelry, for example, are very interesting to observe, but you may not know what to do with these items back home. Consequently, you may want to watch demonstrations for artistic talents and technical details rather than purchase the demonstrated products which may look out of place in your tastefully decorated home. You may feel you really don't have a place to display or use such unique. Indeed, unless you collect a lot of tourist kitsch, your home decor and wardrobe may not support the introduction of traditional Indian designs and colors however interesting the handwork may be. This observation goes beyond cultural preferences. Like China, India generally lacks design talent that is oriented to international tastes. At the same time, you will find a few shops, such as Ravissant in Delhi and Mumbai, that offer top quality items designed for an international audience.

In terms of sheer volume, India is a shopper's paradise. Its major shopping strengths include:

❑ **Jewelry:** Indian's love jewelry, especially gold necklaces, rings, earrings, and bangles. Much of it is made in bright colored 22k gold. You'll also find lots of jewelry using precious and semi-precious stones, especially diamonds, rubies, sapphires, emeralds, and pearls. Also, look for unique tribal and enameled jewelry associated with workshops in Jaipur. Much of the jewelry is made in traditional Indian designs which may be perfect for a special outfit or too ethnic for your jewelry tastes. At the same time, many top Indian jewelers design jewelry for export to Western markets. Many of these shops can be found in and around the major five-star hotels. Some of India's best jewelers are found in Mumbai, Delhi, Agra, and Jaipur. For loose stones, visit Agra. For enameled jewelry, try Jaipur. For pearls, head for Hyderabad.

When shopping for jewelry in India, keep these observations in mind. First, sellers of jewelry may tell you boastfully that the setting is handmade—the implication being that handmade is more valuable than multiple pieces made from a precision die. Don't get carried away with the value of "made by hand." Just as not only the age, but also the quality of workmanship, gives value to an antique, the same holds true as for the worth of "handmade" in jewelry. The exquisite craftsmanship in a beautifully created handmade piece of jewelry can add to its value, but a lot of Indian jewelry does not meet this quality standard. But, like poorly tailored clothes, much of this jewelry is churned out by amateur hands, with a decided look of crude workmanship. So carefully examine the quality of the setting before being swayed by the old "handmade" sales pitch.

Second, old pieces of Indian jewelry will almost certainly be 22k-24k gold. The 14k gold jewelry we are used to seeing so much in the States isn't really considered gold by most Indians—too much alloy in it—and thus they do not work with what they may feel is the equivalent of costume jewelry. Indian jewelry traditionally formed a woman's wealth in times when she could not legally own property. This, combined with a mistrust of banks, made jewelry an important asset—not just adornment. So nearly purse gold (24k) had value. But pure gold is soft—too soft to be used as a setting for stones. The prongs are apt to loosen and the stones fall out from the settings. An 18k setting is a good compromise—high gold content, but enough alloy to give it greater strength for settings. If jewelry is higher than 18k and has gemstones set in it, the prongs holding the stone should not be a higher gold content than 18k. It is possible to have a ring, for example, that is 22k but the prongs are 18k.

❏ **Handicrafts:** India is a paradise for a large variety of handicrafts. Spend an hour in a government or C.I.E. emporium and you will quickly see the large range of handicrafts available in India. Look for sandalwood carvings, inlaid wood boxes, stuffed toys, puppets, pottery, papier mache products, brassware, copper items, silver, enamelware, embroidery, ceramics, marble plates and boxes, bidriware, and carved panels. Colors are often very bright and vibrant, with the generous use of reds, oranges, yellows, and greens.

❏ **Textiles:** India is rightly famous for its woven silks, brocades, sarees, embroidery, hand blocked prints, ethnic dresses, and wool shawls. In every city you will find emporiums, shops, and bazaars that offer a wide range of attractive textiles that have been produced in villages and factories. You may want to purchase silks by the meter and have them tailored into blouses, shirts, or dresses or home decorative items, such as pillows, placemats, and wall hangings.

❏ **Furniture:** Furniture is one of the best buys in India. Indeed, India is a treasure-trove for colonial-style furniture, both old and reproduction. Several shops and warehouses specialize in offering a wide range of Indian, British Raj, Portuguese, and Sri Lankan furniture. Some of the best buys are on reconditioned old furniture as well as reproduction furniture. If you have something you would like to have made, bring a photo or design to India. You'll find several places that will reproduce exactly what you want at very reasonable prices, including shipping. Also, expect to find cane furniture, lac furniture, patio furniture, and unique decorative furniture plated with white metal and silver.

❏ **Antiques and collectibles:** You can still find some good quality antiques and collectibles in India. Look for many collectibles from the British Raj period, especially in Mumbai. Keep in mind that the government restricts the export of antiques—nothing over 100 years old without special permission.

❏ **Paintings and sculptures:** India has a very vibrant art community that produces attractive traditional and contemporary paintings and sculptures as well as traditional Mughal paintings in miniature. Look for many private art galleries in Mumbai, Delhi, and Chennai that display some of India's leading artists, including many from India's major art center in Calcutta. At the same time, you're find lots of tourist art in the form of miniature paintings on paper and bone, especially in Udaipur and Agra. Traditional miniature ivory paintings have been replaced with bone because of the international ban on the import and export of ivory products.

❏ **Carpets:** You can't miss carpets in India. They, along with the ubiquitous and aggressive Kashmiri rug merchants, seem to be everywhere you shop. Most government and private emporiums and numerous shops in hotel shopping arcades offer a wide variety of carpets. However, don't be pressured into buying something you really don't need or want. Be sure to shop around to compare quality and prices. And bargain hard for such purchases—your initial offer should be no more than half of the asking price. India's major carpet centers are found in Bhadohi, Agra, Amritsar, Jaipur, Gwalior, and Kashmir. Carpets are normally produced in three varieties: Persian (Ispahan and Kashan), Turkoman, and Ambusson (French). Also look for colorful durries.

❏ **Leather goods:** Many shops offer a wide range of locally produced leather goods, especially shoes, briefcases, handbags, wallets, and belts. Some letter bags and shoes are obvious knock-offs of popular European designer goods. The leather quality, designs, and workmanship vary greatly, depending on the particular shop. In general, leather goods are relatively inexpensive and quality is mediocre to average. While you'll find leather goods in all cities, especially in the emporiums, Chennai is one of India's major leather centers.

The list goes on and on, with silver crafts, metal ornaments, bidriware, enameling, pottery, terracotta, stone craft, sculptures, and wood lacquer work. You'll find many attractive shopping treasures in India as you explore this fascinating country's emporiums, shops, and bazaars. The real fun of shopping in India is discovering new and unusual items that will integrate well with your home and wardrobe while, at the same time, meeting many interesting artisans and shopkeepers. As you will quickly discover, shopping will become one of your favorite memories of India—if you do it right.

5

Rules For Success

S hopping in India follows its own set of rules and logic that differs from shopping in many other countries. On the one hand, there's lots of shopping available for all kinds of local handcrafted products, which ostensibly makes India a shopper's paradise. On the other hand, there are lots of shopping pitfalls in India, where it's not always easy to "read" the shopping situation. Indeed, what you see is not always what you get and vice versa.

Our task in this chapter is to make some sense out of India's shopping culture so that you can acquire your treasures with confidence and ease. Properly oriented, you should be better able to effectively navigate your way through India's many emporiums, shops, and markets.

THREE PRICING/PRODUCT CULTURES

The five shopping cultures we identified in Chapter 4 revolve around three pricing and product cultures. Depending on where you shop, expect to encounter three very distinct styles of shopping, each with its own set of rules and related pitfalls. The first one appears more like the one you are probably used to back home—fixed prices where items are displayed with price tags and purchases result in signed receipts. This shopping culture is primarily found in **government emporiums and shops in hotel shopping arcades**. You'll probably feel comfortable shopping in these places because you know exactly what to pay for particular items and you feel confident that the goods presented are genuine. You primarily go to these places without the assistance of a guide who sometimes tries to steer you away from such shops because they are not noted for paying commissions. Occasionally you may encounter a special sale in these places, but in general prices are fixed and product integrity is relatively predictable. Even in these shops, if you are buying an expensive item, a piece of jewelry for example, it is reasonable to ask if *"a discount is possible"* or *"if you can do any better on the price."* It is not unusual to get a 10 or 15 percent discount. During India's festive season (September to December), many of these places offer special discounts that can run from 5 percent to 50 percent.

The second shopping culture centers around **private emporiums and shops that pay commissions to bus drivers, tour guides, and street touts** for bringing you to their shop. The commissions range anywhere from 2 percent to 40 percent of your shopping total; in many shops the standard commission is 30 to 40 percent. You, in effect, indirectly pay this commission to these middlemen because you are shopping in a place that has already inflated their "fixed" prices by 30 to 40 percent. Many of these places are easily identifiable: emporiums frequented by many tourists who arrive by tour bus, private car, taxi, or auto-rickshaw. In Delhi, the upscale Saga Department Store is a favorite of drivers and guides. In other cities, the Cottage Industries Emporiums (CIE), operated by the same company as Saga Department Store, are favorites. Many of the new shops in heavily-touristed areas, such as Agra and Jaipur, fit into this familiar commission pattern. These driver- and guide-friendly emporiums and shops usually have many drivers and guides hanging around the front or in the back awaiting their commissions as you conclude your shopping up front. While most of these places claim to have fixed prices, they are

❑ Commissions paid by shops to drivers, guides, and touts range from 2 percent to 40 percent of your shopping total; 30 to 40 percent is often the norm.

❑ If you arrive at a shop by yourself, let the salespeople know you have come tout-free. If you ask for a discount, you may receive 10 to 40 percent off the already inflated fixed price!

❑ Don't expect large discounts except in some markets and bazaars. Most shops in India do not like to bargain or give discounts.

❑ To determine fair prices, visit government emporiums in each city prior to venturing into the markets, shops, and private emporiums.

only fixed if you arrive at the shop with a commission-hungry driver, guide, or tout. If you arrive by yourself, let the salespeople know you have come tout-free. Ask for a discount since you are not interested in paying the fixed price that already includes someone else's commission. In many cases, you will receive a 10 to 40 percent discount!

The third shopping culture involves price uncertainty. This culture is primarily found in **markets and bazaars** where shopping requires strong bargaining skills. The difference between the first quoted price and what you finally pay could be 20 to 60 percent, depending on how well you bargain and how flexible the vendor is with his pricing.

A good rule of thumb for shopping in India is that most prices are negotiable, unless you are shopping at a government emporium. But discounting is often minimal. When in doubt, always ask for a discount. Start the process by asking the classic *"Is it possible?"* question:

> *"It is possible to do any better on the price?"*

A shopkeeper may be able to shave off 5 or 10 percent, depending on your method of payment and whether or not you require packing and shipping services. However, don't expect large discounts. In general, shops in India do not like to bargain or give discounts. Markets and bazaars, however, are a different story.

PLAN AND COMPARE PRICES

You should approach India with a well organized shopping plan. Your plan should include a list of items you want to purchase as well as a list of shopping areas and specific shops you wish to visit. Use this book as a starting point for identifying possible products and specific shops. List the items you wish to purchase and the people for whom you are buying as well as the comparison prices you gathered before you left home. This well organized shopping plan will enable you to make the most of your shopping time in India.

However, if you're uncertain about what to buy in India and decide to "wait and see" what's available, you can quickly do your planning and comparative shopping immediately upon arriving in India. We strongly recommend visiting government emporiums in each city prior to venturing into the markets, shops, and private emporiums. However, make sure you are visiting a real government emporium—not one that may confuse you with a name that sounds like it belongs to the government. For example, the well appointed Cottage Industries Emporiums (C.I.E.) are run by a very wealthy and entrepreneurial Kashmiri family—not by the government.

PRICE TAGS JUST FOR YOU

Bargaining does take place in some places you will visit in India. While most stores display price tags on items, except for the truly "fixed price" government emporiums, don't take such labeling as a sign of the final price you should pay. Rather, treat stated prices as starting prices from which you begin a bargaining process to determine the final price **you** will pay. In fact, many shops put price tags on items because they know tourists tend to pay what's marked on the tag. Don't let these tags dissuade you from negotiating a price that can be 10 to 20 percent less than what is marked on the tag. However, many shops will not bargain or discount since they feel no need to do so given their regular clientele that pays full price. When in doubt, always pose the polite *"Is it possible?"* question.

ANATOMY OF SHOPS AND SHOPPING

Many shops in India, including some in what are ostensibly upscale hotel shopping arcades, are simply unappealing at first glance to visitors who come from shopping cultures with nice window and counter displays and professional customer service. In India, shops tend to be crammed with goods that are not particularly well displayed and customer service leaves much to be desired—either none at all or extremely aggressive! Indeed, you may become initially disoriented as you enter a huge emporium or small shop. You may need to take a few minutes just aligning your eyes to the helter-skelter layout of the shop and ask if they have an upper or lower level and how to find the stairs or elevator that takes you to the different levels. In so doing, you may discover a "diamond in the rough." In other words, don't take first visual impressions as a sign of a good or bad shop. You'll need to probe much deeper into the shop for the really good stuff!

Throughout our shopping in India, we identified 21 rules that seem applicable in many shopping situations, from emporiums to small shops and markets. They include:

1. **Don't judge a shop by what it looks like on the outside:** Remember, this is not a shopping culture

that is big on retail presentation skills. Many of India's best shops are literally holes in the wall. But once you enter, you may discover it's filled with great treasures. In addition, the shop may have a larger warehouse or factory that is filled with shopping treasures. Learn to poke around and ask questions about the true extent of their inventory.

2. **Don't judge a shop by the first room you see.** Large shops, such as emporiums, have unique characteristics that demand further investigation. They often include several separate rooms, each acting as a kind of "department" displaying different items. The first room you enter is not necessary representative of the shop. It may include a demonstration area, lots of large items such as marble table tops in Agra, cheap jewelry and T-shirts, or many tacky handicraft items. Many shops tend to turn off visitors with what is displayed in the first room. Be sure to go further in the shop and explore all of the rooms. You may be pleasantly surprised to find one or two rooms in the back of the shop have exactly what appeals to you. Indeed, you may conclude that the emporium or shop is really a 3 in 1 shop—three different shops operating simultaneously, from the worst to the best. Indeed, the best stuff is usually not found in the first room. Welcome to India's convoluted retail display talents!

3. **If you're not seeing what you like, ask to see the "good stuff."** This rule is especially applicable in shops that have a jewelry section. Many shops display a few average quality pieces but keep their "good stuff" in a back room or safe. If you appear to be a serious buyer, or one who has the financial means to afford more expensive pieces, the shopkeeper or manager may share his secret with you: *"We have more in the back room. Would you like to see my special collection?"* You then follow him to a separate room where a locked safe or display counter is opened and you see the "best of the best" the shop literally keeps under lock and key. You may be amazed at what you see. An emporium or shop that has tacky handicrafts and poor quality jewelry may all of a sudden reveal top quality items. Again, don't judge a shop by its front door, room, or displays. You need to probe deeper into what may become the secrets of a shop reserved for people who have both

the interest and means to afford the best of the best. Shop personnel will often "size you up" as you browse through a shop to determine if you warrant an invitation to visit the back room. If they don't extend an invitation, you might ask for an invitation to visit the back room with this question: *"Is there more? Do you have a special room or collection?"*

4. **The best designed products tend to be found in the most upscale shops found in hotel shopping arcades and in a few noted shops found in upscale suburbs.** Most of the large shopping emporiums and jewelry stores include products with traditional ethnic designs and colors. While they may be interesting to see, many of these products may not integrate well in your home or wardrobe. The best designs will be found in the most upscale hotel shopping arcades where shops tend to cater to Western tastes of international travelers. The Khazana shops in the Taj Group hotels, for example, are noted for their selection of well designed products that especially appeal to upscale international travelers.

5. **Skip the demonstration area unless you have the interest as well as the time to kill.** Many emporiums and shops have a demonstration area where you can see craftsmen weave, polish stores, carve, and produce inlaid marble table tops. After seeing two or three of these demonstrations to learn how products are produced, and to speculate about their sweatshop conditions, you can probably skip most other demonstrations. They are great time killers that primarily set you up for a high pressured salesperson who wants you to buy the item being demonstrated. In many shops, the demonstration area is located out front or in the first room where you may feel obligated to watch since it seems to be the prerequisite step to entering the shop—the walkway literally goes through the demonstration section! Don't feel obligated to hang around long. Just bypass the area and go directly into the second room. If asked *"You want to see demonstration?"*, say *"No, I've seen it already. Where's your really good stuff?"* Since you may appear to know what your doing, you may be taken directly to the back room (Rule #3) for a "private showing."

6. **Don't accept all the drinks offered.** Many shops will offer you tea or a soft drink. This is a nice customer service gesture, but its aim is to keep you around longer with the hope that you will buy something as well as to make you feel indebted. Unless you are really thirsty, you may want to skip the drinks and get directly down to business. This also is a good way to pick up a bug because of the less than sanitary dish-washing practices.

7. **Don't expect to get much of a discount, but always ask for a discount even when told the emporium or shop has "fixed prices."** Most shops are reluctant to bargain or give discounts. They see themselves as fixed-price operations. They may at best give you a 5 to 10 percent discount, but only if you ask. Always pose the polite *"Is it possible?"* question: *"Is it possible to do better on this price?"* After all, anything is possible in India and the future often looks bright for those who are patient and persistent. The response might be *"We can give you a 5 percent discount if you pay cash."* You might response with another "possibility" question: *"Is it possible to do 10 percent?"* If the response is *"No,"* you might nicely point out that *"Since I just arrived today, I think I need to look around more. Maybe I'll come back later."* Chances are you may end up with a 10 percent discount. After all, once you leave the shop, there's a good chance you will never come back—truly a lost opportunity. If, on the other hand, you correctly "read" an emporium or shop as one that is probably giving 30 to 40 commissions to drivers, guides, and touts (just survey the parking area for such signs), and you have found this shop on your own (point out that it was recommended in your guidebook and not by your driver or guide), you have a lot more room to bargain. Go for a 30 to 40 percent discount but be willing to settle for 20 percent if you truly love the item.

8. **Avoid shopping near most major tourist sites.** Many of the market stalls and small shops that oper-ate near popular tourist sites, such as a Taj Mahal, offer inferior quality products at highly inflated prices. Indeed, you may pay 50 percent more in these shops for the same item found in a government emporium or shop in town or at your hotel. Many of these places

also are the havens for drivers, guides, and touts who will tell you they know a great place to shop where *"The prices really good."* They may even tell you the shop is run by their uncle, although such familial bounds are more commission-driven than blood-related! The prices are really good only for *them* because they will be raking in a 30 to 40 percent commission on your purchase. Seldom will you find a "good deal" in such shops which are basically tourist traps.

9. **Crowds at emporiums and shops are not necessarily a good indicator they are desirable places for you to shop.** Often the least crowded shops will be the best places to shop because they refuse to pay commissions to drivers, guides, and touts. Unfortunately, many of these places may be on the verge of going out of business because they have been boycotted by these tourist middlemen. Crowded shops often mean many tourists have been brought to the shops because the shopkeepers encourage drivers, guides, and touts to do so for 30-40 percent commissions. Many of the places offer poor quality products at highly inflated prices.

10. **Quickly get rid of aggressive and pestering touts.** Touts are a real nuisance in India. They seem to abound in heavily touristed areas and aggressively attach themselves to tourists. There is nothing good for you that can come from being led around by a tout. Unfortunately, many visitors don't know how to deal with touts and thus may encourage the very people they hope to avoid. Tourists who feel they should be culturally sensitive and not offend the locals tend to stop and talk with touts and try to convince them that they are really not interested in their special services. After awhile, many visitors give in to a persistent tout in hopes of getting rid of him; greedy and wishful thinking tourists may actually convince themselves that they may indeed get a great deal from the tout's so-called uncle! Hope does not spring eternal with touts. Don't worry about being culturally sensitive with these people. You have to do more than just say *"No."* Being seasoned and persistent touts, they know *"No"* does not mean *"No"* if they keep pestering you. The first mistake you can make with a tout is to acknowledge his presence by engaging in a

conversation or giving him eye contact. Ignore the person by moving on without saying a word and mumble something in an incomprehensible foreign language (make one up so he can't understand what you are saying!). If he becomes a real nuisance, look him in the eye, shout at him loudly and clearly, become animated by waving your hands and arms like a madman, and say: *"No, go away. Get out of here. I want to be left alone."* Immediately turn around and walk away. You'll probably startle him and he'll go away. Best of all, the word will quickly go out to other touts that you are a waste of their time. You might also embarrass them.

11. **Avoid most rug and textile demonstrations.** If you want to really kill some time and feel like a captive shopper, agree to see the special rug or textile demonstration offered by an emporium or shop. You may want to experience one of these demonstrations while in India, at least for the cultural experience or to learn what you should avoid in the future. However, sitting through more than one such demonstration is really a foolish waste of time. Many of these demonstrations will keep you captive for an hour or more. As the demonstrator unrolls each carpet or textile, he'll probably ask you if you want to *"Keep or take away?"* This not-so-subtle game often leaves you with a pile of "keepers" at the end of the demonstration. You'll then have to go through another round of *"Keep or take away?"* that may result in your feeling pressured to purchase something in your "keeper" pile just to get out of this captive shop. If you fail to designate at least one "keeper," the demonstrator will probably keep you in the shop forever demonstrating everything that is in inventory! At this point it's probably time to feign an illness to excuse yourself. When asked if you want to see the demonstration, it's best to say *"No, I've already seen several"* and keep moving without engaging the person in a conversation or giving him eye contact. Remember, this is the tout that resides *in* the shop! If they persist by saying they have the best quality rugs or textiles and that you must really see their demonstration, excuse yourself by saying *"I'm feeling a bit ill. I need to go back to my hotel."*

12. **When entering a Kashmiri rug, shawl, and papier mache shop, be prepared with an "exit strategy."** The Kashmiri's are unquestionably India's most enterprising and aggressive merchants. They also seem to have a monopoly on tourist emporiums and shops. You'll instantly know if you are in one of these shops if you see three prevalent products that usually go together in these shops: rugs, shawls, and papier mache items. The shops also seem to be over-staffed with friends and relatives. We like many of these merchants because they are friendly and informative. At the same time, many others are very aggressive and oppressive. Their customer service skills may instantly turn you off as they pester you to buy something or see their rug and shawl demonstrations. Many of them also have highly inflated prices which they "doth protest too much" with the old tourist line that we have *"Very good prices here."* For example, it's not unusual to pay 50 to 100 percent more in one of these shops for the same items found in a government emporium. If you do find something you like in such a shop, shop around first and then try to bargain hard for as big a discount as possible. They may tell you they have "fixed prices," but everything is negotiable in most of these shops. Let them know you're a savvy shopper because you've done your research and know exactly what the going price should be. At the same time, you may feel like a captive in these shops as they try to get you to sit through a demonstration of their rugs and shawls. Be prepared to say *"No"* and exit the shop. But they may keep talking to you in the hopes of keeping you in the shop. Don't worry; it's not impolite to walk out the door while the person is still talking to you. After all, the so-called conversation you are abandoning is always the same predictable and tired sales pitch: *"Good quality, best prices and selections. You buy here."*

13. **Avoid going to a shop with a guide, driver, or street tout.** Guides, drivers, and street touts in heavily trafficked tourist areas are notorious for getting 30 to 40 percent commissions on everything their "guests" buy in particular shops. Given the high competition for similar products in such areas, especially in the Golden Triangle of Delhi, Agra, and Jaipur, many shops cannot survive unless they encourage guides,

drivers, and street touts to bring them customers. Shops that refuse to pay commissions or only give a nominal 2 to 5 percent commission are either very famous word-of-mouth shops or shops with few customers. Many of the latter shops quickly go out of business because they are boycotted by the middleman who steer tourist traffic into shops that pay them the highest commissions. Needless to say, shops that pay such high commissions often offer a combination of poor quality goods (tourist kitsch) and highly inflated prices. You are the one who indirectly pays the 30 to 40 percent commission because it's already added into the shop's "fixed price." Many of the commission-paying shops also have good quality products. If you find something you really like in one of these shops, plan to return to the shop later without your driver or guide. It's best to do this by getting a business card and telling the salesperson you may return; ask if they will pick you up at your hotel for a return visit. Alternatively, if you don't have the time to come back, let the salesperson know you expect a discount and that you did not come to their shop on the recommendation of your driver or a guide or tout (if they are mentioned in this book, show them the section where their name appears). Chances are your driver or guide may still get a nominal commission (5 to 10 percent rather than 30 to 40 percent), but at least his commission will have to be discounted since you will probably get a discount from the shop (10 to 30 percent) when you approach it in this manner.

14. **Don't be too quick to dismiss a shop because of its customer service**. Shops seem to have lots of turn-offs for tourists, from poor displays and tacky products to aggressive salespeople and an atmosphere of suspicion and distrust. As you may quickly discover, many of the ostensible "turn off" shops may have some hidden treasures. Take an in-depth look before you rush out of such a shop.

15. **Customer service varies considerably from one type of shop to another**. The most aggressive sales-people tend to be found the private emporiums and tourist shops, especially Kashmiri shops used to dealing with bus loads of tourists. Government shops tend to be very laid back; indeed, you may sometimes

need to wake up a sleeping salesperson in order to get assistance! The best quality shops tend to have trained staffs that give quality service.

16. **Ask questions and shop in reputable places.** You must be inquisitive and ask for recommendations from the right people. India offers many great shopping opportunities in places that have good reputations for quality and service. Seek out these places in earnest. Many are identified in this book. Others can be found by asking your hotel concierge or networking with a few quality shops. However, do not ask this question of your driver or guide; they tend to equate quality with commissions, a form of self-interest rightly understood. For example, ask a top jeweler where he might recommend that you shop for top quality furniture, art, or textiles. He knows where top quality lies and will probably share his view with you. Many concierges are objective about quality but others may get commissions, especially if they give you a card with their name and ask you to give it to the shop manager. They may say their card will get you a discount, but in reality that card will probably set him up for getting a commission on your purchases.

17. **Always ask for accurate and detailed receipts.** You may later need receipts for Customs and for tracking your purchase if later you have a problem relating to shipping or authenticity. Make sure you receive an official signed receipt. If the shop says they ran out of receipts, ask them to type you a receipt on their letterhead or give you a temporary receipt. They can send an official receipt to your hotel room or put it in the mail to your home address. Never purchase an expensive item without a receipt.

18. **Pay with credit cards whenever possible.** Especially if you are buying high-ticket items that could possibly be problematic in terms of shipping and authenticity, pay for your purchases with a credit card. Although they are not obligated to do so, in many cases, the credit card company will assist you should you have a problem with your purchase. If you dispute the charge with a letter of complaint, the credit card company will contact the shop and ask for a resolution. This "long arm of the credit card company" may help you

resolve any problems with the shop. At the same time, expect to pay more for using credit cards and traveler's checks than paying in cash. Your best deals are in using U.S. dollars.

19. **Photograph any purchases that will or might be shipped, as well as anything in the shop you are uncertain about purchasing at this time, and take the shop's business card with information on any future purchases.** If you are having items shipped, be sure to take a photo of each purchase *before* it gets wrapped. This will help you with Customs back home (just show them a photo of what's in the shipment for duty assessment purposes) as well as with any insurance claims or problem with switching of goods. Try to take a photo of the salesperson alongside your purchase. This may prove to be an invaluable visual record of your transaction. The photos also are fun to review prior to receiving your shipment—Christmas is coming in July! Also, if you are uncertain about purchasing a particular item, ask the salesperson if you can take a photo for future reference. You may later decide to call or fax the shop and tell them what you want. Ask them to write the item on the back of their business card along with the price. Indeed, we often purchase several items by fax and email after we get home and have had a chance to think about items we left behind. Most shops are experienced in fulfilling such "long distance" requests. Having information written on the back of a business card, along with a photo of the item(s), should make your long distance shopping very easy.

20. **Get full information on the shop, including its name, address, phone number, fax number, email, and Website.** You may need this information later if you (1) have problems with shipping or authenticity of your purchase, or (2) wish to purchase an item you left behind or want to purchase more of the same item. Ask if a shop has a Website. Some shops are beginning to discover the wonders of long-distance e-commerce by including some of their best inventory on their Website. You can later shop via the Internet.

21. **If you're having your purchases shipped, be sure to spell out *all* the details to prevent any costly**

errors. Assume nothing since you may later discover you did not clearly communicate your intentions. While many shops are used to shipping abroad, even they make mistakes. The process can take a long time because communication is not always clear, even though you left India with what you thought was a clear understanding of the process. For example, don't just ask a shop to ship your goods to your home address. Be specific. Tell them you (1) need to receive them by a specific date, (2) want your goods insured against both loss and breakage, (3) expect them shipped to a specific airport or seaport, and (4) wish to have other items consolidated in your shipment. If you decide to consolidate, make sure you arrange to have the items shipped to the shop along with a detailed list of what will be coming, from where, and the value of each item. Also, provide them with a set of pictures of these other items. The more details you can give the shop on your shipment, the less likely things will go awry. For example, if you fail to specify that you want your shipment to arrive at the Port of Baltimore, chances are they will make an error and ship it to the Port of Boston. Be redundant. Leave the shop a copy of your shipping instructions, along with photos and a list of items, and then fax them this same information as soon as you get home. Restate exactly your understanding of what is being shipped, how, and when. Underline or put in caps the name of the port or airport you expect to receive the shipment. Do not assume the shop knows a great deal about the geography of your country! At the same time, shops often encounter difficulties at their end, such as securing government permits, consolidating shipments, and transferring money. Often faxes don't work and calling by telephone or using email can be frustrating. In the end, this will all work out and you will probably get your shipment. But this whole process can be frustrating.

PRACTICE 12 RULES OF BARGAINING

While some bargaining takes place in shops, most bargaining occurs in markets and bazaars where prices are anything but fixed. If you are not an experienced haggler, here are some tips that can help you appear to be a seasoned shopper.

In general, you want to achieve two goals in this haggling process: **establish the value of an item and get the best possible price**. The following bargaining rules generally work well.

1. **Do your research before initiating the process.** Compare prices among various shops, starting with the fixed-price items in department stores. Spot-check price ranges among shops in and around your hotel. Also, refer to your research done with catalogs and discount houses back home to determine if the discount is sufficient to warrant purchasing the item abroad rather than at home.

2. **Determine the exact item you want.** Select the particular item you want and then focus your bargaining around that one item without expressing excessive interest and commitment. Even though you may be excited by the item and want it very badly, once the merchant knows you are committed to buying this one item, you weaken your bargaining position. Express a passing interest; indicate through eye contact with other items in the shop that you are not necessarily committed to the one item. As you ask about the other items, you should get some sense concerning the willingness of the merchant to discount prices.

3. **Set a ceiling price you are willing to pay.** Before engaging in serious negotiations, set in your mind the maximum amount you are willing to pay, which may be 20 percent more than you figured the item should sell for based on your research. However, if you find something you love that is really unique, be prepared to pay whatever you must. In many situations you will find unique items not available anywhere else. Consider buying **now** since the item may be gone when you return. Bargain as hard as you can and then pay what you have to—even though it may seem painful—for the privilege of owning a unique item. Remember, it only hurts once. After you return home you will most likely enjoy your wonderful purchase and forget how painful it seemed at the time to buy it at less than your expected discount. Above all, do not pass up an item you really love just because the bargaining process does not fall in your favor. It is very easy to be *"penny wise but pound foolish"* in India simply

because the bargaining process is such an ego-involved activity. You may return home forever regretting that you failed to buy a lovely item just because you refused to "give" on the last $5 of haggling. In the end, put your ego aside, give in, and buy what you really want. Only you and the merchant will know who really won, and once you return home the $5 will seem to be such an insignificant amount. Chances are you still got a good bargain compared to what you would pay elsewhere if, indeed, you could find a similar item!

4. **Play a role**. Shopping in India involves playing the roles of buyer and seller. Indians tend to be terrific role players, more so than Westerners. Therefore, it is to your advantage to carefully structure your personality and behavior to play the role of buyer. If you approach sellers by just "being yourself"—open, honest, somewhat naive, and with your own unique personality—you may be quickly walked over by a seasoned seller. Once you enter a shop, think of yourself as an actor walking on stage to play the lead role as a shrewd buyer, bargainer, and trader.

5. **Establish good will and a personal relationship**. A shrewd buyer also is charming, polite, personable, and friendly. You should have a sense of humor, smile, and be light-hearted during the bargaining process. But be careful about eye contact which can be threatening. Keep it to a minimum. Sellers often prefer to establish a personal relationship so that the bargaining process can take place on a friendly, face-saving basis. In the end, both the buyer and seller should come out as winners. This cannot be done if you approach the buyer in very serious and harsh terms. You should start by exchanging pleasantries concerning the weather, your trip, the city, or the nice items in the shop. After exchanging professional cards or determining your status, the shopkeeper will know what roles should be played in the coming transaction.

6. **Let the seller make the first offer.** If the merchant starts by asking you *"How much do you want to pay?"*, avoid answering; immediately turn the question around: *"How much are you asking?"* Remember, many merchants try to get you to pay as much as you are willing and able to pay—not what the value of the

item is or what he or she is willing to take. You should never reveal your ability or willingness to pay a certain price. Keep the seller guessing, thinking that you may lose interest or not buy the item because it appears too expensive. Always get the merchant to initiate the bargaining process. In so doing, the merchant must take the defensive as you shift to the offensive.

7. **Take your time, being deliberately slow in order to get the merchant to invest his or her time in you.** The more you indicate that you are impatient and in a hurry, the more you are likely to pay. When negotiating a price, **time** is usually in your favor. Many shopkeepers also see time as a positive force in the bargaining process. Some try to keep you in their shop by serving you tea, coffee, soft drinks, or liquor while negotiating the price. Be careful; this nice little ritual may soften you somewhat on the bargaining process as you begin establishing a more personal relationship with the merchant. The longer you stay in control prolonging the negotiation, the better the price should be. Although some merchants may deserve it, **never** insult them. Merchants need to "keep face" as much as you do in the process of giving and getting the very best price.

8. **Use odd numbers in offering the merchant at least 40 percent less than what he or she initially offers.** Avoid stating round numbers, such as 60, 70, or 100. Instead, offer $62.50, $73.85, or $81.13. Such numbers impress upon others that you may be a seasoned haggler who knows value and expects to do well in this negotiation. Your offer will probably be 15 percent less than the value you determined for the item. For example, if the merchant asks $100, offer $62.50, knowing the final price should probably be $75.00. The merchant will probably counter with only a 10 percent discount—$90. At this point you will need to go back and forth with another two or three offers and counter-offers.

9. **Appear disappointed and take your time again.** Never appear upset or angry with the seller. Keep your cool at all times by slowly sitting down and carefully examining the item. Shake your head a little and say, *"Gee, that's too bad. That's much more than I had planned*

to spend. I like it, but I really can't go that high." Appear to be a sympathetic listener as the seller attempts to explain why he or she cannot budge more on the price. Make sure you do not accuse the merchant of being a thief, even though he may be one! Use a little charm, if you can, for the way you conduct the bargaining process will affect the final price. This should be a civil negotiation in which you nicely bring the price down, the seller "saves face," and everyone goes away feeling good about the deal.

10. **Counter with a new offer at a 35 percent discount.** Punch several keys on your calculator, which indicates that you are doing some serious thinking. Then say something like *"This is really the best I can do. It's a lovely item, but $67.25 is really all I can pay."* At this point the merchant will probably counter with a 20 percent discount—$80.

11. **Be patient, persistent, and take your time again by carefully examining the item.** Respond by saying *"That's a little better, but it's still too much. I want to look around a little more."* Then start to get up and look toward the door. At this point the merchant has invested some time in this exchange, and he or she is getting close to a possible sale. The merchant will either let you walk out the door or try to stop you with another counter-offer. If you walk out the door, you can always return to get the $80 price. But most likely the merchant will try to stop you, especially if there is still some bargaining room. The merchant is likely to say: *"You don't want to waste your time looking elsewhere. I'll give you the best price anywhere—just for you. Okay, $75. That's my final price."*

12. **Be creative for the final negotiation.** You could try for $70, but chances are $75 will be the final price with this merchant. Yet, there may still be some room for negotiating **extras**. At this point get up and walk around the shop and examine other items; try to appear as if you are losing interest in the item you were bargaining for. While walking around, identify a $5-10 item you like which might make a nice gift for a friend or relative, which you could possibly include in the final deal. Wander back to the $75 item and look as if your interest is waning and per-

haps you need to leave. Then start to probe the possibility of including the extras while agreeing on the $75: *"Okay, I might go $75, but only if you include this with it."* The *this* would be the $5-10 item you eyed. You might also negotiate with your credit card. Chances are the merchant is expecting cash on the $75 discounted price and may add a 2-5 percent *commission* if you want to use your credit card. In this case, you might respond to the $75 by saying, *"Okay, I'll go with the $75, but only if I can use my credit card."* You may get your way, your bank will float you a loan in the interim, and in case you later learn there is a problem with your purchase—such as misrepresentation—the credit card company may even help you. Finally, you may want to negotiate packing and delivery processes. If it is a fragile item, insist that it be packed well so you can take it with you on the airplane or have it shipped. If it is a large item, insist that the shop deliver it to your hotel or to your shipper. If the shop is shipping it by air or sea, try to get them to agree to absorb some of the freight and insurance costs.

This slow, civil, methodical, and sometimes charming approach to bargaining works well in many situations. However, merchants do differ in how they handle the haggling process. In some cases, your timing may be right: the merchant is in need of cash flow that day and thus he or she is willing to give you the price you want, with little or no bargaining. Others will not give more than a 10 to 20 percent discount unless you are a friend of a friend who is then eligible for the special "family discount." And others are not good businessmen, are unpredictable, lack motivation, or are just moody; they refuse to budge on their prices even though your offer is fair compared to the going prices in other shops. In these situations, unless it's a unique item you can find nowhere else, it is best to leave the shop and find one which is more receptive to the traditional haggling process.

Bargaining in traditional markets requires a different approach and may result in larger discounts. In contrast to the numerous polite merchants you encounter in shops, sellers in open-air markets tend to be lower-class, earthy, expressive, pushy, and persistent as they attempt to sell you many things you cannot use or have no desire to even inspect.

In contrast to our previous bargaining rules, successful bargaining in markets should involve **little time** and a great deal of **movement**. If you are interested in an item, ask the price, counter with a price you are willing to pay, and be relatively firm with this price. Since there is a great deal of competition in these markets, it is to your advantage to spend very little time with any one vendor. State your offer and slowly move on to the next vendor. Sellers know they will probably lose you to the competition, so they need to quickly conclude a deal before someone else gets to you; they are motivated to give you large discounts. You also can be a little more aggressive and obnoxious and less charming in these places. If, for example, an item is quoted at $10, offer $3 or $4 and move on toward the next vendor. Chances are the seller will immediately drop the price to $7. If you counter with $5 and are moving while stating your offer, the seller will probably agree to your offer. But be sure you want the item. Once your offer is accepted, you are expected to carry through with the purchase. These markets are great places to accumulate junk while successfully practicing your bargaining skills!

Bargain For Needs, Not Greed

One word of caution for those who are just starting to learn the fine art of bargaining. **Be sure you really want an item before you initiate the bargaining process**. Many tourists learn to bargain effectively, and then get carried away with their new-found skill. Rather than use this skill to get what they want, they enjoy the process of bargaining so much that they buy many unnecessary items. After all, they got such *"a good deal"* and thus could not resist buying the item. You do not need to fill your suitcases with junk in demonstrating this ego-gratifying skill. If used properly, your new bargaining skills will lead to some excellent buys on items you really need and want.

Examine Your Goods Carefully

Before you commence the bargaining process, carefully examine the item, being sure that you understand the quality of the item for which you are negotiating. Then, after you settle on a final price, make sure you are getting the goods you agreed upon. You should carefully observe the handling of items, including the actual packing process. If at all possible, take the items with you when you leave the shop. If not, take photos and insist on a detailed receipt.

Beware Of Scams

Although one hopes this will never happen, you may be unfortunate in encountering unscrupulous merchants who take advantage of you. This is more likely to happen at private shops and markets that are set up to cater to the tourist trade. The most frequent scams to watch out for include:

1. **Misrepresenting quality goods.** Be especially cautious in jewelry stores and antique shops. Sometimes so-called expensive antiques are excellent copies and worth no more than a fraction of the quoted price. Precious stones, such as rubies, may not be as precious as they appear. Accordingly, you may pay $2,000 for what appears to be a ruby worth $10,000 back home, but in fact you just bought a $25 red spinal. Pearls come in many different qualities, so know your pearls before negotiating a price. Some merchants try to sell "new antiques" at "old antique" prices. Many of the fakes are outstanding reproductions, often fooling even the experts. You may want to simply shop for reproductions.

2. **Goods not shipped.** The shop may agree to ship your goods home, but once you leave they conveniently forget to do so. You wait and wait, write letters of inquiry, and receive no replies. Regardless of all your efforts to communicate with the shop, you may never receive the goods you paid for.

Your best line of defense against these and other possible scams is to be very careful wherever you go and whatever you do in relation to handling money. A few precautions should help avoid some of these problems:

1. **Do not trust anyone with your money** unless you have proper assurances they are giving you exactly what you agreed upon.

2. **Do your homework** so you can determine quality and value as well as anticipate certain types of scams.

3. **Examine the goods carefully**, assuming something may be or will go wrong.

4. **Watch very carefully how the merchant handles items** from the moment they leave your hands until they get wrapped and into a bag.

5. **Request receipts** that list specific items and the prices you paid. Although most shops are willing to "give you a receipt" specifying whatever price you want them to write for purposes of deceiving Customs, avoid such pettiness because Customs officials know better, and you may need a receipt with the real price to claim your goods, seek a refund, or put in an insurance claim. Be sure to make your own notation on the back of the receipt indicating the item and its cost in dollars. The approximate dollar value will help you keep track of your spending as you go as well as assist as you fill out your Customs declaration. If the shop is to ship, be sure you have a shipping receipt which also includes insurance against both loss and damage.

6. **Take pictures of your purchases.** Before anything gets packed, be sure to take a photo of the item with the person who sold it to you. If you later have a problem with your purchase, you'll at least have visual evidence of what you purchased and with whom.

7. **Gain possible protection against scams by using credit cards** for payment, especially for big ticket items which could present problems, even though using them may cost you more. Though credit card companies are not obligated to help you, many will assist if a shop has defrauded you. However, you must be able to substantiate your claim.

If you are victimized, all is not necessarily lost. You should report the problem immediately to the local authorities or your credit card company. While inconvenient and time consuming, nonetheless, these steps should help you get satisfactory results.

PACK RIGHT FOR INDIA

Serious shoppers pack differently from many other types of travelers. Since you may want to take many small purchases with you, it's a good idea to come to India with at least one nearly empty suitcase filled with bubble wrap and packing supplies—tape, knife, scissors, black magic marker, rope, extra straps, stapler, notebook, envelopes, and business cards. We often find shops pack goods to disguise rather than to protect. The bubble wrap and tape will come in very handy when you must repack your purchases to protect them from airline baggage handlers. Depending on your luggage allowance, you may want to have some purchases repacked into a large cardboard or wood box that can be checked through as luggage. If you purchase a long but lightweight item, you'll find the extra strap to be useful. Whatever you do, make sure everything you purchase and take with you has been properly repacked. It's best that you do this repacking yourself rather than rely on someone else who may not understand what you mean by safe and secure packing. Use the notebook to take notes about your purchases. Staple the shop's receipt and business card together and file it in an envelope from which you can retrieve the information if questioned about your purchases at Customs.

You also are well advised to take a comfortable pair of walking shoes since you will probably be doing lots of walking in India.

And remember to travel in India with a calculator and business cards. You'll need the calculator to figure prices and look the part of a "savvy shopper." Business cards come in handy for taking notes, leaving contact information, and impressing others.

PART III

Nine Indias For Treasures and Pleasures

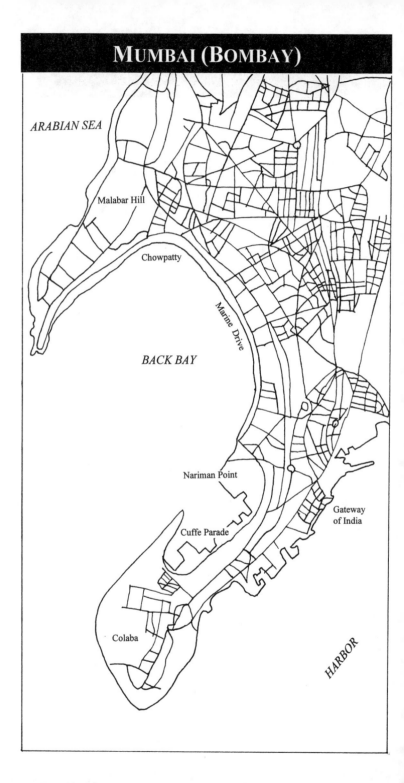

MUMBAI (BOMBAY)

ARABIAN SEA

Malabar Hill

Chowpatty

Marine Drive

BACK BAY

Nariman Point

Gateway of India

Cuffe Parade

Colaba

HARBOR

6

Mumbai
(Bombay)

I f you arrive at an airport and all the signs say you are in Mumbai, don't panic! You have indeed arrived in Bombay. Officially known as Mumbai since 1996, Bombay is to India what Shanghai is to China and New York is to the United States—its major financial, commercial, transportation, and communication center as well as its great ethnic and linguistic melting pot. It's India's center for banking, diamonds, and industry. Nearly 45 percent of the country's trade and commerce flows via Mumbai. Ringed by over 3,000 factories, the city boasts the country's best harbor and port facilities. It's also the center for India's famous movie industry ("Bollywood") which produces over 300 movies each year—the world's largest output, as well as it's growing satellite and television industries.

BEAUTY AND HOPE FROM A DISTANCE

While combining elements of high-rise and financial Manhattan and glamorous Hollywood with a heavy dose of Victorian colonial architecture, Mumbai is still very much a Third World city. It's chaotic; you can't safely drink the water; its slums and squalor are atrocious; and the beggars really do come through your rolled down windows at traffic stops! Yet, it's also one of

India's most attractive, vibrant, and contradictory cities. View busy and glittering Marine Drive—also dubbed the "Queen's Necklace"—from the Kamal Nehru Park on Malabar Hill at night and you will discover Mumbai is especially beautiful when viewed from a distance. The city's favorite deity, Lord Ganesha, the remover of obstacles, seems to be ever present in this unique City of Hope.

INDIA'S MOST WESTERNIZED CITY

Representing India's most Western and cosmopolitan community, Mumbai looks and feels different from other Indian cities with its grand yet worn museum of British colonial architecture, wide streets and parks, tall buildings, and fashionable hotels, restaurants, and shops. Its British colonial architecture is especially impressive—massive Victorian Gothic stone buildings, some combining Indian architectural elements, seemingly constructed to last forever—true monuments to India's colonial past and examples of construction that can survive India's harsh people and climatic environments where maintenance and paint seem to be luxuries.

Mumbai was not always like this. In fact, during the first half of the 20th century Bombay was one of the great cities of the East with well laid out roads, an excellent public transportation system, and reliable water and electricity—a true showcase of the British colonial empire. But no more. After World War II and Independence, the city succumbed to chaos attendant with too many people and too little attention given to the delivery of municipal services. Cities devastated by the war or overwhelmed by refugees, such as Singapore and Hong Kong, soon eclipsed India's urban centers and became the grand and model cities of Asia. Mumbai, along with Delhi and Calcutta, slide into an abyss of chaos and deterioration, with only its colonial architecture to remind the world that these were at one time great cities of the East. Compared to these other Asian cities, India's major cities wallowed in chaos

❑ Mumbai looks and feels different from other Indian cities.

❑ This used to be one of the great cities of the East. But no more, having been eclipsed by the great success stories of Singapore and Hong Kong.

❑ Mumbai has a well deserved reputation of being India's party town. Energetic and hip, the city never seems to stop.

❑ The city is a melting pot of different ethnic and linguistic groups.

❑ This is a city of hope, a place where poor immigrants have pulled themselves up from poverty and into Mumbai's huge middle and upper classes.

and mismanagement.

Like other major cities in India, Mumbai has become a kind of street-level theater which offers a colorful, chaotic, noisy, and often amazing visual feast—immigrants, slums, congestion, broken streets, makeshift construction, and sputtering, pollution belching vehicles. Rough and crumbling, everything seems to be in a state of disrepair. The city's questionable services testify to the fact that this remains a city struggling to survive as an urban entity.

However, behind this visual facade lies a series of oases consisting of fine hotels, restaurants, shops, and entertainment establishments that especially appeal to the tastes of the local middle and upper classes and to many travelers who wish to graduate from Mumbai's steamy, chaotic, and exhausting streets. As you will quickly discover, not everything in Mumbai is in the eye of the beholder. There are some real appealing treasures and pleasures in Mumbai, but you must first go beyond the noisy and visual street-level chaos to discover which doors open to the city's best oases of beauty and tranquility.

The city is very Western in terms of the many pleasures it offers business people and visitors—fine hotels, restaurants, and entertainment. Indeed, Mumbai has a well deserved reputation of being India's party town. Energetic and hip, the city never seems to stop.

A STRUGGLING CITY OF HOPE

Despite its Western facade, Mumbai shares many of the same characteristics so readily found in other Indian cities—it's big, crowded, congested, noisy, makeshift, worn, and dirty. Its not-so-charming chaos can wear on you after a while. Constantly under construction or reconstruction, little in this city would pass building codes found in most developed countries. Mumbai also boasts India's largest slum, numerous beggars, pesky touts, endless traffic jams, and a great deal of air pollution. Compared to other Indian cities, it does have fewer cows wandering the streets, which is a blessing for drivers and pedestrians.

The problems of Mumbai are similar to many large urban centers found in other Third World countries. The city is a melting pot of different ethnic and linguistic groups that have helped to both build and disassemble this city. It has long attracted numerous immigrants, such as the Parsis, Gujaratis, and south Indians, who make up their own sizable and powerful communities. But Mumbai's commercial and industrial successes also have served as magnets which attract hundreds of rural poor to Mumbai's infamous slum each day. Indeed, over 50 percent of Mumbai's population lacks electricity and running water. But for many of them, this also is a city of hope, a place where poor immigrants have pulled themselves up from poverty and into Mumbai's huge middle and upper classes. Being India's most entrepreneurial city, people understand Mumbai is about the pursuit and pleasure of money. In the meantime, evidence of this struggle between poverty and hope is everywhere.

Mumbai also is a paradoxical city in great transition. What you see is not always what you get, and what you get may be more than what you bargained for. The population, along with businesses and hotels, are increasingly moving to the less congested and more reasonably priced suburbs. Becoming self-contained and more comfortable and convenient communities than central Mumbai, the suburbs are taking on a decided Western character complete with their own shopping centers, restaurants, and nightlife. The new planned city of Vassa, located just two hours from the city, is destined to play a major role in the transformation of the old Mumbai into a new community that is more Western than Indian in character. From all of Mumbai's chaos may come some semblance of urban order.

VISITING MUMBAI

So why visit Mumbai? Because it exhibits a different facet of India; because it's a fascinating city; because of its many fine shopping and dining opportunities; because it's a party city; because it's there; because it's one of the best places to enter or exit the country; and because it reveals a lot about India's future. While this may not be a ringing endorsement of Mumbai, it does mean you don't need to spend a great deal of time here unless you are doing business in India or you are a shopaholic or enjoy sampling great restaurants and a nonstop nightlife. While tourists find few outstanding sightseeing opportunities in Mumbai, they do have a chance to do some interesting shopping and enjoy many comforts of travel not found elsewhere in India, from dining in fine restaurants and pub crawling to enjoying the decadence of five-star hotels. Three to four days in Mumbai will probably be sufficient for most visitors.

SURPRISING MUMBAI

Mumbai is actually made up of seven islands which have been merged through land reclamation during the past 150 years. Located on the Western coast and stretching 22 kilometers into the Arabian Sea, from a distance Mumbai could pass for Miami or Rio. But it really doesn't. It's probably closer to aging Havana.

India's largest city of 15 million people, Mumbai is a noisy and throbbing metropolis of people and vehicles. This huge melting pot is home to India's largest middle class along with many wealthy and famous personalities. If you are somebody in India, you probably maintain a residence in Mumbai. Different from any other city in India, Mumbai is especially noted as India's main commercial, financial, and industrial center. It's especially noted for its auto and pharmaceutical industries. India's stock market is located here along with the headquarters of many national companies and multinational corporations. It's also India's most westernized city—a city of movie studios, fashion shows, beauty pageants, designer labels, cell phones, and bars. It's also India's center for the fast growing television and satellite industries. It has the look and feel of a Western city.

THE BASICS

LOCATION

Facing the Arabian Sea, Mumbai is located on a reclaimed peninsula along India's west coast, north of Goa and south of Gujarat. Boasting India's best port facilities, the city is a beehive of international trade and commerce. Most major businesses maintain extensive operations in Mumbai because of this city's strategic location, financial infrastructure, and communication networks.

CLIMATE AND WHEN TO VISIT

Mumbai can be hot, humid, balmy, rainy, cold, and very pleasant, depending on the time of year you visit. It gets very hot and humid between March and mid-June. Located further south than Delhi and the cities of Rajasthan, it has a more tropical climate. Then the monsoon rains hit and continue into September. Occasional flooding also can add to the heat and human misery index. October brings blue skies, cool sea breezes, and generally very pleasant, although sometimes balmy, weather. For us, the best time to visit Mumbai is between October and February. November, December, and January are especially delightful months in Mumbai.

POPULATION

Mumbai's population of 15 million makes it India's largest city and one of the world's three largest urban areas. Drawn from many areas of India, the population is ethnically and linguistically very diverse. Such diversity is recognized in the local school system that provides instruction in ten different languages, although the city has four major spoken languages: Hindi, Marathi, Gujarati, and English. It's also a population exhibiting extremes in wealth and poverty. Some of the world's wealthiest people live here. At the same time, urban poverty is very widespread with nearly 50 percent of the population living on the streets and in slums lacking electricity and running water. Basic city services appear overwhelmed by the sheer size of Mumbai's population, although the city does not experience frequent electrical outages often found in other cities. More so than in most other Indian cities, Mumbai's population tends to be very entrepreneurial—a real buying and selling culture. Mumbai residents have a reputation for being hard-working and ambitious. It is their City of Hope.

GETTING THERE

The largest number of international flights into India land in Mumbai. Indeed, Mumbai is the international gateway city to India. Because it's so easy to enter India by way of Mumbai, you may want to make Mumbai your gateway city to India. It's a good place to start your Indian adventure.

If you're coming to Mumbai from other parts of India, you'll find excellent air connections into Mumbai from other cities. In fact, the largest number of domestic flights originate and terminate in Mumbai. Four domestic airlines service Mumbai: India Airlines, Jet Airways, Sahara Indian Airlines, and Skyline NEPC.

Other transportation options include train, bus, and car, although air travel will be most convenient. Indian trains and buses may be more of a cultural experience than you are prepared to undertake.

ARRIVAL AND DEPARTURE

Wow! Welcome to bureaucratic, entrepreneurial, and over-populated India. This could become your first dose of real culture shock. If you arrive by air on an international flight, expect to land in the middle of the night since most international flights from Europe, Asia, and North America get scheduled at that time. If your flight gets delayed and comes in near the arrival time of another flight, which happens frequently, expect to spend a couple of hours navigating through the utter chaos of the airport's immigration, customs, and baggage retrieval sections—literally the airport from hell! The international airport (Sahar) at night can become complete gridlock—an extremely inauspicious introduction to India. This experience will initially test your tolerance for legendary Indian inefficiency, disorganization, and utter chaos. Lacking clear arrival directions (you may end up in the wrong section), waiting in what is ostensibly a line (one big mass of humanity surging toward what may be an exit), and discovering your bags are probably on one of six belts (no signs indicating which belt), you may instantly discover what is undoubtedly the first truth about India: *Nothing is easy in India, from the moment you arrive until the day you depart!* Patience, tolerance, and forgiveness will serve you well. You'll eventually wind through this mess and move on to your hotel, perhaps before sunrise, and via your second cultural experience—an Indian taxi ride.

But, then, you may not experience such chaos and gridlock if your plane lands at a different time and if crowds are thin. In any case, your airport experience may reveal the second truth about India: *This is a paradoxical and anecdotal place—many things appear similar but nothing is the same.* This airport experience may occur again somewhere else in India, but it may not as you sail smoothly through other air terminals. Such experiences in India are simply unpredictable.

Before leaving the belted baggage retrieval area for customs, you'll find a money exchange to the left of the belts. The exchange is more favorable to traveler's checks than to cash. It's best to change some money here since you'll need cash to pay for your ride into the city, unless you're being met by a hotel representative. As you leave customs, you'll see prepaid taxi counters and a huge crowd of people at the exit with many signs bobbing above the heads of bystanders. Look for your name on a homemade sign if you expect someone to meet you at the airport. Look carefully for your name—it could be misspelled!

The international airport is located about 30 kilometers north of the main downtown area, Nariman Point. You can get there by taking the airport bus service (Rs 50 plus Rs 5 per bag) or by taxi. While relatively inexpensive, the bus takes one to two hours, depending on the traffic situation. You may want to take a taxi which costs from Rs 200 to Rs 300, depending on the time of day and whether it's a metered or prepaid taxi. A taxi will take 35 minutes to an hour to make the same trip. You'll find a prepaid taxi counter in the arrival hall. While it costs a little more to take a prepaid taxi, they are still relatively cheap and more convenient than the metered taxis outside which can be a hassle, especially when the driver informs you his meter doesn't work and you'll have to pay his asking price, which can be higher than the prepaid taxi price. As you exit the terminal with your bags, chances are you will be approached by one, two, or three men who will volunteer to carry your bags—one per person regardless of its size—whether you want them to do so or not. They, of course, expect a tip which should be very small. Now you've probably discovered the third truth about India: *Many persistent and pesky people want your money, although their questionable services are neither requested nor required but delivered nonetheless.*

If you arrive at the domestic terminal (Santa Cruz), which is located four kilometers from the international terminal, your transportation choices will be the same as from the international terminal and costs will be very similar.

The trip from the airport to your hotel in the middle of the night will give you some glimpses of what lies ahead in Mumbai and India. At night the city looks seedy—lots of people sleeping in doorways and along sidewalks; buildings, streets, and vehicles look very worn and dilapidated. If you're staying at a five-star hotel, such as the Oberoi or Taj Mahal, it will probably look like an oasis which you will come to adore! This image of Mumbai will change somewhat after the sun rises and millions of people take to the streets in a parade of colorful chaos. But this image never really recedes during your entire stay in India. It's always in the background and repeated in various forms.

When leaving Mumbai on an international flight, plan to check in three hours before departure time. The departure tax, which should be paid before checking in, is Rs 300 per person.

TRANSPORTATION AND GETTING AROUND

Although the traffic in Mumbai at times can be horrendous, in general it flows in its own characteristic way. Your transportation options here are numerous, from auto-rickshaws, buses, and trains to taxis and a car with driver. We prefer taking taxis or hiring a car with driver. Restricted from the city proper, auto-rickshaws only operate in the northern suburbs. Trains do run to the suburbs.

Black and yellow taxis are found throughout the city. They are located at hotels and taxi stands or just cruising along the streets. All taxis are metered, but everyone knows the rate shown on the meter is outdated. Rather than fix or replace the meters, each driver carries a printed conversion chart that shows how much additional must be added to the metered amount to get the final fare. At present the conversion rate is about 1 to 11. For example, if the meter rate says 01:60 (Rs 1.6), the conversion chart will tell you that translates into 18:00 (Rs 18); after midnight this same fare increases to 22:50 (Rs 22.5).

If you are adventuresome and want to rub elbows with the locals, you might try the red single or double-decker buses. They are very cheap (Rs 2) and extremely over-crowded during rush hours. In addition, they are not well marked for English speaking tourists (you see the English destinations marked on the side of the bus, as it passes by you!). One ride may convince you to use taxis or private cars, both of which are relatively inexpensive.

Getting around by taxi or private car is relatively convenient. Taxis charge Rs 10.50 for the first 1.6 km and Rs 6.50 for each additional kilometer. With many rides costing less than US$1, and seldom more than US$3, you may be *"penny wise and pound foolish"* using buses or auto-rickshaws.

❑ All taxis are metered, but everyone knows the rate shown on the meter is very outdated. Each driver carries a printed conversion chart.

❑ Buses are not well marked for English speaking tourists.

❑ For the most convenience in getting around, hire a car and driver. Most taxi drivers will be happy to become your full-day companion.

❑ Drivers often get lost or confused as to where you want to go. Some lack a good sense of direction and end up in the darnest places!

For the most convenience in getting around, especially if you are shopping, hire a car and driver. You should be able to do this for less than Rs 800 per day or Rs 600 for a half day. Most taxi drivers will be happy to become your full-day (8 hours) companion. Indeed, almost every taxi driver will ask you if they can become your car and driver companion for the day. Be sure to negotiate a half-day or full-day rate with them before you decide to use their services. If you hire a hotel car with driver, it may cost you two or three times more than if you negotiated a rate with a taxi driver. Since it's so easy to arrange a car with driver and the cost is relatively inexpensive, you may want to start your first day in Mumbai with a car and driver. Just walk out the front door of your hotel and approach a few of the taxi drivers waiting for customers. You'll have no difficulty making these arrangements on your own since most drivers speak some English and they are very accommodating. The only problem is that some of these drivers get lost or confused as to where you want to go. The problem is complicated by the fact that many of Mumbai's streets have two names. Even long-time residents get confused by the renaming of streets for famous and not-so-famous public figures. Take a good map with you and write down all the addresses for the places you want to go. Don't assume your driver knows where he's always going. Some lack a good sense of direction and end up in the darnest places! Another problem is that some drivers may want to take you to shops that give them commissions. You need to stay in control of your shopping agenda by telling the driver exactly where you want to go. After all, why would you want to take shopping advice from someone who lives in a slum or sleeps in the back seat of his car each night? Would you do that back home? Drivers know what they are doing when they recommend a shop—getting closer to a commission.

TOURS AND TOURIST OFFICES

If you prefer joining a tour, you should have no problem doing so by contacting the concierge or front desk at your hotel for information on various tour groups that offer half-day and full-day tours of Mumbai and the surrounding area. Both the federal and state government tourist offices also provide useful information and services on tours. The Government of India tourist office (Tel. 203-3144) is located at 123 Maharshi Karve Road, just opposite the Churchgate station. It's open Monday through Friday from 8:30am to 6pm and on Saturday from 8:30am to 2pm. It also has a 24-hour counter at the international airport and a counter at the domestic airport (Tel. 614-9200) which closes after the last flight. The Maharashtra Tourism Development Corporation (MTDC), located at CDO Hutments, Madame Cama Road, offers daily (except Monday) tours of the city and nearby areas (Tel. 202-6713 or 202-4627):

- **Mumbai City Tour:** Available as a morning and afternoon tour. 9am to 1pm and 2pm to 6pm.

- **Suburban Tour:** 9:15am to 6pm. Departs from tours division, MTDC, Gateway of India.

- **Open-deck bus tour:** 7:30pm to 8:30pm and 8:35pm to 9:35pm on Saturday and Sunday. Departs from the Hotel Oberoi.

- **Boat trip to Elephanta Caves:** Departs from the Gateway of India every half hour from 8:00am to 2:30pm. Boat ride takes one hour.

TIPPING

Tips are appreciated in Mumbai however large or small. While it is not customary to tip taxi and auto-rickshaw drivers, porters and waiters do expect to receive tips. However, no set amounts or fixed percentages are expected. It's up to you to determine the value of the service. Keep in mind that wages tend to be very low so what may seem to be a small tip to you will probably mean a lot to the recipient. Be sure to set aside enough small change for such tips.

RESOURCES AND VIRTUAL MUMBAI

You'll find lots of good resources on Mumbai once you arrive. The Government of India tourist office offers a free booklet on the city as well as a "What's On" guide to city entertainment. Bookshops have several inexpensive local guides and maps such as the *Travellers Yellow Pages*, *The Road Guide to Mumbai*, and *The Mid-Day Good Food Guide to Mumbai.* If you stay at the Taj Mahal Hotel, be sure to ask the front desk for a copy of *The Taj City Guide* which provides lots of useful information on sightseeing, shopping, and dining.

Before arriving in Mumbai, you may want to access information online about the city. You'll find several excellent Web sites that provide a wide range of information on the city. Some sites, such as Mumbai-Central, also have message boards, discussion groups, and links to other useful sites. We highly recommend visiting these sites as part of your pre-trip planning for Mumbai:

City:	www.mumbainet.com
	www.mumbai-central.com
	www.mumbaizone.com
	www.bombay.indiacity.com
	http://theorytifr.res.in/bombay
Hotels:	www.india-travel.com/mumbai.htm

Restaurants:	*www.mumbainet.com/foodplza/foodplza.htm*
News:	*www.timesofindia.com*
	www.indiatimes.com

GETTING TO KNOW YOU

Mumbai is not a difficult city to figure out and get around in. We recommend familiarizing yourself with a few sections and then take taxis to get around. Most places are within a 20 to 30 minute drive, depending on the traffic, and most taxi rides cost less than US$2.00. Better still, hire a car for a half or full day to take you around the city for sightseeing and shopping. Having a car available for a four or eight hour period is very convenient and relatively inexpensive, especially on a hot or rainy day.

Located on a narrow peninsula, Mumbai has a north-south orientation much like New York City's Manhattan Island. It's best to orient yourself to its various sections. Running north to south, the major sections of interest to visitors include:

❑ **Mahalaxmi:** Known for its popular racecourse and turf club as well as for one of Mumbai's best furniture shops, The Raj. If you're looking for antique or reproduction colonial furniture, it's worth making a trip to the Mahalaxmi area. If not, you can skip this area. If you continue north of this area, you'll be heading for the airport and the suburbs beyond.

❑ **Kemp's Corner:** This is Mumbai's upscale shopping area with boutiques offering the latest in Indian fashions and accessories. Young designers display their collections in small shops. Nearby Cumballa Hill, Breach Candy, and the Beautiful Boulevard (Napeansea Road) offer additional shopping opportunities. Not the greatest shopping opportunities, but an interesting area to explore if you have a few hours to kill. Just be careful of the traffic in this area. It's not very pedestrian-friendly!

❑ **Crawford Market/Zaveri Bazaar/Chor Bazaar:** These are Mumbai's famous market and bazaar areas where you can buy just about anything imaginable, from expensive jewelry to cheap clothes and used electronic goods along with fresh fish and spices. An extremely crowded, congested, and typical dirty market area where the watchwords are "watch your wallet" (the areas are riff with pickpockets), hundreds of small shops and stalls vie for street and sidewalk space. Definitely cultural experiences that will probably not yield much in terms of quality shopping other than perhaps some fine jewelry in the Zaveri (Gold) Bazaar. On a hot day you may decide you have better things to do with your time than cruise through this chaos and congestion! But then it could be "fun" depending on where you come from. Be sure to bargain hard for everything you buy.

❏ **Churchgate:** Mumbai's famous railway station is the central landmark for this area. Here you'll find the city's oldest and most famous saree shops next to each other at Marine Lines (adjacent to the railway tracks) and numerous street stalls offering cheap clothes along what is called "Fashion Street" (a section of Mahatma Gandhi Road bordering the park area on the east side of the train station). A very crowded and congested area, it's as much a cultural experience as a shopping experience.

❏ **Colaba:** This is Mumbai's more popular tourist section. Located near the southern end of the peninsula, it's where most of the city's major hotels, restaurants, shopping, and sightseeing can be found. It's where you will find the Taj Mahal Hotel, the Gateway of India, the Prince of Wales Museum, and numerous tourist shops in and around the hotel and extending to Regal Cinema and the Prince of Wales Museum at Wellingdon Circle. Here you will find street vendors alongside small and large shops offering everything from typical Indian arts and crafts, tourist kitsch, and cheap clothes to nice antiques, jewelry, textiles, and art. You can easily confine 70 percent of your stay in Mumbai to this area. You'll want to occasionally escape into Mumbai's grand oasis, the Taj Mahal Hotel, for tea, a cold drink, or ice cream. Looking out at the Gateway to India, you know you're in a special place that has witnessed some very important parades of history.

❏ **Nariman Point:** This is Mumbai's business center which houses the city's skyscrapers. Here you will find major financial institutions, corporations, and airline offices. It's also home for the city's two five-star Oberoi hotels and their adjacent shopping arcades. Bankers and diamond dealers tend to stay here, although the diamond dealers are moving to the suburbs. If you are in Mumbai for business, you'll most likely want to stay in this area. Be sure to check out the restaurants and shopping at the Oberoi hotels. It doesn't get much better.

❑ **Cuff Parade:** Located at the southern tip of peninsula, this area is most noted for the World Trade Center and its rather tired shopping center.

❑ **Marine Drive, Chowpatty Beach, and Malabar Hill:** Located south of Cumbala Hill and north and west of Nariman Point, these are three of Mumbai's most scenic areas. Marine Drive runs along the seashore from Nariman Point to the foot of Malabar Hill and includes Chowpatty Beach. At night this well lit area becomes known as the "Queen's Necklace." Both Marine Drive and Chowpatty Beach are popular promenades and gathering places for locals. In the evening, Chowpatty Beach takes on a carnival atmosphere. The upscale Malabar Hill area offers nice views of Back Bay, Chowpatty Beach, and Marine Drive and is famous for its Hanging Gardens and the Parsi Towers of Silence (funeral towers where bodies of the Parsi sect are laid out in the open to be picked by vultures and crows).

SHOPPING MUMBAI

While Mumbai is often touted as a shopper's paradise, it's only such if you equate paradise with volume or compare shopping in Mumbai with other cities in India. The truth is that Mumbai offers lots of shopping opportunities but the quality and designs are often repetitious, mediocre, and disappointing. You'll see lots of the same arts and crafts over and over and over again; most clothes and textiles are designed for locals; jewelry designs tend to cater to traditional local tastes; the art is at best okay; and antiques and collectibles tend to be limited. For shoppers, Mumbai is not Bangkok, Singapore, Jakarta, Hong Kong, or even Shanghai. Lots of shopping, yes; but by no stretch of the imagination is it a shopper's paradise.

Shopping in Mumbai is similar in two respects to shopping elsewhere in India. First, expect to encounter several pesky touts along the street who attempt to attach themselves to you. They want to take you to their favorite shops that give them commissions on your purchases. The best way to avoid these people is to tell them firmly that *"I want to be left alone."* They will eventually go away. Whatever you do, don't indicate an interest in them. Second, be sure to bargain in the markets and aggressive emporiums. You should be able to negotiate discounts from 10 to 60 percent. However, many shops tend to be very laid back and do little bargaining.

Mumbai is India's shopping center for everything from inexpensive market and street goods to the latest in imported designer clothes and jewelry. Reflecting both the extreme poverty and wealth of this city, Mumbai's markets and shops have something for everyone. Like China's Shanghai, Mumbai is a relatively sophisticated, fashionable, and wealthy city where shopping is coming of age. The city boasts numerous markets for inexpensive clothes, jewelry, antiques, and household goods and a variety of small shops and hotel shopping arcades that primarily cater to tourists and expatriates in search of arts, crafts, jewelry, antiques, and furniture. Numerous other shops are famous among the local middle and upper classes for exquisite jewelry, textiles, and clothes, especially fashionable sarees.

WHAT TO BUY

Mumbai shops offer a good range of products for shoppers who are especially interested in local products and designs. The major such products include:

❏ **Jewelry:** Mumbai is India's major diamond and gold center. In fact, the largest number of diamonds in the world are cut in India. Numerous jewelry shops, especially ones like **Tribhovandas Bhimji Zaveri** and **Danabhai Jewellers & Sons** in the famous gold market area along Zaveri Bazar Street, offer a wide range of both diamond and gold jewelry in the form of bangles, rings, and necklaces. However, most jewelry you'll find in Mumbai is produced in traditional Indian designs to be worn with sarees and the shops are usually packed with local buyers. This often means big pieces of jewelry in 22 or 24 karat gold. At the same time, a few shops, such as the 135 year old Tribhovandas Bhimji Zaveri, also maintain special lines of jewelry for export to Japan, Europe, and North America. While interesting to view and to watch locals buy, chances are you won't purchase the local jewelry. Don't expect to find much fashionable Western jewelry readily displayed in Mumbai. For exclusive one-of-a-kind pieces that appeal to Westerners, visit the **Ravissant** showroom in the Oberoi Hotel.

❑ **Arts and crafts:** Like other cities in India, Mumbai is well stocked with arts and crafts from all over the country. For the largest and most redundant collection of such items, be sure to visit **Cottage Industries Emporium** near the Regal Cinema, just off Battery Street, and not far from the Taj Mahal Hotel. Its two floors are jam-packed with rugs, yardage, bedspreads, carved doors, elephants, wood inlaid pictures, stuffed animals, and many other arts and crafts typically found throughout India. It also has several art galleries that showcase paintings and sculptures of local artists. Shops like **Popli & Son**, which is located behind the Taj Mahal Hotel on Battery Street, offer an attractive range of gold and silver ethnic jewelry, precious and semi-precious stones, silver artifacts, miniature paintings, and other handicrafts.

❑ **Antiques and collectibles:** Most of Mumbai's antiques and collectibles date from the British colonial period and include everything from silver, ivory, ceramics, prints, boxes to wood carvings, bronzes, and stone sculptures. **Chow Market** has numerous stalls offering antiques and collectibles. You'll find numerous shops offering a wide range of quality antiques, such as **Phillips Antiques** on Madame Cama Road, between the Taj Mahal Hotel and the Prince of Wales Museum, **Natesan's Antiqarts** at the Jehangir Art Gallery building, and **A. K. Essajee** which is located just behind the Taj Mahal Hotel.

❑ **Furniture:** Mumbai is a good place to purchase both old and new furniture. Its shops are especially noted for their colonial furniture, including old Portuguese furniture from Goa. Many of the shops do excellent restoration work. Some of the best such shops include **The Raj** near the racecourse in Mahalaxmi; **Collectors' Corner** at Phillips Antiques; **A. K. Essajee** behind the Taj Mahal Hotel; **Jogeshwari** beyond the airport; **Doshi** at Napecase Road (beyond Kemp's Corner); and **Farida Hoosenally** at 522 Sayani Road. However, many other small shops also have large workshops and warehouses located outside the central business district. Regardless of the size of a shop, ask if they have another shop or warehouse. In many cases, they will have a photo album of items available in their warehouse.

- ❏ **Home furnishings and decorative items** [bai's large middle and upper classes, more a] cater to the domestic needs of these gro[ups] uniquely designed tableware, lamps, potter[y] linens, dishes, and glasses. Many of the[ ] located in and around Kemp's Corner, such[ ] and **Good Earth**.

- ❏ **Clothes and textiles:** Mumbai abounds with clothes and textile shops, from inexpensive street vendors and market stalls to exclusive boutiques, tailor shops, and famous saree shops offering a wide range of textiles. At the low, try the street stalls along "Fashion Street" which are located near Bombay Gymkhana. Exclusive boutiques can be found in the major hotels, such as the Taj Mahal and Oberoi, as well as in and around Kemp's Corner (try **Ravissant** and **Litolier**). Mumbai's oldest and largest saree shops are found along Marine Lines near Church-gate Station: **Indian States**, **Kala Niketan**, and **Roop Milan**. For tailoring and textiles, visit two shops in the Taj Mahal Hotel: **Burlingtons' of Bombay** and **Indian Textiles Company**.

WHERE TO SHOP

MAJOR SHOPPING AREAS

Mumbai's shopping areas are relatively well defined. Once in an area, you can easily walk from one shop to another, although the crowded, broken, beetle-stained, and vendor-occupied sidewalks frequently force you into the street where you must be careful to dodge vehicles. The major shopping areas include:

- ❏ **Taj Mahal Hotel to Wellingdon Circle:** This is the major shopping area for tourists in search of arts, crafts, antiques, furniture, and jewelry. You can easily spend hours shopping in this area. Use the Taj Mahal as your shopping base and oasis since you will probably want to occasionally return there to escape from the heat, noise, pollution, and crowds of the nearby streets. In fact, one of our favorite shopping breaks is a visit to the Sea Lounge on the second floor of the old section of the Taj Mahal Hotel. Having tea, a cold drink, ice cream, or lunch there overlooking the sea and traffic is a very pleasant way to break up your shopping day.

Start your shopping in this area at the Taj Mahal Hotel's shopping arcade. Shops are found in both the old and new wings of this landmark five-star hotel. As you enter the front door, turn left, pass the reception desk on the right, and walk down the long hall. Here you'll find travel agencies, a pharmacy, and several nice shops: **Burlingtons' of Bombay** for quality tailoring, textiles, bedspreads, wall hangings, and T-shirts; **Malabar Boutique** for wonderful clothes, bags, scarves, pillow cases, boxes, purses, jewelry, and furniture; **Taj Art Gallery** for changing exhibits of major artists from all over India; **Indian Textiles Company** for beautiful one-of-a-kind silk and gold fabrics; and **Gazdar** for antiques, jewelry, and silver. In the newer wing of the hotel, which is directly opposite the entrance, you'll find a good bookstore, **Nalanda**, and a branch of **Natesan's Antiqarts** which offers top quality large antiques in the form of temple carvings and bronzes. The remaining shops in this arcade offer a wide assortment of jewelry, handicrafts, carpets, and clothes.

As you leave the hotel, turn to your left and walk to the area behind the hotel. Here you'll find lots of small shops and stalls selling a wide assortment of arts and crafts, including carpets, shells, paintings, stone carved elephants, post cards, bangles, and beads. If you next head toward the Regal Cinema building, which is located opposite the Prince of Wales Museum, you'll see Battery street which is behind the Regal Cinema. This street includes several interesting antique shops. The two best shops here are **A.K. Essajee** (Landsdown House, Below Regency Inn Hotel, Battery Street, Tel. 202-1071) and **Z. N. Exporters** (4, Battery Street, Suleman Chambers, Tel. 202-7256). One of Mumbai's oldest antique shops (over 130 years), **A.K. Essajee** is crammed with antiques: doors, marble tables, glass chandeliers, Portuguese chests, old palace windows, doors, pots, tables, and chairs. This shop also has two other warehouses which include both antiques and reproductions. Ask to see their photo album for samples of other items. **Z. N. Exporters** is a small shop with furniture. It also has another shop four doors away which offers silver, bronze, daggers, and even Russian icons. Ask to see their photo album which includes doors, chairs, chests, and panels in their nearby warehouse. **Popli & Son** (Battery Street, Tel. 285-4757) has an excellent selection of gold and silver ethnic jewelry, precious and semi-precious stones, silver, miniature paintings, and other handicrafts.

Just off of Battery Street, at 34 Chhatrapati Shivaji Maharaj Road near the Gateway to India (Tel. 202-1101), is Mumbai's largest arts and crafts emporium, the **Central Cottage Industries Emporium**. Its two floors are jam-packed with arts and crafts from all over India. Watch your head on the second floor; it has a dangerously low ceiling with head-stopper beams!

Across from Regal Cinema is **Phillips Antiques** (Tel. 202-0564) which is one of Mumbai's oldest (since 1860) and most respected antique shops. Here you'll fine lots of silver, ivory, Burmese lacquerware, ceramics, boxes, and prints. Be sure to ask to see their photo album. Phillips Antiques also has another company, **Collectors' Corner**, that deals in both antique and reproduction furniture. Many dealers come here to source for furniture as well as to use Collectors' Corner for reliable shipping. Nearby is **Amar Gems & Crafts** (1, Abubaker Mansion, Tel. 202-8923) which offers a wide selection of jewelry, silver, carvings, neck pieces, and beads.

Across the street is the Prince of Wales Museum and next to it is the **Jahangir Art Gallery**. Here you'll find two shops worth visiting: **Natesan's Antiqarts** in the basement of the gallery for a fine collection of arts and antiques in bronze, silver, stone, teakwood, and sandalwood, and the **Terrace Art Gallery** on the roof of the building (watch the rather dangerous metal stairs) for paintings (oils) by Chetan. The Cafe Samovar on the first floor is a very popular for lunch.

❏ **Oberoi Hotel and Oberoi Towers Hotel:** Located at Nariman Point, these two adjacent Oberoi hotels offer some of Mumbai's best quality shopping. Within the Oberoi Towers Hotel, an upscale shopping arcade is located just off the hotel lobby. Here you'll find lots of shops offering jewelry (try **Maharani** and **Ahmed Joo** for excellent quality), arts and crafts, carpets, leathergoods, bookstore (**Ritika** for coffee table books), and designer silver and leather (**Ravissant**). Next to Oberoi Hotel is the Oberoi Shopping Centre consisting of two parts: first floor with numerous small upscale shops offering jewelry, carpets, arts and crafts, clothes, leathergoods; and recently renovated second and third floors with very touristy arts and crafts, jewelry, leather, shoe and accessory, and carpet shops. The best quality shops are found on the first floor.

❑ **Kemp's Corner and Breach Candy:** Located north of city center, this is one of Mumbai's more upscale shopping areas for clothes and accessories. However, this whole area tends to be overrated as a major shopping center. You will find a handful of quality shops but not many for all the effort you make in finding this area. Several boutiques primarily appeal to trendy locals. The best way to explore this area is to take a taxi or car to Cumballa Hill. Get off at the hospital, which is just before the flyover, and across the street from the **Good Earth** shop (32, Cornelian Kemp's Corner, 104, August Kranti Marg, Tel. 388-6750). This is one of Mumbai's most attractive home decorative shops which specializes in pottery, glassware, placemats, lamps, candles, fabrics, flatware, and dinner sets. From here, walk south and then cross to the other side of street and walk under the flyover. In the first block after the flyover you will come to a shopping area on the left which is called **Om Chambers**. This center consists of a collection of designer boutiques and jewelry shops. The first building in this complex, **Inter Plaza**, includes more than 20 Indian designers with their small boutiques. Behind this building are two levels of shops offering imported jewelry (**Piaget** and **Chopard**), costume jewelry (**Paja**), and designer jewelry (**Paulomi's Treasure**). If you keep walking south, you will come to two adjacent shops (top of building says "Hotel Kemps Corner")—**Ravissant** (Tel. 368-4934) for exquisite fabrics, bed spreads, and clothes (Indian designs) and a silver designer line; and **Litolier** for classy saris. After these two shops, there's not much else of note for shoppers. Keep walking south to intersection and go to the right. Walk another 10-15 minutes and you come to the **Breach Candy** area which borders the seaside of Marine Drive. Watch where you walk since you face an obstacle course of broken sidewalks, vendors spilling over into the road, and cars parked in your pathway. You won't find much here except for **Arena** (jewelry), **Benzer Department Store**, and several shops specializing in fabrics, sarees, and trendy clothes and a few cafes. It may not be worth the long walk, especially on a hot day, with all the sidewalk obstacles along this busy street of traffic and traffic jams. Also, located nearby is the Beautiful Boulevard on Napean Sea Road with shops offering a wide range of imported name brand goods of primary interest to Mumbai's upper middle and upper classes.

❑ **World Trade Center:** Located south of the Oberoi Hotel, this business and shopping center houses various state handicraft emporiums. A relatively quiet area where you may be able to find some interesting arts, crafts, and gift items. Primarily set up to promote the export of state products. A good place for dealers to shop. Not high on our "must visit" retail shopping list.

❑ **Markets and Bazaars:** Like many other cities in India, Mumbai has numerous traditional markets and bazaars that are a combination of being colorful, congested, and cultural experiences. Four markets in particular are worth visiting for a variety of goods:

- **Chor Bazaar:** Located off Mohamadali Road and near Pydhoni in a Muslim section of the city, this is Mumbai's version of a peoples' flea or second hand market. Also known as "Thieves Market," this extremely congested and noisy area, which often becomes a madhouse of honking vehicles, is filled with small narrow stalls offering lots of junk as well as an occasional antique or noteworthy collectible; however, many so-called antiques are reproductions. Look for hardware, clothes, fans, tools, radios, trunks, antique reproductions, gramophones, carved rosewood furniture, old chandeliers, brass curios, and all types of antiques. Be sure to bargain hard for everything here. Secure your valuables against possible pickpockets who are known to frequent this area. In the end, you may find this area to be more of a cultural experience rather than a good source for shopping. On a hot and steamy day, you'll definitely want to find an oasis after this street-level experience!

- **Crawford Market:** Renamed the Mahatma Phule Market. Located just north of the Victoria Terminus Railway Station, this is Mumbai's main wholesale produce or wet market where locals shop for fruits, vegetables, meat, live animals, spices, and lots of odds and ends. The live, or almost dead, animal section is found at the rear of the market. An interesting traditional market with its ornate Gothic exterior. A visit it will probably become a cultural experience rather than potential buying experience. If you have been to similar markets elsewhere, this is one of those "been there, done that" type of experience you may not need to repeat, especially if your stomach is a bit queasy and if you would like to avoid more crowds!

- **Fashion Street:** A street market located near the university and opposite Bombay Gymkhana. Consists of a long row of small stalls selling cheap clothes and accessories—T-shirts, pants, shirts, blouses, blue jeans, shorts, childrens' clothes. Many are export rejects, factory overruns, and knockoffs. Be sure to look everything over carefully for defects. The name for this street is a misnomer—chances are you'll find lots of dreadful colors and much less than fashionable c-lothes! But they are really cheap, if you bargain hard; 50-60 percent discounts are appropriate. This street market, too, can become a cultural experience.

- **Zaveri Bazaar:** You may have some difficulty locating the major section of the market. Ask your driver to take you to the intersection of Kalbadevi and Sheikh Memon streets (at the Cotton Exchange). Located on Zaveri Bazar Street, this is Mumbai's main gold market. Both sides of this extremely congested and narrow street (more like a pedestrian lane since vendors spill into the street) are lined with gold and jewelry shops with armed guards as well as street vendors selling watches, hardware, belts, clothes, and fruits. Most of the jewelry (gold, silver, and stones made into bangles, bracelets, necklaces, rings, and ear rings) is produced in traditional Indian designs which are appropriately worn with the saree. While most of the shops sell similar types of gold and jewelry, you will find a few stand-out shops here. If you only stop at one place, make sure it's **Tribhovandas Bhimji Zaveri** (241-43, Zaveri Bazar, Tel. 342-5001). The ground and first floors of this well respected 135 year old shop are filled with a wide range of traditional Indian jewelry, including many large and heavy show pieces. The second floor is devoted to silver and Western style jewelry using precious and semi precious stones, especially diamonds. You also should visit **Danabhai Jewellers & Sons** at 290/92, Zaveri Bazar, Tel. 205-7000). Several silver shops can be found along a side street, Mumbadevi Road. The Brass Bazaar also is located in this area.

❑ **Department Stores:** Mumbai has a few department stores but they primarily cater to local residents with lots of clothes and household goods—especially pots and pans. Save your time. Most are not even worth the cultural experience. The major department stores include:

- **Akbarallys:** 45 V. Nariman Road, Tel. 204-3921.

- **The Bombay Store:** Sir P.M. Road, Tel. 288-5048.

- **Shopper's Stop:** 211 D, S.V. Road, Andheri (West), Tel. 624-0451.

❑ **Handicraft Emporiums:** Several standard handicraft emporiums are found in Mumbai. The best and most comprehensive is the **Central Cottage Industries Emporium** at 34 Chhatrapati Shivaiji Maharaj Marg (Tel. 202-2491) which is located within a five minute walk from the Taj Mahal Hotel and just down the street from Wellingdon Circle, behind the Regal Cinema, and across from Battery Street. Also, look for the **Khadi and Village Industries Emporium** found at 286 Dadabhai Naoroji Road, and the **Gujarat Government Handicrafts Emporium** located at Khetan Bhavan, J. N. Tata Road. Other state handicraft emporiums can be found at the **World Trade Center**.

BEST OF THE BEST

The best quality shopping tends to be found in and around Mumbai's three top hotels—Oberoi Hotel, Oberoi Towers, and the Taj Mahal Hotel. Certain product lines, such as arts and crafts, antiques, jewelry, and clothes tend to congregate in the same sections of the city. A few outstanding shops are located outside the main business section, with some operating from homes. When shopping for antiques and furniture, remember that many unassuming small retail shops also may have factories and warehouses elsewhere in Mumbai or outside the city. These other operations tend to cater to wholesalers and others who require reliable shipping and exporting. In some cases, these shops may have branch shops, factories, and warehouses in other cities, especially Delhi.

We found the following shops to be some of Mumbai's best for uniqueness and quality:

ANTIQUES AND OBJECTS D'ART

Shops and markets throughout Mumbai offer a wide range of antiques and objets d'art, from jewelry and small collectibles to furniture and huge architectural pieces from palaces. Some verge on being flea market junk, especially when shopping in the Chor Bazar. But you will find lots of quality antiques, many dating from the Raj period, in several of Mumbai's antique shops. Many of the antique shops also source for dealers as well as maintain factories that produce new furniture for export. When visiting an antique shop, always ask if they have another shop, warehouse, or factory or a "catalog" (photo album) of other things they sell. You may be surprised with what you find. Indeed, you may end up on a serendipitous shopping adventure that takes you from a tiny shop to a large warehouse or factory on the outskirts of Mumbai. We found the following antique shops to be well worth visiting. Many have catalogs, additional shops, warehouses, and factories:

❏ **Phillips Antiques:** *Opposite the Regal Cinema and the Prince of Wales Museum, in the heritage Indian Mercantile Mansion on Madame Cama Road, Tel. 202-0564 or Fax 202-5579. Web site: www.phillipsantiques.com.* Operating since 1860, this is the place for serious collectors of everything from prints, engravings, porcelain, Burmese lacquerware, and old glass to coins, buttons, rings, jade, ivory, vases, bowls, and miniature paintings. The shop is literally a treasure trove of small collectibles dating from the 18th and 19th centuries. Excellent quality and very reliable. Also offers antique furniture through its export division, Collectors' Corner, which is located on the second floor of this building; ask to see their photo albums which include doors, tables, columns, and cement garden pieces. Especially noted for their colonial furniture which is housed at a different location within 30-35 minutes by car from this shop. One of the best places for packing and shipping.

❏ **Natesan's Antiqarts:** *Two locations: Lobby shopping arcade of Taj Mahal Hotel, Tel. 202-4165; basement of Jehangir Art Gallery, Tel. 285-2700 or Fax 285-2121.* Offers one-of-a-kind pieces, from sculptures and wood carvings to chests and boxes, in bronze, silver, stone, teakwood, and sandalwood. Includes some handicrafts. Most are large and heavy pieces that need to be shipped by sea freight.

The largest selection is found at the Jehangir Art Gallery. Also has shops in Bangalore, Trivandrum, New Delhi, and London. Manufactures bronze figures and teakwood furniture for export from its factory in Bangalore. A top quality shop in operation for over 65 years.

❑ **A. K. Essajee/Essajee & Son:** *Ground Floor, Landsdown House, Below Regency Inn Hotel, Battery Street, Tel. 202-1071 or Fax 287-3371.* This 120 year old dusty shop offers a large selection of old chests, doors, marble tables, glass chandeliers, pots, tables, chairs, palace windows, and small collectibles. Also manufactures new furniture. Ask to see their photo album for examples. Has two warehouses, one behind the Taj Mahal Hotel and another at Marine Lines.

❑ **Gazdar:** *Taj Mahal Hotel Shopping Arcade, Tel. 202-3666 or Fax 283-6498.* Offers a unique collection of objets d'art—antique jewelry, silver, watches, enamel figures, and carved wood panels. Also manufactures its own line of European-style jewelry. Views itself as the "Tiffany's of India" with many contemporary pieces made with rubies, diamonds, emeralds, and pearls. A well established and reputable shop in operation since 1930.

❑ **Z. N. Exporters:** *4, Battery Street, Suleman Chambers, Behind Regal Cinema, Tel. 204-7256 or Fax 204-8889.* This small shop actually consists of two shops. The first shop is crammed with furniture—doors, chairs, chests, and panels. Ask to see their photo album which has examples of furniture available in their warehouse which is located two blocks away. The second shop is four doors away and includes lots of silver, bronze, daggers, and even Russian icons!

❑ **Almari (Zewar Exports):** *Vasant Vehar, 8, M. L. Dahanukar Marg (Carmichael Road),Tel. 497-3426 or Fax 497-3427.* This is not an easy place to find given its residential location, but it's worth the adventure. Please call ahead for directions and hours (usually 10am to 6pm, and closed on Sundays). Located in a big old house, the upstairs rooms are filled with quality furniture and antiques from all over India. Includes mirrors, carvings, boxes, tables, chests, and lamps. A separate shop downstairs offers a wide range of folk art as well as costume jewelry, scarves, bags, and fashion accessories.

FURNITURE

Furniture and antiques often get mixed together in India. Many shops that offer antique furniture (see above) also do restoration work as well as produce new furniture for export. You'll have little difficulty finding a good range of colonial and Portuguese furniture in Mumbai. Two shops in particular are well worth visiting:

❑ **The Raj**: *Opposite the Racecourse at Wellington Sports Club, Volga House, 1-C, K. Khade Marg, Mahalaxmi, Tel. 495-2626 or Fax 495-1146.* If you visit only one furniture shop in India, make sure it's The Raj. Dealers, expatriates, and collectors love this exceptional place for attractive original and reproduction British, Portuguese, Dutch Colonial, and Indian-style furniture. A "must see" shop, you can easily do all of your furniture shopping at The Raj. This expansive two-storey shop/warehouse is filled with old furniture—chairs, tables, desks, doors, beds, and pillars. While some of the old furniture is reconditioned, most are reproductions with some being made from old wood taken from dismantled houses. The craftsmanship is excellent and the finishes are well done. Be sure to visit the upstairs showrooms where you will most likely bump into foreign dealers who are exporting this furniture to Europe and North America where prices will be five to ten times higher than here at the source. Very experienced at shipping furniture abroad. Be sure to pick up a copy of their brochure/catalog which also includes information on their showroom in Delhi.

❑ **Collectors' Corner**: *Opposite Regal Cinema and the Prince of Wales Museum, in the heritage Indian Mercantile Mansion on Madame Cama Road, Tel. 202-0564 or Fax 202-5579.* Web site: *www.phillipsantiques.com.* As part of Phillips Antiques, Collectors' Corner offers both antique and reproduction furniture. You can view some of their collection online by visiting their Web site. The offices are located on the second floor of Phillips Antiques. Go there to examine the photo albums or to meet the manager or his assistants. If you are interested in exploring further, they will arrange to take you to their warehouse which is 30-35 minutes away. Collectors' Corner also will source furniture for their clients. If you have a particular piece of furniture in mind, chances are they can either find it for you or make it themselves. A very well respected and reliable company also known for its shipping expertise.

ART

While Calcutta is India's major art center, you will find some quality art in Mumbai. A few galleries in the city offer paintings of artists from all over India as well as Mumbai. Be careful when you see a sign that says "Art Gallery." It usually refers to a clothing store! For starters, try these galleries and shops:

❑ **Taj Art Gallery:** *Taj Mahal Hotel shopping arcade.* Located next to the Malabar Boutique, in the old section of the hotel, this gallery changes art exhibits each week. Represents major contemporary artists from all over India who primarily work in oils.

❑ **Jehangir Art Gallery**: *Located next to the Prince of Wales Museum.* Includes changing exhibits of leading Indian artists.

❑ **Treasure Art Gallery:** *Jehangir Art Gallery (roof top).* This long established (over 30 years) gallery represents the paintings of the aging artist Chetan. Most are oil paintings of rural and urban scenes ranging in price from US$50 to US$400. Watch your step in getting to this gallery. It's located above the popular Cafe Samovar, but you get to it by going through the building near the cafe and climbing the rather dangerous outdoor metal stairs to get to the roof top entrance to the gallery.

❑ **Gallery Chemould:** *Jehangir Art Gallery.* Includes monthly changing exhibits of up and coming contemporary artists. Often disappointing exhibits.

❑ **Popli & Son:** Behind the Taj Mahal Hotel on Battery Street, Tel. 202-2321. Includes silk paintings as well as miniature ivory paintings along with lots of jewelry and handicrafts.

JEWELRY

Much of the jewelry you'll see in Mumbai is in 22 karat gold and made in local designs as bangles, rings, and necklaces to be worn with sarees. Many of these pieces are big and clunky.

However, some jewelry stores also offer separate lines of Western designed jewelry using diamonds and previous and semi-precious stones. The following jewelry stores are worth visiting:

- ☑ **Tribhovandas Bhimji Zaveri:** *241-43, Zaveri Bazar, Tel. 342-5001 or Fax 343-5656.* This is Mumbai's most famous jewelry and gold shop located in the heart of the congested gold market (Zaveri Bazar) area. It's also reputed to be India's largest showroom. Operating since 1865, this five-storey shop is a shopper's paradise for both Indian and Western jewelry; indeed, you can shop for both lines of jewelry simultaneously. The first three floors showcase a large variety of jewelry. The ground floor primarily presents traditional Indian jewelry, especially bangles and large gold necklaces and rings. You may be more interested in the next two floors. The first floor has a large collection of diamond jewelry, necklaces, rings, earrings, and bracelets. The second floor is primarily devoted to silver articles and a Western designer collection called the "Empress" line of jewelry. This beautiful collection, crafted by a leading Japanese designer, is exported throughout the world and represents some of India's finest Western-style jewelry. This shop has something for everyone, including numerous show-stopper pieces for the rich and famous.

- ❑ **Danabhai Jewellers Sons:** *290/92, Zaveri Bazar, Tel. 208- 7000.* Located across the street from Tribhovandas Bhimji Zaveri, this is one of the nicer jewelry showrooms in the Zaveri Bazar area. Includes lots of traditional Indian gold jewelry.

- ❑ **Arena:** *69 Bhulahai Desai Road, Breach Candy, Tel. 368-1122 or Fax 368-1133.* Located opposite the U.S. Consulate, this classy showroom displays lots of traditionally designed Indian jewelry. Offers a large collection of gold chains as well as a very attractive collection of jewelry using diamonds, rubies, and emeralds. A relatively new shop related to the nearby Benzar Department Store.

- ☑ **Gazdar:** *Taj Mahal Hotel Shopping Arcade, Tel. 202-3666 or Fax 283-6498.* Likes to refer to themselves as the "Tiffany's of India." A combination jewelry, objets d'art, and antique shop operating since 1933. While some designs may look old-fashioned, most pieces are very attractive, detailed, and of excellent quality. Has its own factory where it produces many contemporary pieces using rubies, diamonds, emeralds, and pearls. Especially noted for their use color and designs that suggest movement.

❑ **Treasured Jewels:** *64, Oberoi Shopping Plaza, The Oberoi Hotel, Tel/Fax 284-6170, ext. 6864.* This small shop offers an excellent collection of gold neck pieces and jewelry as well as enamel elephants and purses.

❑ **Paja:** *15, Om Chambers, Kemp's Corner, Tel. 369-1050.* This small shop produces its own costume jewelry. Offers attractively designed earrings, necklaces, and bracelets. Most are made with silver and then gold plated.

❑ **Ahmed Joo:** *L-25, Hotel Oberoi Towers, Tel. 283-6467.* Small shop offering a beautiful collection of jewelry.

❑ **Unigem:** *12, Dharam Palace, Hughes Road, Tel/Fax 364-1196.* India's only all diamond jewelry showroom. Offers international jewelry designs.

TEXTILES, SAREES, AND TAILORING

Numerous shops in Mumbai offer excellent collections of textiles, sarees, and tailoring services, from the very ordinary to haute couture. Some of Mumbai's best shops include:

❑ **Indian Textiles Company:** *Taj Mahal Hotel shopping arcade, Tel. 202-8783.* Exquisite collection of fine textiles designed by this well known company. Includes printed, handwoven, and gold embroidered silks. Great materials for making clothing and gorgeous bedspreads. Purchase by the meter. Does not offer tailoring services. Also has a showroom in New Delhi (R-61, Greater Kailash - I).

❑ **Ravissant:** *Abhay Chambers, Kemp's Corner, Tel. 368-4934 or Fax 368-4935.* This is India's haute couture textile and clothing boutique. Produces gorgeous fabrics, bedspreads, pillows, and clothes from its New Delhi factory which also exports abroad. The beautiful fabrics and designs are simply outstanding. Ask to see their photo album (catalog) of bedspreads. You may want to order a custom-made bedspread to your own specifications. Most bedspreads range in price from US$250 to US$400. This shop also showcases its uniquely designed silver tableware and accessories which it has been producing since 1993.

❑ **Indian States:** *Jorawar Bhuvan, 93, Maharshi Karve Road, Marine Lines, Tel. 200-8989 or Fax 208-6745.* This well established and popular shop is jam-packed with sarees, textiles, and ready-made pajamas. Offers the traditional Chaniya Choli (long skirt with top), Panajuwi (dress) and hand painted silk scarves. Beautiful fabrics.

❑ **Kala Niketan:** 95, *Maharshi Karve Road, Marine Lines, Tel. 200-5001 or Fax 200-0229.* The large three-storey shop is a real education in Indian fabrics and clothes for women. It specializes in sarees, silk material, shawls, and handicrafts. The ground floor is primarily devoted to sarees from all over India. The gold sarees from Bangalore and the Muslim wedding materials are especially interesting. The salespeople will be happy to roll out the fabrics on the demonstration tables. The first floor includes silk fabric which can be purchased by the meter and hand-painted shawls. The third floor, which must be entered from a side entrance with an elevator, includes some nondescript handicraft items which are not particularly appealing.

❑ **Burlingtons' of Bombay:** *Taj Mahal Hotel shopping arcade, Tel. 202-5593 or Fax 363-4300.* If you want tailoring done or ready-made clothes, Burlingtons' is the place to go. They do good quality tailoring and they are relatively fast. They also offer an excellent selection of fabrics for shirts, suits, and dresses. Tailored shirts cost less than US$15. The ground floor of this shop primarily has men's clothes, including ready-made shirts. The first floor is a lady's boutique. It also includes many nice designer-style dresses, bedspreads, and patch work wall hangings made in villages.

HOUSEWARES, GIFT ITEMS, SILVER

❑ **Malabar Boutique:** *Taj Mahal Hotel shopping arcade.* One of our favorite shops. This long established small boutique is a great place to shop for clothes, fabric (silk and cotton), bags, scarves, pillow cases, boxes, purses, ceramics, furniture, and antiques. Has its own workshop where they produce their unique designs. Tasteful selections by its Canadian owner. Popular shop with local residents, both Indian and expat.

❑ **Good Earth:** *3, Cornelian Kemp's Corner, 104, August Kranti Marg, Tel. 388-6750 or Fax 389-1529.* Located across the street from the hospital, this attractive home decorative shop offers a nice selection of dinner sets, flatware, placemats, glasses, pottery, pillows, lamps, candles, and fabrics. Popular shop with locals who appreciate contemporary home design. Also has a shop in Delhi at the Qutub Enclave.

❑ **Ravissant:** *L-14, Oberoi Tower's Shopping Arcade, Tel. 284-2586, Ext. 6658.* Offers uniquely designed silver and leather accessories for home and office. Uses Western designers for producing export quality products. Very expensive but top quality.

❑ **Prabhu Hira:** *Hotel Oberoi Towers, F/D2, Tel. 287-0124, Ext. 6701.* This large shop is jam-packed with all types of silver plated serving pieces, goblets, vases, and bowls. A good place to pick up last minute gift items.

CARPETS, LEATHER, AND ACCESSORIES

Numerous shops in and around the major hotels and shopping centers are filled with ubiquitous carpets and leather goods. Shops behind the Taj Mahal Hotel and in the Oberoi Towers Shopping Centre offer a disproportionate number of these goods. Be sure to bargain hard in these shops since they tend to be run by Kashmiri merchants who are used to setting initial high prices in anticipation of haggling with customers.

❑ **Ravissant:** *L-14, Oberoi Tower's Shopping Arcade, Tel. 284-2586, Ext. 6658.* See comments above on this shop for leather goods.

❑ **Cheemo:** *F-61 H.C. Level, Oberoi Towers Shopping Centre, Tel. 285-3497.* This attractive shop is filled with name-brand leather shoes and handbags such as Versace, Gucci, DKNY, Prada, Moschino, Fendi, and Picasso. A great place to buy decent quality knock-offs at reasonable prices.

❑ **Jolly:** *F-63-74, Oberoi Towers Shopping Centre, Tel. 204-1230.* This relatively large shop offers a nice selection of matching shoes and small handbags. Designer quality leather goods.

HANDICRAFTS

Most of the handicraft shops are found in and around the major hotels and shopping centers, especially in the Oberoi Towers Shopping Centre and behind the Taj Mahal Hotel. Some of the best collections of handicrafts can be found at the following shops:

❑ **Central Cottage Industries Emporium:** *34 Chhatrapati Shivaiji Maharaj Marg, Tel. 202-2491.* Offers Mumbai's most comprehensive collection of arts and crafts from all over India. An expansive two-storey building crammed with rugs, fabrics, bedspreads, carved doors, elephants, in-laid wood pictures, stuffed animals, silver, marble, papier mache, furniture, bags, pottery, brass, jewelry, and much much more.

❑ **World Trade Centre:** *Located at Cuff Parade.* The first two floors of this building include numerous state handi-craft shops and emporiums offering a wide range of representative arts and crafts for export. A maze of shops offering lots of touristy items in a very quiet setting.

ACCOMMODATIONS

Except for Mumbai's deluxe hotels, accommodations in this city are nothing to write home about. Hotels here tend to be more expensive than elsewhere in India. The Oberoi, Oberoi Towers, Taj Mahal, and Leela Kempinski maintain the highest international standards which also are reflected in their high prices (US$250-$350 per night). You'll immediately see a major difference in the quality of facilities, services, and service between these hotels and other properties.

The best hotels, which primarily cater to businesspeople and upscale tourists, are found in the central business district. Juhu Beach, which is far from the city center (west of the airport), also has several hotels. None, however, are of the quality found in the central business district. Your best location for shopping, sightseeing, and dining will be the Colaba and Nariman Point sections of the city. While you'll pay more for accommodations here, you'll quickly discover how nice it is to have a convenient oasis nearby!

DELUXE HOTELS (5-STARS)

❑ **The Oberoi Hotel:** *Nariman Point, Mumbai, 400021, Maharashtra, Tel. 91-22-202-5757 or Fax 91-22-204-3282, USA & Canada Toll Free 800-562-3764.* The Oberoi is a real class operation and our personal choice for Mumbai. Overlooking the Arabian Sea and located in the heart of the commercial and banking districts, the main shopping area is only a short distance away. A member of Leading Hotels of the World, the elegant Oberoi offers the service and amenities expected in a 5-star hotel. A personal butler is at hand for guests who prefer this personalized service and the concierge is at your service. The 350 room and suite hotel is formal but warm. The lobby area is spacious and well lighted by day by the soaring atrium and exudes warmth by night. Rooms are well appointed with writing table, armoire outfitted with the television and a large safe, fax machine and laptop connections, a dressing room for luggage, closet and mini-bar and a beautiful marble bath with a shower stall separate from the tub. Although the hotel filters its water to a potable level, it continues to provide complimentary bottled water at bedside.

Service is impeccable. The staff goes out of its way to be helpful. Guests receive personalized stationery as an extra touch which reflects attention to detail everywhere.

The Brasserie offers all day and evening dining with an ambience more pleasant than a coffee shop but with the value usually found there. The Rotisserie and Sea Grill promotes Continental cuisine and features grilled and roast meats, poultry, and fresh seafood. The lobster thermidor is outstanding and the vegetables steamed perfectly. The Kandahar showcases Indian cuisine from various regions of the country, and blends traditional sauces recast to appeal to universal palettes. The glass-fronted kitchen permits a view of the tandoors and the charcoal grill.

For the shopper, the Oberoi offers a wide array of shops within the hotel complex. A few steps across the lobby and you are in the Oberoi Tower shopping arcade —a mix of upscale jewelry, silver, leather and craft shops. Right next door are the two Oberoi shopping centers. Includes convention facilities and health club.

❑ **The Oberoi Towers**: *Nariman Point, Mumbai 400021, Maharashtra, Tel. 91-22-202-4343 or Fax 91-22-204-3284, USA & Canada Toll Free 800-562-3764*. Centrally located on Marine Drive overlooking the Arabian Sea and adjoining the Oberoi, this 600 room tower caters to both the upwardly mobile business traveler as well as the upscale leisure traveler. The lobby is spacious and the recently renovated guestrooms are decorated in soft, pastel hues and equipped with refrigerator, mini bar, direct dial phones and individually controlled air conditioning. The coffee shop has been replaced by Bombay's first Hard Rock Cafe. One of the most popular restaurants is Casa Mexicana featuring piquant Mexican cuisine from nachos to fajitas. One of the newest restaurants in the Towers is Indian Jones—offering an array of specialities from various Asian regions, the setting itself is reason to enjoy a meal here. A shopping arcade offering a variety of upscale boutiques is located on the ground floor. Next door, between the Oberoi Towers and the Oberoi, are two Oberoi Shopping Centers. Taken together, over 200 shops are available to the traveler only a few steps from the hotel lobby.

❑ **Taj Mahal Hotel**: *Apollo Bunder, Mumbai, 400 039, Maharashtra, Tel. 91-22-202-3366 or Fax 91-22-287-2711, USA & Canada Toll Free 800-458-8825*. Located on the seafront, adjacent to the Gateway of India, the Taj Mahal Hotel is as much a landmark as home to luxurious accommodation, fine dining and hospitable service. A member of the Leading Hotels of the World, the Taj, with its 600 guestrooms and 40 suites is actually two hotels in one. The Old Wing is the original building and the New Wing is actually a 19 story tower. All the guestrooms and suites in the Old Wing are unique—no two are alike in decor or furnishings. In the Old Wing, find your room via either the elevator or the majestic staircase which leads to an interior veranda on each floor. The wide verandas serve as galleries for artwork and antique furniture. Rooms in the Old Wing face either the sea or overlook the garden and outdoor swimming pool. Rooms in the Tower Wing are slightly less expensive and have contemporary decor. Whether you choose a standard room or a suite in either wing, all offer modern comforts. Try the Zodiac Grill where the food is superb and white gloved waiters click their heels and nearly stand at attention as the meal is served. Or watch the boats leave the jetty from a window table in the Sea Lounge as you cool off with a dish of the Taj's homemade ice cream. There are several nice shops located in both the old and the new wings. Includes meeting facilities and fitness center.

❏ **The Leela Kempinski:** *Sahar, Mumbai 400059, Maharashtra, Tel. 91-22-836-3636 or Fax 91-22-836-0606.* Located near the airport (25 kilometers from the city's business center), this well maintained five-star property is especially popular with businesspeople and airline employees. Offers 425 spacious rooms and 32 suites, 4 restaurants, 2 bars, health facilities, business center, and conference facilities.

❏ **President Hotel:** *90 Cuffe Parade, Colaba, Maharashta, 91-22-215-0808 or Fax 91-22-215-1201.* Especially popular with businesspeople with its location near the World Trade Center, it offers excellent service and business amenities. Includes 310 rooms, 34 suites, 3 restaurants, health facilities, and business center. Especially popular for its buffet breakfast. Not full 5-star.

❏ **Centaur Hotel:** *Juhu Tara Road, Juhu Beach, Maharashtra, Tel. 91-22-611-3040 or Fax 91-22-611-6343.* The most expensive hotel in Juhu Beach, this beachfront property is located far from the city center. Offers 365 rooms, 20 suites, 3 restaurants, health facilities, and business services. Not full 5-star.

FIRST CLASS HOTELS (4-STAR AND FADING)

❏ **Ambassador:** *Veer Nariman Road, Churchgate, Mumbai 400020, Maharashtra, Tel. 91-22-204-1131 or Fax 91-22-204-0004.* An older property noted for its revolving restaurant which offers excellent views of the city and the Arabian Sea. 123 rooms, 4 suites, 3 restaurants, bar, and coffee shop.

❏ **Holiday Inn:** *Balraj Sahani Marg, Juhu Beach, Mumbai 400049, Maharashtra, Tel. 91-22-620-4444 or Fax 91-22-620-4452.* Located outside the city center, this modern hotel offers 174 rooms, 16 suites, 2 restaurants, bar, coffee shop, health facilities, and business services.

❑ **Nataraj:** *135 Netaji Subhash Road, Mumbai 400020, Maharashta, Tel. 91-22-204-4161 or Fax 91-22-204-3864.* Centrally located along Marine Drive, this hotel has nice views of the Arabian Sea. The small rooms are modest but clean. Includes 69 rooms, 6 suites, restaurant, bar, and bookstore.

❑ **Ramada Palm Grove:** *Juhu Beach, Mumbai 400049, Maharashta, Tel. 91-22-611-2323 or Fax 91-22-611-3682.* Offers relatively large rooms; a few have limited views of the beach. 112 rooms, 2 suites, restaurant, bar, health facilities, and business services.

❑ **Fariyas:** *25, off Arthur Bunder Road, Colaba, Mumbai 400005, Maharashtra, Tel. 91-22-204-2911 or Fax 91-22-283-4992.* Located near the Gateway of India, this hotel offers a good range of facilities for its price range. Somewhat worn. 88 rooms, 4 suites, restaurant, bar, health facilities, and meeting rooms.

❑ **Ritz:** *5 Jamshedij Tata Road, Mumbai 400020, Maharashtra, Tel. 91-22-285-0500 or Fax 91-22-285-0494.* Located just off Marine Drive, this older hotel is in a good location. A little worn and old fashioned but clean. 66 rooms, 6 suites, 2 restaurants, and a coffee shop.

RESTAURANTS

Mumbai has some of the best restaurants in all of India. Being a cosmopolitan city, Mumbai's restaurants offer a wide range of international cuisines, from French, Italian, and American to Chinese, Japanese, and Thai. Seafood restaurants are especially popular in Mumbai. Many of the best Indian and international restaurants will be found in the top hotels. For the latest information on the city's best restaurants, check with your hotel concierge as well as acquire a copy of Rashmi Uday Singh's *The Mid-Day Good Food Guide to Mumbai* which is available in many bookstores and hotel shops. Reservations are essential for many of these popular restaurants.

❑ **Mewar:** *Oberoi Towers, Tel. 202-4343.* This well appointed restaurant serves wonderful Indian dishes in a truly regal setting. Try the prawns in coconut shell (*jhinga pardanashin*). Dinner only.

❑ **Rotisserie and Sea Grill:** *Oberoi Hotel, Tel. 202-5757.* One of Mumbai's best restaurants for seafood. Serves a terrific lobster thermidor. Also serves excellent steaks. Lunch and dinner. Great service.

❑ **Kandahar:** *Oberoi Hotel, Tel. 202-5757.* Very popular and elegant Indian restaurant. Lunch and dinner.

❑ **Zodiac Grill:** *Taj Mahal Hotel, Tel. 202-3366.* One of India's best Continental restaurants. Elegant dining accompanied by unforgettable service—a show by itself with white-gloved waiters. Lunch and dinner.

❑ **Thai Pavillion:** *Hotel President, 90 Cuffe Parade, Colaba, Tel. 215-0808, Ext. 5621.* Wonderful authentic Thai dishes served in an elegant setting by very attentive waiters. One of Mumbai's most popular specialty restaurants. Lunch and dinner.

❑ **Casa Mexicana:** *Oberoi Towers, Tel. 202-4343.* Very popular Mexican restaurant offering a good range of standard Mexican dishes. Colorful setting and nice atmosphere. Lunch (big buffet) and dinner.

❑ **Gaylord:** *Veer Nariman Road, Churchgate, Tel. 282-1259.* For more than 40 years this well established and reliable restaurant has been delighting diners with its Continental and Indian dishes. Known for its roast lamb, chicken, and kebab dishes. Breakfast, lunch, and dinner.

❑ **Chetana:** *34 K. Dubash Marg, Kala Ghoda, Tel. 284-4968.* This cozy restaurant serves excellent vegetarian Rajasthani and Gujarati thali for lunch and Rajasthani dishes for dinner. Attached to a craftshop and bookstore.

❑ **China Garden:** *Om Chambers, 123 A. K. Marg, Kemp's Corner, Tel. 363-0841.* This very popular, award winning pan-Asian restaurant is always crowded with trendy locals, including movie stars. Excellent seafood and vegetarian dishes. Lunch and dinner.

❑ **Trishna:** *7 Ropewalk Lane, next to Commerce House, Kala Ghoda, Fort, Tel. 267-2176.* This very small but popular seafood restaurant has become a trendy place for upscale visitors and local VIPs. Famous for their huge crabs. Lunch and dinner.

❑ **Ling's Pavilion:** *19/21 Mahakavi Bhushan Marg, Behind Regal Cinema, Tel. 285-0023.* This popular Chinese restaurant is famous for its seafood dishes. The house speciality is crabs. Lunch and dinner.

❑ **Tanjore:** *Taj Mahal Hotel, Tel. 202-3366.* This elegant North Indian restaurant is famous for its food, dance, and live music. Famous for its tandoori and crab dishes. Also serves South Indian cuisine. Lunch and dinner.

❑ **Kyber:** *145, MG Road, Kala Ghoda, Tel. 267-3227.* A very popular North Indian restaurant, especially for its Islamic ambience and waiters in Pathan tribal dress. Excellent for kebabs and rotis. Lunch and dinner.

❑ **Under the Over Bistro Grill:** *36 Altamount Road, Kemp's Corner, Tel. 386-1393.* This small bistro serves delicious Continental, Italian, Mexican, and American dishes. Great desserts. Popular with young professionals and artists. Lunch and dinner.

❑ **Goa Portuguese:** *Opposite Mahim Head Post Office, Near Hinduja Hospital, Kataria Road, Mahim, Tel. 444-0202.* This popular Goan, Portuguese, and Continental restaurant serves excellent stuffed crabs and lobsters. Live Goan music after 9pm. Lunch and dinner.

SEEING THE SITES

In addition to shopping and dining, there's plenty to see and do in and around Mumbai to occupy at least two days of sightseeing. You may want to join half- or full-day tours to see the major sites. Mumbai's most popular sites include:

❑ **Gateway of India:** Located at Apollo Bunder, opposite the Taj Mahal Hotel and overlooking the Arabian Sea, this impressive stone archway is the city's major symbol. Originally built of plaster in 1911 to welcome George V and Queen Mary to India, it was rebuilt in 1927 in its present massive stone arch form. This structure attracts hundreds of visitors each day who stroll along the sidewalks to enjoy the sea breeze and views. You can take a launch from here to see the docks. Launches also operate hourly from here for the six mile ride (one hour) to the island of the Elephanta Caves.

❑ **Prince of Wales Museum:** This marvelous architectural structure houses one of the world's best collections of Indian art. Built in 1905 of gray basalt and yellow sandstone in the Indo-Saracenic style to commemorate, the visit of the Prince of Wales, who later became King George V, this rambling three-storey museum is divided into three major sections—art, archaeology, and natural history. Spend a couple of hours here and you'll learn a great deal about the past 400 years of Indian history through the many nice displays which include English descriptions. Includes art, jewelry, terracotta figurines, icons, weapons, miniature paintings, and prehistoric pottery.

☑ **Victoria Terminus (Chhatrapati Shivaji Terminus):** Also known as Bori Bunder and often referred to as simply "VT", this is truly a working railway station with trains and people everywhere! It's also a marvelous architectural monument to a by-gone era. Built in 1888 in a grand Gothic style mixed with Indian architecture, this is India's largest and most impressive railway station. It's the headquarters for the Central Railway System. Nearly 1000 trains carrying 3 million passengers pass through "VT" daily; over a half million are local commuters. From a distance, because of the station's impressive stained-glass windows, Corinthian columns, turrets, spires, and arches, visitors may mistake the building for a large cathedral. The station is a colorful and crowded mix of migrant families, beggars, pickpockets, vendors, porters, and tourists.

❑ **Jehangir Art Gallery:** Located next to the Prince of Wales Museum in Kala Ghoda, this is the city's most important center for contemporary Indian artists. Operated by the Bombay Art Society, the gallery rents space to artists who put on exhibitions of varying quality. The gallery also include two shops (Natesan's and Terrace Art Gallery) as well as a popular restaurant, Cafe Samovar. The avant-garde character of this gallery may or may not appeal to you. Open daily from 11am to 7pm.

❑ **National Gallery of Modern Art:** *M. G. Road.* Located across the street from the Prince of Wales Museum, this four-storey circular building houses modern Indian art exhibits. Open Tuesday to Sunday, 10am to 5pm.

- ❑ **Flora Fountain:** Built in 1869, this landmark stands at Mumbai's busiest business intersection which is surrounded by major banks, corporate offices, shops, and the Stock Exchange. Now called Hutatma Chowk, it commemorates those who died in India's struggle for independence.

- ❑ **Mani Bhavan:** *19 Laburnam Road, Tel. 362-7864.* This was once Gandhi's home in Bombay when he visited here between 1917 and 1934. It now serves as a museum of Gandhi and his times. Includes a research institute, library, photos, and furniture. Open daily 9:30am to 6pm.

- ❑ **Hanging Gardens (Sir Pherozshah Mehta Gardens):** Located at the top of the exclusive residential area of Malabar Hill, these gardens date from 1881. Landscaped on top of the city's three reservoirs, these well maintained gardens are popular with joggers and sightseers. Enjoy the hedges and bushes shaped into animal figures, panoramic views of Backbay and the city, and terrific sunsets.

- ❑ **Kamal Nehru Park:** Adjacent to the Hanging Gardens, this pleasant area includes the huge Old Lady's Shoe for children, a lovely pavilion and surrounding grounds, and a magnificent view of Marine Drive. Best place to view the "Queen's Necklace" at night.

- ❑ **Marine Drive:** This is Mumbai's seaside promenade with the Arabian Sea to the west and high rise buildings to the east. Stretching from Nariman Point in the south to Chowpatty Beach in the north, Marine Drive becomes known as the "Queens Necklace" with its bright lights at night. It's best seen from Kamala Nehru Park. Horse-drawn carriages operate at both ends of this promenade. Look for the Taraporevala Aquarium which is the largest such exhibition in India.

- ❑ **Chowpatty Beach:** Located at the north end of Marine Drive, which is at the foot of Malabar Hill, this popular beach is a cultural experience for many visitors. The beach is the center for Hindu ceremonies, snake charmers, monkey-trainers, balloon sellers, masseurs, and shooting galleries. Especially lively in the evening. Watch out for pickpockets and eunuchs.

❏ **The Elephanta Caves:** Located on an island 11 kilometers from the Gateway of India, these impressive caves
with their stone sculptures were originally built in the
6th century A.D. The most impressive sculpture is a six-
meter tall, three-headed bust of Lord Shiva. The main
cave includes nine carvings, mostly of Shiva in different
settings. You can reach the island by regular motor
launches which leave hourly, between 8am and 2:30pm,
from the Gateway of India. Air-conditioned catamarans
leave from the Gateway at 10am and depart from the
island at 2pm. The trip takes about one hour each way.

❏ **Major markets:** As we already examined under shop-
ping, the following markets are especially popular with
visitors; they are included on many city tours: Fashion
Street, Crawford Market (Mahatma Jyotiba Phule
Market), Chor Bazaar (Thieves Market), and Zaveri
Bazaar (Gold Market).

ENTERTAINMENT

Mumbai is known as India's party city with its profusion of
trendy beer bars, pubs, discotheques, gymkhanas, and clubs
which are frequented by young professionals, older businessmen, models, and movie stars. Primarily attached to hotels and
restaurants, many of these places only admit couples. Expect
very noisy places with loud rock music. For peace and quiet, try
the hotel bars and lounges. The following are some of the most
popular such night spots in Mumbai:

❏ **1900:** *Taj Mahal Hotel, Tel. 202-3366.* Open for its up-
market members and guests. Open 8:30pm to 2am.

❏ **H.Q.:** *Above Cafe Royal, 166, Mahatma Gandhi Road,
Opposite Regal Cinema, Tel. 202-0560.* Couples only.
Dance floor.

❏ **Studio:** 16, Marzban Road, Next to Sterling Cinema,
Tel. 207-7270. Couples only. Movie theme pub.

❏ **Tavern:** *Fariyas Hotel, 25, Off Arthur Bunder Road,
Colaba, Tel. 204-2911.* English-style pub with loud rock
music. Couples only. Open 6:30pm to 11:30pm

❑ **Razzberry Rhinoceros:** *Juhu Hotel, Juhu, Tel. 618-4014.* Hard rock cafe style discotheque with live bands on certain nights. Couples only.

❑ **Jazz By the Bay:** *143 Marine Drive, Tel. 285-1876.* Mumbai's only jazz club. Open until 12:30am.

❑ **Cyclone:** *Leela Kempinski Hotel, Sahar, Tel. 836-3636.* One of the city's best discos. Primarily open to hotel guests and members and their guests.

❑ **The Cellar:** *Oberoi Towers, Tel. 202-4343.* Small but popular dance floor in a classy setting. Open 10pm to 1am.

❑ **The Pub:** *Rasna Restaurant, Churchgate.* American-style pub with dance floor.

Hotel bars and lounges offer quieter venues for relaxing after a day on Mumbai's hectic streets. These three have nice views of the city and the Arabian Sea:

❑ **The Bay View Bar:** *The Oberoi, Tel. 202-5757.*

❑ **The Ambassador Hotel:** *Rooftop garden bar, Tel. 204-1131.* Open 6:30pm to 11:30pm.

❑ **Sea Lounge:** *Taj Mahal Hotel, Tel. 202-3366.* Open 10am to 12:30pm. Primarily open for coffee, tea, and sandwiches.

Mumbai also offers more refined entertainment, from classic to modern, in the form of music, theater, and dance. For a sampling of "what's on," check the daily *Times of India* for a current listing of upcoming cultural events or ask your hotel concierge for details. Also, check the menu on your in-room television set for information on such events from the Maharashtra Tourism Development Corporation. Major performances are usually held in several theaters and auditoriums (Tata Theater, Little Theater, Experimental Theater, Godrej Dance Academy Theater, Drama Opera Arts Complex) of the **National Center For the Performing Arts** (NCPA, located at the tip of Nariman Point, Tel. 283-3737) as well as at the **Nehru Center Auditorium** (Dr. Annie Besant Road, Worli, Tel. 492-8237).

7

Delhi

Welcome to the bustling and sprawling medieval and modern metropolis of Delhi. Consisting of two cities—the modern capital of New Delhi and the traditional walled city of Old Delhi—this is one of India's major gateway cities. It's a city of politics, bureaucracy, history, art, culture, and fine hotels, restaurants, and shopping. While not a particularly attractive city, with a preponderance of uninspired architecture and worn buildings, it does have its own distinctive character and rhythm—wide tree-lined streets and traffic circles in New Delhi and narrow crowded streets, historical monuments, and attractive Mughal architecture in Old Delhi. A big city of over 10 million people spread over 579 square miles, there's lots to see and do here. You'll need at least three days to do the basics but plan on five days to do the place justice. You'll need that time to discover Delhi's real shopping treasures as well as sample its many travel pleasures.

GETTING TO KNOW YOU

Like so much of India, you can find a great deal that is wrong with Delhi. The traffic is often terrible and it's a dirty, dusty city (from handling the money to touching handrails, you'll

DELHI

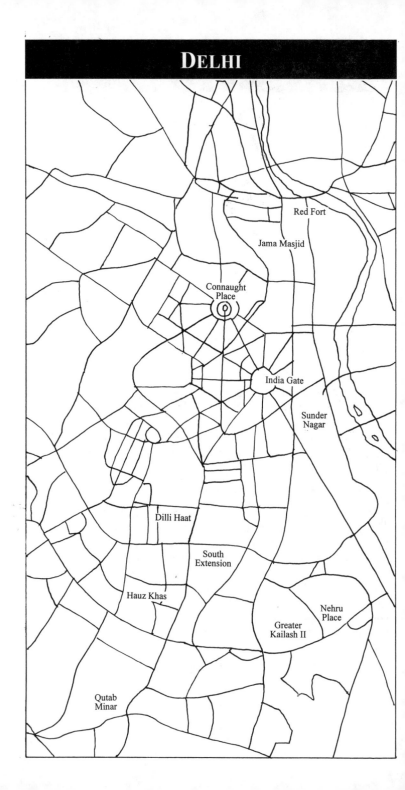

have difficulty keeping your hands clean). Everything seems to be in the process of being completed or deteriorating—nothing ever seems finished, completed, or maintained. Even the cars, buses, and trucks look like they have been in a demolition derby as they weave in and out of the traffic, occasionally collecting another well deserved scratch and dent to add to their already fractured bodies. Don't be surprised if you become involved in a few traffic "accidents" during your stay in Delhi. Frequent minor fender-benders result in the perpetrator receiving only an evil eye from the recipient rather than an out-of-the-vehicle assessment of the damage or even a legal or financial settlement. Determining quality in Delhi is real easy—you know it when you see it because there's so little quality on display in the city's crumbling streets and its rumpled vehicles.

> ❏ Determining quality in Delhi is real easy–you know it when you see it.
>
> ❏ At times you'll see amazing street scenes, some almost Biblical, and think you're on a movie set in another century or era.
>
> ❏ Some observers may tell you Delhi is not the "real India." Don't believe them. This is India at its best and its worst.
>
> ❏ Given the sprawling nature of this city, it's best to view it from a north-south, old and new orientation.
>
> ❏ The central part of the city looks and feels different from other parts of Delhi.

But like the rest of India, there is something very charming and magical about this place for those who have become tolerant and accepting of India's many challenges. The electricity frequently fails, but it soon comes back on either with backup generators or restored city power (it's a good idea to carry a flashlight). You'll frequently encounter a bureaucratic mentality of passing the buck (*"It's not my job—go over there."*), but eventually your problems get solved or redefined. The beggars and touts are aggressive, but they will leave you alone if you ignore them and don't establish eye contact. At times you'll see amazing street scenes, some almost Biblical, and think you're on a movie set in another century or era.

Accordingly, it's best to approach the city as a unique adventure where you expect the worst but are always pleasantly surprised that good and unexpected things do indeed happen to you! Delhi will grow on you after a while, once you settle into its Third World rhythm and find your oases for an occasional escape into a familiar world of order, comfort, sanity, and maybe some unexpected but well deserved decadence.

Some observers may tell you Delhi is not the "real India." Don't believe them. This is India at its best and its worst. It's just a little different from other parts of the country.

Delhi is a melting pot of many peoples and cultures. After

Mumbai and Calcutta, it's India's third largest city. Delhi is a visual feast of colorful people, lumbering vehicles, old inspiring architecture, and unique street level activity. There's never a dull moment here as you navigate Delhi's many crowded, crumbling, noisy, and chaotic streets and sidewalks, visit its numerous sites, and encounter its many street urchins and touts at intersections and at tourist sites and shops. Like so many other cities in India, Delhi presents an amazing street drama of people, animals, and vehicles. It's a city you won't want to miss as you experience both the old and the new of Delhi and India.

Given the sprawling nature of this city, it's best to view it from a north-south, old and new orientation. The northern part consists of Old Delhi with its distinctive and massive Red Fort, Jama Masjid, city gates, and narrow and congested streets of buses, cars, auto-rickshaws, bullock carts, wandering cows, and an occasional elephant. Historically, it represents the influence of various Mughal dynasties in Delhi.

Central and southern Delhi are part of New Delhi which historically represents the British colonial legacy with its emphasis on grand architecture and urban planning. Attempting to bring order out of chaos, the central part of the city looks and feels different from most other parts of Delhi. It's centered at the circular Connaught Place and extends south and east to India Gate, parliament buildings, major hotels, and the diplomatic enclave (Chanakyapuri). Here, as you move south of congested Connaught Place, you will find wider streets with traffic circles and painted curbs. The feel to this part of the city is one of less congestion, open spaces, and greenery. It feels planned and regulated rather than typically spontaneous and chaotic.

The southern part of the city extends south and east of the railroad tracks and encompasses, Lodi Gardens, Dilli Haat, Ring Road, Hauz Khas Village, Greater Kailash I, Greater Kailash II, New Friends Colony, and Qutab Minar areas. Here you will find a combination of crowded and congested streets, neighborhood markets spilling onto the streets, local shopping centers, and upscale residential enclaves of Delhi's upper-middle and upper-classes called "colonies." At times this section of the city reminds one of the chaos found in much of Old Delhi to the north.

A TALE OF MANY CITIES

Delhi has long functioned as a center of political and dynastic power, although never as significant as today. With a history dating more than 3,000 years, Delhi has been the site for numerous cities that rose and fell with the fate of various local and invading rulers. Since the 11th century, Delhi was the site for at least 15 different cities and their dynastic rulers. The whole area is filled with hundreds of monuments and ruins from the various cities, from gates and walls to mosques and forts. The famous Qutab Minar victory monument, for example, dates from the Qutab Minar dynasty which was founded in 1193. But some of the most enduring structures date from the 16th century when the Mughal ruler Emperor Shah Jahan of Taj Mahal fame transferred his seat of power from Agra to the newly constructed city of Shahjahanabad which is now known as Old Delhi, a very densely populated area of congested streets, narrow lanes, crumbling buildings, and separate communities of Muslims, Sikhs, and Hindus. Lal Quila, or the Red Fort, became the symbol of this city and remains so to this day. It was here where the British defeated local rulers and uprisings, most notably the Indian Mutiny in 1857, and established their rule for the next 90 years. But it was never a really great city. For the next 50 years Delhi continued to function as one of India's urban backwaters.

It wasn't until 1911, when the British transferred the capital of their colonial empire from Calcutta to Delhi, that this city began acquiring a new look. To reflect its power and seemingly permanent presence, the British Raj embarked on constructing a modern planned city of 26 square kilometers, complete with wide tree-lined boulevards, monuments, gardens, and basic municipal services, literally a monument to the British empire. Completed nearly 20 years later, to accommodate a population of 70,000, the city also was designed for future expansion, although nowhere near its current level. With independence, Delhi continued to function as the capital and symbol of modern India.

Like Mumbai and so many other large cities in India, Delhi has succumbed to the chaos attendant with excess population and the deterioration of urban services. While its grand monuments, wide boulevards, new commercial buildings, and five-star hotels suggest that this is a city of hope, its slums, congestion, disrepair, and filth also remind you that this, too, is a Third World city of hard living for millions of people.

But there is a lot more to Delhi than what meets the eye in the chaos of its heady streets. Like so many other places in India, Delhi has many faces and it exudes numerous contradictions. If you seek out the best of the best in Delhi, you'll discover a very vibrant city that has a great deal to offer visitors. You may have to dodge vehicles, on occasion step over pavement dwellers, wait patiently for cows to cross traffic, push and shove your way through crowds, and escape from annoying touts, persistent beggars, and street noise, but the rewards are oases of fine hotels, restaurants, shops, entertainment, art, and culture. Indeed, you'll encounter some of the best shopping in all of India in Delhi—better than in the reputed shopper's paradise of Mumbai. While you have to work at discovering the best of the best in Delhi, always remember, nothing comes easy in India; for those who persist, the rewards are often well worth the struggle and suffering! Unlike others who claim this is not the real India and recommend quickly passing through Delhi, we find this city well worth your serious attention. It may not be the real India—if indeed there is such a thing—but thank God it's close! Stay and shop here a few days and this city may well become your favorite destination in all of India.

THE BASICS

LOCATION

Situated on the west bank of the Yamuna River, Delhi is located in the center of the northern region. It's approximately 1440 kilometers northeast of Mumbai and 1550 kilometers northwest of Calcutta (2 hours by air or 18 hours by train from either location). It's the central city in India's most popular "Golden Triangle" of cities—Delhi, Agra, and Jaipur. Each of these other cities is approximately four hours from Delhi by road—200 kilometers to Agra and 261 kilometers to Jaipur. Many visitors stay a few days in Delhi and then venture on to Agra for a day or two to see the Taj Mahal and then on to the fascinating Rajasthan "Pink City" of Jaipur. From Delhi, they also may venture on to Varanasi (765 kilometers), Bhopal (741 kilometers), Jammu (586 kilometers), Jodhpur (604 kilometers), Lucknow (569 kilometers), and Udaipur (635 kilometers).

CLIMATE AND WHEN TO VISIT

If you arrive in Delhi between April and June, you may feel you'll die from the heat! Indeed, the temperature can reach over 100°F during May and June. This is one very sweltering hot place. The best time to visit Delhi is between October and March, with November, December, and January being the coolest months; you may need a sweater or jacket for the cool evenings and mornings in December and January when temperatures can fall below 20°F. February is especially pleasant with bright skies and springtime temperatures. The rainy season occurs from mid-June to mid-September.

POPULATION

Delhi's population of nearly 10 million people makes it the third largest city in India. It's also India's fastest growing large urban center. Similar in many respects to Mumbai, Delhi's population is very diverse, drawn from many regions of the country. The city is a magnet for rural migrants who come here in search of new opportunities. However, approximately one-third of the population, or nearly 3 million people, live on the streets or in slum and squatter settlements. The main languages here include Hindi, Urdu, Punjabi, and English. As for religion, Delhi's population is overwhelmingly Hindu (84%) with Muslim (8%), Sikh (6%), and Christian (1%) minorities.

ARRIVAL AND DEPARTURE

Like Mumbai, Delhi is serviced by several major international airlines. In fact, many visitors start their India adventure in Delhi because of its strategic gateway location. Given its Westernized character, Delhi is a relatively easy place to ease yourself into India.

If you arrive by air on an international flight, you will land at Indira Gandhi International Airport which is located approximately 20 kilometers southwest of the city center. If you arrive on a domestic flight, you'll land at the Palam terminal which is about 4 kilometers from the international airport. At both airports you'll find convenient prepaid taxi booths where you can arrange for a taxi into the city. The cost ranges from about Rs 150 to Rs 250, depending on the distance. You'll also find shuttle buses and metered taxis. Depending on the time of day, it takes from 30 to 75 minutes to get from the airport to the center of the city.

If you arrive by train, you'll either arrive at the Old Delhi Station (in the heart of the city) or the New Delhi Station (located just north of Connaught Place). If you plan to travel to Agra, you may want to take the train from New Delhi. This is a much safer alternative than driving a car on the hair-raising, vehicle-strewn road to Agra. The train trip takes about two hours. The best train is the air-conditioned *Shatabdi Express* which departs from New Delhi at 6:15am and arrives in Agra at 8:10am; the train departs Agra at 8:21pm and arrives in New Delhi at 10pm. The *Taj Express* leaves later (7:15am) and takes longer (arrives 9:45am); it also departs earlier from Agra

(6:45pm and arrives in New Delhi at 9:45pm). The *Shatabdi Express* also goes to Jaipur (5:50am departure, arriving at 10:20am); it departs Jaipur at 5:50pm and arrives in Delhi at 10:15pm.

TRANSPORTATION AND GETTING AROUND

Welcome to one of the slowest and most riotous road shows in India—overcrowded trucks, buses, cars, motorcycles, bullock carts, auto-rickshaws, bicycle rickshaws, horses, cows, elephants, goats, and dogs all vie for the road in what appears to be a case of urban madness. Except for the traffic jams, and if you avoid transportation modes you don't understand, you'll have no trouble getting around Delhi. Buses, taxis, auto-rickshaws, and assortment of other transportation modes are plentiful and cheap. However, despite being an inexpensive cultural experience, we do not recommend using buses—they tend to be crowded, hot, dirty, and time consuming. Auto-rickshaws may seem like cheap fun, but their novelty may quickly wear off when caught in a hot, noisy, and highly polluted traffic jam; indeed, you'll quickly discover it's no longer fun when you have to sit in the traffic breathing in the exhaust fumes from other pollution belching vehicles. We much prefer using taxis or hiring a car with driver, preferably ones with air-conditioning. Metered yellow-top taxis are easy to find, especially at hotel taxi stands and along the streets—ask the hotel doorman to call a cab or just flag them down. Since many meters have not been recalibrated to reflect current taxi rates, don't be surprised if your taxi driver adds a 100 percent surcharge to the amount that appears on the meter to accurately reflect the current rate. Most taxi rides within the city are very inexpensive—Rs 50 to Rs 120 (US$1.20 to US$3.00). Expect many taxi drivers to ask if you need a car for a half- or full-day. Most are eager to act as your car and driver for the day. Expect to pay from Rs 700 to Rs 900 (US$16 to US$22) for a full-day or eight-hour service. You also can arrange for a car and driver through your hotel, travel agent, or taxi company. If you plan to stop at several locations as well as do shopping, you will probably find a car and driver to be most convenient.

While it is convenient and safe to take the train from Delhi to Agra and Jaipur, you may want to rent a car with driver for this trip. You would be insane to try and drive it on your own. Several taxi and tour companies can arrange for a car and driver. Ask at your hotel or the Government of India Tourist Office for information on such transportation.

Tours and Tourist Offices

Visiting Delhi and the surrounding area can be very convenient and relatively inexpensive if you take advantage of numerous local tourist services. The **Government of India Tourist Office** is located at 88 Janpath (open Monday to Friday, 9am to 6pm, and Saturday, 9am to 2pm, Tel. 332-0008) which is just south of Connaught Place and a block north of the grand looking Central Cottage Industries Emporium building. While it has limited resources, the personnel here try to be very helpful. It's important that you ask questions rather than just look for printed information. This is a full-fledged tourist information and assistance center. It will help you with everything, including lost baggage, hotel reservations, tour guides, approved tour operators, and meditation courses. This office has its own cadre of nearly 350 trained and licensed tour guides which you can inexpensively hire by the half- or full-day (four or eight hours). If you're looking for brochures, you'll need to ask at the desk since they are not well displayed. We careful of the numerous touts and taxi drivers who hang out in front of this rather dreadful looking building; they are persistent and annoying. Arrange your travel plans inside this office rather than along the street! This office, as well as the **Delhi Tourism Development Corporation** (N Block, Connaught Place, Tel. 331-3637), maintains 24-hour tour counters at both the international and domestic airports. They can help you book a room should you arrive in Delhi without hotel reservations. The Government of India Tourist Office also operates the prepaid taxi counters at these airports. Most state governments maintain tourist information centers in Delhi.

You'll find tour agents in most major hotels and around Connaught Circus, Paharganj, Rajendra Place, and Nehru Place. Some of the major tour companies include **American Express** (Tel. 332-4119), **Sita World Travel** (Tel. 331-1122), **Mercury Travels** (Tel. 436-2608), **Dilly Tours** (Tel. 351-2297), **Oriental Travels** (Tel. 332-7214), **Royal Expeditions** (Tel. 623-8545), **Thomas Cook** (Tel. 332-8468), **Trade Winds** (Tel. 332-1822), **Travelite** (Tel. 332-3830), and **Wanderlust** (Tel. 687-5200). Most of these companies can arrange tours within the city as well as to Agra, Jaipur, and other parts of India.

Shopping Hours and Closing Days

Shops are generally open from 10am to 7pm, although some keep shorter (11am to 5:30pm) or longer hours (9am to 9pm). Not all shops are open the same days of the week. When you plan your shopping itinerary, make sure you know which areas close on Sunday, Monday, Tuesday, Wednesday, and Friday:

➤ **Closed Sunday:** Connaught Place, Janpath, Baba Kharak Singh Marg, Jor Bagh, Khan Market, Nehru Place, Sunder Nagar, Yashwant Place, Chandni Chowk, and Sadar Bazar.

➤ **Closed Monday:** Defense Colony, INA. Market, Jangpura, Karol Bagh, Lajpat Nagar, Sarojini Nagar, and South Extension.

➤ **Closed Tuesday:** Greater Kailash, Green Park, Hauz Khas, Kalkaji, Safdarjung Enclave, Vasant Vihar, Shahdara, and Yusuf Sarai.

➤ **Closed Wednesday:** Gopinath Bazar, Rajouri Garden, Delhi Canti, Janakpuri, and Tilak Nagar.

➤ **Closed Friday:** Subhash Nagar, Moti Nagar, Kirti Nagar, and Raja Garden.

RESOURCES

Once you arrive in Delhi, you'll find numerous publications summarizing Delhi's major treasures and pleasures. Look for the following publications that are available in bookstores, newsstands, and hotel kiosks:

City Companion: New Delhi
Delhi Diary
Delhi: The Complete City Guide and Magazine
Discover Delhi
Eating Out
First City
HEREdelhi

If you stay at a Taj hotel, pick up a copy of *The Taj City Guide*. Most of these publications summarize the major attractions, recommend restaurants, identify shops, and include a calendar of upcoming events, including sports and entertainment.

Prior to arriving in India, you may want to check out several Websites identified in Chapter 2 (page 36-37). Some sites will take you directly to useful Delhi sites, especially the government's tourism site: *www.tourindia.com*

GETTING TO KNOW YOU

It's relatively easy to orient yourself to Delhi. The old medieval section of the city is Old Delhi in the north with its Red Fort, narrow streets, and mosque. New Delhi, consisting of Central and South Delhi, sprawls to the south where most of the major commercial buildings, government buildings, embassies, shopping centers, hotels, and restaurants are found. You'll definitely want to explore a few areas in Old Delhi, but most of your time will probably be spent exploring the treasures and pleasures found in the central and southern sections of New Delhi.

The best way to see and shop Delhi is to rent a car and driver for the day. Begin with Old Delhi, which is in an arrested state of disrepair and where the crowds and congestion are most prominent. But this place also has real character and some of Delhi's most inspiring architecture. Start out by visiting the **Red Fort** (Lal Qila) and then proceed to other highlights of Old Delhi, such as Jama Masjid, Chandni Chowk, and the Charity Birds Hospital. Altogether, you should be able to see most of Old Delhi in a long half a day (four to six hours); most of your time will probably be spent at the Red Fort. Except for the bazaar area (Chatta Chowk) within the Red Fort, there's not much worthwhile shopping in Old Delhi. Visit the main thoroughfare, **Chandni Chowk**, for the cultural and photographic experience—crumbling old buildings, crowds, and unusual commercial activities that can quickly disorient first-time visitors. However, don't expect to do much quality shopping here, although you may find some antiques, jewelry, and textiles worth buying.

From Old Delhi, head south to the center of New Delhi—**Connaught Place**, which is also referred to as Connaught Circle and surrounded by the rim street of Connaught Circus. This busy central business and tourist district, noted for its distinctive and decaying old white pillared colonial buildings as well as tout-infested underground shopping center (Palika Bazaar), is filled with small tourist shops, street vendors, travel agencies, art galleries, government offices, restaurants, budget hotels, and cinemas. You can easily spend a half day exploring this fascinating and bustling area. Visit the many shops along the three streets that surround the circle as well as explore the underground shopping center and the buildings along the main streets that run south and southwest of the circle like spokes in a wheel—Janpath and Baba Kharak Sansad Marg streets. **Janpath** is really the main street for shoppers. Running directly south from the circle, both sides of the street are lined with shops as well as the India Government Tourist Office (88 Janpath) and the recently renovated old Hotel Imperial (behind the Tibetan Market). The major shopping highlights here include the huge, colorful, and relatively new **Central Cottage Industries Emporium** (STC Building, Janpath), with its six floors of intense shopping, and the **Tibetan Market**, with its 100+ stalls offering handicrafts and souvenirs, which lines the street opposite the Emporium and in front of the Hotel Imperial. Nearby **Baba Kharak Sansad Marg** (just southwest of Connaught Circle near Parliament Street) houses the arts and crafts emporiums of twenty states; the Rajasthan and Gujarat government handicraft emporiums are the best of the bunch. Be sure to stop in the Hotel Imperial for additional shopping and perhaps have tea or lunch. Its impressive restoration makes this one of Delhi's most interesting hotels. Better still, you may want to stay at this award-winning hotel which is so centrally located near Connaught Place.

From here, you may want to head southeast along **Kasturba Gandhi Marg** or south along Janpath to Windsor Place and then southeast along **Ashoka Road** until you come to one of Delhi's major sightseeing highlights and India's great memorial to those who died in World War I—**India Gate**. Anchoring the east end of the expansive and open boulevard called Rajpath, **India's Parliament House**, the Rashtrapati Bhawan, anchors the west end of this boulevard. Relatively clean and often freshly painted for obvious window-dressing purposes, this whole area also is noted for its wide streets and numerous traffic circles that lace through Delhi's diplomatic quarters.

If you continue south, you enter South Delhi near **Lodi Gardens** and **Dilli Haat** (a market-style arts, crafts, food, and cultural exhibition grounds). If you go southeast along Zakr Hussain Road, you'll come to one of Delhi's best shopping centers for arts, antiques, crafts, and jewelry, **Sunder Nagar Market**. The whole area southwest, south, and southeast of Rajpath is home to five top hotels which offer some of Delhi's best quality shopping and dining: Oberoi, Hyatt Regency, Taj Palace, Taj Mahal, and Maurya Sheraton. Be sure to put these five hotels on your shopping list; visit them early during your stay in Delhi to get a good idea what's available for quality shopping, especially the upscale shopping arcades at the Oberoi and Hyatt Regency hotels which house some of Delhi's best quality shopping. Altogether, you can easily spend two to three days exploring the many sights and shops of Central Delhi.

South Delhi, which basically extends south of Lodi Gardens and Dilli Haat, offers several interesting sightseeing and shopping opportunities. This area of the city is noted for its housing and commercial estates, large apartment complexes, and huge shopping and commercial complexes. One of the most important and best preserved sights is the **Qutab Minar Complex** which is located south of these area's best shopping center, Hauz Khas Village. If you enjoy history and old ruins, Qutab Minar is well worth visiting. Built in the 12th and 13th centuries, it consists of a huge (234 feet and 5 storeys) victory tower, mosque, and tomb.

Shoppers in South Delhi head for **Hauz Khas Village**, and for good reasons. While access to this area is somewhat difficult (have your driver or taxi park just before the entrance to Hauz Khas Village), it's well worth the stop. Although Hauz Khas's absolutely chaotic narrow streets and lanes of cars, motorbikes, bicycles, cows, push carts, mud, and cow dung may initially dissuade you from exploring this unique and illogical shopping area, don't give up too soon. Explore its main street but make sure you wander through the narrow meandering back lanes that are lined with some wonderful small shops and restaurants. Like pealing a banana, the whole area takes on a different complexion after an hour or two. Here you'll discover some wonderful small shops offering excellent quality arts, crafts, silver, jewelry, trendy clothes, furniture, and home decorative items. Plan to spend at least two hours here—preferably three or four, including time for lunch or dinner.

Directly east and southeast of Hauz Khas Village are two other interesting areas for shopping—Greater Kailash I and Greater Kailash II. Although there are many upscale residential shops in this area, we primarily visit Greater Kailash II for one very hard-to-find shop (drivers have difficulty finding it, even with a phone number, Tel. 642-9384)—**Mehra's Art Palace** (M-1, Main Market, Greater Kailash II, Tel. 648-4194)—which is one of India's oldest, best quality, and reliable shops for arts, crafts, antiques, and furniture. The shop is actually a crowded three-storey showroom for its several expansive warehouses which are located on the outskirts of the city. The warehouses primarily offer large pieces of furniture and stone garden statuary. Many major dealers from abroad start and finish their Indian buying spree here. Some may even spend three to four days just buying from Mehra's various warehouses. If you are a dealer, you'll think you've died and gone to furniture, antique, and craft heaven—no need to source elsewhere since Mehra seems to have everything and does such reliable packing and shipping. Indeed, some shoppers' only interest in coming to New Delhi is Mehra's showroom at Greater Kailash II!

Just northeast of Greater Kailash I, or immediately southeast of the intersection of Ring Road and Mathura Road is **New**

Friends Colony. This is one of Delhi's upscale residential and shopping areas. Indeed, many of New Delhi's rich and famous live in the surrounding walled residential areas. The highlight of this area is **Ravissant** (50 & 51 Commercial Complex, Tel. 683-7278), India's haute couture boutique for fabulous textiles, jewelry, and silver. This is their main shop and headquarters office for their three other shops in India (two in Mumbai and one at the Oberoi Hotel in Delhi). Other major shopping complexes, which are primarily of interest to locals, is the **South Extension Market**, which straddles Ring Road, and the huge **Nehru Place** just east of Great Kailash I on Chiragh Delhi Road.

Good hotels are hard to find in South Delhi. The best ones in this area are the five-star **Hyatt Regency**, with its wonderful shopping arcade (great for jewelry), located just northeast of Hauz Khas Village, and the relatively new and impressive four-star **Park Royal Hotel** at Nehru Place.

SHOPPING DELHI

Some of India's best shopping is found in Delhi. In fact, we prefer it to Mumbai which is reputed to be India's major shopping center. Like many other cities in India, Delhi is a relatively easy place to shop—if you know what to buy and where to go. Since the city does not have huge Western-style shopping centers and much of the shopping is geared for the local middle class, it's relatively easy to locate Delhi's best quality shops. They tend to be attached to the major hotel shopping arcades and concentrated in and around Delhi's major shopping districts—Connaught Circle, Sunder Nagar Market, and Hauz Khas Village. A few quality shops also can be found in Greater Kailash II and New Friends Colony. While you will find a few markets and bazaars in Delhi, most are of limited shopping interest to visitors, although many are cultural curiosities.

Don't expect to do a lot of bargaining in Delhi, except among street vendors and in bazaars. Many retail shops will give a 5-10 percent, perhaps even a 20 percent, discount if you ask and bargain hard. They are most likely to give you a discount based upon your payment method—a discount if you pay with cash rather than use a credit card or traveler's check. The government's Central Cottage Industries Emporium has only fixed prices which tend to be very reasonable compared to prices in private shops and emporiums. Shops run by Kashmiri merchants, which usually have lots of carpets and papier maiche items, are more likely to bargain. You also can expect to get deeper discounts from popular tourist shops that usually pay drivers and touts a 30 percent commission on everything their "guests" purchase—if you arrive at these shops on your own. Try to get the 30 percent to pass directly to you as your discount.

You'll find lots of department stores and handicraft emporiums throughout New Delhi. However, be very cautious where you go and what you pay, especially any places recommended by drivers and touts who may be getting a 30 percent commission on everything you buy. Places, such as the upscale Saga Department Store (B-5, Jangpura, Main Mathura Road), seem to be on every drivers' and touts' "must visit" list. Operated by a very enterprising and successful group of Kashmiris, this impressive department store also has some of the highest prices anywhere in India. Expect to pay 30-60 percent more here on comparable items found in other places, such as the government's Central Cottage Industries Emporium on Janpath. However, if you fall in love with something you can find nowhere else, you may still consider it a bargain.

WHAT TO BUY

Similar to Mumbai, you'll find a good range of products to choose from in Delhi. Arts, crafts, antiques, furniture, jewelry, and textiles are especially good buys.

❏ **Arts and crafts:** Delhi abounds with emporiums and shops selling a wide range of arts and crafts from all over India. Look for lots of small items, such a inlaid wood boxes, sandalwood carvings, stuffed toys, puppets, pottery, and paper maiche boxes and napkin rings. There are no surprises here—lots of the same arts and crafts you've probably seen elsewhere in India. Many of same places also offer furniture, antiques, home decorative items, textiles, and clothes. For the best selections, and prices, go to the government's **Central Cottage Industries Emporium** (Tel. 332-1577) on Janpath. Twenty various state handicraft emporiums along **Baba Kharak Sansad Marg** (just southwest of Connaught Circle near Parliament Street) also offer a wide range of arts and crafts, including textiles and other products, from all over India. Many of the shops that line the arcade at the **Red Fort** in Old Delhi, **under the Safderjung flyover** (opposite the old airport and on the Jorbagh side of

Aurobindo Marg), and at **Sunder Nagar Market** also offer a wide range of arts and crafts. **Dilli Haat**, across the street from the INA Market, offers arts and crafts from many parts of India. However, keep in mind that most of these shops and emporiums offer many traditional arts and crafts that may not be particularly stylish for Western tastes. If you are looking for different styles and designs, you'll have to shop elsewhere, especially in the hotel shops and Hauz Khas Village. For example, some of Delhi's best quality arts and crafts can be found at the **Khazana** shops at both the Taj Mahal Hotel (Tel. 301-6162) and Taj Palace Hotel (Tel. 301-0404), in numerous shops at both the **Oberoi and Hyatt Regency hotel** shopping arcades, and in several shops in the **Hauz Khas Village** shopping area, especially at **Jharokha** (Tel. 686-4638) and **Natural Selections** (Tel. 685-8192). The shop at the **Crafts Museum** (Pragati Maidan Village complex on Mathura Road, Tel. 331-9817) offers excellent quality pottery, shawls, and paintings. For a very unique and expensive collection of arts and crafts, visit **Lotus** (Tel. 436-3030, ext. 1074) as the Oberoi Hotel. This Bangkok-based company, which now has production facilities in India, offers some of the most exquisite pieces, including stunning jewelry and accessories, you will find anywhere in the world. Dealers especially like shopping at **Mehra's Art Palace** in Greater Kailash II (Tel. 648-4194) and at **Goel Export** at S-443, School Block, Shakarpur (Tel. 327-6525).

❑ **Art:** Delhi has a very active art community and numerous good quality art galleries representing some of India's top artists. Be sure to pick up a copy of the monthly publication *HEREdelhi*. It provides an excellent overview of the current art scene, including Delhi's many art galleries and exhibitions. Some of Delhi's best art galleries include **Kumar Gallery/Art India** (Oberoi Hotel, Hyatt Regency Hotel, Sunder Nagar Market, and a large gallery at the owner's home in South Delhi, by appointment with Vinit Kumar at Oberoi shop, Tel. 436-2826); **Dhoomi Mal Gallery** (8-A, Connaught Place, Tel. 332-8316); **Art Today** (Hamilton House, A-1 Connaught Place, Tel. 332-0689); and the **Centre For Contemporary Art** (E-2, Connaught Place, Tel. 336-5126). **Hauz Khas Village** also has numerous art galleries worth exploring, especially the **Delhi Art Gallery** (Tel. 696-7619) and **Jharokha** (Tel. 686-4638).

❑ **Antiques and collectibles:** Several shops throughout Delhi offer a wide range of antiques and collectibles. Many of the shops, such as Kumar Gallery and Bharany's, have nice collections of old tribal (Bastar) Khond sculptures. In Old Delhi, the major antique centers are along the main thoroughfare, **Chandni Chowk**, and within the arcade of the **Red Fort** (visit Gulzari Lal and Sons and the Himalayan Art Gallery). Within New Delhi, head for **Sunder Nagar Market**. This shopping center is jam-packed with shops selling antiques and collectibles. Some of the best shops here are **Natesan's Antiqarts** (Tel. 464-9320), **Bharany's** (Tel. 461-8528), **Kumar Gallery** (Tel. 461-1113), and **Rare Arts**. **Mehra's Art Palace** (M-1, Main Market, Greater Kailash 2, Tel. 648-4194), also offers a good range of antiques, from small collectibles to huge architectural pieces. Several shops in the major hotel shopping arcades, such as **Anvita Art Gallery** (The Oberoi Hotel, Tel. 436-2651), also offer good quality antiques and collectibles.

❑ **Furniture:** Delhi is a great place to buy both antique and reproduction furniture. Since most shops are experienced in shipping furniture abroad and sea freight from Delhi is relatively inexpensive, you don't have to worry about shipping. If you like something, buy it. Furniture is one of the great buys in Delhi. If you visited **The Raj** in Mumbai, you'll want to also visit their Delhi showroom near Qutab Minar for colonial and ethnic Indian furniture (Ambawata Complex, 1st Floor, opposite Bhulbhulaiya, Mehrauli Village Road, Tel. 667-794). **Kumar Gallery** has one of the best collections of top quality Tibetan furniture in all of Asia; they showcase a few pieces in their retail hotel shops but most of their fabulous collection is found at their home gallery in South Delhi (for serious buyers by invitation only, Tel. 436-2826). For antique furniture, be sure to visit **Mehra's Art Palace** (Tel. 648-4194) and one or two of their factory farms on the outskirts of the city (by invitation). **Goel Exports** (S-443, School Block, Sharkarpur, Tel. 327-6525) also has a large collection of antique furniture; be sure to visit their four upper floors. At Hauz Khas, make a special effort to visit **Natural Selections** (also known as Creative Looms and Crafts, 1, Hauz Khas Village, Tel. 685-8192) for a good collection of old and reconditioned furniture.

❑ **Jewelry:** Many of Delhi's best jewelry shops are found in and around Connaught Circle and in the shopping arcades of the city's top hotels, especially the Hyatt Regency and Oberoi. In the Connaught Circle area, many of the jewelry shops carry traditional 22k gold jewelry appropriate for local buyers. Some of the best shops include **Krishna & Sons Jewellers** (26-F, Connaught Place, Tel. 332-3557) and **Ivory Mart Jewellers** (22-F, Connaught Place, Tel. 331-0197). Sunder Nagar Market also has some excellent jewelry stores, especially **Jagan Nath Hem Chand Jewellers** (Tel. 464-5925) and **La Boutique** (Tel. 461-9066). At Hauz Khas Village, visit **Silver Smith** (Haveli No. 29A, Tel. 696-7128) for good quality ethnic silver jewelry. But it's the Hyatt Regency Hotel that has the largest concentration of jewelry stores. If you're in the market for quality jewelry, we recommend spending some time in this shopping arcade. The quality and designs here are generally very good compared to other places in Delhi. The two-level shopping arcade includes **Be Jewelled** (stunning pieces, L-83, Tel. 618-1066), **Regency Jewellers, J. H. Jewellers, Jaipur Jewels Palace, Shantivijay Jewellers, Shalki Jewels, Shanti Bros. Jewellers, Khanna Gems, Jewels Paradise,** and **Swati Gems**. The **Khazana** shops at the Taj Mahal Hotel and Taj Palace Hotel also carry good quality jewelry. At the Oberoi Hotel, look for **Shantivijay Jewellers** (Tel. 436-1249). At the Hotel Maurya Sheraton, **Precious Arts & Jewels** (#14, Tel. 302-3180) offers good selections. For tribal jewelry, visit **Lall's Copper and Brass Palace** and **The Studio** at Sunder Nagar Market. For very unique jewelry, be sure to visit **Ravissant** (Oberoi Hotel, Tel. 436-3030, ext. 1071, and 50 & 51 Commercial Complex, New Friends Colony, Tel. 683-7278) and **Lotus** (Oberoi Hotel, Tel. 436-3030, ext. 1074). You'll find jewelry in most arts and crafts emporiums. However, you'll have to judge the quality for yourself. If you visit the shops under the Safdarjung Flyover (opposite old airport), see the jewelry selections at **Padma Jewels Ltd., The Arts and Crafts Store** (Tel. 469-3115) and **Mughal Jewels and Crafts Emporium** (Tel. 462-8892). Expats recommend several reliable jewelers: **Nimal V. J.** (B-7 Connaught Place, Tel. 373-9254), **Ramayana Cottage Emporium** (N-12, Greater Kailash I, Tel. 621-6864), **Shree Jewelers** (Le Meridien Hotel, Tel. 371-7637), and **Vasudev and Sons** (Stutee Building, Karol Bagh, Tel. 575-2523).

❑ **Brass and bronze:** Most arts and crafts emporiums have a selection of brass and bronze items. Be sure to visit the numerous brass and bronze shops at **Sunder Nagar Market** which offer a wide range of brass and bronze items, from large boxes and candlesticks to small temple toys.

❑ **Carpets:** Kashmiris operate numerous carpet shops throughout Delhi. After a while, these shops all look and feel the same. It's okay to be paranoid in these places. The rug merchants tend to be very aggressive and difficult to escape from. They can easily subject you to an hour of ritual tea drinking and carpet rolling as well as ruin your shopping day. Whatever you do, make sure you bargain hard for carpets; don't be afraid to say *"No, I'm not interested"* or *"I have too many carpets already!"* Most arts and crafts emporiums, which are run by Kashmiris, have a carpet section. You may want to start your carpet shopping adventure by visiting the **Central Cottage Industries Emporium** on Janpath (Tel. 332-1577) which has a large carpet section where carpets are sold at fixed prices; this place should give you an idea of the going market rates for carpets. Other shops worth visiting include **Tibet House** (16, Jor Bagh, Lodi Road, Tel. 461-1515, **Maharaja Arts** (F-213/D MB Road, Lado Sarai, Tel. 686-4151), and two carpet shops in Hauz Khas Village—**Cashmeri Gallerie** (Tel. 685-4503) and **Shikara** (Tel. 685-1220). You'll also find a carpet section in the **Khazana** shops of the Tai Mahal Hotel and Taj Palace Hotel.

❑ **Home furnishings, decorative items, and gifts:** The always reliable **Central Cottage Industries Emporium** on Janpath has a good range of home furnishings and decorative items, although the quality is average and designs tend to be uninspired. Hauz Khas Village has several home furnishing and decorative shops. Look for **Aavaran, Works of Art, The Choice, Natural Selections, Jharokha, Ogaan** (go to very back of shop). Expats recommend **C. Lal and Sons** in Jor Bagh for Indian gifts and **The Shop** in Connaught Place for nice placemats, napkins, and tablecloths. The tasteful **Khazana** shops at the Taj Mahal Hotel and Taj Palace Hotel are filled with wonderful home furnishings, decorative pieces, and tasteful gift items. Upscale **Ravissant** offers an exclusive collection beautiful of bedspreads, pillows, bone china, glassware, and collectors silver in its large shop at New Friends Colony (Tel. 683-7278).

❑ **Clothes and textiles:** Most major hotels have tailors that can make garments within 24 to 48 hours. Expats recommend several reliable tailors: **Vedi Tailors** (Connaught Place, between D and E block); **Jyoti Wazir** (C-515 Defense Colony, Tel. 469-8143), **Krishna's Cloth House** (Khan Market), **Tailors of Taste** (Tel. 696-3437), and **B. Rai Sons** (B-52 Khan Market). For beautiful women's cotton clothes, visit **Anokhi** (in Santushti and Khan Market). For unique clothes made by local designers, be sure to visit **Santushti Market** (upscale shopping area run by Air Force wives in the diplomatic enclave near the Samrut Hotel) as well as several boutiques in Hauz Khas Village. The first shop on the right as you enter Hauz Khas Village, **Ogaan**, offers gorgeous sarees and accessories. The **Khazana** shops at the Taj Mahal Hotel and Taj Palace Hotel offer attractive men's clothing and saris. The **Saga Department Store** (8-5, Jangpura, Main Mathura Road) has its own line of stylish men's and women's clothes, although prices tend to be highly inflated for cloths as well as everything else in this classy department store frequented by commission-hungry drivers and tour guides. For good quality silk, visit **Banaras House** (N-13, Connaught Place, Tel. 331-4751 and at the Oberoi Hotel shopping arcade), and **Handloom House** (9A-Block, Connaught Place, Tel. 332-3057). For nice quality fabrics, sarees, shawls, and scarves, **Kalpana** (F-5, Connaught Place, Tel. 371-3738). One of Delhi's oldest fabric shops, **Ram Chandra Krishan Chandra** (Gali Parante Wali, Old Delhi, Tel. 327-7869), offers three floors of silks and hand loomed fabrics. If you're interested in antique textiles, one of the best places in all of India is **Bharany's** (14, Sunder Nagar Market, Tel. 461-8528); it includes many rare pieces of interest to collectors. For uniquely designed pillow covers, tablecloths, sari borders, and old embroidery pieces, be sure to visit **Sen Sation** at the Hyatt Regency Hotel (Tel. 618-1234, ext. 1880) and Hilton Hotel (Tel. 332-0101, ext. 2185) shopping arcades. For inexpensive clothes, try the many stalls that make up the **Tibetan Market** in front of the Hotel Imperial and across the street from the Central Cottage Industries Emporium on Janpath. The **Central Cottage Industries Emporium** at Janpath has a huge section of textiles and clothes on the second and third floors; go to the fifth and sixth floors for menswear and children clothes. For some of the best textiles and clothes, be sure to visit the exclusive **Ravissant** at New Friends Colony (Tel. 683-7278).

☐ Toys: The **Central Cottage Industries Emporium** has a nice selection of locally produced toys on the third floor. Expats highly recommend **Chaudhary's** (in Khan Market and Greater Kailash I, M Block) for nice toys.

WHERE TO SHOP

Delhi offers a variety of shopping venues from hotel shopping arcades and handicraft emporiums to shopping centers, department stores, street shops, markets, and bazaars. What it lacks are huge enclosed air-conditioned shopping malls with specialty shops that are so characteristic of shopping in Bangkok, Singapore, Hong Kong, Japan, and the United States.

Much of Delhi's shopping is a mixture of markets and bazaars which often function as open-air shopping centers. Market lovers encounter a wide range of shopping venues, from the helter-skelter of **Chandni Chowk** in Old Delhi and the **Tibetan Market** on Janpath to the underground **Palika Bazaar** at Connaught Circle, the open-air cultural center called **Dilli Haat**, the antique center at **Sunder Nagar Market**, and the upscale boutiques at **Santushti Market**. In Delhi you will encounter everything from traditional inexpensive street stalls to upscale boutiques in lovely garden settings. Many of the most popular markets offering everything from clothes, jewelry, and souvenirs to antiques, books, and tailoring are located in and around central Delhi: **Janpath, Sarojini Nagar, Jor Bagh, Connaught Place, South Extension, Khan Market, Dilli Haat, Santushti Market**, and **Sunder Nagar**.

In general, the best quality shops tend to be found in the major five-star hotels and in Sunder Nagar Market and Hauz Khas Village. You'll also discover many other good quality shops outside these areas.

OLD DELHI

☐ **Red Fort:** Although somewhat touristy, the nearly 40 small shops that crowd into the arched arcade area offer a wide range of arts and crafts and a few antiques. The shops offer lots of brassware, wood boxes, silver, jewelry, paintings, purses, sandalwood carvings, and tribal art. Our favorite shop here is the last one on the right which is next to the restaurants—**Gulzari Lal & Sons**. It offers many genuine antiques as well as good quality arts and crafts. Best of all, this shop is part of a much larger operation called **Goel Exports**. If you are interested in antique furniture and other arts and crafts, ask to visit their other shop and warehouse which is located at S-443, School Block, Shakarpur (Tel. 327-6525). Many dealers go there because of the wide range and volume of items available for export. Goel Exports also has another warehouse. Other shops worth visiting in the Red Fort are **Delhi Arts** for jewelry, paintings, purses, brassware, temple toys, sandalwood carvings, and handicrafts (#34, Tel. 326-5680), **Himalayan Art Gallery** (#19-A), and **Kashmir Art Palace**.

❑ **Chandni Chowk:** This is one of the cultural experiences which may or may not add up to worthwhile shopping for you. Also known as Silver Street, Chandni Chowk is one of Old Delhi's most crowded and colorful bazaars. The shops here wholesale numerous products, including gold and silver jewelry, 'zari' work, spices, textiles, grains, and much more. Given the high level of competition, it's expected that you bargain hard for everything. Many people view Chandni Chowk as a major tourist attraction rather than a significant shopping destination. You'll have lots of photo opportunities here as taxis, cows, auto-rickshaws, bicycles, horse carriages, and bullock carts compete with pedestrians for space on this crowded street. The best shows may be the enterprising pavement astrologers, photographers, doctors, and shoemakers who ply their trades.

CENTRAL DELHI

❑ **Connaught Place:** This much touted traditional shopping area may have seen better days but we haven't seen them in over seven years. It's worn and somewhat intimidating with all the touts, beggars, pests, pickpockets, and idle people hanging around the circle. Be careful where you step since numerous sidewalk vendors selling books, textiles, food, handicrafts, and paintings occupy a good portion of the pavement. Also, watch out for the enterprising shoeshine operators who follow you

around trying to get your business—even if you wear
tennis shoes or sandals! They are known for the old trick
of making a mess of pedestrians' shoes and then pointing
out that you need to hire them to clean the mess, which
could consist of a heavy layer of good old cow dung
readily available curbside. Nonetheless, Connaught Place
at least should be on your short shopping list. It includes
several well established shops that are especially popular
with locals and tourists. Here you'll find numerous
jewelry, clothing, gallery, book, and arts and crafts shops
lining the two main streets that make up the circle.
Don't expect to find the latest in fashionable jewelry or
clothing here. Much of what you see will be in traditional local designs and colors. Some of the best shops
here are **Krishna and Sons Jewellers** (26-F, Connaught
Place, Tel. 332-3557), Nirmal V.J. (B-7 Connaught
Place, Tel. 373-9254), and **Ivory Mart Jewellers** (22F,
Connaught Place, Tel. 331-0197) for jewelry; **Kalpana**
(F-5, Connaught Place, Tel. 371-3738) for nice quality
fabrics, sarees, shawls, and scarves; **Glamour** (F-20,
Connaught Place) for fabrics and scarves; **M. A. R-
amzana** (16-E, Connaught Place, Tel. 332-2108) for
Kashmiri carpets, handicrafts, jewelry, and scarves; **Ivory
Palace** (F-16, Connaught Place) for a nice selection of
handicrafts, gems, and paintings; **Dhoomi Mal Gallery**
(8-A, Connaught Place, Tel. 332-8316) and **Art Today**
(Hamilton House, A-1, Connaught Place, Tel. 332-0689)
for excellent quality paintings and sculptures; and the
New Book Depot for a nice selection of books.

Don't forget the underground shopping bazaar which
has entrances and exits at the circle. Called the **Palika
Bazaar**, it's filled with hundreds of small shops offering
everything from shoes, watches, videos, music, jewelry,
clothing, and accessories to brassware, luggage, and electronics. Chances are you won't find anything worthwhile
here. If you do, be sure to bargain hard since prices will
most likely be inflated. It's a rather dingy and dirty place
with shopkeepers constantly pestering you with such
inane sales pitches as *"Hello, sir"*, *"Excuse me"*, and *"Come
inside."* But you may want to go underground for the
cultural experience. One word of caution: despite the
obvious security (metal detectors at the entrance), this
shopping bazaar has been the target of terrorist bomb-
ings by separatist groups who have inflicted a death toll
on shoppers. Depending on India's current political
climate, you may or may not want to go underground to

peek or shop. Sometimes it can get you killed! Above
ground you'll find a Pizza Hut and Wimpy's to escape
from the street traffic and the terror of the touts. While
there are numerous shops in and around Connaught
Place, you may be able to finish this area within one to
two hours. It's not high on our shopping list.

❑ **Janpath:** Connected to the center of Connaught Circle
and running south for several kilometers, the first
kilometer of this shopping street is worth exploring. The
main attraction in the government's **Central Cottage
Industries Emporium** (Tel. 332-6790) on the east side
of Janpath which is across the street from the Hotel
Imperial and Tibetan Market. Like the old government
Friendship Stores in China, this modern six-storey
building is jam-packed with products from all over India.
You'll find everything from textiles and ready-made
clothes for adults and children to jewelry, brassware,
paintings, carvings, inlaid boxes, furniture, toys, pottery,
and marble stoneware. The quality is generally good and
the prices both fixed and reasonable. You may want to
make this one of your first shopping stops in Delhi in
order to get an overview of what's available and at what
price. Many other emporiums and department stores,
such as CIE near Hauz Khas and Saga Department Store
on Mathura Road, may appear to be government-run,
but in reality they are private operations run primarily
by enterprising Kashmiri companies. Prices in these
other places are often 10 to 50 percent higher and for
good reason; some pay tour guides and bus and taxi
drivers 30 to 50 percent commissions for bringing them
customers, i.e., unsuspecting tourists. You also may want
to visit the **Tibetan Market** which is located across the
street from the Central Cottage Industries Emporium
and in front of the Hotel Imperial. Consisting of a string
of more than 100 small stalls spilling onto the sidewalk
along Janpath, the market is a fun place to shop for
inexpensive clothes, brass, beads, bags, and a variety of
souvenirs. Since most stalls sell similar items, be sure to
compare asking prices and bargain hard for everything.
For jewelry, look for **Tribhovandas** (2 Scindia House,
Janpath, Tel. 331-3337).

❑ **Baba Kharak Sansad Marg:** Running southwest of
Connaught Circle and not far from Janpath, this street
is home to 14 state emporiums that showcase a wide

range of products produced in their states. The three best emporiums are those representing Rajasthan, Gujarat, and Delhi.

❑ **Sunder Nagar Market:** This is really a street-front shopping center rather than a market or bazaar in the traditional sense of the term, although shopping often takes on a bazaar character. Located near the Oberoi Hotel, set back from Dr. Zakir Hussain Road and southeast of India Gate, this is one of our favorite shopping areas for arts, antiques, textiles, handicrafts, and jewelry. You can easily spend two to three hours exploring the many dusty and cluttered shops, and then you'll probably want to return later to further explore its many treasures. Most of the shops poorly display their products in windows as well as in their shops. You'll have to go into each shop and carefully look around for appealing treasures. In many cluttered shops, this will be real work! Some of the best shops here include: **India Arts Corner** (#30, Tel. 461-8257) for an excellent selection of quality arts, crafts, jewelry, prints, and white marble pots and vases painted in gold and enamel; **Treasures India** (#28, Tel. 464-3207) for furniture, paintings, brass, marble vases, carvings, and silk scarves; **Nav-Rattan Arts, Friends Electric Co., Modern Crafts,** and **India Arts Palace** for brass items; **La Boutique** (#20, Tel. 463-2099) for a nice selection of handicrafts, jewelry, and objects d'art; **Bharany's** (#14, Tel. 461-8528) for a terrific collection of antique textiles, tribal art, enameled jewelry, and shawls; **Natesan's Antiqarts** (#13, Tel. 464-9320) for antique carvings, bronze figures, and sandalwood; **Kumar Gallery** (#11, Tel. 461-1113) for a collection of fine oil paintings and tribal sculptures; **Ladakh Art Gallery** for silver jewelry; **Lall's Copper and Brass Palace** (#31, Tel. 462-7625) for an unusual and bazaar-style collection of tribal jewelry, brass, boxes, and textiles (everything is piled high in this thoroughly disorganized shop!); **Jagan Nath Hem Chand Jewellers** (#7, Tel. 464-5925) for excellent quality jewelry, custom made pieces (manufactures in own factory), and loose stones; **The Studio** (#4, Tel. 461-9360) for lots of contemporary silver and tribal jewelry; and **Rare Arts** (in a building by itself in the center of the compound) for jewelry and small silver and brass pieces.

- ❑ **Oberoi Hotel Shopping Arcade:** Located on the first floor of the Oberoi Hotel to the left, just after the reception desk, this is one of Delhi's most upscale shopping centers. It's a mixture of a few top quality shops and a few typical Kashmiri carpet and shawl shops. The best shops include **Art India** (Tel. 463-1195) which is a branch shop of Kumar. You'll find an excellent selection of paintings, prints, and tribal sculptures. If you're interested in seeing Kumar's terrific collection of art and Tibetan chests, contact Vinit Kumar who is often in this shop. His impressive galleries are located in the family compound in South Delhi. **Banaras House Limited** offers an excellent collection of textiles and fabrics. **Shantivijay Jewellers** (Tel. 436-1249) is a very nice jewelry shop which also has a branch in the Hyatt Regency shopping arcade. **Ravissant** (Tel. 430-4071) offers its own unique and exquisite collection of silver, leather, and fabrics. **Lotus**, a new-comer to Delhi from Bangkok, presents a fabulous collection of uniquely designed silver pieces, gold jewelry, cigar boxes, trays, and elephant purses at knock-your-socks-off prices. **Anvita Art Gallery** (Tel. 436-2651) offers unique silver and bronze pieces, textiles, paintings, and tribal jewelry and sculptures. The remaining shops here include three over-priced Kashmiri carpet shops (Shagoon Emporium, Ali Shah, and Indo Kashmir Carpet Factory), a tailor (-Intercontinental Man's Shop), and a couple of jewelers (Jewel and Indian Arts Gallery).

- ❑ **Taj Mahal and Taj Palace Hotel Shops:** Both of the Taj hotels limit their shopping arcade to one shop—the upscale handicraft and clothing emporium **Khazana**. These fine quality shops are attached to each of the Taj hotels. A central buyer in Delhi purchases for all of the shops. Each shop is beautifully laid out with nice displays, attractive products, and attentive service. The shops are well stocked with an eclectic mix of local products: leather bags, furniture (both small and large), silk, sarees, carpets, paintings, books, and arts and crafts. These shops also include a men's clothing section. If you're not staying at a Taj hotel, you should at least stop by one of these hotels to see a Khazana shop. You're likely to encounter them at Taj hotels elsewhere in India.

- ❑ **Maurya Sheraton Hotel Shopping Arcade:** This hotel has two small shopping arcades offering jewelry, art, carpets, and books. The best shops are **Precious Arts and Jewels** (#14, Tel. 302-3180, ext. 1956) for nicely designed jewelry and loose stones (ask to see the gold jewelry and stones locked in the safe); this shop also operates two other jewelry shops in the hotel—**Art and Jewel Co.** and **Juwella**. **Kumar Gallery** (Tel. 302-3148) offers nice quality miniature paintings, tribal sculptures, and Tibetan chests.

❑ **Le Meridien Hotel Shopping Arcade:** The first two floors in the huge and dark atrium of this hotel house 25 shops offering jewelry, cloths, handicrafts, rugs, shawls, tribal silver, and books. The four jewelry shops on the ground floor offer some interesting pieces. **Shree Jewelers** (Tel. 371-7637) comes highly recommended.

❑ **Hilton Hotel Shopping Arcade:** The first and second floor shopping arcade has shops offering carpets, clothes, jewelry and books. Be sure to stop at the **San Sation** shop for beautiful sarees and pillow covers.

❑ **Santushti Shopping Centre:** Located in the diplomatic section of town, across from the Samrat Hotel and in the Willingdon Airforce Camp, this shopping complex has several shops offering clothes, jewelry, home furnishings, leather goods, and fabrics. It has a lovely setting with well-maintained gardens and a wonderful restaurant, Santushti.

❑ **Below Safdarjung Flyover:** Located across from the old airport, this is one of the most unique shopping areas in Delhi which is overlooked by many visitors. Several shops are literally housed under the flyover; you can hear the traffic rumble overhead while in the shops. Most of the shops offer arts, crafts, and jewelry and operate like handicraft emporiums. Be sure to visit **Padma Jewels, The Arts & Crafts Store** (Tel. 462-5698), a very large emporium filled with brass items, jewelry, clothes, musical instruments, stone sculptures, screens, boxes, sandalwood carvings, marble plates, tables, and carpets. Popular with Japanese visitors, this shop is run by Jains rather than Kashmiris. **Mughal Jewels and Crafts** (Tel. 462-8892) specializes in jewelry and handicrafts. It designs and manufactures its own jewelry. The shop also carries a nice selection of clothes, screens, sandalwood carvings, paintings, brass items, Indian jade, marble plates, and leather goods. Claims it always undersells the government's Central Cottage Industries Emporium.

SOUTH DELHI

❏ **Hauz Khas Village:** This area seems to have no logic— just lots of chaos! But it's home to some Delhi's major shopping treasures. Shops turnover frequently and new ones come on board as they try to make it in this popular upscale shopping area. The area requires lots of mindless wandering through what at times feels like a medieval community. The dusty and potholed main street is utter chaos with people, cows, cars, bicycles, and motorbikes trying to slowly squeeze through the mess. However, don't spend too much time on the main thoroughfare. Most of the really interesting shops are found in the side streets and small lanes. You may want to set aside at least three hours to explore this area. It has lots of good small restaurants (Thai, Italian, Mexican) for lunch or dinner. Hauz Khas Village is home to numerous arts, crafts, jewelry, clothing, furniture, home decorative, silver, and leather shops as well as numerous art galleries. This is modern India where new styles and designs are on display. It's a fun place to shop and dine. Our favorite shops here include: **Natural Selections** (#1, Tel. 685-8192) offers an excellent collection of old furniture and home decorative items; they also have warehouses with additional furniture (ask if you don't see what you want at this shop). **Jharokha** (#24, Tel. 686-4638) is a combination arts, crafts, and home decorative shop and art gallery. It's three floors include excellent quality pottery, boxes, paper, bed covers, linens, rugs, paintings, and sculptures. **Delhi Art Gallery** (#13, Tel. 696-7619) is jam-packed with paintings from many contemporary Indian artists; older and more valuable pieces of art are stored in the back room (need to ask to see). **Silver Smith** (Naveli No. 29A, Tel. 696-7128) has a nice collection of ethnic silver which it sells fixed price by weight. **Ogaan** (H-2, Tel. 696-7595), an upscale boutique, has gorgeous designer sarees and accessories at the front of its shop; it also offers contemporary pottery and tableware at the rear of the shop. **Aavaran** (#1, Tel. 651-2260) is a great place for attractive Rajasthan handicrafts and home decorative items.

❑ **Hyatt Regency Shopping Arcade:** If you're in the market for jewelry, there's no better place to go than to this large two-storey shopping arcade. Known for its concentration of quality jewelry stores, this shopping arcade also has a few other noted shops offering art, antiques, textiles, and carpets. For jewelry, be sure to stop at the first shop off the lobby—**Be Jewelled** (L-83, Tel. 618-1066). Their exclusive designs are stunning. Another fine jeweler here is **Shantivijay Jewels** which is located on the lower level. Other jewelers here include **Regency Jewellers, Varun Gems, Sital Dass Sons, Abhusham Neeraj Enterprise, J. H. Jewellers, Shalk Jewels, Shanti Bros. Jewellers, Khanna Gems**, and **Jewels Paradise**. Nice Rajasthan silver and neck pieces can be found a **Jaipur Jewels Palace** and **Jawahrat E. Hind**. For contemporary art, tribal sculptures, and Tibetan chests, be sure to visit **Kumar Gallery** (Tel. 39203148). **Bharany's** of Sunder Nagar Market also has a shop on the lower level offering textiles, jewelry, carvings, silver, and tribal sculptures. For silk pillow covers, scarves, and neckties, stop at **Silk India**. One of the most distinctive shops here is **Sen Sation** (Tel. 618-1234, ext. 1880) with its uniquely designed pillow, bed, and table covers in muted colors. Several Kashmiri rug merchants have shops here: **Kashmir Carpet Palace, Shaw Art Palace**, and **Smeer & Sourabh**.

❑ **Greater Kailash II:** This upscale residential area includes several home-based boutiques. One of the best shops in all of India is located here: **Mehra's Art Palace** (M-1, Main Market, Tel. 648-4194). It's jam-packed with quality antiques, brass objects, arts, and crafts. If you're interested in old furniture, chests, doors, and marble garden pieces, ask to be taken to their warehouse (Mehra Farm) which is about 25 minutes from this shop on the outskirts of the city. A "must visit" shopping destination.

❑ **Dilli Haat:** Located across the street from the popular INA Market and near Lodi Gardens, the Dilli Haat complex offers a mixture of shopping, dining, and entertainment that represents the diversity of India's various states. It's essentially an upscale food and crafts bazaar with changing exhibits every three weeks. The exhibition grounds consist of several stalls where craftsmen from all over India display and sell their products (clothes, textiles, handicrafts, jewelry). The food section consists of 24 stalls operated by the state tourism corporations. Cultural performances take place in the open-air cultural complex. Opening at 10:30am, Dilli Haat also is a popular place for breakfast. Current food and dance programs are usually listed on banners at the front of the complex.

❑ **New Friends Colony:** Located southeast of the Rim Road, just off Mathura Road, this shopping complex primarily caters to Delhi's upper-middle and upper classes who live in the walled residential areas and flats of South Delhi. Our favorite shop here is **Ravissant** (50 & 51, Commercial Complex, Tel. 683-7278) with its exquisite collection of jewelry, textiles, bedding, and tableware.

❑ **Qutab Minar:** Located near the Qutab Minar complex are a few shops and shopping areas worth visiting. **Qutab Colonnade** (H 5/6 Mehrauli Road, Tel. 696-7537) is a restored haveli (mansion) with shopping offering artifacts and clothes. **The Raj** (Ambawata Complex, 1st Floor, opposite Bhulbhulaiya, Mehrauli Village Road, Tel. 66794) offers a wonderful collection of restored Indian and colonial furniture. If you're interested in having furniture made, be sure to visit here. **Maharaja Arts** (F-213/D MB Road, Lado Sarai, next to Qutab Minar, Tel. 686-4151) has one of the largest carpet factories and showrooms in Delhi.

❑ **South Extension Market:** Located on both sides of Ring Road (Part I and Part II), this popular shopping center and market primarily caters to local residents, especially the upper middle class. It includes numerous outlets offering name brand clothes, leather goods, jewelry, and home decorative items. It also includes several of Delhi's largest department stores.

BEST OF THE BEST

Several of our top shops offer a wide variety of items rather than specialize in one or two items. Thus, several names appear frequently for different products: Khazana, Kumar Gallery, Ravissant, Jharokha, and Central Cottage Industries Emporium. The best shopping in Delhi is concentrated in a few major shopping areas. If you have limited time in Delhi, you may want to concentrate your shopping efforts on the following shops which we found to be some of the city's best for uniqueness and quality.

ANTIQUES AND OBJECTS D'ART

❑ **Mehra Art Palace:** *M-1, Main Market, Greater Kailash II, Tel. 648-4194 or Fax 646-9160.* In operation for more than 50 years, this reliable shop is a favorite of dealers. It's always at the very top of our shopping list, the place we'll visit on either our first or second day and often return to on our last day in Delhi. It's where we get some of our most unique antique and home decorative pieces as well as best buys in India. Many people are in awe of the massive collections available here and at the "Mehra Farms." Expect to find a treasure-trove of wood, brass, and silver collectibles at this shop; be sure to visit all three densely packed floors. The Gujarat puppets, temple toys, and carvings, when available, are terrific discoveries. Like a tip of the iceberg, this shop provides a glimpse of what you may soon discover is a huge inventory of antique furniture and other large collectibles which can be found at Mehra's Farms located 25 minutes from this shop. You'll need to ask to be taken to this expansive warehouse, which is only one of three such places operated by Mehra. Very good and reliable shippers who may well serve as your shipping consolidation point in India. Very easy to work with both in India and from abroad. This is where experience really shows.

❑ **Art India/Kumar Gallery/Sainik Farms:** *Four retail locations plus the farm: Art India at Oberoi Hotel (Tel. 436-2826 or Fax 463-1195); Kumar Gallery at Hyatt Regency Hotel, 11 Sunder Nagar Market (Tel. 461-1113 or Fax 463-1195), and Hotel Maurya Sheraton (Tel. 302-3148 or Fax 463-1195). Contact Art India for private showing of galleries at the owner's Sainik Farms home compound.* Wow! It doesn't get much better or pricier than at these Kumar shops and galleries. While the Kumar shops are primarily noted as some of India's top art galleries, they also offer antique tribal sculptures (Khond pieces from the Bastar tribal area in Central India), Tibetan chests, and a few other quality collectibles.

❑ **Natesan's Antiqarts:** *13, Sunder Nagar Market, Tel. 464-9320 of Fax 332-5993.* If you visited their shops in Mumbai (or in Bangalore, Trivandrum, and London), you know this is a very impressive one-of-a-kind collector's gallery. Includes large old sculptures, wood carvings, chests, sandalwood, and bronzes. The very old and expensive pieces, for serious buyers, are stored in the back of the shop. A photo album shows some larger pieces, such as old doors, that are for sale.

❑ **Anvita Art Gallery:** *The Oberoi Hotel, Tel. 436-2651.* This small but very attractive shop offers a good selection of quality paintings, silver, bronze figures, and textiles. Includes many nice old pieces of interest to serious collectors.

❑ **Khazana:** *Taj Mahal Hotel (Tel. 301-6162) and Taj Palace Hotel (Tel. 301-0404).* These tastefully laid out shops include some antiques and many objets d'art. While many of the items in these two shops look the same, when it comes to antiques and objets d'art, the collections differ somewhat. The central buyer in Delhi, who has a real eye for quality antiques, furniture, and collectibles, purchases for all of the Taj's Khazana shops throughout the country. It's a good idea to visit each of the shops since each will have a different mix of such items.

FURNITURE

❑ **The Raj:** *Ambawata Complex, 1st Floor, opposite Bhulbhulaiya, Mehrauli Village Road, Tel. 667-794.* If you visited The Raj in Mumbai, you know this is one of India's exceptional furniture showrooms and factories. Specializing in British, Portuguese, Dutch Colonial, and Indian-style furniture—both antique and reproduction—The Raj is very popular with dealers, expatriates, and collectors. The workmanship and finishes are some of best you'll find in India. If you're in the market for antique or reproduction furniture, The Raj may be the perfect place to satisfy all of your furniture needs. Very reputable and reliable. Experienced in packing and shipping worldwide.

❑ **Mehra's Art Palace:** *M-1, Main Market, Greater Kailash II, Tel. 648-4194 or Fax 646-9160.* While the Greater

Kailash II shop has some furniture on display, this shop does not do justice to the huge inventory maintained at the Mehra Farm warehouse on the outskirts of the city. You'll see a few antique doors in the alley behind the shop, but you'll have to take the "by invitation only" journey to Mehra Farm to see what is one of the most impressive operations in India. Primarily set up for dealers and collectors, Mehra Farm has two huge warehouses that are crammed with one of the most incredible collections of antique furniture, accessories, and doors: Goa and Gujarat cabinets, Tibetan chests, Sri Lankan boxes and chests, beds and panels from Goa and Calcutta, and sofas, settees, and tables from all over India. Most of the furniture and doors are in their original state of disrepair. You'll have to literally walk through the warehouses (extremely hot during the hot season) and make your selections. Prices range from US$200 to over US$1,000 for many of the big cabinets and doors. Mehra will do some basic restoration work, but don't expect miracles; what you see is probably what you will get with some basic sanding, filling, and waxing that passes for "restoration." If you need major restoration work, plan to do it at home. Don't forget to visit the small building to the right of the warehouse. It includes a small collection of unrestored painted Tibetan chests. Depending on the current inventory available, here you may be able to make a terrific buy—paying only US$500 to US$800 for a painted Tibetan chest that sells for much more. If you are looking for beautifully restored furniture, it's best to shop at The Raj which specializes in such restoration work. Mehra is good for purchasing old fixer-uppers.

❑ **Natural Selections:** *1, Hauz Khas Village, Tel. 685-8192 or Fax 651-2129.* Offers lots of old restored furniture and home decorative items. Very popular with U.S. embassy personnel who want furniture and accessory pieces they can immediately use as well as serves as tasteful home decorative items. This shop includes large cabinets, beds, chests, carved pillars, and doors along with many small furniture pieces, such as end tables and chests. Offers some painted Tibetan chests but they need lots of restoration work. Be sure to visit the lower level of the shop which is crammed with furniture. If you don't see anything to your liking, ask about their current warehouse inventory. They have three warehouses which are located both inside and outside the city. The warehouses inside the city are crammed to the ceiling with furniture (almost impossible to walk through or fully view the pieces). One warehouse located more than two hours from the city produces reproduction furniture. Works with many dealers but is very much oriented to the local retail market, especially the expat community and visitors from abroad.

❑ **Goel Export:** *S-443, School Block, Shakarpur, Tel. 327-6525 or Fax 327-6503.* Similar in many respects to Mehra's operation, but on a much smaller scale, the first two floors of this multi-storey shop are crammed with old furniture and doors.

❑ **Art India/Kumar Gallery:** *Four retail locations plus home compound: Art India at Oberoi Hotel (Tel. 436-2826 or Fax 463-1195); Kumar Gallery at Hyatt Regency Hotel, 11 Sunder Nagar Market (Tel. 461-1113 or Fax 463-1195), and Hotel Maurya Sheraton (Tel. 302-3148 or Fax 463-1195). Contact Art India for private showing of galleries at the owner's Sainik Farms home compound.* The Kumar group offers a fabulous collection of top quality Tibetan chests. Most of the retail shops have one or two small chests on display. However, most of the collection is found at Kumar's gallery at Sainik Farms. You'll need an appointment to see this collection. These top quality chests command high prices (US$2,000 - US$15,000).

❑ **Khazana:** *Taj Mahal Hotel (Tel. 301-6162) and Taj Palace Hotel (Tel. 301-0404).* While these shops primarily offer arts, crafts, clothes, and jewelry, you'll also find a small collection of quality tables, chairs, chests, and doors.

ART

❑ **Art India/Kumar Gallery:** *Four retail locations plus the farm: Art India at Oberoi Hotel (Tel. 436-2826 or Fax 463-1195); Kumar Gallery at Hyatt Regency Hotel, 11 Sunder Nagar Market (Tel. 461-1113 or Fax 463-1195), and Hotel Maurya Sheraton (Tel. 302-3148 or Fax 463-1195). Contact Art India for private showing of galleries at the owner's Sainik Farms home compound.* Kumar is one of the important supporters and promoters of contemporary Indian artists. They work with a group of twenty established artists as well as a few up and coming artists. Each shop offers a selection of paintings. However, the largest collection of paintings and sculptures are found at its Sainik Farms gallery which consists of a separate building housing art. Serious buyers need an appointment to view this collection. The Hyatt Regency Hotel shop offers a good range of representative art.

❑ **Dhoomi Mal Gallery:** *8-A, Connaught Place, Tel. 332-8316 or Fax 332-8316.* Operating since 1936, this is the oldest art gallery in Delhi (claims to be the oldest in all of Asia). Representing more than 40 artists, the gallery is jam-packed with contemporary oils and sculptures. A good place to sample a wide range of Indian art.

❑ **Art Today:** *Hamilton House, A-1, Connaught Place, Tel. 332-0689 or Fax 371-2998.* Relatively new, this very attractive and modern gallery represents several top artists as well as many up and coming artists. Hosts many exhibitions.

❑ **Delhi Art Gallery:** *13, Hauz Khas Village, Tel. 696-7619.* Climb the narrow stairs and you're rewarded with a very nice selection of contemporary Indian art displayed in several rooms. One room includes a collection of older paintings and drawings. The back room has lots of additional paintings tightly stored on racks—just in case you don't find some in the main gallery. Well worth visiting when visiting the Hauz Khas area.

❑ **Jharokha:** *24, Hauz Khas Village, Tel. 686-4638.* Maintains a small art gallery on the third floor consisting primarily of oil paintings. Look for unique sculptures on the ground floor. One of our favorite shops in Delhi for unique arts and crafts. A quality operation.

JEWELRY

❑ **Be Jewelled:** *L-83, Hyatt Regency Hotel, Tel. 618-1066 or Fax 619-7531.* Produces beautifully designed jewelry, especially large pieces. Does custom work.

❑ **Jagan Nath Hem Chand Jewellers:** *7, Sunder Nagar Market, Tel. 464-5925 or Fax 462-9569.* Designs and manufactures jewelry. Includes a good selection of loose precious and semi-precious stones. Does custom work.

❑ **Lotus:** *Oberoi Hotel, Tel. 436-3030, ext. 1074 or Fax 436-0207.* One of Asia's most unique haute couture shops which specializes in producing gorgeous jewelry fit for the very rich and famous. Includes jewelry and accessory pieces.

❑ **Ravissant:** *50 & 51, Commercial Complex, New Friends Colony, Tel. 683-7278.* Amidst all the beautiful bedding, silks, clothes, silver, bone China, and glassware is a separate room showcasing a collection of stunning Indian jewelry. As with all the Ravissant shops in Delhi and Mumbai, the selections here represent a keen eye for detail and quality.

❑ **Shantivijay Jewellers:** *Oberoi Hotel, Tel. 436-1249 or Fax 436-0534.* Nicely designed contemporary jewelry.

❑ **Ivory Mart Jewellers:** *22F, Connaught Place, Tel. 331-0197.* This large and popular jewelry shop offers a nice selection of traditional Indian jewelry as well as loose stones. Will make jewelry to your specifications (bring your photos or drawing).

❑ **Tribhovandas:** *2 Scindia House, Janpath, Tel. 331-3337.* This large and famous jewelry emporium includes lots of precious gems and gold jewelry, especially large pieces.

TEXTILES, SAREES, CLOTHING

❑ **Ravissant:** *50 & 51, Commercial Complex, New Friends Colony, Tel. 683-7278.* One of the best selections of top quality fabrics, garments, bedspreads, and pillow covers. Exclusive designs and wonderful colors.

❑ **Bharany's:** *14, Sunder Nagar Market, Tel. 461-8528 or Fax 463-4081. Also has a shop at the Hyatt Regency Hotel.* If you're in the market for antique textiles and tapestries, this is the place to shop, especially at their Sunder Nagar Market shop. This famous shop offers some wonderful old Indian textiles, as well as antiques and jewelry, that are definitely collector pieces. Includes lots of folk art and tribal pieces. Many of the tapestries make terrific wall hangings. Owner, shop, and textiles featured in many leading publications. One of the best places in India for old textiles.

❑ **Ram Chandra Krishan Chandra:** *Gali Parante Wali, Old Delhi, Tel. 327-7869.* Located on a very narrow and crowded lane, this is one of Delhi's oldest and most famous fabric shops. Its three floors are jam-packed with silks and hand loomed fabrics.

❑ **Kalpana:** *F-5, Connaught Place, Tel. 371-3738 or Fax 331-5368.* This large and popular silk, saree, and shawl shop offers nice fabrics. Go upstairs for ready-made clothes. You'll need to ask about the shawls.

❑ **Banaras House Limited:** *Oberoi Hotel.* This well established shop offers an excellent collection of textiles and fabrics.

❑ **Khazana:** *Taj Mahal Hotel (Tel. 301-6162) and Taj Palace Hotel (Tel. 301-0404).* Includes a nice range of fabrics and clothes for both women and men.

❑ **Sen Sation:** *Hyatt Regency Hotel, Tel. 618-1234, ext. 1880 or Fax 618-5149.* Produces beautiful pillow, bed, and table covers from saree borders and old embroidered pieces.

❑ **Ogaan:** *H2, Hauz Khas Village, Tel. 696-7595 or Fax 685-3864.* Offers beautifully designed sarees and accessories. Nicely displayed in a very contemporary shop that also includes home decorative items.

HOUSEWARES, GIFT ITEMS, SILVER

❑ **Ravissant:** *50 & 51, Commercial Complex, New Friends Colony, Tel. 683-7278.* Includes an exclusive collection of bone China, glassware, and silver. Introduces new silver collection each year.

❑ **Jharokha:** *24, Hauz Khas Village, Tel. 686-4638.* Offers a terrific selection of quality stationery, pottery, sheets, towels, table linen, silverware, glassware, rugs, candle stands, cushions, cutlery, curios, crockery, baskets, terra cotta, and accessories. A fun place to shop.

❑ **Silver Smith:** *Hauz Khas Village, Haveli No. 29A, Tel. 696-7128.* Small shop offering reasonably priced (by weight) ethnic silver.

CARPETS, LEATHER, AND ACCESSORIES

❑ **Maharaja Arts:** *F-213, D. Lado Sarai, MB Road (next to Qutab Minar), Tel. 685-4731 or Fax 685-4354.* One of the largest carpet factories and showrooms in Delhi.

❑ **Bharat Leather Emporium:** *E-1, Connaught Place, Tel. 332-1252.* Offers a wide selection of locally produced leather products.

❑ **Tibet House:** *16, Jor Bah, Lodi Road, Tel. 461-1515.* Offer a nice selection of good quality carpets.

❑ **Khazana:** *Taj Mahal Hotel (Tel. 301-6162) and Taj Palace Hotel (Tel. 301-0404).* Includes tasteful selections of quality leather and carpets.

HANDICRAFTS

❑ **Central Cottage Industries Emporium:** *Janpath, STC Building, Tel. 332-1909.* This huge emporium is filled with handicraft from all over India. Since everything is fixed price, it's a good idea to shop here first in order to get an idea of quality and pricing.

❑ **Indian Arts Corner:** *30, Sunder Nagar Market, Tel. 461-8257.* This small but well established shop offers a good range of arts and crafts—ivory sculptures, brass pots, papier mache boxes, Tibetan crafts, silver figures, ivory paintings, sandalwood carvings, marble boxes, silk paintings, and enamel figures.

❑ **Padma Jewels, The Arts & Crafts Store:** *1, Below Safdarjung Flyover, Aurobindo Marg, Tel. 469-3115.* This unique and expansive under-the-road handicraft emporium is jam-packed with everything from sandalwood carvings to musical instruments. Good selection of boxes.

❑ **Khazana:** *Taj Mahal Hotel (Tel. 301-6162) and Taj Palace Hotel (Tel. 301-0404).* Offers an excellent selection of good quality handicrafts in a classy gift shop setting.

❑ **CIE (Cottage Industries Exposition Limited):** *M5, Hauz Khas Village, Tel. 686-2611.* This large Kashmiri handicraft emporium, which is one of several successful emporiums in the CIE chain of emporiums found in fourteen cities, is a typical bus and taxi stop—drivers and guides bring tourists here to get commissions. Despite the inflated prices and tourist stop character, CIE offers a good selection of attractive carpets, jewelry, clothes, shawls, silk, accessories, furniture, bronzes, art, miniature paintings, marble inlaid products, and arts and craft of Rajasthan. You may or may not like this one-stop-shop, especially when you know prices, but not selections, are better at the government's Central Cottage Industries Emporium on Janpath.

❑ **Saga Department Store:** *B-5, Jangpura, Main Mathura Road, Tel. 431-6981 or Fax 432-4313.* This is basically an upscale version of CIE. Another aggressive Kashmiri shopping emporium much loved by bus and taxi drivers as well as tour guides who collect their "drive by" commissions. Nice displays of good quality handicrafts that especially appeal to tourists. As might be expected from such an operation, you'll pay highly inflated prices to cover all of their internal and external "overhead."

ACCOMMODATIONS

The hotel scene in Delhi is changing as more and more five-star hotels, operated by Western managers with many years of international experience, open here. Indeed, until the Raddison Hotel near the airport opened in 1998, the most recent five-star hotel to open in Delhi was the Le Meridien in 1989. The local rating system of five- and four-star hotels is not to be trusted in terms of quality. For example, there is a huge different between the five-star Oberoi, Taj Palace, and Hyatt Regency hotels and the so-called five-star Ashok, Best Western Surya, and Vasant Continental. Indeed, the latter three hotels seem to be missing a few points on their stars. Their local management and maintenance systems are quite different from those that operate on international standards. One of Delhi's real surprise hotels is the old, but newly renovated, Hotel Imperial which has justly won several recent tourism awards. We hesitate to recommend many other hotels since so many are poorly maintained or lacking expected services. Not surprising, Delhi's best hotels also tend to be the centers for the best dining and shopping. They are great oases from the crowds, chaos, heat, noise, and filth of the city. The best such hotels include:

❏ **The Oberoi:** *Dr. Zakir Hussain Marg, New Delhi, 110 003, Tel. 91-11-436-3030 or Fax 91-11-436-0484, USA & Canada Toll Free 800-562-3764.* The Oberoi is a first-class operation and a personal favorite in New Delhi. We are fans of Oberoi hotels, as well as the chain's founder, Mohan Singh Oberoi, and the Oberoi New Delhi lives up to our high expectations. Step through the doorway into the lobby and the guest is greeted by the soothing sound of a marble fountain. The seating is casual, yet elegant, and showcased is a repertoire of arts of India. If you want a place where you can escape the hubbub of the city yet be close to the business district, shopping or sightseeing, The Oberoi fits the bill. A member of The Leading Hotels of the World, The Oberoi New Delhi fulfills the expectations of the business or leisure traveler. Each of the 300 guestrooms is a haven of classic elegance and contemporary amenities. Interiors are in subtle, gentle hues and walls are tastefully decorated with Indian prints. The Oberoi combines Western expectations of comfort, convenience, and ambience with understated touches that remind the guest he is in India. A double lock system and round the clock security posted on each floor enhance one's sense of security. In room fax machines and pull out writing ledges at bedside, the desk, and the television console are standard. The personalized, yet unobtrusive attention of the valet adds a special touch. For the business traveler, the Oberoi boasts state of the art communication and a renovated Executive Center is equipped with the latest technology. Two private meeting rooms attached to the business center operate around the clock. Six food and beverage facilities, banquet rooms and conference facilities can accommodate up to 500 people.

Try Baan Thai for Thai food, Kanhadar, the award winning restaurant for Indian cuisine, or LaRochelle—also a top choice—for a continental menu. There is a health club with gymnasium and the hotel overlooks the 18-hole Delhi Golf Club. The shops in corridors off to the left as you enter the lobby offer some of the highest quality goods to be found in Delhi. For antiques, jewelry, or carpets make selections from the shops in the hotel or ask to go to their larger shops located elsewhere in the city. You are just a stone's throw away (though it is across a busy highway and somewhat difficult to get to on foot) from Sunder Nagar Market—a great place to shop for antiques and home decorative items.

❑ **Hotel Imperial:** *Janpath, New Delhi, 110 001, Tel. 91-11-334-1234 or Fax 91-11-334-2255.* If you want a hotel steeped in history but throughly modern in amenities and located so you can step out the door and with a few steps be in the midst of the pulse of the city and near shopping venues galore, Hotel Imperial fits the bill. Located in the middle of eight landscaped acres in the heart of Delhi, the Hotel Imperial has one of the best locations in New Delhi. Close to Connaught Place, it is within easy walking distance of many restaurants and lots of shopping—from the adjacent Tibetan Market and Central Cottage Industries Emporium to a plethora of smaller shops. A short walk from the lobby down a palm lined driveway leads to a world of bazaars, galleries and historical monuments. Winner of several recent customer service awards, the hotel is one of the best kept secrets in Delhi. Recent extensive renovations have given a luxurious look to the 285 guestrooms and suites while retaining the old world charm afforded by the high ceilings, spacious rooms and green palm-fringed grounds. The public areas have also been renovated and restaurants added and updated as well. The regal flourishes of the past blend with modern amenities to provide convenience, comfort, and ambience for today's visitor. Enjoy a meal on the Verandah and recall that Nehru met here frequently with friends or peek into the ballroom and envision Lord Wellington opening the hotel on this spot in 1935. Now after more than 60 years, the service and facilities of the Imperial Hotel still reflect the graciousness of those bygone days. The hotel has been enlarged and thoroughly renovated to meet the standards of the discriminating guests of the new millennium. Conference facilities, business center and fitness facilities available.

❑ **Taj Mahal Hotel:** *Number One Mansingh Road, New Delhi, 110 011, Tel. 91-11-301-6162 or Fax 91-11-301-7299, USA & Canada Toll Free 800-458-8825.* The Taj Mahal Hotel, a member of The Leading Hotels of the World, is located close to the seat of government as well as business and shopping districts and historical sights. Its 300 guestrooms and suites are both tastefully and luxuriously furnished with amenities for both the leisure and business traveler. The guestrooms facing the India Gate and government buildings afford a wonderful evening view of the stately buildings outlined in small lights against the night sky. For those who desire greater exclusivity and pampering, The Taj Club provides up-graded facilities and privileges. These upgrades include: complimentary airport limousine transfer, sit-down check-in and check-out on the Club Floor, early check-in and check-out on an availability basis, welcome drink, 24 hour valet service, complimentary Continental breakfast in the Taj Club lounge, complimentary cocktails and hors d'oeuvres, use of the Club Floor meeting room, tea and coffee throughout the day in the Taj Club lounge, bottle of wine, chocolates, fresh flowers and a fruit basket. Even allergy-free pillows are provided on the Club floors! The Emperor Lounge, beside the main lobby, serves light refreshments. The coffee shop serves a range of Eastern and Western foods in surroundings reminiscent of a south sea island resort—with thatching for a ceiling. The shopping venue, Khazana, which is present in most Taj hotels, offers a wide range of quality Indian crafts, a range of jewelry from inexpensive baubles to fine jewelry, clothing, furniture and decorative items. Includes conference facilities, business center and health facilities.

❑ **Taj Palace Hotel:** *2 Sardar Patel Marg, Diplomatic Enclave, New Delhi, 110 021, Tel. 91-11-301-0404 or Fax 91-11-301-1252, USA & Canada Toll Free 800-458-8825.* Enter the spacious lobby and walk up the wide marble staircase and you will think you are entering a palace. A few more steps and the colorful canopies hung from the ceiling above divans will convince you you're entering an exotic place. A member of the Leading Hotels of the world, the hotel's 421 guestrooms and suites are spacious and tastefully decorated in Western decor with sitting areas and working size desks. Two Club Floors have a private lounge and business center. Rooms on the Business Floor and the two Club Floors have in room fax on request as well as email facility, laptop computer as well as background information on major Indian industries. The luxury Terrace Suites have a terrace garden that expands space available for large gatherings or a private al fresco dining experience. Try the Orient Express award winning restaurant. Set in a railway car, you may feel as if you're in an Agatha Christie novel. Handi, located on the lobby level offers authentic home style food from North and Western India. There is a live "Ghazal" performance every evening. Includes conference facilities, business center and fitness center.

❑ **Maurya Sheraton Hotel & Towers:** *Diplomatic Enclave, New Delhi, 110 021, Tel. 91-11-611-2233 or Fax 91-11-611-3333, USA & Canada Toll Free 800-325-3535.* Located in the Diplomatic Enclave with architecture which gives tribute to the Mauryan Dynasty, this imposing hotel offers luxury, convenience and special services for business travelers. In the large lobby, attractive sitting areas incorporate the colors of a huge folk painting set into the massive overhead dome. Its 500 rooms and 44 uniquely designed suites are designed for comfort. The Sheraton Towers offers eight floors with additional services such as complimentary airport transfers, personalized check-in, use of the Towers Club which includes complimentary full breakfast and Club Hour, use of board rooms, Internet access from each guestroom, interactive television, and even a bon voyage drink at the Welcomgroup airport lounges. The Executive Club offers similar amenities. Kamal Mahal, the conference and banquet center offers sophisticated electronics and professional services. Try the West View restaurant for Western cuisine from around the world or Bukhara for rustic northwest frontier food or Dum Pukht for foods of India's royals. Includes full convention and fitness facilities.

❑ **Hyatt Regency:** *Bhikaji Cama Place, Ring Road, New Delhi, 110 066, Tel. 91-11-688-1234 or Fax 91-11-688-6833, USA & Canada Toll Free 800-233-1234.* A large lobby, clad in soft hues of marble with brass latticed mirrored glass walls overhead, welcomes guests to the Hyatt Regency. A pool connects to a waterfall that spills down to the lower lobby. Handpicked, traditional works of art grace the public areas as well as the 517 guestrooms. Check out the mural-size silver reliefs in the Regency ballroom. The Regency Club floors provide special amenities. Meeting facilities and support are available. Club Olympus is a fully equipped fitness facility. Guests in search of oven-fresh pizzas, al dente pastas and fine wines will head for La Piazza—a casual rustic Italian restaurant. Several quality shops on the lower level.

❑ **Ashok Hotel:** *50B Chanakyapuri, New Delhi 110 021, Tel. 91-11-611-0101 or Fax 91-11-687-3216.* Set in the Diplomatic Enclave, the Ashok is a prominent landmark. The first government owned hotel, its rose colored sandstone exterior with arched and turreted features give it a distinctive appearance and its most enduring feature. From the large sandstone wheel by the entry to artifacts which adorn the spacious, yet low ceiling space of the lobby, you know you are in an Indian hotel. The Ashok offers a choice of 571 guestrooms and suites—most with private balconies. In the morning it is nice to stand on the balcony and listen to the birds who nest in the surrounding trees. Guestrooms are predominantly in Western decor, whereas some deluxe suites have an Indian motif. Guestrooms on several floors have been recently renovated; those that haven't show many signs of being well worn and dimly lit. Includes convention facilities, a business center, fitness facilities available.

❏ **Parkroyal:** Nehru Place, New Delhi, 110 019, Tel. 91-11-622-3344 or Fax 91-11-622-2810. This new hotel in south Delhi is adjacent to the International Trade Towers and the American Shopping Plaza. It seems to be a bit away from the city center, but with a car or taxi this is not a problem. The spacious marble lobby with wood paneled columns welcomes visitors. The 216 well appointed guestrooms and suites are replete with a panoramic view of the city. Try the Delhavi restaurant for authentic Nawabi and Mughlai cuisine or Empress of China for dishes with the emphasis on Szechwan style cuisine. The Lutyen's Club provides attention to business needs, and guests enjoy the Club Lounge with complimentary breakfast and early evening cocktails. Includes conference and business facilities as well as health club.

❏ **New Delhi Hilton:** *Barakhamba Avenue, Connaught Place, New Delhi 100 001, Tel. 91-11-332-0101 or Fax 91-11-332-5335.* Situated at Connaught Place, the New Delhi Hilton is only minutes away from government offices, cultural centers, and shopping malls. It adjoins the commercial complex of the World Trade Center and World Trade Tower. The 445 guestrooms and the 53 designer suites located in an exclusive atrium tower provide expected amenities. There is even an Attorneys' Club Floor for legal professionals! Special rooms have wheelchair access. Three Executive Floors with exclusive Clubroom Lounge serves complimentary breakfast daily. Includes conference facilities and fitness center.

❑ **Claridges:** *12 Aurangzeb Road, New Delhi, 110 011, Tel. 91-11-301-0211 or Fax 91-11-301-0625.* Not far from Connaught Place, this low rise hotel set in an exclusive residential area has a cozy feel. Long-term and repeat visitors appreciate Claridges traditional charm—a reminder of a time when the pace of life was slower and less complicated. One side of the lobby has a British Victorian decor, while the other side replicates an Indian courtyard. The 123 guestrooms and 11 suites are spacious. Some third floor rooms have balconies overlooking the pool. Includes business services and a health club.

Other hotels worth considering include these five- and four-star properties:

❑ **Le Meridien:** *Windsor Place, Janpath, Tel. 91-11-371-0101 or Fax 91-11-371-4545.* Attractive lobby with large, dark atrium with lots of shopping, especially for jewelry.

❑ **Ambassador:** *Sujan Singh Park, Cornwallis Road, New Delhi 110003, 91-11-463-2000 or Fax 91-11-463-2254.* Belonging to the Taj Hotel chain, this old property has a branch of the famous South Indian restaurant, Dasaprakash.

❑ **Oberoi Maidens:** *7 Sham Nath Marg, New Delhi 110054, Tel. 91-11-252-5464 or Fax 91-11-292-9800.* Located right on the line of Old Delhi and New Delhi, this Oberoi property has a hotel training school attached to it. Indeed, this is one of the few places in the world with a working hotel attached to a school. Good value.

❑ **Samrat Hotel:** *Chanakyapuri (behind Ashok Hotel), New Delhi 110021, Tel. 91-11-603-030 or Fax 91-11-687-3216.* Uninspired property but popular with meeting groups and Russian merchants. Guests tend to head for dining and shopping facilities next door at the more inspired, but still gloomy fortress and sister hotel, the Ashok Hotel.

RESTAURANTS

Like Bombay, Delhi is one of India's major centers for fine dining. Within the past few years, most major hotels have paid serious attention to developing the food and beverage side of their businesses. As a result, they have developed a combination of excellent Indian, Continental, and Chinese restaurants, along with some theme restaurants, to cater to the palates of business travelers, tourists, expatriates, and the local upper-middle and upper-classes. A few hotels, such as the Maurya Sheraton, Oberoi, and Taj Mahal, have developed an exceptional set of fine dining restaurants: staying at one of these hotels means never having to go out to eat.

Many of Delhi's restaurants represent the best in the country, offering both fine food and terrific ambience—oases from the hustle and bustle of Delhi's dusty streets. More and more international chefs, especially German, French, Italian, British, and Hong Kong, are in charge of kitchens that turn out Delhi's best Continental and Chinese cuisine. Everything tends to be authentic because most Western food is literally imported from abroad since it's better quality and less expensive to do so than to procure equivalent products in the local markets.

While more expensive than restaurants elsewhere in India, nonetheless, dining out in Delhi is relatively inexpensive by Western standards. A meal for two that might cost US$200 in many major cities in Europe and North America may go for less than US$50 in Delhi. French and Continental dining tends to be very reasonable, especially considering the taxes and costs of importing much of the food as well as the chefs. Consequently, many travelers are pleasantly surprised to discover they can afford to splurge when it comes to fine dining in Delhi.

While some restaurants in the top hotels may prefer jackets for men, most accept smart-casual and casual attire. For dinner, it's a good idea to make reservations since many of the popular restaurants may be fully booked. Here are our picks for the best of the best in Delhi dining:

INDIAN

❑ **Bukhara:** *Maurya Sheraton Hotel, Diplomatic Enclave, Tel. 611-2233, 12:30pm - 3pm and 7:30pm - midnight.* This is one of India's very best Indian (Northwest Frontier cuisine) dining experiences and the flagship restaurant for the famous Bukhara international chain of Indian restaurants.

❑ **Dum Pukht:** *Maurya Sheraton Hotel, Diplomatic Enclave, Tel. 611-2233, 12:30pm - 3pm and 7:30pm - midnight.* Offers the unique Awadh (in Dum Pukht style) cuisine.

❑ **Kandahar:** *The Oberoi, Dr. Zakir Hussain Marg, Tel. 436-3030, 12:30pm - 3pm and 7:30pm - 11:30pm.* Northwest Frontier cuisine served in a beautiful classy setting.

❑ **Frontier:** *Ashok Hotel, 50-B, Chanakyapuri, Tel. 611-0101, ext. 2849, 12:30pm - 2:45pm and 8pm - midnight.* Tandoori cuisine.

❑ **Darbar:** *Ashok Hotel, 50-B, Chanakyapuri, Tel. 611-0101, 12:30pm - 2:30pm and 8pm - 11:30pm.* Indian and Mughlai cuisine.

❑ **Handi:** *Taj Palace Hotel, 2 Sardar Patel Marg, Diplomatic Enclave, Tel. 301-0404, 12:30pm - 3pm, and 7:30pm - midnight.* Muglai and Northwest Frontier cuisine served in elegant surroundings. Buffet lunch and dinner.

❑ **Haveli:** *Taj Mahal Hotel, Tel. 301-6162 (Peshawari), 12:30pm - 3pm and 7:30pm - midnight.* Northern Indian cuisine served in an enchanting old haveli setting.

❑ **Chor Bizarre:** *Hotel Broadway, Asaf Ali Road, Tel. 327-3821, 12:30pm - 3:30pm and 7:30pm - 11:30pm.* Tandoori and Kashmiri cuisine served from tables and chairs collected from various bazaars. Good kebabs.

❑ **Baluchi:** *New Delhi Hilton, Barakhamba Avenue, Tel. 332-0101, 12:30pm - 2:45pm and 7:30pm - midnight.* Northwest Frontier and Tandoori cuisine.

❑ **Dehli Ka Angan:** *Hyatt Regency, Bhikaji Cama Place, Tel. 618-1234, 12 noon - 2:30pm and 7pm - 11:30pm.* Punjabi and Mughlai cuisine. Try the excellent Sunday brunch.

❑ **Pakwan:** *Le Meridien, Windsor Place, Tel. 371-0101, 12:30pm - 3pm and 7:30pm - midnight.* Northwest Frontier cuisine.

❑ **Coconut Grove:** *Ashok Yatri Niwas, 19 Ashok Road, Tel. 332-4511, noon - 3pm and 7pm - 11pm.* South Indian cuisine.

❑ **Delhavi:** *Parkroyal New Delhi, Nehru Place, Tel. 622-3344, ext. 55, noon - 3pm and 7:30pm - 11:30pm.* Mughlai and Nawabi cuisine.

❑ **Sikandra:** *Surya Hotel, New Friends Colony, Tel. 683-5070, 12:30 - 3pm and 8pm - midnight.* Mughlai cuisine.

CONTINENTAL AND FRENCH

❑ **The Orient Express:** *Taj Palace Hotel, 2, Sardar Patel Marg, Tel. 611-0202, 12:30pm - 2:45pm and 7:30pm - 11:45pm.* A converted rail car of Orient Express fame, this exceptional restaurant wins accolades for being the most romantic restaurant in Delhi. Serves four-course, one-price menu which also is one of Delhi's most expensive.

❑ **La Rochelle:** *The Oberoi, Dr. Zakir Hussain Marg, Tel. 436-3030, 12:30pm - 3pm and 7:30pm - 11:45pm.* Once one of Delhi's popular restaurants for French cuisine has been recently changed to fusion cuisine. Run by one of Delhi's very best Western chefs. Elegant setting. Serves large portions

❑ **West View:** *Maurya Sheraton Hotel, Diplomatic Enclave, Tel. 611-2233, 7pm - 11pm.* Western grill. Top floor dining in a beautifully appointed restaurant reminiscent of a cavernous wine cellar. One price menu (with two price options) includes three appetizers, soup, vegetable and meat selections from the grill bar, separate salad and pasta bar, and desert. Grill options include imported steaks, pawns, and salmon (one price option) and local chicken, lamb, and pork (another price option). Go here hungry—it's a ton of excellent food with attentive service.

❑ **Grill Room:** *New Delhi Hilton, Barakhamba Avenue, Tel. 332-0101, 12:30pm - 3pm and 7pm - midnight.* Continental with emphasis on steaks and seafood.

❑ **Captain's Cabin:** *Taj Mahal Hotel, 1, Mansingh Road, Tel. 301-6162, noon - 2:45pm and 7:30 - 11:45pm.* Continental and seafood cuisine. Considered by many to be the best seafood restaurant in the city.

❑ **Longchamp:** *Taj Mahal Hotel, 1, Mansingh Road, Tel. 301-6162, 12:30pm - 2:45pm and 7pm - 11pm.* French cuisine.

❑ **Le Belvedere:** *Le Meridien Hotel, Windsor Place, Tel. 371-0101, 12:30pm - 2:45pm and 7:30pm - midnight.* Continental and Indian cuisine.

❑ **Le Pierre:** *Le Meridien Hotel, Windsor Place, Tel. 371-0101, 12:30pm - 3pm and 7:30pm - midnight.* French cuisine with Delhi's only flambe menu.

❑ **Burgundy**: *Ashok Hotel, 50-B, Chanakyapuri, Tel. 611-0101, Ext. 2842.* French cuisine.

CHINESE

❑ **Bali Hi:** *Maurya Sheraton Hotel, Diplomatic Enclave, Tel. 611-2233, 7:30pm - 12:30am.*

❑ **Tea House of the August Moon:** *Taj Palace Hotel, 2, Sardar Patel Marg, Tel. 611-0202, 12:30pm - 2:45pm and 7:30pm - 11:45pm.* Cantonese, Szechuan, Shanghai, and Haka cuisine.

❑ **House of Ming:** *Taj Mahal Hotel, 1, Mansingh Road, Tel. 301-6162, 12:30pm - 3pm and 8pm - midnight.* Szechuan and Cantonese cuisine.

❑ **Noble House:** *Hotel New Delhi Hilton, Barakhamba Avenue, Tel. 332-0101, 12:30pm - 3pm and 7:30pm - 11:30pm.* Szechuan, Hakka and Cantonese cuisine.

❑ **Empress of China:** *Parkroyal Hotel, Nehru Place, Tel. 622-3344, noon - 3pm and 7:30pm - 11pm.* Szechuan cuisine.

❑ **Taipan:** *The Oberoi, Dr. Zakir Hussain Marg, Tel. 436-3030, 12:30pm - 3pm and 8pm - midnight.* Szechuan and Cantonese cuisine.

❑ **TK's, The Oriental Grill:** *Hyatt Regency, Bhikaji Cama Place, Tel. 618-1234, 12:30pm - 2:30pm and 7pm - 11:30pm.* Chinese, Indonesian, Thai, and Japanese cuisine served Teppanyaki style.

❑ **Jade Garden:** *Claridges Hotel, 12 Aurangzeb Road, Tel. 301-0211, 12:30pm - 2:30pm and 8pm - 11:30pm.* Hunan, Cantonese, and Mandarin cuisine.

Italian, Thai, Japanese, Mexican, and Other

Delhi also is seeing the increasing presence of a variety restaurants offering a range of international cuisine. More and more Japanese, Thai, Mexican, and Italian restaurants are appearing on Delhi's dining scene. Many of these restaurants are found in the major hotels or in the Hauz Khas Village area.

❑ **La Piazza:** *Hyatt Regency Hotel, Bhikaji Cama Place, Tel. 618-1234.* Italian cuisine. One of the most popular new Italian restaurants in the city. Very popular for Sunday brunch.

❑ **Baan Thai:** *Oberoi Hotel, Dr. Zakir Hussain Marg, Tel. 436-3030, 12:30pm - 3pm and 8pm - midnight.* Outstanding Thai cuisine. Considered one of Delhi's very best restaurants. Nice ambience.

❑ **Sukhothai:** *24, Hauz Khas Village, Tel. 685-3846, 12:30 - 3pm and 7:30pm to 11:30pm.* Located on the third floor of Jharokha, one of Delhi's best art and home decorative shops. Good Thai cuisine.

❑ **Cafe Pedro:** *19, Hauz Khas Village, Tel. 696-1789, noon - 3:30pm and 7pm - midnight.* Mexican cuisine.

❑ **Duke's Place:** *Hauz Khas Village, Tel. 686-4909, noon - 3:30pm and 8pm - 11:30pm.* Italian cuisine.

❑ **EGO:** *4, Community Centre, New Friends Colony, Tel. 631-8185, noon - midnight.* Italian cuisine.

❑ **Ichiban:** *9, Pandara Road Market, Tel. 338-6689, noon - 3:30pm and 7pm - midnight.* Chinese and Japanese cuisine.

❑ **Las Meninas:** *The Park, 15 Parliament Street, Tel. 373-3737, noon - 2:45pm and 8pm - 11:45pm.* Spanish cuisine.

❑ **Mezza Luna:** *17, Hauz Khas Village, Tel. 651-2552, 1pm - 3:30pm and 8pm - 11:30pm.* French, Italian, and Swiss cuisine.

❑ **The Blue Elephant:** *New Delhi Hilton, Barakhamba Avenue, Tel. 332-0101, 7:30pm - 1am.* Thai cuisine. Excellent view and ambience.

❑ **T.G.I. Friday's:** *62 Vasant Lok, Vasant Vihar 57, Tel. 614-0964, noon - 11pm.* International cuisine.

❑ **Tokyo:** *Ashok Hotel, 50-B, Chanakyapuri, Tel. 611-0101, 12:30pm - 3:45pm and 7:30pm - 11pm.* Japanese cuisine served in a nice setting. Go upstairs for more traditional seating.

FAST FOOD

Fast food restaurants have been anything but fast in coming to Delhi or, for that matter, India. Indeed, the near absence of such restaurants seems remarkable given their pervasive presence in most major cities of the world. But this is not surprising given India's long-standing closed door policies toward international food and beverage companies. Indeed, only recently have Coca Cola and Pepsi been permitted to operate in India, and at a loss. Nonetheless, you will find a few of these international fast food favorites in Delhi: **Domino's Pizza** (M-40, Greater Kailash II, Tel. 691-6540, 11am - 11pm); **KFC** (20, Community Centre, New Friends Colony, Tel. 692-4544, 11am - 11pm); **McDonald's** (10 Basant Lok Community Centre, Vasant Vihar, 10:30am - 11pm); **Pizza Hut** (No. 1, Convenience Shopping Centre, Street 7, Shanti Niketan, Tel. 687-8002, 11am - 11pm); **Wimpy** (N-6, Janpath, C.P. 1); and **Nirula's** (nine locations).

SEEING THE SITES

In addition to shopping, hotels, and restaurants, there are lots of other things to see and do in Delhi. This is a city of many monuments and museums. If you love sightseeing, or just want to sample the highlights of the city, we recommend joining a half or full-day tour (see our tour recommendations near the beginning of this chapter) or renting a car and driver or hire a licensed government tour guide (contact the Government of India Tourist Office at 88 Janpath; open Monday to Friday, 9am to 6pm, and Saturday, 9am to 2pm, Tel. 332-0008). Delhi's major tourist highlights include:

OLD DELHI

❑ **Lal Qila (Red Fort):** Constructed by Emperor Shah Jahan of Agra fame in 1638, this impressive red sandstone fort of palaces and inner courtyards is one of the best surviving examples of grand Mughal architecture. Highly recommend attending the imaginative sound-and-light show (Purana Quila) which takes place every evening at sunset, except during the rainy season (July to September) and on cold evenings in January. This well done show provides a nice historical overview, beginning with developments at Indraprastha and ending with Indian Independence in 1947. For details, call 462-9365 or 460-3178.

❑ **Chandni Chowk (Silver Street):** Located near the entrance of the Red Fort, this maze of street and alleys is Old Delhi's busiest commercial area. Once, when designed by Shan Jahan's daughter in the 17th century, an attractive area of mansions and gardens which is now dominated by a series of crowded and chaotic markets and crumbling buildings.

❑ **Jama Masjid:** Located opposite the Red Fort, this massive (120 x 201 feet) mosque, with two impressive 130 foot (40 meter) minarets, was completed by Emperor Shah Jahan in 1656. It remains India's largest mosque. Open daily 7am - noon and 2pm - 5pm, although you may want to skip Friday which is prayer day. Can visit minarets.

❑ **Rajghat:** Located not far from the Red Fort, along the banks of the Yumuna River, this is the memorial to the much revered Mahatma Gandhi, the Father of the Nation. The black marble platform marks the spot where Gandhi was cremated in 1948. The grounds also include memorials to Jawaharlal Neher, Lal Bahadur Shastri, Indira Gandhi, and Rajiv Gandhi.

❑ **Charity Bird Hospital:** *Nataji Subhas Marg, across from Lal Qila, 8am - 8pm.* Started by the Jains in 1956, this unique hospital nurses injured pigeons, parrots, sparrows, and other animals. Operates with donations from visitors and contributions from others.

CENTRAL DELHI

❑ **Connaught Place (Rajiv Gandhi Chowk):** The bustling but worn commercial center and shopping arcade of downtown Delhi located new the New Delhi Railway

Station. A major center for offices, shops, restaurants, bars, budget hotels, tourist agencies, and touts. Distinctive British colonial heritage architecture (colonnaded verandas and corridors) characterizes the buildings which are laid out in two concentric circles that also serve as expansive traffic circles. The underground Palika Bazaar is located near the southern side (Janpath) of the circle. Roads radiate in all directions from the circle, with the busiest street being Janpath, which is lined with shops and vendor stalls.

❑ **Crafts Museum:** *Pragati Bhavan, Mathura Road, Tel. 331-7641, 10am - 5pm, closed Monday.* Very nice exhibits of quality crafts from all over India. Includes examples of over 20,000 crafts, from 18th to 20th centuries, displaced in a re-created "Village Complex." Demonstration area with craftsmen at work. Be sure to stop and shop at the crafts shop. Can also purchase from the craftsmen. A great stop on any sightseeing or shopping itinerary.

❑ **Dolls Museum:** *Nehru House, Bahadur Shah Zafar Marg, open 10am - 6pm, closed Monday.* Displays over 6,000 dolls. Popular with collectors and children.

❑ **India Gate:** *The east end of Rajpath.* This impressive 136 foot (42 meter) arch serves as the war memorial to those Indians who died in World War I. Includes an eternal flame in memory of the unknown soldier.

❑ **Jantar Mantar:** *Just south of Connaught Place, off of Parliament Street, and west of Janpath (immediately north of the Hotel Imperial).* A very interesting observatory, with an impressive 40-foot stone sundial at the center, designed by the great astronomer King Sawai Jai Singh II of Jaipur in 1724 for observing the stars and planets.

❑ **National Gallery of Modern Art:** *Jaipur House, near India Gate, Tel. 338-2835, 10am - 5pm (closed Monday).* Housed in the former residence of the Maharaja of Jaipur, this gallery showcases major works by contemporary Indian artists as well as some Western artists who painted on India. Can purchase reproductions at the reception desk.

❑ **National Museum:** *Janpath, Tel. 301-9538, 10am to 5pm, closed Monday.* One of India's very best museums.

Houses a comprehensive collection of Central Asian and Indian artefacts, from prehistoric times to the present. Especially noted for its sculptures and jewelry.

❑ **Nehru Memorial Museum and Library:** *Teen Murti House, Tel. 301-6734, 9:30am - 4:45pm (museum) and 9am - 7pm (library), closed Monday.* Showcases photos, memorabilia, and personal items of Jawaharlal Nehru

❑ **Parliament House:** West end of Rajpath. This architecturally impressive building houses both the upper and lower houses of parliament.

❑ **National Zoological Park:** *Located at the end of Rajpath near Purana Qila, the 15th century fort, and Sunder Nagar Market, 9:30am - 5:30pm, closed Friday.* This 214-acre park is one of the country's best zoological parks with lots of interesting wildlife and pleasant grounds. Includes the largest number of white tigers in captivity. Take peanuts for the birds.

SOUTH DELHI

❑ **Humayun's Tomb:** Built in the 16th century by Emperor Humayun's wife, this white marble and red sandstone tomb with high arched entrances is a good example of Mughal architecture.

❑ **Lodi Gardens:** *Lodi Estate (Lady Willingdon Park).* Popular with morning walkers and picnickers, this relaxing park includes beautifully landscaped gardens and the tombs of the 14th and 15th century Lodi and Sayyed dynasties.

❑ **Dilli Haat:** *Near Lodi Estates and across the street from the INA Market.* India's first permanent fair for crafts, food, and cultural activities.

❑ **Lotus/Bahai Temple:** *Bahapur, Kalkaji, near Nehru Place (9 kilometers southeast of Connaught Place).* Completed in 1986, this distinctively designed Bahai temple, in the shape of a blossoming white lotus flower, is an architectural masterpiece. From a distance, it has similar features to Sydney, Australia's Opera House.

- **National Rail Museum:** *Chanakyapur, Tel. 601-816, 9:30am - 5pm (closed Monday).* An interesting collection of 26 vintage locomotives 17 carriages and salons, including fire engines, carriages, and coaches from the days of the Nizams, Maharajas, and Rajs.

- **Qutab Minar:** This impressive 234 foot (73 meter) red and buff stone victory tower was constructed by Delhi's first Muslim ruler, Qutab-ud-din Aibac, at the end of the 12th century. The popular grounds also include an iron pillar, mosque, tombs, and other interesting structures.

ENTERTAINMENT

Delhi's nightlife tends to be very sedate—nothing like the party city of Mumbai. Most entertainment tends to be centered around the major hotels which have bars, lounges, and discos. Many of the cultural performances take place in the India International Centre (40 Lodi Estate, Tel. 461-9431) as well as several other auditoriums. For information on the latest in art, dance, film, music, and theater, see the "Timeout" section of *First City* as well as the *Delhi Diary*, both of which are available in most major hotels.

Delhi's major entertainment highlights include:

NIGHTCLUBS/DISCOS

- **Annabelles:** New Delhi Hilton, Tel. 332-0101, 10pm - 2am.

- **CJ's:** Le Meridien, Tel. 371-0101, 10pm - 2am.

- **Ghungroo:** Maurya Sheraton Hotel, Tel. 301-0101, 10pm - 3:30am

- **Mirage:** Best Western Surya Hotel, Tel. 6783-5070.

- **My Kind of Place:** Taj Palace Hotel, Tel. 301-0404, 10pm - 2am.

- **Oasis:** The Hyatt Regency, Tel. 618-1234, 10pm - 2am.

- **Someplace Else:** The Park, Tel. 373-3737, 10pm - 2am.

BARS/LOUNGES

❑ **Captain's Cabin:** Taj Mahal Hotel, 1 Mansingh Road, Tel. 301-6162.

❑ **Club Bar:** The Oberoi, Dr. Zakir Hussain Road, Tel. 436-3030.

❑ **Polo Lounge:** Hyatt Regency Hotel, Bhikaiji Cama Place, Ring Road, Tel. 618-1234.

❑ **Viceroy:** Claridges, 12 Aurangzeb Road, Tel. 301-0211.

JAZZ CLUBS

❑ **Jazz Bar:** Maurya Sheraton Hotel, Diplomatic Enclave, Tel. 301-0101.

SOUND AND LIGHT SHOWS

❑ **Red Fort:** One of the best sound and light shows in India. Begins with the dramatic developments at Indrapratha and ends with achieving Independence in 1947. Held nightly, except during the rainy season (July to September) and on cold evenings in January. Conducts both Hindi and English language programs. The English programs take place at 7:30 - 8:30pm (November to January), 8:30 - 9:30pm (February to April and September to October), and 9-10pm (May to August). For details, call 327-4580. Be sure to take mosquito repellant with you.

CULTURE

❑ **Dances of India:** *Parsi Anjuman Hall, Bahadurshan Zafar Marg, opposite Ambedkar Football Stadium, Delhi Gate, Tel. 331-7831 (call for reservations).* Daily performances of six classical, tribal, and folk dances.

8

Varanasi

Welcome to one of India's most unique and fascinating cities, the spiritual center for Hindus. Varanasi is to Hinduism what Jerusalem is to Christianity and Mecca is to Islam—its most holy city. It is also an important religious center for Muslims and Buddhists. But most people go to Varanasi because of its temples and unique waterfront rituals performed by Hindus. Miss these activities and you'll miss what Varanasi is all about—India's spiritual treasures. It's one of India's greatest outdoor cultural theaters. Some people even believe this is the "real" India. It isn't. It's just another dimension of exotic, multi-faceted India.

DOWN ALONG THE SACRED RIVER

You have to see it to believe it. This is a drama with a most unusual and colorful cast of characters. There's never a dull moment here as Varanasi's street and water scenes completely assault one's senses. From sunrise to sunset, each day thousands of Hindus from all over India, as well as from other countries (over 5,000 new arrivals), come to Varanasi to perform rituals in the sacred waters of the Ganges River. Early each morning these pilgrims flock to its banks of concrete and stone staircases (ghats) that lead to the water's edge to worship, meditate, and perform their ritual cleansings as the sun rises. Lined with over 90 bathing ghats, the river is a ritual center: each pilgrim must make ritual dips in five main ghats in order to wash away their sins and to attain enlightenment (*moksha*). Most visit the temples; some consult with priests perched on wooden platforms; others partially disrobe and descend into river to ritualistically wash away their sins; and still others come here to cremate the bodies of loved ones or to both sanctify and celebrate marriage. In the midst of all these sacred activities, boat loads of tourists paddle by photographing this unique parade of daily rituals. At the same time, tourists, pilgrims, sadhus, beggars, vendors, and cows wander through the colorful and sometimes eccentric crowds.

INTO THE OLD CITY AND ITS LANES

Just a few meters behind the ghats lies the old city with its labyrinth of narrow and winding streets, lanes, and alleys lined with aging homes, workshops, shops, stalls, temples, shrines, religious monuments, ashrams, palaces, and museums. This whole area is reminiscent of a medieval city, a Middle Eastern souk, or the chaos of Marrakesh. You can easily get caught up in the crowds and get lost here, but not for long. There are enough tourists and locals wandering through these areas to assist you with a proper exit.

As you will quickly discover, Varanasi's treasures and pleasures are primarily spiritual in nature—more so than any other city in India. If you spend some time here, you'll know there is something very magical and mystical about this place. Like some other Western tourists who come here and "go native" for a few days, you may even undergo your own spiritual transformation in the process!

AN ANCIENT AND TIMELESS CITY

Varanasi is India's oldest city, with a history of over 3,000 years, which also makes it one of the world's oldest continuously inhabited cities. And it shows again and again as you explore the well worn streets, lanes, and waterfront of what is simultaneously a mystical, magical, and maddening old city. Its narrow winding streets and lanes are transversed by a constant stream of mixed humanity that seems to bridge centuries of transportation modes, occupations, classes, and apparel. If it weren't for the honking horns, lumbering motorized vehicles, florescent street lights, and frequent power outages, you could easily forget you are at the dawn of the 21st century or, for that matter, the 20th, 19th, 18th, or 10th centuries. There is a certain timeless character to this place that spans more than two millenniums. It is the most unique and exotic place to visit in India as well as perhaps in the world.

If you've just come from Mumbai or Delhi, where you thought you had encountered a high degree of chaos, poverty, and filth, Varanasi will certainly put these other places in better perspective. You haven't seen anything until you've been in Varanasi. Everything seems magnified here. Indeed, the visual chaos of a city overwhelmed by people could momentarily shock you. Varanasi is steeped in all of the above and to a much greater degree than other cities in India. It's first of all one of India's most chaotic cities —frequently characterized by complete bedlam of people, animals, and vehicles in the old city. Indeed, occasionally the traffic literally grinds to a halt at nonfunctioning intersections as traffic police attempt to unsnarl an amazing, colorful, and noisy web of traffic composed of competing bicycles, cycle-rickshaws, auto-rickshaws, motorcycles, motor-scooters, pushcarts, buses, trucks, cars, pedestrians, cows, and a herd of water buffalo seemingly locked into battle for advancing to the next inch of available pavement. It's an incredible free-for-all that somehow gets untangled and works in the end. Neither pictures nor words—only your presence—could do justice to this amazing sea of bobbing humanity and vehicles.

- ❑ You can easily get caught up in the crowds and get lost here, but not for long.
- ❑ This is simultaneously a mystical, magical, and maddening old city.
- ❑ There's a certain timeless character to this place that spans more than two millenniums.
- ❑ Occasionally the traffic literally grinds to a halt as traffic police appear hopeless in attempting to unsnarl an amazing, colorful, and noisy web of traffic.
- ❑ Varanasi is filled with some of India's poorest people who come here out of destitution.
- ❑ This definitely is a cultural experience sometimes jokingly referred to as the "burning and learning" city, a place noted for its crematories and three universities.

Second, while basically a working class community, Varanasi is filled with some of India's poorest people who come here out of destitution. You may encounter more beggars and touts per meter than in most other places in India. Especially early in the morning near the banks of the Ganges, when tourists arrive to view the sunrise, the beggars line the walkways, seemingly coming out from nowhere in what appears to be a medieval street drama or characters from Les Miserables—old men and

women, young people, children, lepers, and the deformed; you
name it and they will come to you. If the beggars don't get you,
the young touts offering products you neither need nor want
may pester you to death. After all, most pilgrims who come here
have little or no attachment to the material world—only the
tourists offer material satisfaction. Many riverfront arrivals are
simply destitute, having traveled here to be spiritually connected to the next life. Some come here to die, joining the many
hundreds of others whose bodies are consumed on the funeral
pyres along the Ganges River each week. Indeed, Varanasi
easily qualifies as the world's largest outdoor hospice; the
charred remains of over 60,000 bodies are thrown into the river
each year.

Third, this is a very dirty, unsanitary city with open drain-
age ditches filled with trash and frequently used by men as
public urinals; pock-marked streets amply supplied with fresh
cow, horse, and goat dung; piles of fresh garbage alongside the
streets being picked by both humans and animals; restaurants
and cafes that look like breeding grounds for Hepatitis A and B;
and heavy noise and air pollution from the many cars, motorbikes, buses, and trucks that crowd this city's antiquated and
dusty streets. Major sections of the city at times look like they
are in some stage of being condemned or razed.

Is there beauty in this beast? Is this another case of charming chaos best experienced from the window of an air-conditioned car or viewed later in a colorful photo album of exotic
pictures minus the trash, sounds, and smells? Perhaps all of
these negatives can be easily explained away, or risen above,
from a spiritual perspective. Unless you are a devout Hindu
who can transcend all the negatives of Varanasi's material
world, there is nothing particularly attractive about this city. It
definitely is a cultural experience sometimes jokingly referred to
as the "burning and learning city"—a city dominated by
crematories and three universities. Since it has been materially
neglected and abused for the sake of the spiritual world, you
will have to appreciate the city on a very different plane than
what you may be used to when visiting other places in India. If
you can trek through the filth and manage the beggars and
pests, Varanasi may even enlighten you as you focus your
attention on the ritual bathings along the sacred Ganges River
or on the magical moments discovered at temples and even
along the congested streets and lanes of the old city.

To really appreciate Varanasi, you'll need to take a little
time to put this place into a larger spiritual perspective and to
consume the incredible visual feast unfolding before your eyes.
Walk its streets and lanes; take a cycle-rickshaw through rush

hour traffic; cruise the Ganges to view the riverfront rituals; or just sit on the sidelines and watch the parade of fascinating people, faces, and activities, and you'll know you have entered a different place and time. This is definitely a place from which many of your more interesting India travel stories will get told over and over in the years to come!

ARRIVING AND SURVIVING

POPULATION AND LOCATION

Located along the west bank of the sacred Ganges River, Varanasi is 765 kilometers from Delhi, 677 kilometers from Calcutta, 606 kilometers from Agra, 320 kilometers from Lucknow, and 125 kilometers from Allahabad. A city of approximately 1.3 million people, thousands of additional people visit this city each day as pilgrims and tourists.

GETTING THERE

Air connections to Varanasi are not great. Only a few cities are directly connected to Varanasi via **Indian Airlines**: Delhi, Mumbai, Agra, Lucknow, and Kathmandu. If you want to fly from Mumbai to Varanasi, you'll have to change planes in Delhi. Be sure to check on domestic routings before you plan your trip to India. The Varanasi connection may affect your other connections in India. The direct connection to Agra is especially convenient if you are making the Delhi-Jaipur-Agra trip. A few other airlines also link to Varanasi: **ModiLuft**, **Sahara Airlines**, and **U.P. Airways**. The closest airport is 22 kilometers from the city at **Babatpur**.

Varanasi is connected to all major cities by train. The Rajdhani Express train from Delhi takes 9 hours; the Poorva Express takes 12 hours. Two trains connect Calcutta with Varanasi and they take from 11 to 15 hours to make the Calcutta-Varanasi run.

Given the long road distances between Varanasi and such major cities as Delhi and Calcutta, it's most convenient to reach Varanasi by air than by road or train.

ARRIVAL BY AIR

If you arrive by air, you'll land at the small Varanasi Airport at Babatpur which is about 22 kilometers from the city. The arrival area is a small room that also serves as the baggage retrieval and transportation areas. Here you will find porters, luggage carts, and car rental and bus transportation desks. A sign opposite the luggage belt lists the fixed rates for porters and the bus. The bus costs Rs 25 per person and it stops at most major hotels. However, be aware that several freelance guides and taxi drivers also want your business. Many work with the personnel at the bus desk who will give them your bus ticket for a "free" taxi ride to the city. If you are approached by someone who says he represents your hotel, chances are he is working with the taxi drivers and guides (they come in twos); legitimate hotel representatives hold up signs and almost look official. The freelancer will put you in a taxi with a driver and guide who will take you to your hotel for the cost of the bus ride, but during the trip they will try to sell you on their tour services. Since this is their only opportunity to give you a "sales pitch," you may feel pressured to use their services. Don't. Tell them you need to think about it and maybe get back with them after you have had a chance to check into your room. They may at this point plead poverty—they lost money bringing you in from the airport "free". That's their problem. In fact, most of these taxis come back from the airport empty anyway since the fares from the city to the airport (about Rs 325) are figured as one-way out and an empty return. Any business they can drum up this way is really icing on the cake. Don't worry; they are not really losing money on this scheme or it would not continue.

If you get taken into the city by one of these guides and drivers, you may want to use them for some sightseeing. Be sure to bargain for an hourly, half day, or daily rate. They should cost you about Rs 150-200 per hour or US$30-$40 per day, depending on the quality of the guide and car. At the same time, check with your hotel about alternative tour services. You may want to connect with a professional guide rather than one of the airport freelancers.

Leaving the airport can be somewhat confusing since signs and the public address system are next to worthless. After checking in, you'll need to find your gate which is in another section of the building. Just follow the "drinking water" sign to your right, turn left, and you'll eventually find the area on your left. If not, ask where to go. If you haven't gone through security, you know you're not at your gate! Once in your departure lounge, keep an eye on the planes and make friends with some other passengers who look like they might know where they are going. The public address system is garbled. Although the whole area is over staffed, no one seems to be doing anything useful other than creating more chaos by leading passengers one-by-one outside to identify their bags (their so-called system for security). You'll have to walk outside to identify your baggage which will be piled on a baggage cart. If someone approaches you in the departure lounge, or the person who takes you outside says he's your personal "porter" for identifying your bags, ignore his not-so-subtle "please tip me for this service" demeanor. These people are always finding inventive ways to hit up tourists for a few extra rupees.

ORIENTATION

The first thing you need to know about the city is that it's divided into new and old sections. The newer part of the city is a few kilometers west of the river and centered around the Cantonment area (The Mall—this is the major hotel street, not a shopping mall) which is where most of Varanasi's major hotels are located. The streets here are wider and less congested—some even tree-lined—than in the old section of the city. However, during rush hour, which seems to run from 8am to 7pm, it may take over one hour to go the few kilometers from this area to the old city along the river. The traffic here emphasizes once again the old saying that *"Nothing comes easy in India!"*

Many of Varanasi's major attractions are found in the old city which borders on the Ganges River with its concrete and stone ghats that stretch for more than four miles along the river banks. You can't miss this section—it's where all the people, animals, and vehicles seem to congregate along narrow and winding beetle-stained streets, lanes, and alleys that lace the many temples, shrines, ashrams, museums, and shops that are found behind the ghats and temples fronting the river. This is the most congested as well as the dirtiest and noisiest part of the city. If you stay in one of the major hotels in the newer part of the city, getting from there to the banks of river in the old city (about 5 kilometers) may take anywhere from one half hour to one and a half hours, depending on the traffic situation. And traffic can be horrendous during much of the day, especially in mid afternoon. You can expect to spend an hour in this densely packed traffic that often crawls at a snail's pace. In fact, the situation may get so bad that you may want to abandon your vehicle and walk the rest of the way (be careful not to get hit by a vehicle). Traffic very early in the morning (6am), the time when most tourists go to see the sunrise on the river, is much lighter. Indeed, at this hour you can make the trip from the Cantonment area to the river banks within 20 minutes.

NAVIGATING THE CITY

You have numerous alternatives for navigating Varanasi and the nearby Buddhist city of Sarnath. The easiest and most convenient way of tackling this place—our best recommendation—is to hire a car with driver and guide. It's relatively inexpensive to do so and the comfort and convenience factors are well worth the pittance you pay. Expect to spend about Rs 150-200 an hour or Rs 1200 to Rs 1800 a day. That comes to about US$3-5 an hour or US$30-40 a day. After you experience the traffic and crowds, you'll think such charges are the best spent money in Varanasi!

If you want to get closer to the locals and really experience heavy doses of noise and air pollution, rent cycle-rickshaws and horse-drawn tongas or take auto-rickshaws and the buses. We recommend doing so only as a short cultural experience. The trishaws can be great fun and they are cheap (Rs 60 per hour) and the motorized trishaws are faster (Rs 120 per hour), but they are not great fun nor a good deal if you get stuck in the traffic for an hour or more which can easily happen in Varanasi.

Navigating the city on your own is very difficult for two reasons: maps are either nonexistent or incomprehensible (small print and few details make them next to useless) and the city is complete chaos. You need someone who can show you the way through the chaotic labyrinth of streets, lanes, people, animals, and vehicles.

TOURIST OFFICES AND TOURS

Several government tourist offices and information centers operate in Varanasi: **Government of India Tourist Office** (15B, The Mall, Varanasi Cantt, Tel. 43744), **Government of India Tourist Information Counter** (Babatput Airport, open during flight times), **UP Tourist Office** (Parade Kothi, Tel. 43486), and **UP Tourist Information Counter** (Railway Station, Tel. 43670). These offices provide brochures, answer questions, and can arrange tours and guides.

Several tour agencies operate in and around Varanasi. You may want to check with your hotel front desk for recommendations. Some hotels have agency offices in the shopping arcade areas. Two of best agencies include **T.C.I.** (Travel Corporation India, Tel. 346-298) and **SITA World Travel** (Tel. 348-445). You can call these agencies and they will send a representative to your hotel to outline various tour options. Most have a standard set of tours, but you may want to customize a tour around your particular interests and ask for a guide who is very knowledgeable and whose English is very good. We recommend hiring a guide for a full day or a day and a half (depending on how fast you can get your guide to move) which would include covering the usual tourist sites and activities, such as sunrise on the Ganges, a walk through the lanes of the old city, visits to a few temples, and a trip to nearby Sarnath. You also may want to customize your tour to include several shopping destinations as outlined in this chapter as well as a trip to the university and, if time permits, a stop at the Diesel Locomotive Factory. A good evening activity would include a cultural performance (music and dance) on the banks of the river.

GETTING TO KNOW YOU

Previously known as Kashi, the city that illuminates, and also referred to as Banaras by local residents, Vanarasi is a melting pot of religious pilgrims, curious tourists, and a variety of religious and ethnic groups. Located an hour's flight southeast of Delhi, Vanarasi is a city of approximately 1.3 million people. Situated along the Ganges River, this is India's oldest and holiest city. It's a city of over 2,000 temples and shrines, most of which are devoted to Shiva. Thousands of Hindu pilgrims come here each year to visit various temples and to be reborn through ritual cleansings in the polluted waters of the river or to die and be cremated in one of the two open-air crematoriums along the banks of the river. Its more peaceful neighboring city of **Sarnath**, located 11 kilometers north of Vanarasi, is one of Buddhism's most important places—where the Lord Buddha preached his first sermon and revealed Buddhism's doctrine of the eight-fold path. If you visit Varanasi, you definitely should visit Sarnath. The contrasts between Varanasi's Hinduism and Sarnath's Buddhism are quite interesting. Varanasi also is an important center for Muslims who make up 25 percent of the local population. Its **Gynavapi Mosque**, located adjacent to the famous Vishwanath Golden Temple of the Hindus, was built during the 17th century over the ruins of the former Vishwanath Temple. Today, both are heavily guarded by gun-touting security personnel.

Vanarasi is not all about religion. It's also an important center for higher learning, music, silk brocade, carpets, and locomotive production. **Banaras Hindu University**, located in the southern section of the city, is Asia's largest residential university with over 20,000 students. The university also is noted for its excellent music and dance productions, and Varanasi is home to India's most famous musical instrument, the *Sitar*, and its most internationally famous musician, Ravi Shankar. Several silk factories and cooperatives produce the unique Vanarasi silk brocade which is made into bed covers, sarees, shawls, tablecloths, and wall hangings. Vanarasi also is a famous carpet production center; its wool double-knotted carpets appear in many local shops and they are exported abroad. And Vanarasi is the center for the design and production of India's locomotives at the Diesel Locomotive Works Factory and Diesel Locomotive Works Colony southwest of the city.

There's plenty to see and do in Varanasi and neighboring Buddhist center of Sarnath. Most visitors spend two days here which should be enough time for covering the area's major sites and shopping. Three or more days here and you are likely to run out of things to do or you've decided to become a pilgrim!

SHOPPING VARANASI

Most visitors come to Varanasi because of its religious appeal. However, the city also offers some unique shopping opportunities centered around its pilgrims and its famous industries. Given Varanasi's fame for silk and embroidery work, you will most likely be approached by touts who will invite you to their "family" or "uncle's" factory or shop for a cup of tea. Try to resist such invitations since you will most likely waste a lot of time as a "captive" of a well organized demonstration and sales operation—similar in many respects to Kashmiri rug merchants who hold visitors captive with monotonous rug demonstrations and high pressure sales tactics!

Unlike many other large cities in India, Varanasi does not have a major one-stop-shop government emporium where you can compare products and prices. It does have a few small state emporiums, such as **UPICA** (Nadesar, Cantt), **UP Handlooms** (Lahurabir and Bula Nala), **Tantuja** (Bengal Emporium, Dasaswamedh Road), and **Mahatex** (Maharashtra Emporium, Godowlia). Consequently, you're on your own when it comes to shopping in Varanasi. Expect to be approached by many touts and quoted high prices. Be prepared to bargain for everything and to trust no one on prices and quality. Unlike our other cities, we are reluctant to identify the "best of the best" for shopping in Varanasi. While you'll find lots of shopping in Varanasi, it's not particularly exciting and you probably won't have to worry about shipping purchases from Varanasi, unless you purchase a large rug. Much of the shopping is disappointing, with designs being very traditional and ethnic. Nonetheless, you might discover some interesting treasures here.

WHAT TO BUY

☐ **Silk, brocade fabrics, and clothes:** Varanasi is well known throughout India and the world for producing beautiful silk brocades and Banares sarees, many of which are works of art. The most beautiful silks are woven with pure gold and silver, and embroideries come in many unique and elaborate designs. Famous American and European dress designers use Varanasi silk and brocade fabrics in their work, and the elaborate brocades are often used for Indian wedding sarees. Many of the textile shops also operate as silk weaving factories with small cottage looms on display. Visit the **Government Weaving Centre** (Chauka Ghat, Tel. 43834) and **Subhan Ali & Sons** (J. 14/178-A, Qazi Sadullahpura, Tel. 210-189) for weaving demonstrations and displays of sarees, brocade silk, natural silk, embroideries, and dress materials. Some of the best selections are found at two shops in the central Chowk Bazaar area: **Brij Raman Das** and **Ushnak Malmulchan**.

☐ **Ornamental brass work:** This is another Varanasi specialty. Look for numerous functional and decorative pieces, from candle holders to boxes. **Thatheri Bazaar** is well stocked with brass work.

☐ **Carpets:** Varanasi is well known throughout India for its expensive Bhadohi silk carpets. Indeed, many people refer to Varanasi as "the carpet capital of India." **Cottage Industries Exposition Ltd.** (Mint House, Nadesar, Tel. 344026) has a large display of Varanasi carpets amongst its many Kashmiri carpets.

☐ **Musical instruments:** Varanasi is famous for it musicians (Ravi Shankar) and musical instruments. If you're in the market for a sitar, there's no better place in the world to buy a sitar than in Varanasi. Visit one of the master craftsmen: **Radhey Shyam Sharma** (52/34E Luxmi Kund, behind New Imperial Hotel).

☐ **Art:** Varanasi has a budding art community as well as offers art from other areas in India. For good examples of contemporary Indian paintings, visit **ABC Art Gallery** (opposite Tulsi Manas Temple, Durgakund Road, Tel. 310-434, open 3-7pm only in Winter, October - March).

❏ **Crafts/Curios:** Varanasi's bazaars are filled with all types of crafts and curios. It's especially noted for glass beads which it exports worldwide. Head for the city center, around **Chowk**, **Godowlia**, **Vishwanath Lane**, **Gyanvapi**, and **Thatheri Bazaar** for such shopping.

❏ **Pilgrim Paraphenalia:** Many of the small stalls in the bazaars and lanes, especially **Vishwanath Lane**, offer a wide range of personal and religious items for pilgrims. Look for drinking cups, water containers, linga, chalk, make-up, Vishnu figures, clothes, and sashes.

WHERE TO SHOP

Most shopping in Varanasi is found along streets, lanes, and markets of the old city or in a few shops, factories, and hotel shopping arcades in the Cantonment area of the newer city. Shopping in the old city yields few treasures of interest to international travelers—go there for the medieval and bazaar cultural experiences but don't expect to come away with anything in particular. You'll simply have the walk the streets and lanes of this area. The main shopping streets and lanes in the old city are **Chowk**, **Godowlia**, **Vishwanath Lane**, **Gyanvapi**, and **Thatheri Bazar**. In the newer section of the city, the hotels along **The Mall** and the Taj Ganges hotel and a few shops along **The Mint** are the major shopping areas. Altogether, you can shop most of Varanasi within four hours. Here are some of the better places to visit:

❏ **Cottage Industries Exposition Ltd. (CIE):** *Mint House, Nadesar, Tel. 344026.* Located across the street from the Taj Ganges Hotel, this is one of the most interesting arts and crafts emporiums in India. It's housed in a lovely old Maharaja's palace which has variously served as a coin mint, hospital during World War I, and the British Viceroy's residence. Currently operated by Kashmiris (one of more than 30 CIE operations in India), it's filled with Kashmir and Varanasi carpets in the right wing of the building and a variety of Kashmir handicrafts (painted papier mache boxes, eggs, and Christmas ornaments, and placemats and bronze sculptures), clothes (cashmere sweaters, shirts, neckties, sarees), and silk yardage on the left wing of the building. Everything here is nicely displayed, the service is very friendly, and the building itself is well worth the visit. The right wing with the carpets is the most interesting with is marble floor, stained glass windows, and beautifully carved and painted ceiling. Don't be afraid to bargain here. Remember, this is not a fixed-price government emporium. It's a highly entrepreneurial Kashmiri operation.

❏ **Silk Factories:** You'll find several silk factories in Varanasi that have made this city famous for is beautiful and intricately made brocade silk. Most claim to be the largest. Don't believe them. The factories are old family operations that include some looms and production in their buildings. But most of the production is contracted out to other homes and in villages. The factories provide the materials and designs and the contract workers produce accordingly. Some are organized as cooperatives that sell to the government. Many approximate "sweat shops." Visits to these silk factories often reminds one of visiting carpet shops—you get the sit-down presentation involving the constant unrolling of products until the demonstrator thinks you've identified something you like—offers "keep" or "take away" options with each unraveled item. Sometimes you feel like you're a captive of this demonstrator who relentlessly keeps up the act until he literally wears you down. Some people will buy a small item just to get out of the place, or they buy something because they feel sorry for the demonstrator who has put in so much time and effort unrolling pile after pile of material! Don't feel pressured or obligated with such a soft or hard sell. This is all part of the standard sales pitch, which is often very good, even suggesting creative uses of the fabrics just in case you claim you can't use them! We've yet to buy anything at these places simply because we can't use the materials in our home or on our bodies. Regardless of the terrific workmanship or ostensibly inexpensive prices, the colors and designs are simply inappropriate for our tastes and too ethnic to take home; some are dreadful. Five or ten *"Thank you, but no"* or *"I'm not interested"* and a fast walk will get you out of these places without a needless purchase. On the other hand, you might find something that really appeals to you and your decor and wardrobe. Two of the major silk factories include:

- **Mehta International:** *S.20/51, 3B, Varuna Bridge (100 meters from Clarks Varanasi Hotel), Tel. 344489.* One of the oldest and largest producers of brocade silk made into tapestries, bed covers, scarves, sarees, and tablecloths. Uses two traditional forms of weaving that can be seen in the demonstration area: the typical 18th century Jacard system and the ancient (12th century) hand system. Tour of working looms ends with a presentation of products in a large display room. Products are unrolled like rugs as the presenter explains the intricacies of each and compares different quality levels. You, of course, are urged to purchase something lovely for your home. Only problem—few colors, designs, and sizes are appropriate for most western homes. The workmanship is lovely but we can't think what to do with the stuff. Perhaps a souvenir that gets stored in a drawer? Local colors, designs, and sizes appeal to only a few tourists. For example, most bed covers are produced in the size of a perfect square. Maybe this works for beds made in India, but few Western tourists own square beds!

- **Subhan Ali & Sons:** *J. 15/178-A, Qazi Sadullahpura (near Chhavi Mahal Cinema), Tel. 210189.* Represents a community of male Muslim weavers using hand looms. One of the oldest and largest shops around. Includes several buildings of weavers and a demonstration area where you will be invited to sit, have tea, and "just look" at lots of fabrics unrolled before you. The shop is jam-packed with bed covers, scarves, tablecloths, blouses, and silk fabric and brocades. Expect to pay Rs 100 to Rs 800 per meter for silk.

- ❏ **The New Curio Cottage:** *S. 19/3, Mint House, Tel. 347-078 (near Taj Ganges Hotel).* This small but long established shop offers a wide range of antiques and handicrafts. Many of the older pieces are from Bihar. Look for old temple toys, sandalwood carvings, jewelry, enamel pieces, silver trays, textiles, brass items, masks, musical instruments (sitar), and carved panels.

- ❏ **Hotel shopping arcades:** Most four and five-star hotels have small shopping arcades that include arts, crafts, curio, clothes, jewelry, and book shops. The two best shopping arcades are found in Varanasi's two best hotels: Clarks Varanasi and Taj Ganges. The **Hotel Clarks**

Varanasi includes seven small shops offering a good variety of arts and crafts, jewelry, clothes, books, and postcards. The **Taj Ganges** includes one large two-storey Kashmiri emporium (**New Kashmir Stores**) filled with arts, crafts, clothes, silk, shawls, sweaters, and carpets.

❑ **Godowlia:** A big market area in the center of the old city. Filled with shops selling fabrics, clothes, and household goods as well as street vendors offering clothes and footwear. Very crowded and congested areas. Watch out for the honking cars, auto-rickshaws, and cycle-rickshaws, cows, and water buffalo. It's easy to get hit by a vehicle here or step into cow and water buffalo dung.

[handwritten note: Old city market]

❑ **Vishwannth Lane:** Just off Godowlia. Crammed with goods for women (sarees and makeup) and pilgrims.

[handwritten note: Sarees' old city]

ACCOMMODATIONS

Several new budget hotels are currently under construction in Varanasi to accommodate the numerous budget travelers who come to this city. At the same time, you'll find adequate four and five-star accommodations in Varanasi. Hotels, even the best, have an upcountry look to them.

DELUXE HOTELS

❑ **Hotel Clarks Varanasi:** *The Mall, Cantonment, Tel. 542-348-501 or Fax 542-348-186.* Located 20 kilometers from airport and 1 kilometer from railway station. 135 rooms. Facilities: swimming pool, restaurants, coffee shop, bar, shopping arcade. One of Varanasi's oldest and best hotels. Recently refurbished rooms make this a five-star property. Popular with tour groups. Sponsors one of the best evening cultural performances (music and dance) conducted in a 270-year old refectory on the banks of the Ganges. Check dates and times since this ostensibly "daily" program actually gets scheduled based upon guest demand.

❑ **Taj Ganges:** *Raja Bazaar Road at Nadesar Palace Compound, Cantonment, Tel. 542-345-100 or Fax 542-348-067.* Another one of Varanasi's best five-star hotels. Popular with tour groups. Located 21 kilometers from airport. 130 rooms. Facilities: swimming pool, 2 restaurants, 2 bars, tennis court, 2-floor shopping emporium. Conveniently located across the street from the classy Cottage Industries Exposition building. Also arranges cultural performances at the hotel and along the Ganges.

❑ **Varanasi Ashok:** *The Mall, Cantonment, Tel. 542-46020 or Fax 542-348-089.* Located 22 kilometers from airport and 1 kilometer from railway station. This is a government operated hotel. 84 rooms. Facilities: swimming pool, restaurant, shopping arcade.

❑ **Hindustan International:** *C-21/3 Maldahiya, Tel. 542-351-484 or Fax 542-350-931.* Located 24 kilometers from airport and 3 kilometers from railway station. 108 rooms. Facilities: swimming pool, health club, restaurant, coffee shop, bar.

❑ **Hotel Ideal Tops:** *The Mall, Cantonment, Tel. 542-348-091 or Fax 542-348-685.* Located 18 kilometers from airport. 40 rooms. Facilities: restaurant, bar, travel desk.

❑ **Pallavi International:** *Hathwa Place, Chetganj, Tel. 542-356-939 or Fax 542-322-943.* The only heritage hotel in the area. Located 22 kilometers from airport and 1.5 kilometers from railway station. 40 rooms. Facilities: swimming pool, restaurants, travel counter.

STANDARD HOTELS

❑ **Hotel De Paris:** *15 The Mall, Cantonment, Tel. 542-46601.* Located 20 kilometers from airport and 1 kilometer from railway station. 50 rooms. Facilities: 2 restaurants, bar, tennis court, travel counter.

❑ **India:** *59 Patel Nagar, Cantonment, Tel. 542-343-009 or Fax 542-348-327.* Located 18 kilometers from airport and 0.5 kilometers from railway station. 80 rooms, 3 suites. Facilities: restaurants, bar, travel counter.

RESTAURANTS

Varanasi is not noted for inspired cuisine, great restaurants, nor fine dining experiences. Most major hotels serve obligatory buffets for tour groups. Restaurants and cafes in the old city are not particularly noted for their sanitation standards. The best and safest restaurants tend to be found in the major hotels located in the Cantonment area. Among the best are:

❑ **Mandap:** *Taj Ganges Hotel, Nadesar Palace Compound, Cantt.* Indian and Continental cuisine.

❑ **Varuna:** *Taj Ganges Hotel, Nadesar Palace Compound, Cantt.* Indian and Mughlai cuisine.

❑ **Amrapali:** *Clarks Varanasi, The Mall, Cantt.* Indian and Continental cuisine.

❑ **Atithya:** *Varanasi Ashok, The Mall, Cantt.* Indian and Continental cuisine.

❑ **Darpan:** *Hotel Pallavi International, Chetganj.* Multi-cuisine.

❑ **Sindhi Restaurant:** *Opposite the Lalita Cinema.* Located in the center of the city. Indian cuisine (serves thalis).

❑ **Canton Restaurant:** *Hotel Surya.* Indian, Chinese, and Continental cuisine.

❑ **Palm Springs:** *Hotel India.* Indian cuisine.

❑ **Temple Restaurant:** *Dasaswamedh Road, Godowlia.* Popular with tourists for breakfast, lunch, and dinner.

❑ **Ayyar's Cafe:** *Dasaswamedh Road, Godowlia.* South Indian vegetarian cuisines.

❑ **Burger King:** *Varuna Bridge, Cantt.* Not affiliated with the Canadian-American chain. Popular for burgers (vegetarian, mutton, chicken) and shakes. No tables.

SEEING THE SITES

Most of Varanasi's sightseeing focuses on the river, ghats, old city, and nearby city of Sarnath. If you are Hindu, Varanasi is all about religion, death, salvation, and rebirth. If you are Buddhist, Varanasi is a way station along the road to one of Buddhism's most important cities, Sarnath. If you are none of the above, Varanasi and Sarnath will surely educate you about religion and culture in India. Major highlights here include:

❑ **The Ganges and the ghats:** The Ganges River and the nearly 100 ghats that line this river are Varanasi's major attractions. Here you will enter a different world, unlike any you have experienced before. Beginning very early in the morning to late in the evening, thousands of devotees come to the left bank of the river to perform holy rituals in the water, celebrate weddings, participate in cremations, mediate, and seek alms. Hundreds of visitors try to take in all the amazing activities by mingling in the crowds, warding off beggars and touts, cruising the river in small row boats, and taking pictures of the amazing and exotic activities (photography is restricted near the two crematories). The open air crematories process over 200 bodies a day which are then thrown into the sacred river. The sights here are truly amazing. The best times to visit this area is at dawn, as the sun rises over the Ganges, and at dusk, as the sun sets. However, on some mornings the fog is so thick you can hardly see more than five feet ahead. On a clear day, rent a row boat early in the morning to see the river rituals come alive or in the evening to see the sun set. If you are staying in the major hotel section, around The Mall, plan to leave your hotel around 6am (a 20 minute ride) to get to the river in time for the sunrise.

❑ **Temples and mosques:** A very religious city, Varanasi is well known for its 2,000 temples, mosques, and shrines. Viewed from the river bank, it's a city of interesting towers, domes, minarets, and pinnacles. While primarily a Hindu city, nearly 25 percent of the population is Muslim. The city's most famous and sacred temple, **Kashi Vishwanath Temple** (hard to find but located behind the Dashashwamedh and Manikarnika ghats and everyone knows how to find it), is where many pilgrims begin their journey in Varanasi. Devoted to the Lord Shiva, the late 18th century temple is off-limits to non-Hindus. However, the temple can be viewed from the top floor of the house across the lane which also functions as an art gallery and handicraft shop; the owners charge an entrance fee for the less than stellar view—primarily the gilded dome. The nearby **Gyanvapi Mosque** is heavy guarded against possible terrorism of extremist Hindus who consider the area to be a holy Hindu site. Other popular temples include **Kedareshvara**, **Sankat Mochan**, **Shitala**, **Chausath Yogini**, and **Durga** (the Monkey Temple).

❑ **Old City**: You really need to walk the old city to get a sense of its rhythm and character. It can be an exhilarating experience. This place has lots of old world character (worn yet colorful) that often feels like you are in another century. Mark Twain's observation on this city over 100 years ago is still relevant: "Benaras is older than history, older than tradition, older than legend, and looks twice as old as all of them put together." To get the real flavor of the old city with its many temples, mosques, shrines, shops, and bazaars, you should walk its winding streets, lanes, and alleys. It's an interesting experience which will put you in contact with many pilgrims, shopkeepers, and fellow tourists who often look fascinated yet bewildered. At times you may feel lost, but you'll soon emerge into familiar territory near the river or along a main street. The most popular lane in this area is **Vishwanath Lane** (just off of Godowlia Street).

❑ **Benares Hindu University**: Located in the southern part of the city (Lanka) on an expansive tree-lined campus covering 5 square kilometers, this is considered Asia's largest residential university with over 20,000 students (two-thirds live on campus). The university is well noted for the fascinating **Bharat Kala Bhaven**, an art gallery/museum with its permanent collection of textiles and miniature paintings and sculptures (open 11am - 4:30pm and 7:30am - 12:30pm during May and June; closed Sunday and university holidays), and the very tall white marble **New Vishwanath Temple** which stands in a semi-circle. Modeled after the sacred Vishwanath Temple in the old city.

❑ **Ramnagar Fort & Museum**: Located on the right bank of the river, this was once (17th century) the home of the Maharaja of Benares. The Dunbar Hall and royal museum houses memorabilia, from palanquins to costumes and arms. The Dussehra celebration takes place here each fall. A crumbling structure with lots of interesting history and artifacts. Open 9am-noon and 2-5pm.

❑ **Sarnath**: Located 11 kilometers north of Varanasi, this is one of Buddhism's most important sites. It's here, in Deer Park, where the Lord Buddha preached his first sermon over 2,500 year ago after attaining Enlightenment at Bodhgaya. A very peaceful city—especially after chaotic Varanasi—dotted with numerous stupas and ruins, Sarnath is a delightful place to visit. Its history, as well as its ruins, date from the 3rd century B.C. when Emperor Ashoka was responsible for the creation of various stupas, monasteries, and pillar edicts. The red brick archaeological sites are truly impressive. Sarnath's **Archaeological Museum** (9:30am - 5pm, closed Friday) houses many interesting stone statues and artifacts from excavations in the surrounding area; a copy of Ashoka's lion pillar is especially impressive. Be sure to visit **Chau-khandi Stupa**, **Dhamarajika Stupa**, **Dhamet Stupa**, **Ashok Pillar**, and **Moolgandha Kutir Vihara** (temple to Buddha). Just north of Dharmet Stupa is **Deer Park** where you can feed the deer (can purchase carrots from vendors). Sarnath is especially popular with Japanese tourists who are interested in Buddhism's foundations. It's home to the **Central Institute of Higher Tibetan Studies** (near ruins) which offers courses, conducts research, and houses an important library collection.

❑ **Diesel Locomotive Works Factory:** If you're "templed out" and have experienced enough of the crowds, people, and animals, here's a interesting but little known diversion. Located west of the river and northwest of the university, this factory produces India's locomotives.

ENTERTAINMENT

If you haven't had enough daytime entertainment along the river, keep some time open in the evening for cultural performances. One of the most popular such programs is sponsored by the **Clark's Varanasi Hotel** in an 11th century palace along the banks of the Ganges. The program includes prayers, dances, and music. Be sure to check with the hotel for the current schedule (5:30 - 8:30pm, Tel. 348-501). While this excellent program used to be held nightly, its scheduling is now intermittent—depends on demand from tour groups.

Varanasi also is a city of music. Classical music recitals are held twice weekly (Wednesday and Saturday at 8pm) at the **International Music Centre Ashram** (near Dasaswamedh Ghat). Major concerts are occasionally held at **Nagari Natak Mandali**. Ask at your hotel front desk about such programs.

Given the restrictive religious climate in Varanasi, liquor is hard to find outside the bars of major hotels. This very religious city is noted for its vegetarianism, lack of alcohol, and absence of decadent Western entertainment.

Jaipur

Welcome to one of India's most popular tourist destinations for shopping and sightseeing. Located 270 kilometers southwest of Delhi and 230 kilometers west of Agra, Jaipur is the famous pink capital of the colorful parched desert State of Rajasthan. An alluring city of medieval fortresses, palaces, camels, turbaned tribesmen, factories, bazaars, and hundreds of shops offering some of India's best gems, jewelry, and handicrafts, Jaipur is a delightful place to spend a couple of days exploring its many intriguing treasures and pleasures. It's an enchanting city that has many timeless, almost biblical qualities. Indeed, at times you may feel you've been transported into another century, especially when caught up in Jaipur's frenzied bazaars. Above all, Jaipur is a shopper's paradise for locals and foreign visitors alike. Colorful, picturesque, and often dramatic, Jaipur also is a photographer's dream come true!

PINK CITY OF TREASURES AND TOUTS

It's called the "Pink City" but Jaipur looks more salmon and ochre than true pink in color. Originally founded in 1727 by the astronomer-king Jai Singh II to replace the Amber Fort (11 kilometers to the north), the city was laid out according to nine rectangular sections to symbolize the nine divisions of the universe. It included a huge wall with eight imposing gates (20 feet high and 8 feet thick) and a grid of broad streets (110 feet wide), designed for elephant processions, that intersected at the city center, the City Palace. Under royal patronage, traders and artisans were given commercial lanes which continue to this day. The city walls and buildings were painted pink in 1883 in preparation for Prince Albert's visit. Since then, the old walled city of Jaipur has lost some of its walls, but those that still stand have retained a distinctive rose-pink character. The city also has expanded considerably beyond its original pink walls. Today, most quality shops, hotels, and restaurants are located in other parts of this sprawling city.

But for first-time visitors, Jaipur is especially remembered as a unique pink city with walls, forts, palaces, crowded bazaars, distinctive shops, and colorful and strikingly handsome people. The Palace of the Winds (Hawa Mahal), Amber (Amer) Palace, City Palace, and Rambagh Palace (now an upscale hotel) are particularly memorable sites for visitors. And for those who are interested in gems and jewelry, Jaipur is India's capital for precious and semi-precious stones. Just visit the narrow alley between 264 and 268 Johari Bazaar in the Pink City, and you will be at the heart of Jaipur's "gem center." Indeed, at times the whole city appears to be one big shopping emporium for gems, jewelry, and handicrafts. If you are in the market for such products, Jaipur may become one of your favorite shopping destinations in all of India!

> ❏ The old walled city of Jaipur still retains a distinctive rose-pink character.
>
> ❏ Most quality shops, hotels, and restaurants are found outside the walls in this sprawling city.
>
> ❏ Jaipur is India's capital for precious and semi-precious stones.
>
> ❏ Plan to spend at least two days in Jaipur.

At the same time, Jaipur has its down sides—like many other heavily touristed cities in India, it has too much pollution and too many beggars and commission-hungry touts. The pollution is especially noxious near the southern city gates. Here the many pollution-belching trucks, buses, auto-rickshaws, and tempos (bouncing black motorbike taxis) create a haze of filthy air. Given the large number of tourists visiting this city, an equally large number of beggars have descended on the city to work the crowds; many of them belong to professional gangs of beggars who prey on tourists. Touts constantly pester visitors to take them to highly recommended shops that give them a standard 30-40 percent commission. Many shops, of course, encourage such behavior given the highly transient nature of their clientele. Indeed, most shops cannot depend on repeat customers—only repeat touts that bring them new customers for the moment.

Jaipur's treasures and pleasures are many and memorable. To do this city right, plan to spend at least two days immersing yourself in Jaipur's shopping culture and seeing its many unique forts, palaces, mansions, factories, and bazaars.

GETTING TO KNOW YOU

Sprawled over a dry lake bed and surrounded on three sides by the rugged and barren Aravalli Hills—each crowned with a formidable fort—Jaipur is the energetic gateway city to the exotic, fascinating, and timeless desert State of Rajasthan. It's the land of the once powerful Rajput dynasties (7th to 12th centuries) and still proud Rajputs, a kind of fairytale land complete with all the elements that make for great stories and dramatic movie sets—seemingly impenetrable forts, courtly palaces and mansions, expansive estates, brave warriors, talented artisans, bustling markets, bobbing turbans, lumbering elephants, galloping horses, majestic camels, and picturesque desert treks. Indeed, there is never a dull moment in Jaipur and its surrounding area.

The third, and some might say the best, corner in the popular Delhi-Agra-Jaipur "Golden Triangle," Jaipur is a city of great color and contrasts. It's a relatively large city with a population of nearly 1.8 million. Like so many other large cities in India, Jaipur has its own style of bedlam with crowded, chaotic, and polluted streets and a visual feast of colorful people, markets, monuments, and festivals. Proud and handsome looking Rajput men in traditional dress walk the spice-laced streets with bright turbans and long up-turned moustaches. Majestic looking camels, with their heads held high, pull wagons through the city's wide streets while overloaded, noisy, and pollution-belching auto-rickshaws liven up the street drama. This is fascinating street theater that is definitely unique and exotic for first-time visitors.

There is much to see and do in and around Jaipur, from shopping and sightseeing to just relaxing in the desert sun. Plan to spend at least two full days here to do the basics. Three days would be perfect. With five days you can also relax in the decadent splendor of the regal new Rajvilla Resort which is located eight kilometers from the city on the road to Agra. Our advice: don't rush yourself in Jaipur. Like a good wine, it is to be first tasted and then savored for its many exotic flavors. The treasures and pleasures of Jaipur are worth staying around for a few days.

THE BASICS

LOCATION AND POPULATION

The capital and gateway city to the western desert State of Rajasthan, Jaipur lies 270 kilometers southwest of Delhi. Its population of 1.8 million makes it the largest city in Rajasthan. From Jaipur, you can venture east to Agra in the State of Uttar Pradesh or west and southwest to three other popular cities in Rajasthan—Jodhpur, Jaisalmer, and Udaipur. As you will quickly discover, this is one of India's most colorful and fascinating regions. Jaipur will give you an excellent introduction to what lies ahead if you decide to explore Rajasthan further to the west and southwest.

WHEN TO GO

In terms of weather, it's best to visit Jaipur and Rajasthan between October and March which are also the area's most popular tourist months. It can become unbearably hot during the month of June. The July to September monsoon season can be very inconvenient due to rains and floods.

GETTING THERE

You can reach Jaipur from Delhi by air, train, car, or bus. Many visitors prefer the train which also links to Agra and other parts of Rajasthan. Departing daily from New Delhi at either 6am (*Pink City Express*) or 5:50pm (*Shatabdi Express*), the trains take nearly five hours to reach Jaipur. The 237-kilometer train trip from Jaipur to Agra takes nearly seven hours. If you plan to go on to Jodhpur from Jaipur, the train takes four and a half hours. The Jaipur - Udaipur run takes over eleven hours.

We usually take a car and driver to complete the Golden Triangle. The trip takes from four to five hours along a rough road of speed bumps and pot holes. While this may be a foolish way of traveling to Jaipur because of the dangerous road conditions, it is convenient. As your driver dodges trucks, buses, cars, tractor/trailers, auto-rickshaws, motorcycles, bicycles, push carts, bullock carts, elephants, camels, horses, donkeys, cows, water buffalos, goats, dancing muzzled bears, pigs, dogs, vultures, and people—a sort of amazing road zoo interspersed with more than 200 years of transportation modes—he is likely to often repeat the old saying about driving in India that doesn't necessarily inspire confidence: *"When driving in India, you must have good car, good brakes, and good luck!"* If you also can find a good driver, this can be a fascinating, although sometimes nerve-racking, trip by road. In addition to seeing all the road carnage (dead animals and tangled vehicles) alongside the road, you'll pass through many interesting dung-ladden villages and towns. The last one-third of the trip is along a seemingly less dangerous four-lane highway. If you are going on to other cities from Jaipur, plan on the following distances: Agra, 230 kilometers; Jodhpur, 332 kilometers; Udaipur, 374 kilometers; Jaisalmer, 654 kilometers; and Bharatpur, 176 kilometers.

If you fly to Jaipur from New Delhi (**Indian Airlines**), the actual flight time will be about 35-40 minutes. However, you'll probably spend another two hours at the airport. You also can fly to and from Jaipur via Jodhpur (45 minutes), Udaipur (1 hour, 40 minutes), Aurangabad (2 hours, 20 minutes), and Mumbai (1 hour, 30 minutes). Jaipur's **Sanganer Airport** is about 15 kilometers from the city center.

Getting Around

You'll find plenty of taxis, auto-rickshaws, cycle-rickshaws, tempos, and buses to take you around the city and to the outlying areas. Be sure to bargain for your taxis and rickshaws before taking off since they do not have meters. Be forewarned that drivers here have a bad reputation for ripping off tourists with inflated charges. If may be more convenient and economical to hire a car and driver for a half- or full-day. You can arrange for a guide and driver through your hotel tour desk or at the Government of India Tourist Office (Hotel Khasa Kothi, Tel. 373-300) or the Rajasthan Tourist Development Office (Tourist Hotel, M. I. Road, Tel. 376-362).

Tourist Offices and Tours

Several government tourist offices provide some assistance in the form of maps, brochures, contact information, and tours. The **Rajasthan Tourist Development Office** (Tourist Hotel, M. I. Road, Tel. 376362) conducts half-day, full-day, and evening sightseeing tours of the city and surrounding area by coach as well as arranges cars and drivers. The **Government of India Tourist Office** (Hotel Khasa Kothi, Tel. 373-2000, open 9am to 6pm Monday to Friday and 9am to 1pm on Saturday; closed Sunday) offers full-day tours from 9:30am to 5:30pm. Other government tourist information offices include: **Government of Rajasthan Tourist Office** (Jaipur Railway Station, Tel. 315-714, open 24 hours a day); **Government of Rajasthan Tourist Information Bureau** (Central Bus Stand, Sindhi Camp, 10am to 5pm); and **Foreigner's Regional Registration Office** (Rajasthan Police Headquarters, behind Hawa Mahal, Tel. 49391). Private tour companies include: **Sita World Travel** (Tel. 366-809), **Parihar Travel** (Tel. 350-583), **Araveli Safari** (Tel. 373-124), **Karwan Tours** (Tel. 304-854), **Rajasthan Tours** (Tel. 380-824), and **Rajasthan Travel** (Tel. 315-408).

ORIENTATION

Despite the fact that this is one of the better laid out cities in India—done according to an architectural plan with wide main streets—this is still a chaotic, crowded, and dirty city. The wide streets just hold more crowds and contain greater chaos! The two areas of primary interest to visitors are the walled **Pink City**, which includes numerous gates, the City Palace and Museum, the famous Palace of the Winds, and several shops and bazaars; **M. I. Road** (also known as Mirza Ismail Marg), which is Jaipur's main shopping street near the walled Pink City; and **Amer Marg** (Amber Road) which includes numerous handicrafts shops on the way to the Amber Fort. The rest of this sprawling city is dotted with hotels, commercial offices, religious structures, palaces, and mansions.

Because Jaipur is such a large and sprawling city, plan to get around by some form of transportation. This is not an easy city to walk. Even along the major shopping street, M. I. Road, the distances between shops can be long and tiring.

SHOPPING JAIPUR

Shopping is unquestionably one of Jaipur's major attractions. Indeed, there are few places in India that can claim so many shopping opportunities per square kilometer as Jaipur. However, don't expect to do better *quality shopping* in Jaipur than you would in Mumbai or Delhi. While Jaipur offers lots of interesting shopping, the best quality shopping is still centered in Mumbai and Delhi. In this respect, India is no different from most countries: the best shopping tends to gravitate to the largest cities. In Jaipur, you'll have an opportunity to meet artisans and shop directly at various production sources. Chances are you will get "emporiumed-out" after visiting several handicraft emporiums—they all seem to offer the same arts and crafts. After awhile, you may want to close your eyes and hope things dramatically change when you open them again. Unfortunately, they don't. You'll have to go with the flow. Fortunately, the flow is both colorful and fascinating in Jaipur.

For many visitors, shopping is the number one reason for visiting this city. Both the walled city and adjacent M. I. Road, which runs southwest from Ajmeri Gate, are lined with shops and factories offering a tremendous range of gems, jewelry, carpets, handicrafts, copy antiques, leather footwear, fabrics, blue-pottery, and papier mache products. Further north is Amer Road with its many handicraft shops. For jewelry connoisseurs, Jaipur is rightly famous for its unique *kundan* (stones set in gold) and *meenakari* (enameled-ware) jewelry. In many shops and factories, especially within the walled city, you can see artisans at work. Within the many bazaars of the walled city, expect to be approached by people who want to take you to their shop. Don't be led into a gem factory by a street tout or rickshaw driver who invariably gets a 30-40 percent commission on your purchase, which is added to your shopping tab.

One of the maddening aspects of shopping in Jaipur are street addresses. Many shops along the M. I. Road do not have building numbers. Consequently, you may spend a lot of time going up and down this long road trying to identify a particular shop. You may need to ask three or four people if they know where the shop is located before figuring out the exact location.

Be prepared to bargain hard for everything in Jaipur, especially in the bazaars. Since shops are used to inflating prices for tourists, you should be able to negotiate at least a 10 percent discount; 20 to 50 percent discounts also are possible. Remember, these's lots of competition in Jaipur with many shops selling the same types and quality of goods, and you are dealing with many seasoned entrepreneurs who know you are here today and gone tomorrow.

Most shops are open from 10:30am to 7:30pm and are closed on Sunday. Opening and closing days vary for the bazaars within the walled city.

WHAT TO BUY

- ❑ **Gems:** Jaipur is India's major gem cutting and polishing center and one of the world's most important gem producers. Wholesalers from all over the world come to Jaipur to purchase gems. In fact, most stones cut and polished for India's domestic and export gem and jewelry trade come from Jaipur's factories. Dominated by the Muslim community, gem cutting and polishing is still done the old fashioned way—by hand. Here you will find a wide range of precious and semi-precious stones in the shops and markets—rubies, sapphires, emeralds, diamonds, and other stones. Since Jaipur is the center for gem cutting, expect to get your best shopping buy on gems. For a good overview of Jaipur's gem work, visit the many shops in and around the **Johari Bazaar** of the Pink City as well as in shops along **M. I. Road** that offer both gems and jewelry. Precious stones are sold in a narrow alley, **Haldion ka Rasta**, just off Johari Bazaar. Semi-precious stones are found along another nearby alley called **Gopalji ka Rasta**. Expect to encounter young men hawking bags of loose stones at Johari Bazaar. Many of these enterprising sales-men, who may be on their lunch break, are actually factory workers who are trying to unload stones they pocketed while at work. If you know your stones (examine them carefully), you can get some real good deals on the street. But be very careful when buying gems in Jaipur. In some shops the quality is not good and synthetic stones may be offered as the real thing.

❑ **Jewelry:** You'll find lots of jewelry in Jaipur but do not confuse the fact that Jaipur is a gem cutting center with the actual production of jewelry. Here's an important fact few people know: very little jewelry is actually produced in Jaipur, except for the famous enameled gold jewelry which is made in Jaipur. Most jewelry you see in Jaipur's shops and markets is produced elsewhere. Therefore, while gems are a good buy in Jaipur, jewelry may not be. If you've come to Jaipur with the idea of getting good buys on jewelry, think again. You may be able to do much better on jewelry purchases in Agra, Delhi, or Mumbai. Again, gems—not jewelry—are the best buys in Jaipur. Look toward Agra for good buys on jewelry. However, Jaipur does excel in one category of jewelry—tribal jewelry. Some of the best jewelry selections and more reliable shops in Jaipur, as well as India, are found at the **Gem Palace** (M. I. Road, Tel. 374-175) and **Amrapali** (M. I. Road, Tel. 377-940).

❏ **Handicrafts:** Jaipur offers a profusion of handicrafts reflecting the strong crafts tradition in the state of Rajasthan. Here you will find everything from brass figures, pottery, marble statuary, and metal ware to copy antiques, wood carvings, and stone sculptures. The various markets (bazaar) within the Pink City, as well as the many handicraft emporiums outside the city gates, are chuck-full of every conceivable handicraft. You may want to first visit the government handicraft emporium, **Rasathali** (the Rajasthan Government Handicraft Emporium, opposite Ajmeri Gate, M. I. Road, Tel. 367-176), which· has fixed prices accompanied by questionable service, before venturing into the bazaars to haggle for handicrafts. Also, check out two other government emporiums on M. I. Road: **Khadi Ghar** (M. I. Road, Tel. 373-745) and **Handloom House** (Rituraj Building, M. I. Road, Tel. 367-176). However, some of the best handicraft shops are operated in the private sector. Two of the best such handicraft shops include **Manglam Arts** (Govind Nagar, Amber Palace Road, Tel. 41176) and **Silver and Art Palace** (Kachcha Bandha, Amer Road, Tel. 43980).

❏ **Textiles:** Jaipur is well known for its unique tie-dyed (bandhani) and hand-blocked cotton and silk fabrics. While many of the fabrics can be found in the bazaars, you may want to go to the actual production sources. Two villages outside Jaipur are especially famous for producing the hand-blocked fabrics: **Sanganer** (10 kilometers from Jaipur on Kota Road) and **Bagre** (30 kilometers from Jaipur on Ajmer Road). Here you can see families producing the fabrics. Within the city, visit **Arawali Exports** (717 Jagdish Colony, Ramgarh Mor, Amber Road, Tel. 605-131) for a good selection of silk fabrics. Also, stop at the **Handloom House** (Rituraj Building, M. I. Road), **Handloom Haveli** (Lalpura House, Sansar Ch Road), **Rajasthan Fabrics & Arts** (near the city gate (Tel. 41432), and **Anokhi** (2 Yudhistra Marg, behind the Secretariat, Tel. 381-619). Within the walled city, Within the walled city, visit **Bapu Bazaar, Chaupar Bazaar, Nehru Bazaar, and Kishanpal Bazaar** for textiles.

❑ **Carpets and rugs:** Jaipur also is well known for its wool carpets and cotton durries. Some of the carpet and rug shops also offer hand-blocked cotton and silk fabrics. Good selections can be found at **Carpet Mahal and Textile Mahal** (outside Zorawar Singh Gate, Amber Road, Tel. 541-546); **Channi Carpets and Textiles** (Mount Road, opposite Ramgarh Road); **Ankur Exports** (opposite the Rambagh Palace, Tel. 515-212), **Baja Enterprises** (Chand Hira Building, M. I. Road, Tel. 362-804), **Art Age** (2-Bhawani Singh Road, Tel. 381-720), and **Maharaja** (Chandpol, near Smode Haveli). Within the walled city, visit **Subhash Chowk** (see Achral House), and **Tripolia Bazaar** (especially Chaganlal Mangilal at 135, Tripolia Bazaar).

❑ **Blue pottery:** The region is well known for its distinctive blue pottery. Most handicraft emporiums carry this pottery. Also, try **Jaipur Blue Pottery Art Center** on Amer Road, near Jain Mandir (Tel. 48952), **Neerja International** at S-19, Niti Marg, Bhwani Singh Road (Tel. 380-395), and **Kripal Singh** (B-18a Siva Marg, Bani Park).

❑ **Other discoveries:** Jaipur also boasts numerous art galleries and boutiques. Art can be found at **Art Fair** (U-2, Chameliwala Market, opposite the post office on M.I. Road, Tel. 362-915), **Maharaja Art Emporium** (Hawa Mahal Bazaar, Tel. 47592, and **Juneja Art Gallery** (Railway Crossing, Lane 6, Raja Park, Tel. 46362). For men's and women's boutiques, try **Nayika** (Thalia Building, M. I. Road, Tel. 367-334) and **Soma** (5, Gaurav Nagar, Civil Lines, Tel. 382-986). Jaipur also is known for its marble statues, papier mache puppets, lacquerware, Krishna-art miniature paintings, bed linens, and cotton quilts.

Artisans At Work

One of the highlights of shopping in Jaipur is to actually see artisans producing the very products you may want to purchase. While you will find many retail shops in Jaipur, many of these same shops also function as factories which polish gems and produce carpets, rugs, textiles, and handicrafts for both the wholesale and retail markets. In one respect, Jaipur is one big jewelry and handicraft factory town. Many dealers from abroad visit these places to make bulk purchases for export.

Here are some of the major places where you can see artisans at work:

Block printing, handmade paper, and blue pottery	Sanganer Village
Carpets	Achrol House Subhash Chowk
Gems and jewelry	Johari Bazaar
Lac workers	Maniharon Ka Rasta Tripolia Bazaar
Marble carvings	Khajanewalon Ka Rasta
Rajasthani Jootis	Ramganj Bazaar
Tie-dyed textiles	Johari Bazaar

WHERE TO SHOP

Most shopping in Jaipur is concentrated in four areas: within the walls of the Pink City, along M. I. Road and Amer Road, and at hotel shopping arcades. You'll also find shops and vendor stalls at the various sites, such as the Amber Fort.

❑ **The Pink City:** Shopping within the Pink City can be magical and enchanting. Here you find yourself in a traditional crowded market atmosphere where you can search for goods in densely packed shops, and haggle with vendors. Most shopping within the city walls is concentrated in a series of bazaars which specialize in particular products. The largest bazaar is **Johari Bazaar** which is primarily known for its gems, jewelry, fabrics, and sarees. If you're looking for precious and semi-precious stones, be sure to check out the commerce taking place along two narrow alleys near Johari Bazaar—**Haldion ka Rasta** (on opposite side of Johari Bazaar) for precious stones and **Gopalji ka Rasta** (runs west from Johari Bazaar) for semi-precious stones. Other popular bazaars include: **Ramgang Bazaar** (applique and embroidery), **Tripolia** (brassware, carvings, lacquerware), **Bapu** (textiles, perfumes, camel-skin shoes), **Chandpol** (bangles and trinkets), **Kishanpal** (tie-dye textiles), **Ramganj** (shoes), and **Nehru** (textiles, perfumes, camel-skin shoes).

❏ **M. I. Road:** Also referred to as Mirza Ismail Marg, M. I. Road runs southwest of Ajmeri Gate. This wide and long street houses many of Jaipur's best jewelry and handicraft shops. You can easily spend a half day going up and down this street. Indeed, you may need to spend much of that time just trying to find local shops that have no street numbers! Three of Jaipur's best jewelry shops are located here: **The Gem Palace** (Tel. 374-175), **Amrapali** (Tel. 377-940), and **Bhandari Jewellers** (Tel. 61150). Some of Jaipur's best government handicraft emporiums also are located on M. I. Road: **Rajasthali** (Rajasthan Government Handicraft Emporium, across from Ajmeri Gate, Tel. 367-176), **Khadi Ghar** (Tel. 373-745), and **Handloom House** (Rituraj Building). Also, look for **Miss India** (Tel. 371-414) for silver ear rings, bracelets, tribal jewelry, and copies of old silver pieces, and **M. B. Sons** (Tel. 302 001) for a wide selection of jewelry.

❏ **Amer Road:** Running north of the Pink City from Zorawar Gate and on the way to Amber (Amer) Fort, Amber Road includes several handicraft shops, such as **Manglam Arts** (Tel. 41176), **Antiquariat** (Tel. 365-2049), **Silver and Art Palace** (Tel. 43980), **All Rajasthan Cottage Industries** (Tel. 49372), **Maharaja Textile Printers** (Tel. 42935), **Geeta Enterprises** (Tel. 45437), and **Anand Handicrafts** (Tel. 47935).

❏ **Hotel shopping arcades:** Jaipur's two major hotels have shopping arcades that are well worth visiting. The **Rajputana Palace Sheraton Hotel** on Palace Road has a nice shopping arcade in the courtyard at the lower level. It includes jewelry, boutique, leather, carpet, and handicraft shops, such as two **Antiquariat** shops which offer good quality paintings, sandalwood, knives, marble pots, silver, and jewelry; **Channi** for clothes, purses, bed covers, and scarves; **Ritu's** for clothes and leather goods; **Paniharin Arts and Jewels** for jewelry; **Sadak Ali and Bross** for carpets; and **Kashmir Handicrafts** for carpets and handicrafts.

The elegant **Rambagh Palace Hotel** offers one of the best collections of quality jewelry stores in Jaipur, some of which are branch shops of stores in the city along M. I. Road. The best shops are found on the upper level, to both the left and right of the reception counter and near the main restaurant. Some of the shops are only open during the evening, between 7:30 and 10pm, after guests staying at the hotel have returned from a day of touring or when outside guests come for dinner. Three of the best jewelry shops here are **Mugal India** (near travel desk at reception area, Tel. 521-572; its sister shop is on M. I. Road and is called Bhandari Jewellers); **The Gem Palace** (Tel. 381-633; main shop on M. I. Road and other branch shops located at Hotel Mansingh and Hotel Clarks Amer); and **Adinath** (Tel. 381-593). You'll find several other jewelry shops at the back of the hotel and on the lower level facing the main road. Many of these shops are open during the day. Look for **Lall's Gems International, S. Gulab Chand Lunia & Co. Jewellers**, and several aggressive handicraft shops facing the road, to the right of the hotel entrance.

BEST OF THE BEST

We found the following shops to be particularly good for quality and selections. However, we are less certain about reliability, especially if you plan to have your purchases packed and shipped from Jaipur. Since most of your purchases will probably be small items that will fit into your purse or suitcase, or can be worn—jewelry, textiles, handicrafts—plan to take them with you.

GEMS AND JEWELRY

❑ **The Gem Palace:** *M. I. Road, Tel. 374-175 or Fax 373-586. Also has branch shops at the Hotel Rambagh Palace (Tel. 381-633), Hotel Mansingh (Tel. 376-266), and Hotel Clarks Amer (Tel. 550-726).* This is Jaipur's oldest (155 years) and best gem and jewelry shop. It's where the rich and famous shop for top quality jewelry and where dealers from around the world come to purchase top quality gems and jewelry. Both Jacqueline Onassis and Princess Diana shopped here. You can spend anywhere from US$2 to US$2 million on gems and jewelry. The first floor displays a wide range of jewelry, from tribal gold and silver pieces to large necklaces, earrings, and rings appropriate for both Indians and Westerners as well as some textiles. Look for some really beautiful and distinctive enamel jewelry set with diamonds—both new and antique pieces. The really high-end jewelry is locked in the safe from where it gets displayed in the back room for serious shoppers—you'll have to ask to see the really "good stuff." The second floor is devoted to a museum.

❑ **Amrapali:** *M. I. Road, Tel. 377-940 or Fax 375-802.* Wonderful selection of old tribal jewelry on the first floor and gorgeous gold jewelry on the second floor, much of it with a decided ethnic look. Designs special jewelry for Miss India. Works with nearly 800 wholesalers around the world in supplying shops abroad with new jewelry. Also includes nice chests, masks, furniture, and other home decorative and antique items on the first floor. One of our favorite shops in India.

❑ **Bhandari Jewellers:** *M. I. Road, near York Hotel, Tel. 61150. Also has branch shop, called Mughal India, at the Rambagh Palace Hotel, Tel. 521-572.* Nicely crafted jewelry using emeralds and rubies. Guarantees everything. M. I. Road store also offers carpets, paintings, sandalwood carvings, and old silver. If you arrive here without a tour guide, expect to receive a 25 percent discount.

❑ **Adinath:** *250, The Rambagh Palace Hotel, Tel. 521-593, open from 7:30pm to 10pm.* A small but very nice shop for quality silver, gold, and gems. Delightful to work with.

❑ **Silver and Art Palace:** *Kachcha Bandha, Amer Road, Tel. 43980.* See next section on arts and crafts.

❑ **Antiquariat:** *Amber Road, Tel. 44259. Also has two shops in the shopping arcade at the Rajputana Palace Sheraton Hotel.* See next section on arts and crafts.

Arts and Crafts

❑ **Silver and Art Palace:** *Kachcha Bandha, Amer Road, Tel. 43980.* This very popular, award-winning, and successful shop is jam-packed with a wide selection of handicrafts, including silver boxes, sandalwood carvings, paintings, and rugs, as well as lots of interesting gems and jewelry.

The back room includes a beautiful collection of old and new enamel gold jewelry as well as an excellent selection of gemstones. Numerous foreign dealers purchase gems here. While many guides and bus drivers stop here with their clients, they do not receive the typical Jaipur commission for doing so (a nominal 2-4 percent rather than an outrageous 30-40 percent).

❑ **Manglam Arts:** *Govind Nagar, Amber Palace Road, Tel. 41176.* Filled with a nice selection of quality antiques, arts, and crafts. Includes miniature paintings on paper, marble, silk, ivory, cotton, and wood; hand woven durries; brass, wood, ivory, marble, and silver carvings; furniture; architectural pieces (doors and columns); puppets; linens; bed covers; cushions; textiles; and bags.

❑ **Khazana:** *Jai Mahal Palace Hotel. Jacob Road, Civil Lines, Tel. 371-616.* Another Khazana shop which is part of the Taj Mahal Hotel group. Nice selection of clothes, leather goods, bags, antiques, handicrafts, silver, jewelry, quilts, shawls, and durries.

❑ **Antiquariat:** *Amber Road, Tel. 44259. Also has two shops in the shopping arcade at the Rajputana Palace Sheraton Hotel.* Offers a nice selection of quality gems, jewelry, ivory, paintings, carpets, sandalwood, silver, and marble. One shop at the Rajputana Palace Sheraton Hotel is primarily devoted to jewelry and loose stones, including lots of nice ruby and sapphire rings as well as necklaces and antique gold.

❑ **Rajasthali:** *Rajasthan Government Handicraft Emporium, opposite Ajmeri Gate, M. I. Road, Tel. 367176.* Jam-packed with handicrafts and other products from all over Rajasthan—jewelry, bangles, shoes, brass, paintings, pottery, textiles, puppets, papier mache boxes, shawls, bed covers, wall hangings, carpets, durries, furniture, and ready-made clothes. Rather lethargic large staff that lacks the energy and enthusiasm of the more entrepreneurial Silver and Art Palace. You may want to come here first to check the fixed prices before venturing off to the bazaars and private handicraft emporiums. You may find the prices to be lower here; some prices also are higher here—depending on your bargaining skills elsewhere.

TEXTILES AND CARPETS

❑ **Arawali Exports:** *717 Jagdish Colony, Ramgarh Mor, Amber Road, Tel. 605-131.* Offers a good selection of silk fabrics.

❑ **Anokhi:** *2 Yudhistra Marg, behind the Secretariat, Tel. 381-619.* Includes an excellent selection of quality textiles: block-printed fabrics, tablecloths, bed covers, bags, and scarves.

❑ **Channi Carpets and Textiles:** *Mount Road, opposite Ramgarh Road, Tel. 40414.* Primarily engaged in carpet weaving which is done by Muslim children. Includes a good selection of silk block prints. Explore five halls for viewing and buying carpets and prints.

❑ **Pandey Textile Printer:** *Near New Bridge, Sanganer, Tel. 550-710.* Includes a good selection of printed table cloths, bed covers, sarees, dress material, and napkins. Offers very unique patterns and colors not found elsewhere in India.

❑ **Handloom House:** *Rituraj Building, M. I. Road.* Includes a large selection of textiles sold by the meter. Look for bed covers and clothes. Limited selections.

❑ **Satguru's:** *36, Jagdish Colony, Mount Road near Ramgad Mor,* Tel. 46146. This huge textile shop specializes in old embroidery and block prints. Includes bed covers, table cloths, scarves, sarees, wall hangings, and more. Popular with tour buses.

ACCOMMODATIONS

Jaipur offers a wide variety of accommodations, from modern luxury hotels and resorts to intriguing palace hotels and converted mansions (haveli). The three royal palace hotels (Rambagh, Jai Mahal, and Raj Mahal) are all run by the Taj Group. Jaipur's best hotels and resorts include:

❑ **Rambagh Palace:** *Bhawani Singh Road, Jaipur, 302 005, Rajasthan, Tel. 91-141-381-919 or Fax 91-141-381-098, USA & Canada Toll Free 800-458-8825.* Resplendent in its 47 acres, the Rambagh Palace was converted to a hotel in 1957 and is managed by the Taj Group. The 83 guestrooms are well appointed and refurbished with every modern amenity. Each of the 19 luxury rooms is quite spacious and decorated with individual themes. Reserve one of the royal suites—the Princes Suite, the Maharani Suite, and the Maharaja Suite were the former personal chambers of the royal family. The Suvarna Mahal is a regal dining room serving excellent food. Many patrons—both locals and foreign visitors—come from outside the hotel to dine here. The Neel Mahal, open round the clock is decorated in shades of blue with white marble which looks cool even when the mercury soars. Panghat, an outdoor amphitheater, stages Rajasthani folk programs. Indoor swimming pool, jogging track, fitness center and meeting rooms.

❑ **Rajvilas:** *Goner Road, Jaipur, 303 012, Tel: 91-141-64-0101 or Fax 91-141-64-0202, USA & Canada Toll Free 800-562-3764.* An Oberoi hotel and member of The Leading Hotels of the World, Rajvilas is set in tranquil countryside 8 kilometers from Jaipur's city center. The richly detailed fort-setting was constructed using fine finishes and craftsmanship to create an elegant luxury hotel steeped in the romance of Jaipur's opulent heritage. The 54 deluxe guestrooms are arranged in clusters of 4 and 6 rooms with a private central courtyard. The 14 luxury tents are beautifully appointed with teak wood flooring and amenities most guests have never imagined could be found in a tent! Or splurge on a villa—actually two villas with a private swimming pool or the ultimate Royal Villa. Chauffeur driven cars provide complimentary transfers between the hotel and the airport or railway station. A helipad is available on the resort for guests arriving by helicopter. The Surya Mahal restaurant serves fine ·Continental and Asian cuisine—the approach is to offer light fusion cooking with elements from different Asian countries as well as authentic Rajasthani thalis. Meeting facilities, recreational facilities and full spa facilities available. Everything about Rajvilas is first class. If you have enjoyed the tropical ambience of the Aman Resorts in Asia, you will surely want to experience the Rajasthan desert setting of Rajvilas in Jaipur.

❑ **Rajputana Palace Sheraton:** *Palace Road, Jaipur, 302 006, Rajasthan, Tel. 91-141-360-011 or Fax 91-141-367-*

848, USA & Canada Toll Free 800-325-3535. Part of the Welcomgroup chain, the Rajputana Palace Sheraton is located on 6 acres in the heart of Jaipur. A new hotel, rather than a conversion of an old palace, it provides the modern amenities expected by today's traveler in a traditional setting. The lobby is large and welcoming, light and cheery with its white walls and cream marble floors. Comfortable seating areas are strategically placed around a large fountain. The Sheraton's 218 guestrooms and 17 suites are attractively and comfortably furnished in soft hues. The Executive Club features separate check-in at the Executive Club reception desk, lounge facilities with complimentary continental breakfast, a communication center with secretarial services, and meeting rooms. Jal Mahal is a multi-cuisine buffet restaurant. Peshawri, a top of the line speciality restaurant serves the famous North West Frontier cuisine for lunch and dinner. The Chandravanshi Pavilion provides a-la-carte choices anytime—day or night. There is an outdoor shopping arcade on the lower level and outdoor cultural shows are presented in the evening. Conference and banquet facilities, health club and fitness center.

❑ **The Trident:** *Amber Fort Road, Jaipur, Rajasthan, 302 002, Tel. 91-141-630-101 or Fax 91-141-630-303, USA & Canada Toll Free 800-562-3764.* Situated at the base of the Amber Fort and overlooking scenic Jal Mahal on Mansagar Lake, the Trident is a five minute drive from Jaipur. Trident hotels are the mid-range line of the Oberoi Group. The pink facade of The Trident reflects traditional Rajasthani style of architecture. Each of the 140 rooms has its own balcony and is furnished in earth tones and indigo hues. There are non-smoking areas as well as guestrooms for disabled persons. Restaurants serve Asian and European cuisine. Conference room and swimming pool.

Two other palace hotels include:

❑ **The Jai Mahal Palace:** *Jacob Road, Civil Lines, Tel. 91-141-371-616 or Fax 91-141-365-237.* Includes 102 rooms with excellent views of the city.

❑ **The Raj Mahal Palace:** *Sardar Patel Marg, C-Scheme, Tel. 91-141-381-676 or 91-141-381-887.* A small but intimate property with only 21 rooms.

Deluxe hotels include the following:

- ❏ **Jaipur Ashok:** *Jai Singh Circle, Bani Park, Tel. 91-141-320-091 or Fax 91-141-322-999.* A government-operated property with 99 rooms.

- ❏ **Holiday Inn Jaipur:** *Amer Road, Tel. 91-141-509-000 or Fax 91-141-609-090.* Includes 72 rooms.

- ❏ **Mansingh:** *Sansar Chandra Road, 91-141-378-771 or Fax 91-141-377-582.* Includes 91 rooms.

- ❏ **Clarks Amer:** *Jawaharlal Nehru Marg, Tel. 91-141-550-701 or Fax 91-141-550-013.* Includes 202 rooms.

RESTAURANTS

Jaipur's best restaurants are found in the major hotels as well as along M. I. Road and at Raja Park. Many hotel restaurants, to accommodate large tour groups, also serve buffets for breakfast, lunch, and dinner. Expect to find North Indian, Chinese, and Continental cuisine but very few Rajasthani dishes. Jaipur has a large concentration of vegetarian restaurants.

- ❏ **Suvarna Mahal:** *Rambagh Palace, Bhawani Singh Road, Tel. 381-919.* This fine dining restaurant serves Indian, Chinese, and Continental specialties in an elegant and romantic dining room with high ceilings and wall tapestries. Open for lunch and dinner.

- ❏ **Niros:** *M. I. Road, Tel. 374-493.* This extremely popular and reliable restaurant with both locals and visitors has been in operation for over 50 years. Offers excellent Indian, Chinese, and Continental cuisine. Expect to stand in line for a table, but the line moves relatively quickly. Open for lunch and dinner.

- ❏ **Copper Chimney:** *M. I. Road, opposite post office, Tel. 374-493.* Offers Indian, Chinese, and Continental cuisine at quality and prices similar to Niros. After all, the kitchen here is operated by the former chef at Niros. Open for lunch and dinner.

- ❏ **Chanakya:** *4, A. B. Kashi Bhawan, M.I. Road, Tel. 376-161.* North Indian and Continental cuisine. The largest vegetarian restaurant in Rajasthan (seats 1,250 in five dining halls!). Excellent service. Open for lunch and dinner.

❑ **Shivir:** *M. I. Road, Government Hostel Junction, Tel. 378-771.* Indian cuisine served in a rooftop restaurant with a good view of the city.

❑ **Natraj:** *M. I. Road, Tel. 375-804.* North Indian, Chinese, and continental cuisine.

❑ **Chandravanshi Pavilion:** *Welcomgroup Rajputana Palace Sheraton, Tel. 360-011.* Open 24-hours a day, this restaurant serves a wide variety of excellent Indian and Continental dishes. Nice atmosphere and good service.

❑ **LMB (Laxmi Mishthan Bhandar):** *Johari Bazaar, Tel. 565-8344.* Very popular restaurant serving excellent vegetarian dishes at reasonable prices.

❑ **Handi Restaurant:** *M. I. Road, opposite the post office, Tel. 364-839.* Really basic restaurant (complete with plastic chairs and bamboo walls), but it serves excellent barbecue chicken and kebabs.

DINNER THEATERS

❑ **Panghat:** *Rambagh Palace, Bhawani Singh Road, Tel. 381-919.* Thaili dinner with a traditional Rajasthan show (singers, dancers, puppets) staged in an open-air amphitheater.

❑ **Chokhi Dhani:** *Tonk Road (22 kilometers from Jaipur), Tel. 550-118.* This traditional Rajasthan dinner and show (singers, dancers, puppets, jugglers) takes place in a traditional village complex where guests sit on the floor and eat vegetarian dishes with their hands.

SEEING THE SITES

Sightseeing in Jaipur is all about palaces, forts, and museums. If you're interested in history and architecture, Jaipur has a lot to offer in these departments. The major attractions include:

❑ **Palace of the Winds (Hawa Mahal):** *Pink City, Siredeori Bazar.* This rose-pink colored five-storey pyramid building, with its distinctive overhanging latticed balconies, is one of Jaipur's major "Pink City" symbols. Viewed on the west side of the street, just north of Johari Bazaar, it's an imposing architectural facade. It was once used by the court ladies to view the street and market activity in privacy. Unfortunately, most visitors only view the facade from the street. If you visit the City Palace Museum (entrance on Gangauri Bazaar), you also can tour the interior of the building. Hire a guide for Rs 50. He will take you through each level and explain the history and use of the building. From the top, you can get great views of city. Just beware of the aggressive monkeys that have claimed the building as their own!

❑ **Amber Fort:** *11 kilometers north of Jaipur, 9am - 4:30pm.* Also referred to as the Palace of Amber or just Amer, this grand and seemingly impenetrable fort served as the capital of the Kachhawah Rajputs for 600 years prior to establishing Jaipur in 1727. Within the massive stone walls lie several red sandstone and white marble pavilions, royal apartments, palace courtyards, finely carved lattice windows, sculptured pillars, doors, gates, and a pool. The fort also includes several handicraft and souvenir shops as well as a rug demonstration area—and lots of irritating touts—near the entrance. Many visitors make a grand entrance to the fort on top of a brightly adorned elephant, accompanied by musicians, from the foot of the fort to the main gate and into the courtyard—similar to the grand entrance made by many honored guests centuries ago. With over 50 elephants relieving themselves as they take hundreds of visitors up and down the narrow road to the fort each day, be very careful where you walk. The road and entrance often becomes a smelly stream of elephant urine and dung. Expect to encounter a unique and often amusing combination of car and elephant traffic jams at the entrance to the fort. Also nearby is the small **Kali Temple**.

❑ **Nahargarh Fort:** *Northwest of the Pink City, 10am - 4:30pm.* Also known as Tiger Fort. Located at the top of a 600-foot hill overlooking the city, this fort was built in 1734 for the defense of the city. A pleasant place to visit, with fewer crowds. Includes panoramic views of the city below.

❑ **City Palace and Museum:** *Enter along Gangauri Bazaar,*
9:30am - 4:30pm. Located at the center of the Pink City,
the City Palace was constructed in 1728. Today, half of
the palace remains a private residence. In addition to
viewing several buildings in the compound, the museum
displays numerous items from the royal household:
jewelry, arms, dresses, elephant seats, chariots, and
carriages. Just opposite the museum is the back side of
the popular "Palace of the Winds."

❑ **Rambagh Palace:** *Bhawani Singh Road.* This once
luxurious palace was converted into one of Jaipur's top
hotels. Interesting architecture and grounds as well as
excellent shopping and restaurants in the evening.

❑ **Jantar Mantar:** *Near the entrance to the City Palace,*
9:30am - 4:30pm. Built in 1726 to the specification of Jai
Singh II, this observatory of masonry, marble, and brass
has several interesting scientific instruments for analyz-
ing celestial data. Each instrument has its own function,
from giving the time to measuring the longitude and
latitude of celestial bodies.

ENTERTAINMENT

There's not much going on in the streets of Jaipur at night.
Instead, most evening entertainment is centered in the major
hotels. The **Welcomgroup Rajputana Palace Sheraton** (Tel.
368-254), for example, offers a daily cultural program of music
and dance between 7pm and 9pm. Regular cultural programs
also are presented at **Ravindra Manch** (Ram Nivas Garden,
Tel. 49061) and **Jawahar Kala Kendra** (Jawahar Lal Nehru
Building, Tel. 51051). Dinner theaters (see above under
"Restaurants"), such as **Panghat** (Tel. 381-919) at the Rambagh Palace Hotel and **Chokhi Dhani** (Tel. 550-118) along
Tonk Road outside Jaipur, offer interesting cultural programs
while dining under the stars. Bars at the major hotels also serve
as popular meeting places in the evening.

Jodhpur

Located on the edge of the Great Indian Thar Desert, Jodhpur is one of India's pleasant surprises. It's the gateway city to the Desert Triangle which includes the fascinating, exotic, and legendary medieval cities of Jaisalmer and Bikaner. The second largest city in the State of Rajasthan, with a population of nearly 800,000, Jodhpur retains its distinctive character with its impressive fortresses, especially the magnificent Mehrangarh Fort, marble palaces, temples, narrow streets, and bustling bazaars. In many respects, Jodhpur is a shopper's paradise, offering some of India's best shopping. However, many tourists by-pass this intriguing city on their way to nearby Jaisalmer in the west, Udaipur in the south, or Jaipur in the east. Plan to spend a couple of days here. It's time well worth spent.

SURPRISING JODHPUR

Jodhpur was founded by Rao Jodha, the chief of the Rathore clan of Rajputs, in 1459 after the sacking of nearby Mandore, which had served for nearly three centuries as the capital of the state of Marwar, the "Land of the Dead." The stronghold of the fierce Rathore clan, Jodhpur and its rulers at one time acquired great wealth due to the city's strategic location along the rich camel caravan routes of the Thar Desert.

You will most likely enjoy the people and pace of life in Jodhpur. The city is much less hectic than Jaipur. It's a friendlier city with less traffic and air pollution and few, if any, beggars. The city is especially known for its vibrant culture; schools of art and music; talented craftsmen who work as textile dyers, metal engravers, and die-makers; a massive fort overlooking the city; the grand Umaid Bhawan Palace which now serves as a five-star hotel; and lots of great shopping. The famous tailored Jodhpur "breeches" have all but disappeared. It's a city that retains many of its ancient traditions despite its sprawling and modern character. Jodhpur also has a significant military presence which you will occasionally be reminded of when you hear noisy jets and helicopters, and occasional bombs going off, in the surrounding area.

THE BASICS

LOCATION AND POPULATION

After Jaipur, Jodhpur is the second largest city in the State of Rajasthan with a population of nearly 800,000. The city is located 575 kilometers west of Agra, 275 kilometers north of Udaipur, and 602 kilometers southwest of Delhi. As the gateway to the Desert Triangle, Jodhpur is 285 kilometers from Jaisalmer and 245 kilometers from Bikaner.

WHEN TO GO

Situated on the edge of the Thar desert, Jodhpur is a very hot and dry city. The best months to visit are between October and March, although the coolest months are January and February.

GETTING THERE

Indian Airlines flies four times a week to Jodhpur from Mumbai, Delhi, Jaipur, and Udaipur. You usually make connections for Jodhpur through Jaipur and Udaipur. The airport is located about 5 kilometers from the city center. It costs about Rs 180 to take a taxi from the airport to the city but less to return to the airport from the city.

Trains do connect to Jodhpur through Delhi, Agra, Jaisalmer, Jaipur, Udaipur, and Ahmedabad. Expect long train journeys. The connection from Jaipur to Jodhpur takes less than 5 hours. The express train from Mumbai to Jodhpur takes 10 hours. The trip from Jodhpur to Agra takes about 20 hours.

Jodhpur is easily accessible by **road** to other cities. Jodhpur is 575 kilometers west of Agra; 275 kilometers north of Udaipur; and 602 kilometers southwest of Delhi.

GETTING AROUND

You can easily get around Jodhpur by taxi, auto-rickshaw, or bicycle. Since taxis and auto-rickshaws are unmetered, you need to bargain for your rides. Most auto-rickshaw trips within the city cost around Rs 20. Most taxis have fixed rates for various destinations. Ask before you get into the taxi. Bicycles can be rented by the hour at Sojati Gate. Like in other cities, we recommend hiring a car with driver by the half or full-day. You can arrange a car through your hotel tour desk.

TOURIST OFFICES AND TOURS

Local sightseeing can be arranged through the **Rajasthan Tourism** desk at the Hotel Gloomar (High Court Road, Tel. 45084 or 44010). Daily tours of the city and environs (Fort, Jaswant Memorial, Umaid Bhawan, and Mandor) depart from the hotel at 9am and 2pm. You also may want to consider taking a camel safari. Some of Jodhpur's major tour operators include **Aravali Safari and Tours** (Tel. 35944), **Poly Travels** (Tel. 45210), **Rajasthan Tours** (Tel. 36295), **Tourist Guide Service** (Tel. 33054), and **Travel Corporation of India** (Tel. 39052).

ORIENTATION

Jodhpur is a relatively pleasant and easy city to get around in. The city is basically divided into two sections—the new city and the old walled city. The new city lies southeast of the old walled city. Here you'll find the tourist office, major hotels, railway station, and the major handicraft and furniture emporiums. The main roads outside the old walled city are **Umaid Bhavan Road** which leads to the Umaid Bhavan Palace Hotel and several handicraft and furniture shops; **High Court Road** which parallels the railway and runs along the southern wall of the old city and Sojai Gate and includes several handicraft and furniture shops; and **Station Road** that runs south of the Sojati Gate and passes through Sakhari Bazaar and includes several leather shops.

The old city is distinctive for its nearly 10-kilometer stone wall, with eight massive gates, that snakes along the northwest section of Jodhpur. The walls also encompass temples, a clock tower, and Meherangarh Fort. The narrow streets in the medieval city are crammed with small shops. The best bazaar here is the **Sardar Bazaar**. The famous Meherangarh Fort towers over the center of the old city.

The best shopping is found along the main roads of the new city. The old city is an interesting cultural experience but don't expect to do much shopping there, even though you'll find lots of shops lining the narrow streets. The central market, or **Ghasmandi Bazaar**, is very popular with visitors. It's divided into various sections, starting with the general market area near the clock tower: cloth, ivory, bamboo, jewelry, silks, spice, fruit and vegetables, and sweets. The really "good stuff" is found elsewhere—outside these city walls.

BOUNTIFUL TREASURES

Jodhpur is especially known for its shopping and its wholesale and export operations. Many dealers from Europe and North America by-pass other cities in India and come directly to Jodhpur to do most of their shopping. They may spend five days here selecting enough items to fill at least one container of goods. In fact, Jodhpur is reputed to do more wholesaling and exporting of handicrafts and furniture than any other city in India. Responding to export markets, many of the factories and shops in Jodhpur design furniture and metal work products that are appropriate for Western tastes.

As a major shopping center, Jodhpur is well known for several types of products:

❑ **Handicrafts and antiques:** Jodhpur abounds with numerous handicrafts and antiques offered by some of India's best handicraft emporiums. But these are more than just handicraft emporiums. They represent numerous types of products produced in Jodhpur and the State of Rajasthan, and they are organized for exporting large qualities newly produced handicrafts and antique reproductions. Most of these places offer a large selection of textiles, silver, jewelry, instruments, pottery, boxes, carved ducks, metal work, marble figures, paintings, copper, brass, antique reproductions, ivory, embroidered shoes, figurines, insignias in white German metal, Badlas (zinc water bottles encased in a thick cloth), bed covers, wall hangings, puppets, sandalwood carvings, clothes, old doors, and lots of furniture, both old and new. For a good overview, including excellent handicraft selections, visit of **Rajasthan Art Emporium** (Heritage House Rae-ka-Bagh). Other wonderful places include **Lalji Handi-crafts** (Umaid Bhawan Palace Road); **Sun City Art Exporters** (formerly known as Jodhpur Art Exporters; 5, Umaid Bhawan Palace Road); **Rajasthan Arts and Crafts House** (Umaid Bhawan Palace Road), **Abani Handicrafts** (Anand Bhawan, High Court Road), and **Abani Art Emporium** (inside Umaid Bhawan Palace). Many of these shops and emporiums do a great deal of exporting abroad since many dealers come to Jodhpur to do their buying. Within the old city, **Tripolia Bazaar** is noted for handicrafts.

❑ **Furniture:** Some of the best selections of furniture in India can be found in shops and warehouses along Umaid Bhawan Palace Road and High Court Road. The one-kilometer long **Lalji Handicrafts** shop on Umaid Bhawan Road is well worth visiting. Other so-called handicraft emporiums, such as **Rajasthan Art Empo-rium, Suncity Art Exporters**, and **Abani Handicrafts**.

❑ **Textiles:** Look for Jodhpur's famous Bandhani and Lahariya (tie and dye textiles) as well as block screens and prints. Many these can be found in **Kapra Bazaar** within the old walled city and near **Sojati Gate**. For good quality silks and sarees, be sure to visit **Lucky Store** (Sojati Gate), **Prakash Silk Stores** (opposite Sojati Gate), and **Bhagatram Ishwarlal** (across the street from Prakash Silk Stores). Try **Kanda Falsa** area for tie and dye sarees.

❑ **Carpets and durries:** Carpets and durries can be found in several shops along **High Court Road**.

❑ **Leather goods:** Look for camel shoes in **Mochi Bazaar** in the walled city and along **Station Road**.

❑ **Jewelry and silver:** Discover unique silver jewelry in **Sarafa Bazaar** within the old city and in shops along **Station Road**.

TREASURES WITHOUT TOUTS

What is nice about shopping in Jodhpur is the fact that the city has fewer touts because it also has fewer tourists. Nonetheless, some shops do give commissions to drivers and guides, but it's closer to 10 percent rather than the standard 30-40 percent found in many highly touristed cities. Since there's less pressure to buy here, you'll probably do lots of browsing in some of the large shops.

While you'll find numerous small shops in the various bazaars within the old walled city (Tropolia, Sardar, Nai Sarah, and Station Road in the Sojati Gate area), most are not as worthwhile to visit as the bazaars in Jaipur and Udaipur. However, if you visit only one bazaar, go to **Sardar Market** which is the city's best bazaar with its general merchandise. Other bazaars specialize in particular products: **Sojati Gate** (emporia and gift shops), **Tripolia Bazaar** (local handicrafts), **Mochi Bazaar** (embroidered shoes), **Khanda Falsa** (tie and dye sarees), and **Lakhara Bazaar** (lac work and bangles).

Like a dealer, you may be able to do most of your shopping at a few handicraft and furniture shops, such as **Lalji Handicrafts**, **Rajasthan Art Emporium**, **Suncity Art Exporters**, and **Abani Handicrafts**, as well as at a few quality shops in the Umaid Bhawan Palace Hotel—**Abani Art Emporium**, **Jawaharat**, and **Jain Art Emporium**).

ACCOMMODATIONS

Jodhpur has several heritage hotels worth considering when booking accommodations in this city. The best hotels include:

❑ **Umaid Bahawan Palace Hotel:** *Jodhpur 342006, Rajasthan, Tel. 91-291-33316 or Fax 91-291-635-373.* A Welcomgroup property, this is one of the great palace hotels in India. An example of tasteful Art Deco-style architecture in the 1930s, this opulent palace of rose sandstone and marble is the place to stay in Jodhpur. Much of the palace has been converted to a five-star hotel, although it does have a museum and the family of the current Maharaja of Jodhpur still resides in the upper wings of the palace. Includes 94 spacious rooms, 30 suites, 3 restaurants, shops, tennis courts, health club, sports facilities, and much more. This is true decadence you may not want to leave for the hot and narrow streets of the old walled city! Expensive but not unreasonable at US$200 a night for a standard double.

❏ **Ratanada Polo Palace:** *Residency Road, Jodhpur, Rajasthan, Tel. 91-291-31910 or Fax 91-291-33118.* Owned by the son of India's famous polo player, Raorajahanut Singh, this is a popular but very standard business hotel located on the road to the airport. Includes 80 rooms, 9 suites, restaurant, shops, and business services.

❏ **Ajit Bhawan:** *Near Circuit House, Jodhpur 324006, Rajasthan, Tel. 91-291-61240 or Fax 91-291-637-774.* A heritage hotel. Owned by the Maharajah's uncle, Maharajah Swaroop Singh. This converted small palace offers spacious rooms in a very charming desert-village setting that is popular with visitors. Offers several stone cottages in a garden setting. Includes 52 rooms, 11 suites, restaurant, and sports facilities. Sponsors village safaris. Good value.

❏ **Maharaja Resorts:** *Sardar Samand Palace, 55 kilometers from Jodhpur, Tel. 91-291-33316 or Fax 91-291-35373.* A heritage hotel. Includes 18 rooms, restaurant, and bar.

❏ **Sardarsamand Lake Resort:** *Located 60 kilometers southeast of Jodhpur. Make reservations through the Umaid Bhawan Palace Hotel, Tel. 91-291-33316 or Fax 91-291-35373.* This is the lake side hunting lodge of the former Maharaja of Jodhpur. Includes 10 rooms, restaurant, and sports facilities.

RESTAURANTS

Jodhpur's best restaurants are found in the major hotels. These include:

❏ **Marwar Hall:** *Umaid Bhawan Palace Hotel, Tel. 33316.* This opulent restaurant with chandeliers and vaulted ceiling, serves excellent Continental and Indian dishes, including local dishes. Buffet-style dining.

❏ **Khamaghani:** *Ratanada Polo Palace Hotel, Residency Road, Tel. 31910.* Serves Indian, Chinese, and Continental cuisine in a classy and relaxed setting decorated with sarees.

❏ **On the Rocks:** *Ajit Bhawan Hotel, Tel. 612-410.* Serves a popular buffet in a pleasant courtyard. Includes Indian and Chinese dishes along with Rajasthani specialties.

❏ **Kalinga Restaurant:** *Hotel Adarsh Niwas, Tel. 26936.* A popular restaurant with budget travelers. Serves Continental, Tandoor, and Mughlai cuisine.

❏ **Mid Town:** Shanti Bhawan Lodge, Station Road, Tel. 37001. Located near the railway station, this very clean and popular restaurant serves excellent vegetarian dishes. Includes Rajasthani, South Indian, Chinese, and Continental specialties.

SEEING THE SITES

Aside from shopping, there's not a lot to do in Jodhpur. Sightseeing centers around a fort, palace, and the walled city. You can easily cover the highlights of the area within a day, or even less. Major attractions include:

❏ **Mehrangarh Fort:** Located above the heart of the old walled city, this fort was built in 1459 when the capital was moved from nearby Mandore to present-day Jodhpur. Located 5 kilometers from the city center and perched on a stone hill some 121 meters above the city, this massive fortress has walls 6 to 36 meters high and 3 to 21 meters wide. The fort includes eight gates and three main palaces (Moti Mahal, Phool Mahal, Sheesh Mahal) adorned with beautifully carved panels, delicate latticed windows, and pierced screens of red sandstone. Includes an very interesting palace museum (open 9am - 5pm daily in winter and 8am - 6pm in the summer) with lots of memorabilia displayed in 18 different sections, from palanquins to paintings. If you choose to walk up to the fort, it's a challenging 30-minute climb. One of India's most impressive fortresses.

❏ **Umaid Bhawan Palace Museum:** *Umaid Bhawa Palace Hotel, Open daily 9am - 5pm.* Located two kilometers southeast of the city center at the top of a hill, this impressive palace was built between 1923 and 1945, providing employment for 3,000 famine-stricken people in 1923. Located on 26 acres, this rose sandstone and marble palace is 195 meters long and 103 meters wide.

While most of the palace functions as a hotel or residence of the royal family, part of it includes a museum which includes old clocks and watches, books, hunting trophies, scrolls, royal treaties, and a decorated Durbar Hall.

❑ **Mandore Gardens:** *Mandore, 10 kilometers north of Jodhpur, gardens open daily from sunrise to sunset and museum open Saturday - Thursday from 10am to 4pm.* The gardens stand where the old capital of Marwar once stood. Includes a manicured pathway through lush green lawns with shade trees on each side. Includes rock-carved sculptures (Hall of Heros) of 16 figures carved from a single piece of stone and a small museum displaying sculptures as well as ivory and lacquer pieces. A popular spot for picnics.

❑ **Jaswant Thada:** *Near Meherangarh Fort, Open daily 8am - 6pm.* Located 5 kilometers from the city, this pure white marble memorial was built in 1899 by the widow of Maharaja Jaswant Singh II. The memorial serves as a crematorium for royalty. Includes a genealogy and portraits of the rulers of Jodhpur. Famous for its rare 15-cm think, pure slabs of white marble.

ENTERTAINMENT

Not much goes on at night in Jodhpur. Hotel bars, such as the **Trophy Bar** at the Umaid Bhawan Palace Hotel, provide some entertainment until closing time at 11pm. Many of the city's bazaars do stay open until late at night.

Udaipur

I f you've equated the State of Rajasthan with desert-bound fortress cities, Udaipur will come as a pleasant surprise. Located on three lakes with fairytale white marble palaces, temples, havelis, and lush gardens, and surrounded by green forested hills, Udaipur is one of India's most romantic places. Founded in 1599 by Maharana Udai Singh, the leader of the royal house of Mewar which is now known as Udaipur, this is an attractive and friendly city of nearly 350,000 inhabitants. While it is justly famous for the Lake Palace Hotel, museums, and palaces, it is also known for its vibrant art community and craftspeople. In Udaipur, you can stroll the streets and window shop for a large variety of arts and crafts that are unique to Udaipur and the surrounding area. Plan to spend a couple of days here enjoying this lakeside community of artists and craftspeople. It's a favorite destination of most tourists.

SURPRISING UDAIPUR

In many respects Udaipur feels like a small town. Known as the "City of Dreams" and "The Venice of India," Udaipur lacks the extreme traffic congestion, air pollution, and noise found in many other Indian cities. It's pleasant to just walk the narrow and winding streets of the old city and leisurely shop for Udaipur's unique miniature paintings and craft items. Indeed, shopping may become your favorite pastime as you slip into Udaipur's pleasant ambience.

THE BASICS

LOCATION AND POPULATION

Udaipur is one of the largest cities in the State of Rajasthan with a population of nearly 350,000. Located in the southern part of the state, Udaipur is 630 kilometers southwest of Agra, 406 kilometers southwest of Jaipur, and 275 kilometers south of Jodhpur.

WHEN TO GO

The best months to visit Udaipur are between October and March. The coolest months are January and February.

GETTING THERE

Indian Airlines has daily flights to Udaipur from Delhi, Jaipur, Mumbai, Jodhpur, and Aurangabad. **UP Air** flies daily from Delhi, Mumbai, and Jaipur. **Dabok Airport** is located 21 kilometers from the city center. Taxis from the airport to the city cost Rs 200 and take about 40 minutes. If your flight arrives late in the evening, taxis may be difficult to find. Unfortunately, the airport does not have buses or auto-rickshaws. On occasion, especially during busy holidays, arriving passengers do get stranded at the airport!

The city also is connected by **rail** to Delhi (21 hours), Jaipur, Ajmer, Chittaur, Jodhpur, and Ahmedabad. The railway station is located 4 kilometers from the city center.

Several **express buses** service Jodhpur from Delhi, Ahmedabad, Jaipur, and Jodhpur. However, the trip by road can be long, tiring, and dangerous. For example, Jodhpur to Udaipur which is only 275 kilometers, takes 7 hours. We prefer flying.

GETTING AROUND

Taxis and auto-rickshaws are plentiful in Udaipur. However, most meters don't work and prices tend to be expensive. The drivers usually quote a flat rate which may be listed on a chart. Taxis go for over Rs 100 per hour. You'll find posted rates at many hotels. In many cases, you'll need to bargain for a ride. Auto-rickshaws usually charge Rs 30 an hour when you use them for the day. Also, look for cycle-rickshaws and *tongas* (horse carriages). You can rent bicycles.

As in most of our other cities, we recommend hiring a car with driver by the half or full-day. You can arrange a car through your hotel tour desk.

TOURIST OFFICES AND TOURS

The Government of Rajasthan's **Tourist Information Centre** is located at Pateh Memorial Suraj Pole (Tel. 411-535). Look for **Tourist Information Counters** at Dabok Airport and the railway station. For tours of the city and surrounding area, contact **Aravali Safari** (Tel. 420-282), **Lake End Tours** (Tel. 523-611), **Meera Tour and Travels** (Tel. 415-249), **Rajasthan Tours** (Tel. 525-777), **Srinath Travel** (Tel. 529-391), and **TBS Tours and Travels** (Tel. 29661).

ORIENTATION

Udaipur consists of an old and new city. Most of your activities will probably focus on the old city which was once bounded by walls. Today, only the remains of these walls exit. This section of the city lies immediately to the east of Lake Pichola. The famous marble white Lake Palace Hotel sits in the lake, directly across from the City Palace and the Shivniwas Palace Hotel. The center of the city is at **Chetak Circle**, located in the northeast section of the city. The winding and hilly streets and lanes of the old city are lined with tall whitewashed houses with entrances decorated with folk art and windows made of stained glass. You'll find lots of shops and old havelis with large courtyards in this area. It's best to explore this interesting area on foot. However, watch where you step. Public sanitation standards in this city leave a lot to be desired.

The best shopping is found along the main roads of the old city. Look for these shopping areas: **Hathipol**, **Chetak Circle**, **Clock Tower**, **Palace Road**, **Bapu Bazaar**, and **City Market**.

UDAIPUR'S UNIQUE TREASURES

Udaipur is well known for its artists and craftspeople. Several art schools in the city train individuals who produce traditional Rajput-Mughal-style **miniature paintings** which are produced on a variety of mediums, such as ivory, bone, paper, silk, marble, and wood. However, since the use of ivory is now banned, many of the miniature paintings are done on bone which looks like ivory and is actually more durable. Udaipur also is famous for producing **furniture** covered with silver and inlaid with mother of pearl and bone. Also look for antique silver jewelry, clothes, Udaipur- and Gujarati-style embroidery, shoes, wood toys, stuffed toys, tie and dye sarees and turbans, hand-painted textiles, wall hangings, ivory and sandalwood carvings, and cane and carved furniture. Most of these products are made in Udaipur or in nearby villages.

TREASURES AMONGST THE TOUTS

With the increasing number of tourists have come more and more touts who steer tourists into particular shops. As a result, many of the fixed-price government emporiums tend to be very quiet because commission-hungry drivers, guides, and street touts have boycotted these places. At the same time, prices may seem very high in small shops, especially those that offer miniature paintings. Since many drivers, guides, and touts expect a 25-30 percent commission on steering customers to shops, prices are often grossly inflated. Consequently, plan to do some hard bargaining in the bazaars, especially the popular but tout thick Hathipol Market, and small shops that line the major shopping streets. You may be able to negotiate a 25 to 30 percent discount if you claim you have arrived at the shop tout-free!

Don't be discouraged from asking the *"Is it possible to do better on this price?"* question even if the shop claims to have "fixed prices"—remind them that you found the shop on your own and not with a driver, guide, or street tout who might try to hit them up for a commission on your purchases. Emporiums have fixed prices but some private emporiums may discount on large ticket items.

Udaipur's main shopping center is at **Chetak Circle**. Here you'll find one of the first shops you should visit—**Rajasthan Government Handicrafts Emporium** (26, Chetak Circle, open 10am - 7pm). This shop has a large selection of attractive pottery, paintings, silver jewelry, textiles, wall hangings, brass, sandalwood, bed covers, quilts, dolls, the table cloths at fixed prices. The emporium continues to embattle touts by putting a sign up that warns customers to avoid touts who get a 20-25 percent commission. It's best to start your Udaipur shopping adventure here so you can get a good idea of comparative pricing of goods. You may be shocked at the prices in other shops and disappointed at what you paid if you shopped elsewhere before coming here first.

Other good places to shop include the following:

❏ **Manglam Arts:** *Sukhadia Circle, Tel. 28239.* This is a branch shop of one of our favorite handicraft, antique, and furniture shops in Jaipur and Agra. This very nice two-level shop is chucked-full of good quality paintings, silver, furniture, knives, doors, windows, and inlaid bone, ivory, and mother of pearl boxes. Unlike its other shops, this one tends to specialize in art and furniture. You can see a painting demonstration on the first floor (tour groups come here to see it) and observe the making of the unique silver furniture at the workshop on the roof of the building. Manglam Arts claims to be one of the largest exporters of this type of furniture which you may or may not find particularly attractive. It may look tacky in your home or make a perfect accent piece! Nonetheless, this is one of Udaipur's best shops for good quality handicrafts, art, furniture, and antiques.

❏ **Apollo Arts:** *Near Hathipol Market.* One of Udaipur's oldest and most reputable family shops that introduced batik art to Udaipur. Good for batik wall-hangings and miniature paintings on bone.

❏ **Art Centre:** *Aychario Ki Pole, Jagdish Road, Near Jagdish Temple.* Includes an interesting demonstration/workshop area for one of Udaipur's best artists, Kanhaiya Soni, and his students. Does beautiful detailed work in bone and wood.

❏ **Artist Kanhaiya Soni Art Center:** *Jagdish Road, Tel. 524-944.* Offers a good quality and selections of miniature paintings.

❏ **Rajasthan Art School:** Located inside the City Palace, this shop offers a good selection of jewelry, textiles, paintings, silver, sandalwood, stones, clothes, and shoes.

❏ **University of Arts:** *166 City Palace Road, Tel. 422-591.* Offers some of Udaipur's best quality puppets.

❏ **Ashok Art:** *96 Patwa Street, near Jagdish Temple.* A good place to watch artists at work producing miniature paintings.

- **Cottage Industry Exposition (C.I.E.):** *City Palace, Tel. 28111.* Another one of the popular Kashmiri-operated handicraft emporiums with nice displays and a large carpet section.

- **Hathipol Market:** This is the main market for tourists. Even though touts heavily prowl this area and will want to take you to their favorite places, this is still a good market to explore. Be sure to bargain hard for clothes, silk paintings, and antiques. Skip the over-priced jewelry and batiks which are better buys elsewhere.

ACCOMMODATIONS

Udaipur is a great place to relax in the luxury of a palace hotel. Many of these palaces operate like resorts, offering a variety of sports opportunities, such as boating, horseback riding, and camel safaris. Indeed, the city offers several interesting palace hotels that are well worth considering for at least the cultural experience. Since the top two palace hotels have few rooms and are often fully booked, be sure to make reservations well in advance of your arrival date. These and many other hotels also offer cultural programs that primarily consist of puppet shows and folk dances. Udaipur's best **palace hotels** include:

- **Taj Lake Palace Hotel:** *Lake Pichola, Udaipur 313001, Rajasthan, Tel. 91-294-527-961 or Fax 91-294-527-974.* This is Udaipur's most spectacular palace hotel. Located on Pichola Lake and accessible by boat, this elegant 250-year old white marble palace is the favorite of VIPs and upscale travelers. Most rooms have a lake view. Includes 76 rooms, 8 suites, restaurant, bar, shops, pool, and health and sports facilities. Expect to pay US$125-$150 per night for a standard double to stay in such opulence.

- **Shivniwas Palace:** *City Palace, Udaipur 313001, Rajasthan, Tel. 91-294-528-016 or Fax 91-294-528-006.* Located next door to the City Palace. Formerly a royal guesthouse, this property offers excellent views of Lake Pichola. The gorgeous suites are very regal and expensive. Includes 13 rooms, 18 suites, restaurant, bar, health club, pool, and sports facilities. Standard rooms go for around US$100. Expect to pay US$200 to US$500 for the various suites.

❑ **Fateh Prakash Palace:** *City Palace, Udaipur 313001, Rajasthan, Tel. 91-294-528-008 or Fax 91-294-528-012.* A former grand palace built around 1900. Includes 9 rooms, 6 suites, multicuisine restaurant, pool, fitness center, and sports opportunities. Rooms have excellent views of Lake Pichola.

❑ **Laxmi Vilas Palace:** *Fateh Sagar Road, Udaipur 313001, Rajasthan, Tel. 91-294-529-711 or Fax 91-294-525-536.* This former royal guesthouse includes 54 rooms, 10 suites, restaurant, bar, pool, and tennis courts.

❑ **Shikarbadi Hotel:** *Gorendhan Vilas, Udaipur 313001, Rajasthan, Tel. 91-294-528-008 or Fax 91-294-528-012.* Includes 31 rooms, pool, unique puppet shows, and sports opportunities.

The following **standard hotels** offer a good range of accommodations:

❑ **Rajdarshan:** *18, Pannadhai Marg, Udaipur 313001, Rajasthan, Tel. 91-294-526-601 or Fax 91-294-524-588.* Includes 52 rooms, restaurant, bar, and pool.

❑ **Hill Top Palace:** *5, Ambavgarh, Pateh Sagar, Udaipur 313001, Rajasthan, Tel. 91-294-561-664 or Fax 91-294-525-106.* Includes 62 rooms with restaurant and bar. Sponsors puppet show and folk dances.

❑ **Oriental Palace Resorts:** *Main Road, Udaipur 313001, Rajasthan, Tel. 91-294-412-373 or Fax 91-294-411-238.* Includes 35 rooms with restaurant and bar.

❑ **Rangniwas Palace Hotel:** *Udaipur 313001, Rajasthan, Tel. 91-294-523-891 or Fax 91-294-.* Includes 24 rooms with restaurant and pool. Offers puppet shows, folk dances, and horse and camel safaris.

RESTAURANTS

Udaipur's best restaurants are found in the major hotels. These include:

❑ **Gallery Restaurant:** *Fateh Prakash Palace, City Palace Complex, Tel. 16219 or 528-016.* Udaipur's most elegant and romantic restaurant with a wonderful view of Lake Pichola and its palaces. Serves excellent Continental cuisine accompanied by classical Indian musicians. Reservations essential. Coat and tie required. Also serves afternoon tea from 3 to 5pm.

❑ **Neel Kamal:** *Taj Lake Palace Hotel, Tel. 527-961.* This small dining room offers Continental and Indian cuisine as well as several Rajasthani dishes. Nonguests need reservations.

❑ **Berry's:** *Near Chetak Circle, Tel. 25132.* Popular restaurant for Indian, Chinese, and Continental dishes. Especially popular for its ice cream.

❑ **Roof Garden Cafe:** *Across from the City Palace and around the corner from the Rang Niwas Palace Hotel.* Excellent food and service accompanied by live Rajasthani folk music in the evening. Unique decor with its umbrella-covered roof patio.

❑ **Parkview Restaurant:** *Opposite the Town Hall and park in the main section of town.* Popular for its reasonably priced North Indian, Chinese, and Continental dishes.

❑ **Shilpi:** *Near Shilpgram Village, Rani Road, Tel. 522-475.* Pleasant and casual garden restaurant serving Indian and Chinese cuisine.

SEEING THE SITES

Udaipur's lovely setting yields many attractive sites. Most of them are found within close proximity of each other near the lakes. It's a pleasant area to tour by bicycle (your hotel should have rentals available).

You can easily cover the major sites in and around Udaipur within a day. They primarily center around museums, palaces, and gardens:

❑ **City Palace and Museum:** *City Palace Complex, Open daily 9:30am - 4:30pm.* Built in 1725, this is the largest palace in Rajasthan. It, along with adjacent buildings which have been converted to palace hotels, once served as the residence and offices of the maharanas of Udaipur. Overlooking Lake Pichola, this is a sprawling structure of ornate arches, cupolas, and white filigreed balconies and windows, with a labyrinth of narrow walkways and courtyards. The many rooms and museum display a large collection of paintings, porcelain, toys, inlaid glasswork, and antique furniture. Given the size and complexity of this structure, you may want to purchase the excellent guidebook available at the entrance and/or hire a guide to help you get through it all. Guides are available at the gate.

❑ **Lake Pichola:** Surrounded by hills, palaces, temples, bathing ghats, and embankments, this beautiful lake includes two island palaces: Jag Niwas and Jag Mandir. Jag Niwas, which once served as the summer residence for the Newar princes, has been converted to a five-star hotel. While the Jag Niwas is a beautiful white marble structure from a distance, you need to be staying at the Lake Palace Hotel or have dinner reservations in order to see the place. Access to the hotel is strictly controlled from a boat launch area near the base of the City Palace Museum. Jag Mandir Palace is located at the southern end of the lake.

❑ **Folk Art and Puppet Museum (Bharatiya Lok Kala Mandal):** A famous folk art museum displaying puppets from India and around the world. Also include musical instruments and tribal items. The museum offers hourly (almost) puppet shows. Includes a small training center (to left of entrance) where you can see puppets being made. Open from 9am to 6pm.

❑ **Jagdish Temple:** *150 meters north of the entrance to the City Palace.* Built in 1651 by Maharana Jagat Singh I and dedicated to Lord Vishnu. This Indo-Aryan style structure is Udaipur's largest and best temple. Intricately carved with a brass image of the Garuda.

❑ **Sahelion-ki-Bar:** *Saheli Marg, open 8am - 7pm.* Located near Sukhadia Circle, this is one of Udaipur's best gardens. Known as the Garden of the Maids of Honor, it includes beautiful landscaped gardens with a lovely lotus pond, four marble elephants, and several fountains. It also includes a pool pavilion and a unusual Community Science Center with sea monsters, stuffed bats, and neanderthal heads.

❑ **Crystal Gallery:** *Located inside Fateh Prakash Palace.* A fabulous collection of crystal by the former maharana. Includes several rooms of crystal furniture, picture frames, mirrors, vases, lighting fixtures, trays, and much more. Also includes silver and gold objects as well as a bejeweled throne.

❑ **Shilpgram:** Located 4½ kilometers west of Udaipur, this crafts village and performing arts center serves as a living ethnographic museum. Depicts the lifestyles of folk and tribal communities of India's West Zone—Rajasthan, Goa, Gujarat, Maharashtra, Daman and Diu, and Dadra and Nagar Haveli. You can observe craftsmen weaving textiles, carving, and making stuffed toys in a re-created village setting complete with 26 authentic huts. The area also includes shrines, a museum, and a folk art gallery. Camel rides available. Very quiet area since drivers, guides, and touts tend to boycott this "no commission" operation. The place comes alive in December when an annual fair is held here with artists and craftsmen from all over India in attendance.

ENTERTAINMENT

Udaipur offers some of the best cultural shows in all of Rajasthan. Many of the major hotels regularly put on puppet shows as well as Rajasthan musical and dance performance. Between August and April, one hour Rajasthani folk dance and music performances are held at 7pm, Monday through Saturday, at the **Meera Kala Mandir** (Tel. 583-176), Sector 11, Hiran Magari (near the Pars Theatre). Most major hotels have bars. One of the best, with an excellent view of Lake Pichola, is at the **Shivniwas Hotel** (open 11am - 11pm).

Hyderabad

I f you've spent most of your time visiting northern India in such places as Delhi, Varanasi, Agra, and Jaipur, Hyderabad may come as a pleasant surprise. Located in the South and serving as the capital of the State of Andhra Pradesh, Hyderabad is India's fifth largest city with a population of 4.2 million. Known as the Istanbul of India, because of its Muslim architecture and culture, and the pearl capital of India, because of its thriving pearl industry, Hyderabad also is a relatively neat and clean city. It's also one of the major Muslim strongholds in the South. If you enjoy seeing historical sites and shopping for pearls, jewelry, textiles, and handicrafts, Hyderabad may be the perfect place to visit in southern India.

A COSMOPOLITAN SOUTHERN CITY

South India is different. Not only is the climate warmer and more humid than in the North, but it's a relatively wealthier region of the country. The peoples, cultures, and cuisines also differ from other areas of the country.

Hyderabad is a unique city. Juxtaposing the old and the new, Hyderabad has the look and feel of a Muslim city. Reflecting its Islamic roots, many of its old buildings are more than 400 years old. Attractive minarets and domes of mosques and public buildings dot the city landscape. Add to this the city's lakeside and riverfront location, wide streets, new construction, new international airport, and well maintained public areas, and Hyderabad takes on a distinct character of its own.

At present few tourists include Hyderabad on their travel itineraries. This in part reflects the southern character of travel: tour groups and tourists primarily go to the south to see famous temples and temple complexes. Since Hyderabad is not a major temple center, nor is it on the way to other major tourist spots, it is normally by-passed by the average culture-oriented tourist. This is not to say it lacks an important history nor has little to offer international visitors. Indeed, Hyderabad boasts the largest fortress in the south, the spectacular hilltop Golconda Fort with its seven kilometers of walls and bastions, and includes many other interesting historical and architectural sites. The lack of tourists also reflects the fact that Hyderabad remains an undiscovered shopper's paradise.

Hyderabad is primarily a business city on two fronts. Wholesalers and jewelers from all over India, as well as from abroad, come to Hyderabad to deal in pearls. In fact, Hyderabad is a world-famous center for polishing, piercing, sorting, grading, and stringing pearls. Over 90 percent of all pearls in India are reported to at some stage pass through Hyderabad; a very high percentage of pearls from abroad also come to Hyderabad where the city's famous skilled pearl artisans and cheap labor are responsible for making the city one of the world's most important pearl centers. Second, within the past few years, Hyderabad has increasingly become an important high-tech center in India. As more and more computer companies move to Hyderabad, the city should become India's new high-tech center rivaling the premier high-tech status now held by Bangalore.

Hyderabad also is one of the cleanest and neatest cities in India. The city administration has made major efforts to clean up the city's streets and sidewalks with its army of street cleaners and painters. While many local residents see this as politically motivated and thus temporary, at least until the next election, it is a significant departure from many other cities in

- ❑ Hyderabad is India's fifth largest city with 4.2 million people.

- ❑ Hyderabad has the look and feel of a Muslim city.

- ❑ By-passed by the average culture-oriented tourist, Hyderabad remains an undiscovered shopper's paradise.

- ❑ Over 90 percent of all pearls in India at some stage pass through Hyderabad.

- ❑ Within the past few years, Hyderabad has become an important high-tech center.

- ❑ This is one of the cleanest and neatest cities in India.

India which tend to be appallingly trashy and chaotic. The near absence of animals wandering the streets and a civic campaign to keep the city clean seem to have made a difference in Hyderabad's sanitation standards. Nonetheless, the city is at time extremely crowded, congested, and chaotic, especially in the old city around Charminar and in the northern twin city of Secunderabad. The market areas are especially chaotic. While the streets and sidewalks may appear relatively clean, the city is victim to heavy air pollution due to the presence of so many pollution-belching auto-rickshaws, motorcycles, motorscooters, buses, trucks, and cars.

GETTING TO KNOW YOU

Located two hours south of New Delhi and one hour northwest of Chennai by air, Hyderabad is situated at the top center of the southern region. Its lakeside and riverside location—along with its mix of many old buildings in medieval, Moghul, Colonial, and Indo-Saracenic styles adjacent to modern hotels and commercial buildings—make this visually an especially interesting urban center that blends old world charm with a frenzy of modern urban activity.

Hyderabad's history dates from the establishment of the Muslim and Turkoman dynasty of Qutb Shahi and is closely tied to the evolution of the city's pearl trade. In 1512 Quli Qutb Shab established the fortress city of Golconda in what is now **Golconda Fort**. Located 13 kilometers from the city and the largest fortress in southern India, this massive structure with its eight gates and 70 bastions, was partially abandoned in 1589 due to inadequate water supplies and frequent epidemics of cholera and the plague. In that year the fifth Quli Qutb Shahi ruler, Mohammad, moved the capital to the banks of the River Musi. Here the **Charminar**, often referred to as the "Arc de Triomphe of the East," was constructed at the city center along with four main roads that intersected at the imposing monument. Fascinated with pearls, local rulers assembled top artisans to the banks of the **River Musi** where they eventually developed Hyderabad's traditional pearl trade which now draws thousands of local and international visitors to this city each year. Today's pearl trade remains centered in the hundreds of small pearl shops that surround the Charminar and constitute the city's famous "Pearl Market" along **Pathergatti Road**.

Hyderabad actually consists of two separate cities that blend together—**Secunderbad** in the north and **Hyderabad** in the south. Connected as a twin city just north of Hussain Sagar

Lake at Tank Bund, Secunderbad was established as a British cantonment as a result of an alliance between the local ruler (Nizam) and the British East India Company in 1798. Today, except for the imaginary line drawn across the Tank Bund, Secunderbad blends into Hyderabad as part of the larger metropolis. It is perhaps most noteworthy for its several congested commercial streets lined with shops offering pearls, textiles, handicrafts, and a large array of local products.

Hyderabad is where most of the action is—major hotels, restaurants, sites, markets, and shops. The city also is divided into the old and new parts. The newer part lies north of the River Musi and includes most of the city's major hotels and government and commercial buildings as well as a few of its major landmark buildings, such as the Birla Planetarium, Birla Mandir (temple), Osmania University, King Koti Palace, and the legislative building as well as Hyderabad's popular lakeside promenade, the Tank Bund, with its 33 statutes of famous state personalities and a statute of Buddha at the center of the lake.

The old city is located south of the River Musi and is best identified with the massive but graceful Charminar, the arch with four 175-foot high minarets, that symbolizes the city and serves as the landmark for Hyderabad's major pearl, bangle, textile, and handicraft markets. It also includes the adjacent mosque, **Mecca Masjid**, the eclectic riverfront **Salar Jung Museum**, the **High Court** building with its impressive minarets, and the popular **Nehru Zoological Park**.

Most visitors to Hyderabad head for the old city. There they focus attention on Charminar and its surrounding pearl, bangle, textile, and handicraft markets, the city's architectural masterpieces, and Salar Jung Museum. Many of them also visit the Golconda Fort which is located 13 kilometers west of Charminar and on the north side of the River Musi.

Given Hyderabad's combination of sightseeing and shopping attractions, there is plenty to see and do here for at least two days. Serious pearl shoppers may need an extra day or two to cover Hyderabad's many (in the hundreds) pearl shops.

ARRIVING AND SURVIVING

WHEN TO VISIT

Welcome to the South where it gets really really hot and humid. The best time to visit Hyderabad is during the relatively coolest part of the year—October to February. If you miss these months, expect to encounter an inferno!

GETTING THERE

Hyderabad is well connected to major cities such as Delhi, Mumbai, Calcutta, Chennai, Bangalore, Visakhapatnam, and Nagpur. Indian Airlines and private airlines, such as Jet Airways and NEPC, operate daily and weekly flights into Hyderabad. In 1997 Hyderabad's **Rajiv Gandhi Airport** was upgraded to an international airport.

Hyderabad is connected to many major cities by train. However, the distances tend to be long. For example, the two express trains from Delhi take 26 to 33 hours to reach Hyderabad. The train from Chennai takes 14 hours, and the train from Mumbai takes 17 hours. Calcutta is 30 hours away by train.

AIRPORT TO CITY

The airport is located at Begampet which is north of the city. It takes about 20 minutes to get there from most major city hotels. Getting into the city is relatively easy. As soon as you exit the arrival hall, you'll see lots of people waiting to help you. Look for the "Prepaid Taxi" stand which has a sign posted with the rates to various parts of the city. Most taxi rides from the airport to the major hotels cost Rs 110. You pay the driver upon arrival at your location.

ORIENTATION

Since Hyderabad is not a major tourist destination, it doesn't promote itself well. Indeed, it lacks good maps and weekly tourist guides to help orient visitors to this city and its outlying areas. A few local pearl shops produce booklets and fliers to help visitors get around. Most of these are available at the major hotels or directly from the companies.

The first thing you need to know about the city is that it is divided into two major sections with the River Musi dividing the old city in the south from the newer section of the city and the adjacent city of Secunderabad in the north. You will probably want to initially explore the rather compact old city area which is filled with important historical sites and shopping bazaars, especially in and around the Charminar. Much of this very crowded and congested market area should be explored on foot. Like many Indian markets, they quickly become a colorful cultural experience where you have a chance to come into contact with many of the locals and encounter another set of pesky beggars. The area north of the River Musi is very spread out and thus will require more time to explore by vehicle.

NAVIGATING THE CITY

Hyderabad is not a difficult city to get around in if you rent a car with driver and avoid rush hour situations. Hotel travel desks rent cars with drivers for as little as Rs 650 (Rs 900 if air conditioned) for an eight-hour day. No taxis operate in the city. Alternatively, you can get around by bus, auto-rickshaw, or cycle-rickshaw. However, given the high levels of air pollution and relatively inexpensive transportation costs, we recommend renting a car with driver. Better still, splurge for an air-conditioned car in order to avoid the full force of the noxious auto fumes that blanket the city's streets and are constantly pumped through car windows.

TOUR INFORMATION AND AGENCIES

Tourist information on Hyderabad is best found in a few guides and brochures available at most major hotels: *Tourist Guide to Hyderabad*, a small blue advertising booklet produced by Krishna Pearls; a **map and fliers** produced by Kedarnathji Motiwale, one of the city's most respected pearl dealers; a flier, called *Hyderabad*, produced by The Government of India Tourist Office which summarizes tourist highlights in and around Hyderabad; and *Channel 6*, an 80-page guide to sites, entertainment, and shopping found in bookshops (Rs 10) and in many hotel rooms. *Channel 6* is definitely the most useful guide. The publisher also maintains its own Web site:

www.allindia.com/channel6

For assistance with your travel plans, including arrangements for tours and renting cars and drivers, contact your hotel travel desk or the following:

A. P. Tourism Development Corporation
Yatri Nivas Sardar Patel Road
Secunderabad 500003
Tel. 816-375 or 460-1519

Government of India Tourist Office
Sandozi Building Street No. 1 Himayatnagar
Hyderabad 600029
Tel. 763-0037

State Tourism Information Bureau
Gagan Vihar, Mozamjahi Road
Hyderabad 500001
Tel. 473-2554 or 473-2555

International Travel House Limited
ITC Bhadrachalam House, 106, S. P. Road
Secunderabad 500003
Tel. 814-320 or 869-301

SHOPPING HYDERABAD

In many respects Hyderabad is a shopper's paradise. It is first
and foremost India's center for the pearl trade. It also is an
important center for unique handicrafts, handloom textiles, and
jewelry. Plan to set aside at least one full day for shopping
Hyderabad's many markets, shops, and emporiums. If you are
a real dedicated shopper for pearls, you may need two or more
days to cover the hundreds of pearl shops that line Hyderabad's
streets. Unlike shopping in many other major cities in India,
you may discover you are the only foreigner visiting these
shops. For the most part, shoppers in Hyderabad are either
locals or Indians from other parts of the country.

WHAT TO BUY

There's plenty to shop for in Hyderabad. The city and its
surrounding area produce many unique items that are best
found in the city shops. Among them are:

❏ **Pearls:** This is what puts Hyderabad on both India's and
the world's shopping map. Hyderabad is all about the
buying and selling of pearls. The city has a 400-year long
tradition of being India's center for the pearl trade.
Originally patronized by local rulers who were fascinated
with pearls, Hyderabad has developed the skills and
expertise, as well as offers the most inexpensive labor, to
sort, polish, drill, and string pearls from all over the
world. In Hyderabad you will find all grades and kinds of
pearls, from fresh water, black Tahitian, and South Seas
pearls to cultured Japanese pearls and rare Basra pearls.
For the most part, however, the natural or fresh water
pearls come from China and the cultured pearls are
imported from Japan. Most of them are imported by

traders in Mumbai and then shipped to Hyderabad where most pearls are then drilled by talented families in the village of Chandampet which is located about 80 kilometers from Hyderabad. The pearls available on the local market come in four shapes: rice, seed, round, and flower. But it's also "buyer beware" in Hyderabad. While shops claim you can purchase pearls in Hyderabad at one-tenth to one-eight of their price in London and other major cities of the world, don't take such assertions as fact since they are based on comparing apples to oranges. You have to cut through a lot of local pearl hype. We're not as impressed with the product as most shopkeepers and dealers, and we get tired of hearing the same exaggerated stories about their so-called excellent quality pearls. As you will quickly discover, the problem with pearls in Hyderabad is one of quality. Good stuff is hard to find, or at least it's not found in most retail shops. Before you make any pearl purchases, make sure you know something about the quality of pearls. If not, you may get a quick and expensive but inaccurate "local" education from some fast-talking pearl merchant who assumes you are a novice at this game. While savvy diamond buyers look for the 4Cs in diamonds (clarity, cut, carat weight, and color), savvy pearl shoppers should look for the 4Ss in pearls: shape, size, shining (luster), and smoothness. Many pearls found in the shops of Hyderabad fail when assessed according to these 4Ss. We generally find the following problems with pearls in most shops:

1. Shapes tend to be very irregular.
2. Colors and sizes vary considerably on the same strand.
3. Flaws are very apparent, especially in color and pittedness.

Overall, the pearls have a very rough look to them. Many look like they didn't pass the test for export. Even when you ask to see the very best pearls a shop has to offer, the results are often pearls that are average to mediocre in quality. Pearl merchants may try to give you a song-and-dance routine about natural or fresh water pearls and how they are the best in the world, but don't believe them; many are either lying to you or they haven't been exposed to good quality pearls. Also, beware of so-called "semi-cultured" pearls, a widely used but inaccurate term to describe a third type of pearl (after natural and cultured) found in Hyderabad. The so-called "semi-cultured" pearls are nothing more than man-made or simulated (made of plastic and glass) pearls. To use the term "semi-cultured" to describe pearls is indicative of the perils of purchasing pearls in Hyderabad. These are simply simulated pearls. You will be hard-pressed to find top quality pearls you might be used to finding in shops back home. If you are a connoisseur of Mikimoto pearls, forget about finding such top quality pearls in Hyderabad. In the end, you could be paying just as much for poor quality pearls in Hyderabad as you would in London or elsewhere in the world.

❑ Hyderabad has 400-year long tradition of being India's center for the pearl trade.

❑ It's "buyer beware" when shopping for pearls. You have to cut through a lot of "pearl hype" to find the good stuff which is hard to locate in most retail shops.

❑ Savvy pearl shoppers look for the 4Ss in pearls: shape, size, shining (luster), and smoothness. Look very very carefully before buying any pearls.

❑ Pearl merchants may try to give you a song-and-dance routine about natural or fresh water pearls and how they are the best in the world–don't believe them.

❑ Most so-called "semi-cultured" pearls are actually made of plastic or glass!

❑ Natural pearls are sold by karat weight; cultured pearls are sold by gram weight.

Our shopping advice for buying pearls Hyderabad is three-fold: (1) Hyderabad is not the place for novices to learn about pearls—learn about pearls *before* arriving in Hyderabad so you know what you're doing as well as how to recognize con artists (they assume you're probably "pearl dumb"); (2) shop with a very reputable pearl dealer; and (3) examine each pearl carefully according to the 4Ss. If you just wander from one pearl shop to another, or if you willingly go to the favorite shops of a guide or driver, you are likely to make some expensive shopping mistakes.

On the other hand, if you are not particularly interested in purchasing top quality pearls, you can get some very good buys on average to mediocre pearls in the shops of Hyderabad. There is nothing wrong with buying less than top quality pearls as long as you know what you are getting and are getting what you pay for.

When you do purchase pearls, dealers usually sell them two different ways: natural pearls are sold by karat weight; cultured pearls are sold by gram weight. When you comparative shop for pearls, do so by either the karat or gram weights and considering the 4Ss.

Pearls seem to be everywhere in Hyderabad. While pearl and jewelry shops proliferate throughout the city, all major and minor pearl dealers have shops in the city's "Pearl Market". This so-called market is concentrated along a one-half kilometer stretch of **Pathergatti Road** which passes through Charminar and meets Lad Market in the old city. Here you'll find more than 100 shops offering strung pearls and jewelry. Major dealers, such as **Mangatrai Pearls**, **Kedarnathji Motiwale**, **Omprakash & Sons**, and **Krishna Pearls**, maintain branch shops in this area. You can easily spend a day browsing through the many pearl shops in this section of the city.

❏ **Jewelry**: While some pearl shops only offer loose or strung pearls, many shops also offer pearl jewelry that incorporates gold clasps and precious and semi-precious stones. Some stores also specialize in producing beautiful traditional Indian gold jewelry and rings, bracelets, pins, and necklaces made with precious and semi-precious stones. For a great selection of both pearl and traditional gold jewelry, be sure to visit the two large showrooms at the famous **Mangatrai Pearls** and **Mangatrai Jewellery** (Bashir Bagh Road, Tel. 235-728 or 211-082; also check out their third location: **Mangatrai Ramkumar**, Pathergatti Road, Tel. 457-7339).

❏ **Bangles**: Numerous shops in Hyderabad offer a wide assortment of colorful bangles. They range from inexpensive and colorful glass bangles on a wax base to the more famous Hyderabadi bangle inlaid with pearls and semi-precious stones. **Lad Bazaar**, immediately to the west of Charminar, is packed with small shops offering a wide range of bangles. The colorful and cheap Rs 10 glass bangles make fun gifts for both children and adults. We especially like the popular **M. A. Jabbar Bangles Stores** (21-2-266, Lad Bazar, Tel. 524-980) for its wonderful variety of inexpensive bangles and imitation jewelry. Most major pearl and jewelry stores will carry high-end bangles studded with pearls and precious and semi-precious stones.

❏ **Bidriware**: Begun nearly 500 years ago in the historic city of Bidar, Karnataka, Bidri is handcrafted inlaid silver metal work done on the oxidized black surface of an alloy of zinc and copper. Craftspeople develop intricate inlaid designs, which synthesize Persian motifs and Indian artistic traditions, using silver and sometimes gold wires. The result is a distinctive black and silver metal product used as decorative handicraft pieces. Most of the Bidriware comes in the form of boxes, vases, bowls, trays, ornament plates, toys, jars, bangles, brooches, buttons, animal figures, and jewelry. Like many other Indian handicrafts, you may find these pieces especially interesting for their unique craftsmanship and motifs. You may have difficulty deciding on what to do with an acquisition since bidriware is more an acquired taste. However, if you collect knick-knacks or are looking for small gift items, bidriware may be just what you're looking for.

❑ **Hand-woven textiles:** Like many other areas in India, Hyderabad is famous for its own unique handloomed cottons and silks. Hyderabad cotton and silk sarees, also known as Pochampalli sarees, are especially popular. Also look for Venkatgiri cottons, Lepakshi printed sarees, Dharmavaram silks, Madhavaram cotton sarees, and Himroo cotton and silk mixtures. You'll find numerous shops throughout the city offering these and many other kinds of silk and cotton fabrics. Two of the best, and busiest, places for textiles and sarees are the extremely popular **Kalanjali** (5-10-194 Hill Fort Road, Saifabad, Tel. 231-147) and **Chandana Bros.** (Patny Centre, Secunderabad, Tel. 810-470). You'll love the traditional and contemporary designs and ready-made garments at Kalanjali, and you'll definitely be treated to a cultural experience (buying fabrics) at Chandana Bros. Both of these large shops are well worth visiting. You also might want to visit two famous, but much sleepier, government operated shops (you can definitely tell the difference between public and private sector commerce!): **APCO Handloom House** (Metro Estate, Abids, Tel. 232-809) and **Handloom House** (5-5-395, Mukharamjahi Road, Nampally, Tel. 461-6165). The first shop is operated by the Andhra Pradesh State Handloom Weaver's Co-operative Society. The second shop is sponsored by the Government of India. These two shops also have a large selection of upholstery materials, rugs, and tie and dye materials which are not available in most other shops.

❑ **Other discoveries:** Also look for Warangal and Eluru carpets, Mahbubnagar mats, silver filigree work of Karimnagar, Kondapalli toys, wall hangings, paintings, perfumes (attars), Kalamkari prints (found in textiles and wall hangings), sandalwood carvings, furniture, leather, carpets, and lots of brass, bronze, and inlaid wood products in Hyderabad's markets and handicraft shops. Good selections of these and other products are available at **Kalanjali** (5-10-194 Hill Fort Road, Saifabad, Tel. 231-147) and **Lepakshi Handicrafts Emporium** (Gun-foundry, Tel. 235-028).

WHERE TO SHOP

You'll find plenty of places to shop in Hyderabad and adjacent Secunderabad to keep you busy for at least two solid days, if not three days. The major shopping streets in Secunderabad include M. G. Road and Rashtrapati Road; in Hyderabad shopping tends to be centered around Abids, Basheerbagh, Nampally, Sultan Bazar, and Charminar. Unlike many other major cities in India, most quality shopping in Hyderabad is found in markets and in a few key street shops.

❑ **Markets:** While Hyderabad has lots of local markets selling food and household goods, it has two specialty markets of interest to shoppers in search of unique local products. Both markets meet at the famous Charminar arch in the old city:

➤ **Pearl Market:** Look for a one-half kilometer section of Pathergatti Road that starts at the Charminar and runs north toward the river. Both sides of the street are lined with numerous shops offering a wide range of pearls strung in different shapes and sizes as well as pearl jewelry. Three of the oldest and most reputable shops in this area are **Mangatrai Ramkumar** (22-6-191 Pathergatti Road, Tel. 457-7339), **Kedarnathji Motiwale** (22-1-17, Beside Bata, Pathergatti Road, Tel. 4566667), and **Sri Omprakash & Sons** (Machali Kaman, Pathergatti Road, Tel. 525-744).

➤ **Bangle Market:** Hyderabad's famous lacquer and glass bangle market, **Lad Bazar**, begins at the Charminar arch and runs west for several blocks. This narrow and congested street (some call it an alley) is jam-packed with dedicated shoppers dodging cars, auto-rickshaws, cycle-rickshaws, and bicycles as they browse through the many small bangle and costume jewelry shops (they sell those so-called "semi-cultured" pearls) lining both sides of the street. Adjacent to the Mecca Mesjid, this area is frequented by Muslim women veiled and dressed in distinctive black garments. This market also is very famous for being the only place to purchase the traditional bridal costume, the khopada joda, and several bridal accessories. Expect to encounter several persistent beggars, young women (Banjara gypsies) with rent-a-babies, who relentlessly pursue you around the Charminar.

Located in and around these two markets are additional bazaars famous for their perfume and attar dealers as well as for herbs, spices, silver, lace, and used items. The whole area is one big traditional shopping center that draws thousands of shoppers each day.

❑ **Handicraft emporiums:** Hyderabad has several private and government-sponsored handicraft emporiums. Like in most other major cities throughout India, many of these places are operated by Kashmiris. The two best places for handicrafts are **Kalanjali** and **Lepakshi Handicrafts Emporium**. We'll discuss these two shops along with several others when we examine the "best of the best" in handicraft shopping.

❑ **Hotel shopping arcades:** While most major hotels in Hyderabad have shopping arcades, most of these places are very small (1-2 shops) and offer the typical range of handicrafts found in most hotel shopping arcades. Many are operated by aggressive Kashmiris who pester you to buy their rugs, scarfs, shawls, and papier mache items. However, there is one exception in the case of Hyderabad. A few combination pearl, jewelry, and handicraft shops operate in these hotels. The most prevalent such shop is the widely advertised **Krishna Pearls** which is found in four hotels and operates under slightly different names:

➤ **Krishna Pearls and Handicrafts:** Grand Kakatiya Hotels and Towers

➤ **Krishna Pearls:** The Krishna Oberoi and Hotel Green Park

➤ **Palladio:** Holiday Inn Krishna

This company also publishes the small booklet *Tourist Guide to Hyderabad*. We've visited each of their shops and don't feel comfortable recommending them as a reliable source for pearls, jewelry, or handicrafts; you'll have to judge for yourself. Their personnel tend to be very aggressive; prices seem inflated even when given the store discount; quality is not exceptional despite their claims to the contrary; and their "pearl stories" tend to be disingenuous. Be very careful in all shops. Be sure to shop around before deciding to make a purchase. You simply need to know your alternatives before dealing with these rather slick entrepreneurs.

BEST OF THE BEST

PEARLS AND JEWELRY

Since pearls and jewelry are two of Hyderabad's most sought after shopping treasures, you'll literally find hundreds of shops offering a wide range of pearls and jewelry. Among the best are:

❑ **Mangatrai Pearls and Mangatrai Jewellery:** *5-9-46 Basheerbagh, Opposite Hotel Nagarjuna and State Assembly Building, Hyderabad, Tel. 235-728 or Fax 212-370.* Web site: *www.madeinindia.com/mangatrai.* Established over 80 years ago, this is one of Hyderabad's largest and most respected pearl and jewelry dealers. It's frequented by numerous celebrities. If you have time to visit only one pearl and jewelry shop in Hyderabad, make sure its Mangatrai. This place is usually packed with buyers from all over India. The shop is actually divided into two sections. The shop on the right is called **Mangatrai Pearls** and it specializes in pearls. It claims to be the largest pearl dealer in Asia. The selections and quality here are generally better than in most other shops, and they carry more high-end pearls, including South Seas and Tahitian black pearls. Also, the sales personnel will sit down with you to explain differences in quality and prices (sold by grams and karat weight) and answer any questions you may have concerning their pearls and jewelry. The shop on the left deals in both traditional Indian and Western jewelry made with gold and using precious and semi-precious stones. While most of the gems used in the rings, necklaces, earrings, bangles, and bracelets are cut in Jaipur, all the jewelry is designed by

Mangatrai. You'll find many large jewelry pieces here, especially in traditional Indian designs. Mangatrai also maintains a third shop in the Pearl Market of the old city: **Mangatrai Ramkumar Pearls Dealer**, 22-6-191 Pathergatti Road, Tel. 457-7339.

❑ **Kedarnathji Motiwale:** *22-1-17, Beside Bata, Pathergatti Road, Tel. 456-6667; and 36, Babukhan Estate, Basheere-bagh, Hyderabad, Tel. 599-158.* This is Hyderabad's oldest pearl dealer which has been operating for more than 100 years. It's also one of the city's most respected dealers who has a reputation for honesty and integrity. Its two small shops, run by father and son, offer a limited range of pearls and jewelry. Friendly and helpful service. This company also publishes useful tourist information, including a map of the city, a flier on Hyderabad's major sightseeing attractions, and articles about the pearl trade and the perils of purchasing pearls from unscrupulous pearl dealers. Be sure to pick up their "tourist packet" when you visit either of their shops.

❑ **Sri Omprakash & Sons:** *Machali Kaman, Pathergatti Road, Tel. 525-744; and 7-1-938, Kingsway Circle, R. P. Road, Secunderabad, Tel. 770-4068.* This is another one of Hyderabad's oldest and most respected pearl dealers. Their two small shops include a limited selection of pearls and jewelry. Not as friendly or helpful as the first two shops.

❑ **Chandana Bros. Jewellers:** *Patny Centre, Secunderabad, Tel. 810-470.* Recently (1998) opened next door to its huge fabric and saree emporium (Chandana Bros.), this jewelry store offers an excellent selection of traditional Indian jewelry, especially large gold neck pieces. Very little English spoken here.

Other noted pearl and jewelry dealers include:

❑ **Vijay Pearls Dealers:** *11, Unity House, Hotel Emerald Lane, Abid Road, Hyderabad.*

❑ **Sri Ram Jewellery:** *4-1-857, Abid Road, Hyderabad.*

❑ **P. Satyanarayanan & Sons Jewellers:** *Opposite Gandhi Medical College, Basheerbagh, Hyderabad, Tel. 241-654.*

- **Boorgu Jewellers Pearls Shoppe:** *Parklane, Opposite Chenoy Trade Centre, Secunderabad, Tel. 813-251.*

- **Boorgu Gems and Pearls:** *Opposite Amrutha Topaz, Panjagutta, Hyderabad, Tel. 395-844.*

- **K. Chandrakanth Pearls Dealer & Jewellers:** *21-2131/7-8, Charkaman, Opposite Agra Hotel, Hyderabad.*

- **Dwarakadas Mukundas & Sons Jewellers:** *4-3-355/1, Bank Street, Hyderabad.*

- **Jagadamba Jewellers & Pearls:** *Gupta Estate, Baa-sheer-bag, Hyderabad.*

- **Agarwala's Jewellers & Pearls:** *Opposite Gandhi Medical College, Basheerbagh, Hyderabad, Tel. 237-621.*

- **Vithaldas and Sons:** *Machli Kaman, Charminar.*

- **Raj Jewellers:** *1-6-56 Gandhi Statue, Mahatma Gandhi Road, Secunderabad, Tel. 812-350.*

- **Kishandas and Company:** *Begumpet, Cross Roads, Begumpet.*

- **Vandana Pearls Dealer:** *Royal Plaza C-9, K. S. Lane Sultan Bazar, Hyderabad, Tel. 475-4212.*

- **Tibarunal and Sons:** *Opposite Nizam College, Bashirbagh Cross Roads.*

- **Meena Jewellers:** *Deccan Towers, Opposite Nizam College, Bashirbagh Cross Roads.*

- **K. Liluram Jewellers:** *21-2-182 Charkaman, Hyderabad, Tel. 441-2137.*

- **Pradeep Pearls & Exports:** *206 A Block Maheshwari Towers, Adjacent to Sindhuja Super Market, Road No. 1, Banjara Hills, Tel. 332-8815.*

- **Saincher Jewellers:** *Lower Ground Floor Amrutha Mall, Somajiguda, Hyderabad, Tel. 330-1443.*

❑ **Meera Pearls & Jewellers:** *55 Babukhan Estate Basheer-bagh, Hyderabad, Tel. 235-614.*

FURNITURE AND ANTIQUES

Unlike many other major cities, Hyderabad does not have a lot to offer in these categories. You will find lots of new furniture in handicraft emporiums but much of it is extremely ethnic and gaudy. One shop offers excellent antique furniture:

❑ **Antiquity:** *37, Santoshima Colony, West Marredpally Main Road, Secunderabad, Tel. 780-202 or Fax 770-4460, 10am - 8pm.* Somewhat difficult to find in Secunderabad, none-theless, your persistence in finding this relatively new shop (opened three years ago) will be rewarded with some nice selections of antique furniture. This two-storey building is filled with a combination of old and new furniture, panels, brackets, swings, tables, chairs, beds, pillars, and gorgeous carved doors with lintels. Prices here are excellent. Panels that go for Rs 6,000 in Delhi sell here for Rs 1850. And beautifully carved doors that may cost Rs 140,000 in Delhi go for Rs 50,000 here. If you're in the market for old furniture and home decorative items, this shop is well worth visiting. Some-what difficult to communicate long-distance by phone or fax, the shop eventually delivers if you are persistent. Uses a reliable local shipper—Tetra Marine. Ask to speak with Mr. Christy who speaks good English and is helpful.

HANDICRAFTS

Hyderabad offers its share of handicraft shops, from large emporiums to small hotel kiosks. If you're in the market for local handicrafts, try these places:

❑ **Kalanjali:** *5-10-194 Hill Fort Road, Saifabad, Hyderabad, Tel. 231-147.* Located opposite the public gardens and the State Assembly Building, this is Hyderabad's best shop for textiles, clothes, and handicrafts. This attractive 3-storey building may be the only place you want to shop in Hyderabad! The ground floor includes two rooms filled with good quality clothes for men, women, children; textiles; sarees; and bed covers. It has a very good selection of children's clothes. The designs and colors are exceptionally attractive, some of the best we've seen in India. The first floor includes a wide range of handicrafts, including sandalwood, marble, and soapstone carvings; brass figures; Bidriware; pottery and stoneware; toys and dolls; wall hangings, leather; miniature paintings; and books. This section also has a nice selection of unique handmade paper writing cards (Rs 8-13 each) in attractive geometric designs and colors. The second floor is devoted to larger home furnishing items such as furniture, woodcarvings, inlaid wood pictures, carved panels, and screens.

❑ **Lepakshi Handicrafts Emporium:** *Gunfoundry, Hyderabad, Tel. 235028 or Fax 040-243094.* This is the state government-sponsored handicraft emporium. A well established, popular, but somewhat worn two-storey shop, it's filled with all kinds of handicrafts from Andra Pradash and other parts of India. The ground floor is primarily dedicated to brass items, Bidriware, bangles, inlaid wood pictures, furniture, textiles, soapstone carvings, and jewelry. The first floor includes woodcarvings, toys, dolls, leather goods, tribal Banjara items, woolen carpets, cotton durries, wall hangings, Kalamkari and ikat bedspreads, shawls, tie and dye ikat fabric, Kashmiri walnut furniture, and papier mache items. Overall, this is not an exciting shop. Many of its items verge on being tacky, especially when compared to the nice selections and displays found at the more upscale Kalanjali.

Other handicraft emporiums, none of which are particularly noteworthy, include:

➤ **Central Cottage Industries Corporation of India**
94 Minerva Commercial Complex
S.D. Road, Secunderabad
Tel. 845-242

➤ **Cottage Industries Exposition Ltd.**
'Snehalata' 6-3-8871 Greenlands Road
Begumpet, Hyderabad
Tel. 331-1302

➤ **Gurjari** (Gujarat State Handicrafts Emporium)
Hotel Sarovar Complex
5-9-22 Secretariat Road, Hyderabad
Tel. 240-149

> ➢ **Cauvery Arts and Crafts Emporium**
> (Government of Karnataka Enterprise)
> Seven Hills Plaza
> Sarojini Devi Road, Secunderabad
> Tel. 810-604

TEXTILES AND SILK

❑ **Kalanjali:** *5-10-194 Hill Fort Road, Saifabad, Hyderabad, Tel. 231-147.* The ground floor of this attractive three-storey shop includes two rooms filled with the best quality, colors, and designs for fabric and ready-made clothes. Beautiful sarees. Excellent collection of ready-made children's clothes. Very stylish designs and contemporary colors. You'll see a world of difference between this shop and the more traditional shops in Hyderabad. Especially appeals to the color and design tastes of international visitors.

❑ **Chandana Bros.:** *Patny Centre, Secunderabad, Tel. 810-470.* This is as much a cultural experience in buying fabrics and sarees as it is a good opportunity to examine a wide range of textiles. This is one of the most popular fabric shops around. It's wall-to-wall fabrics as well as wall-to-wall customers. Sales people roll out fabrics on what look like covered blackjack tables found in casinos. The open upstairs area is devoted to silk and cotton sarees. The downstairs area includes saree fabric as well as bolts of fabric for men's suits and shirts. If you want to see how the locals shop for fabrics and sarees, this is the best show in town! Not much English spoken here but the personnel try very hard to be helpful. Next door is the newly opened Chandana Bros. Jewellers that specializes in traditional gold Indian jewelry that looks gorgeous with the sarees purchased in this shop.

❑ **Handloom House:** *5-5-395, Mukharamjahi Road, Nampally, Hyderabad, Tel. 461-6165.* Also known as the All India Handloom House, this 3-storey textile emporium is sponsored by the Government of India. It includes a large selection of sarees, home furnishings material, wall hangings, bed covers, rugs, neckties, and shirts. Most items are produced through government-sponsored cooperatives. Includes ikat designs. Not a particularly exciting place to visit—drab displays and inert personnel (some napping at their counters). A typical quiet government operation.

❑ **APCO Handloom House:** *Metro Estate, Abids, Hyderabad, Tel. 232-809.* Operated by the Andhra Pradesh State Handloom Weaver's Co-operative Society Ltd., this place is a little hard to find. Once you arrive at Metro Estate, look for signs near the rear that lead upstairs and across to another building. Here you'll find a large shop offering a wide range of textiles and clothes produced in Andhra Pradesh. Look for tie and dye (ikat) material, cottons, silks, ready-made dresses and shirts, bed sheets, upholstery material, and carpets. Most of the upholstery materials and carpets are exported. Another quiet operation like the Handloom House, but has a little better energy and customer service.

Other shops offering a good range of silks and sarees include:

❑ **Fancy Silks:** *4-1-970-C/17 Ahuja Estate Three Aces Complex, Palace Heights Road, Abids, Hyderabad, Tel. 596-639.*

❑ **Gianey's Silks & Sarees:** *Opposite Pulla Reddy Sweets, Abids Road, Hyderabad, Tel. 516-982.*

❑ **Dulhan:** *Behind Metro Footwear, Station Road, Abids, Hyderabad, Tel. 460-0426.*

❑ **Murali Saree Emporium:** *House No. 17-32 Srinagar Colony, adjacent to Shubhodaya High School, Dilsukhnagar, Hyderabad, Tel. 406-7062.*

❑ **Pochampally Silks & Sarees:** *Tilak Road, Abids, Hyderabad, Tel. 232-446.*

ACCOMMODATIONS

Since Hyderabad is primarily a business city, most of its top hotels are geared toward the business traveler who enjoys the comfort and amenities of fine hotels. Most of the city's best restaurants also are found in these top hotels.

DELUXE HOTELS

- ❑ **Grand Kakatiya Hotel & Towers:** *Begumpet, Hyderabad, 500 016, Tel. 91-40-331-0132 or Fax 91-40-331-1045.* This hotel follows the Welcomgroup tradition of honoring glorious Indian dynasties of the past—the Kakatiya Dynasty of the South. The Grand Kakatiya is located just six minutes from the airport in the heart of Hyderabad. The lobby is spacious and welcoming with several attractive artifacts that remind the guest this is India. Deluxe, Executive Club, Tower or suite, The Kakatiya gives the traveler or businessperson the largest choice of rooms in Hyderabad. At the Towers guests receive complimentary airport transfer, sit-down check-in at the Towers lounge, use of the Towers Club Lounge as well as office and meeting rooms, butler and valet service, and complimentary Club Hour at the Towers Lounge. The Executive Club provides similar amenities. The Deccan Pavilion serves a wide variety of food round-the-clock from a choice of five kitchens. When we arrived in the wee morning hours because of a delayed flight and requested a large portion of hash browns (which was really a side order item) we were served an entire plate covered with great hash brown potatoes. Three restaurants serving different regional varieties of Indian foods are popular. Conference, business facilities, and health club.

- ❑ **Taj Residency:** *Banjara Hills, Road No. 1, Hyderabad 500034, Tel. 91-40-399-999 or Fax 91-40-392-218. Tel. 1-800-458-8825 (from the USA only).* Situated on Banjara Hills, and overlooking a private lake, the Taj Residency is a 10-minute drive from the city's business and shopping districts. The lobby is warm and welcoming. Its 116 rooms include standard rooms and Residency floor rooms. Residency floor guests may request in-room fax machines and enjoy access to the Residency Lounge—a place of quiet to work or relax and where complimentary breakfast is served each morning. The Waterside Café, overlooking the lake, serves Continental, Indian, and Chinese cuisines. Dakhni serves Hyderabadi and Andhra cuisine and Kabab-e-Bahar serves kebabs and is open only for dinner. Considered a business hotel, the Taj Residency offers a fully equipped Business Center for the business traveler and a comfortable respite for the tourist who enjoys service and amenities. A small handicraft shop operates off the lobby area.

❑ **The Krishna Oberoi:** *Road No. 1, Banjara Hills, Hyderabad 500034, Tel. 91-40-392-323 or Fax 91-40-393-079. Tel. 1-800-5-OBEROI (from the USA only).* Also situated in Banjara Hills, the Krishna Oberoi is a 10 minute drive from Hyderabad's business and shopping districts. The spacious lobby and wide corridor leading to the restaurants provide vistas of the hotel's tropical foliage. The 22 rooms include the Presidential Suite with private swimming pool and deluxe suites which open onto terrace gardens. Rooms are comfortable and well appointed. The attractive Gardenia coffee shop is open for breakfast, lunch, and dinner. For informal dining with a variety of cuisines, the Szechuan Garden for Chinese cuisine, and Firdaus serves Indian cuisine. Conference facilities, meeting rooms, and a 24-hour business center cater to the business traveler. A below ground shopping arcade has only one operational shop offering a mixture of pearls, jewelry, and handicrafts.

❑ **Holiday Inn Krishna:** *Road No. 1, Banjara Hills, Hyderabad 500034, Tel. 91-40-339-3939 or Fax 91-40-339-2684. Tel. 1-800-465-4329 (from the USA only).* The third hotel considered 5-star luxury located in Banjana Hills, The Holiday Inn Krishna is also conveniently located to the business and shopping districts. Though structured as an atrium hotel, it is not structured to allow outside light to filter through. The 140 guest rooms include the Holiday Inn options of king leisure, twin studio or double rooms, or one of four executive suites. The Club Select floor provides a separate lounge, complimentary airport transfers, tea/coffee service, buffet breakfast, extended check-out, hi-tea in the evening, happy hour and a discount on business center services. There is a separate non-smoking wing as well as wheel chair accommodation available. The Blue Flower restaurant serves an array of international cuisines and an Italian restaurant, Mama Mia, will be open by the time this is off press. Extensive banquet and convention facilities are available.

❑ **Hindustan International:** *C-21/3 Maldahiya, Tel. 91-40-351-484 or 91-40-351-490; Fax 91-40-350-931.* Located 24 kilometers from airport and 3 kilometers from railway station. 108 rooms. Facilities: swimming pool, health club, restaurant, coffee shop, bar.

❑ **Hotel Ideal Tops:** *The Mall, Cantonment, Tel. 91-40-348-091 or Fax 91-40-348-685.* 18 kilometers from airport and 0.5 kilometers from railway station. 40 rooms. Facilities: restaurant, bar, travel counter, car rental.

❑ **Pallavi International:** *Hathwa Place, Chetganj, Tel. 91-40-356-939 or Fax 91-40-322-943.* The only heritage hotel in the area. Located 22 kilometers from airport and 1.5 kilometers from railway station. 40 rooms. Facilities: swimming pool, restaurants, travel counter.

STANDARD HOTELS

❑ **Hotel De Paris:** *15 The Mall, Cantonment, Tel. 91-40-46601.* Located 20 kilometers from airport and 1 kilometer from railway station. 50 rooms. Facilities: 2 restaurants, bar, tennis court, travel counter.

❑ **India:** *59 Patel Nagar, Cantonment, Tel. 91-40-343-009 or Fax 91-40-348-327.* Located 18 kilometers from airport and 0.5 kilometers from railway station. 80 rooms, 3 suites. Facilities: restaurants, bar, travel counter.

RESTAURANTS

Hyderabad has its own distinctive and rich cuisine which tends to be a bit hot for the uninitiated. Its specialty dishes include *baghara baigan* (eggplants stuffed with spice and cooked in tamarind juice and sesame oil) and *mirchi ka slan* (stuffed green chillies) along with tikka kebabs, *haleem* (mutton and wheat), *khubani ka mitha*, and local *biryani* (rice with meat or chicken and spices. Many of the major hotels serve buffets that include a combination of North Indian, Hyderabadi, South Indian, Chinese, and Continental cuisines. One of the best such buffets is found at the Grand Kakatiya Hotel coffee shop (Deccan Pavillion) which also serves a midnight buffet. Not surprising, like many other cities, the best restaurants in Hyderabad tend to found in the major hotels.

❑ **Firdaus:** *The Krishna Oberoi, Banjara Hills, Road No. 1, Tel. 339-2323.* Offers some of the best Hyderabadi and Indian cuisine in the area.

❑ **Kabab-e-Bahar:** *Taj Residency Hotel, Road No. 1, Banjara Hills, Tel. 399-9999.* Serves excellent barbecue dishes and kebabs in a pleasant outdoor, lakeside setting. Open for dinner only.

❑ **Dakhni:** *Taj Residency Hotel, Road No. 1, Banjara Hills, Tel. 399-9999.* Serves excellent Hyderabadi and Andhra cuisines.

❑ **Szechuan Garden:** *Krishna Oberoi, Banjara Hills, Road No. 1, Tel. 339-2323.* Serves Chinese (Szechuan) cuisine in attractive surroundings.

❑ **Paradise Garden Restaurant:** *Corner of Sardar Patel Road and MG Road, Secunderabad.* Famous for serving both vegetarian and non-vegetarian Hyderabadi cuisine.

❑ **Palace Heights:** *Triveni Complex, Abid Road, Tel. 242-540.* Multi-cuisine served with a great rooftop view of the city.

❑ **The Deccan Pavilion:** *Grand Kakatiya Hotel & Towers, Begumpet, Tel. 331-0132.* Popular coffee shop serving terrific multi-cuisine buffets, including a midnight buffet. Very good service.

❑ **Banjara:** *Banjara Hills.* Serves great Mughlai barbecue.

❑ **Peshawri:** *Grand Kakatiya Hotel & Towers, Begumpet, Tel. 331-0132.* Serves multi-cuisine.

❑ **The Blue Flower:** *Holiday Inn Krishna, Road No. 1, Banjara Hills, Tel. 339-3939.* Serves multi-cuisine.

❑ **Kamat Hotel:** *60/1 Saifabad, opposite Birla Temple, Tel. 232-225.* Popular vegetarian restaurant serving South Indian cuisine.

❑ **Gardenia:** *The Krishna Oberoi, Road No. 1, Banjara Hills, Tel. 339-2323.* Pleasant coffee shop overlooking attractive pool and gardens.

❑ **Waterside Cafe:** *Taj Residency, Banjara Hills, Tel. 339-9999.* Serves Indian, Chinese, and Continental cuisine with a nice view of the hotel's small lake.

SEEING THE SITES

You'll find plenty of interesting sites to visit in and around Hyderabad. The most popular sites include:

❑ **Charminar:** This landmark symbol of the city stands at the center of the old city where the pearl and bangle markets meet along with the less impressive Mecca Masjid. Consisting of a massive arch with four 175-foot high minarets and a small mosque at the top, this impressive monument was allegedly built by the area's fifth king, Muhammad Quli Qutub Shah, as either a talisman to ward off deadly epidemics or in honor of his Hindu wife, Bhagmati. Whatever the case, it looks like an ornate Muslim version of the Arc de Triumphe in Paris. Until recently open to the public, who could climb its 149 winding steps to the top where they could visit a small mosque and get a wonderful view of city, Charminar is now closed due to a recent spate of suicides. It appears Charminar has become a favorite place from which distraught individuals leap to their deaths. At least for now you'll have to view this beautiful edifice from ground level. Charminar is illuminated each evening from 7pm to 9pm.

❑ **Birla Mandir:** Perched on the hilltop of Kalapahad, this landmark temple dedicated to Lord Venkateshwara overlooks Tank Bund and Hussain Sagar Lake. Made from Rajasthan white marble and combining both North and South Indian architectural styles, this impressive temple provides one of the best views of the city.

❑ **Salarjung Museum:** If you're interested in local history relating to a single local notable, visit the 19 rooms of this eclectic museum that houses the personal collection of Nawab Salar Jung II, the Prime Minister to the Nizam of Hyderabad. It reputedly includes over 35,000 antiques and art objects, from furniture, costumes, bronzes, textiles, and glass to ivory, arms, metalware, sculptures, and paintings. Open daily 10am to 5pm. Closed on Fridays.

❑ **Golconda Fort:** Located 13 kilometers west of the city, this is the largest fortress in South India built on a 400-foot high granite hill. Originally built in the 13th century and substantially expanded in the 16th century by the Qutb Shahi kings, the massive solid limestone walls and ramparts extend nearly seven kilometers. Noted for its unique acoustical system. It takes about one and a half hours to tour the fort. It's best to hire local guide to explain the area. A sound and light show is conducted each evening. The old town of Golconda still functions within the outer fort walls and is filled with stalls selling tourist trinkets.

❑ **Qutb Shahi Tombs:** Located one kilometer from Golconda Fort, these are the tombs of the Qutb Shahi rulers. They are domed structures built on square bases with pointed arches. The larger tombs are two-storied. Stop here on the way to Golkonda Fort.

❑ **Mecca Masjid:** Located just off the southwest corner of Charminar, this is one of the largest mosques in South India which can accommodate up to 10,000 worshipers. Famous for its massive door arches and colonnades which are carved from a single slab of granite.

❑ **Osmania University:** Founded in 1917, the university is noted for its beautiful architecture, which is a blend of Hindu (Ajanta) and Perso-Arabic styles in Mughal splendor, and the picturesque Landscape Garden.

❑ **Tank Bund:** Built in the 16th century and linking the cities of Hyderabad and Secunderabad, today this promenade faces the east side of Hussain Sagar Lake. It's lined with 33 bronze statues of famous figures in the state's history. Tank Bund also is a popular gathering place for free Sunday evening cultural programmes, the musical fountains of Lumbini Park, and the massive Buddha statue that stands in the middle of the lake.

❑ **Nehru Zoological Park:** Located south of the Musi River and west of the old city, this 300+ acre park is home to over 3,000 different species of birds and animals. Its popular lion safari park and unique nocturnal zoo draw thousands of people to its gates. Includes the interesting Natural History Museum. Open daily 9am to 5pm. Closed on Mondays.

❑ **Public Gardens:** These well laid out gardens also house some of the city's most impressive and important buildings such as the State Legislative Assembly building, the Jubilee Hall, the Jawahar Bal Bhavan, the Health Museum, and the State Archaeological Museum.

❑ **B. M. Birla Planetarium/Science Museum:** Located in the center of the city, this is India's newest and most modern planetarium. This center for astronomy presents daily sky shows from 10:30am to 3pm except on Thursday when it is closed. The Science Museum is opened daily from 10:30am to 8:15pm but closed the last Tuesday of the month.

ENTERTAINMENT

There's lots going on in Hyderabad, from cultural programs and exhibitions to concerts. Be sure to check the *Channel 6* guide for the latest "What's On" information. Consider attending the spectacular **sound and light show** at Golconda Fort (Tel. 816-375 for details). English language shows take place on Wednesday and Sunday (6:30pm, November - February; 7pm, March - October). The **Ravindra Bharati** puts on regular dance, music, and theatrical performances. Look for art exhibits and free films daily at **Lalit Kala Thoranam** (Public Gardens). The **Alliance Francaise** offers regular cultural programs in French.

If you are into bars and pubs, try the **Atrium Pub** (Holiday Inn Krishna, Road No. 1, Banjara Hills, Tel. 339-3939), **My Choice "Bar"**, The Residency, Public Garden Road, Tel. 320-4060), and **Escape** (Green Park, Greenlands Begumpet, Tel. 291-919).

14

Chennai
(Madras)

Welcome to the gateway city and cultural center of South India. Known as a "Garden City" and serving as the capital of the State of Tamil Nadu, Chennai is one of India's most important cities for classical dance, temples, textiles, art, and cinema. Long called Madras—until a recent name change to Chennai—this is India's fourth largest city with over 4 million inhabitants; it's also South India's largest city. Sprawling 19 kilometers along the Coromandel coast, along the beautiful and expansive Marina Beach, this often sweltering city boasts many surprising treasures and pleasures that are often overlooked by visitors who either bypass the city altogether or only pass through it on a cultural tour to South India's many Hindu temple complexes, especially Madurai, Mahabalipuram, Kanchipuram, Rameswaram Island, and Kanniuyakumri in the State of Tamil Nadu.

MORE THAN HEAT AND TEMPLES

Make no mistake about it—South India is hot and humid, even during the so-called cool season. In Chennai it *really* gets hot and it *really* pours. Indeed, if Chennai could claim three seasons, it would be this variation on the hot season: hot, hotter, and hottest! Facing the Bay of Bengal, which contributes an occasional breeze, Chennai manages to escape some of the worst heat and humidity of South India. The city does function as a gateway city to South India's many fascinating ruins and temple complexes associated with the great Pallava, Chola, and Vijayanagar dynasties that attract thousands of visitors to this area each year.

A very friendly and hospitable city, Chennai has a distinctive culture and colonial history that separates it from the rest of India. Indeed, Chennai is the gateway city to the Dravidian south which exhibits its own unique language, cuisine, social customs, ethnic groups, architecture, and climate. This is a very religious and conservative area where Hinduism plays an important role in the daily lives of the Tamils.

❏ Chennai is the gateway city to the Dravidian south–a region with its own unique language, ethnic groups, architecture, cuisine, customs, and climate.

❏ This is a very religious and conservative area where Hinduism plays an important role in the daily lives of the Tamils.

❏ Chennai functions as an important political, commercial, and manufacturing center for South India.

❏ As the center for Tamil film-making, Chennai produces as many films as Mumbai–nearly 300 each year.

❏ You can easily spend a couple of days discovering Chennai's many shopping treasures.

Chennai also has a rich colonial history involving nearly 300 years of Portuguese, French, and British involvement in the area. Traces of that history are apparent in Chennai's many museums, fortifications, and churches and in its rich Indo-Saracenic style of architecture.

Chennai functions as an important political, commercial, and manufacturing center for South India. With its state legislature and political parties, it's the hotbed for Tamil politics. It's a fast developing commercial center with many low-rise commercial buildings and numerous hotels serving a growing domestic and international business community. It's also a major industrial center with auto, motorcycle, truck, rail coach, and engineering plants; textile mills; cigarette factories; and film studios. As the center for Tamil film-making, Chennai now produces as many films Mumbai—nearly 300 each year.

Shopping is one of Chennai's major pleasures. Emporiums, street shops, hotel boutiques, galleries, and bazaars offer a wide range of local products, from famous Kanchipuram silk, textiles, and furniture to contemporary paintings, inlaid boxes, jewelry, and bronzes. You can easily spend a couple of days discovering Chennai's many shopping treasures.

Many visitors to Chennai often discover they need more time here than they originally allotted. If you want to do

Chennai and the surrounding area properly, plan to spend at least three days here. Four to five days would be even better. Like many other visitors to this friendly city, you may discover there is more to Chennai than just the heat and old Hindu temples.

GETTING TO KNOW YOU

Facing the Bay of Bengal, Chennai is an interesting blend of the old and the new. Originally a small fishing village, in 1639 representatives of the British East India Company established a fort and trading post in this area. The area subsequently became known as George Town with Fort George at its center. Over the next 200 years the British created the city of Madras by acquiring numerous villages in and around Fort George. During the British colonial period, Madras served as the capital of the Madras Presidency which encompassed all of the south, including much of the present states of Maharashtra, Andhra Pradesh, and Orissa, or nearly one-fourth of present day India. European traders and missionaries became permanent fixtures in Madras as they established many of the city's interesting commercial buildings and Christian churches which now stand as landmarks of the foreign presence in Chennai. The trading ethic continues strong to this day as Chennai continues to play an important role in international trade.

If you've come here from other parts of India, one of the first things you notice is the spaciousness of Chennai. To a certain extent, it remains a city of villages, with few buildings of more than ten stories; most are one to two-stories. The size of the city (municipality) itself is officially 170 square kilometers with a population of 4 million. But with suburbs included, Greater Chennai literally sprawls 43 kilometers from north to south and 29 kilometers from east to west with a population closer to 8 million. And the city still has lots of room to expand, although its urban infrastructure—especially water, electricity, and sewage—is extremely strained. Indeed, during the summer months, water is in constant shortage. Frequent power outages and clogged sewage drains, coupled with trash, crumbling roads, unsightly slums, and numerous beggars, make parts of this city less than appealing for local residents and visitors alike. The quality of life improves dramatically when you stay in one of Chennai's oases for business people and tourists—five-star hotels.

At the same time, Chennai suffers from the typical pains found in other large Indian cities: too much traffic and pollution. Despite the spaciousness of the city, its main streets and commercial areas experience a great deal of gridlock and chaos throughout the day. The air and noise pollution is especially bad, particularly along the main thoroughfare of Anna Salai (formerly known as Mount Road). As Chennai continues to grow, these problems are likely to be exacerbated.

Chennai also is a city of trees and gardens. The greenness of this city surprises many visitors who are used to drab congested urban jungles of concrete and wood.

THE BASICS

LOCATION AND POPULATION

Chennai is located on the southeast corner of India. Ethnically and linguistically, the local population, or Tamils, has more in common with the nearby country of Sri Lanka than with many other regions in India. The Tamils are dark-skinned and speak their own distinct language. Chennai's population of 4 million is especially known as being very religious, conservative, and hospitable. Many of the people are genuinely interested in visitors and are eager to be helpful; some may even invite you into their homes. You'll discover a certain easy-going, friendly, and inquisitive nature of the people—more so than in many other places in India. It's often easy to strike up conversations with the locals, if they speak your language or vice versa.

GETTING THERE

It takes some effort to get to Chennai since it is not on the well-worn tourist paths associated with northern India. If you're coming from Hyderabad, the 700 kilometer flight takes about one hour. By train, the trip takes over 14 hours. Flights from both Mumbai and Calcutta take nearly two hours; the flight from Delhi takes two hours and 45 minutes. Trains from Mumbai take 24 hours; from New Delhi, 34 hours; from Calcutta, 28 to 32 hours; and from Hyderabad, over 14 hours. We much prefer the convenience of flying into Chennai.

International flights come into Chennai from Colombo, Dubai, Frankfurt, Jakarta, Kuala Lumpur, London, Mali, Penang, Riyadh, and Singapore.

Located 12 kilometers south of the city center, both the international and domestic airports are next to each other: **Kamarajar National Terminal** and **Aringar Anna International Terminal**. The most convenient way to get from the airport to your city hotel is to go to the prepaid taxi counter as you leave the baggage retrieval area. Purchase a ticket (Rs 220) and then take it to one of the black and yellow cabs waiting outside. Hopefully you'll do better than we did on our last trip—our rickety taxi literally lost a wheel as we left the parking lot of the domestic terminal and turned onto the main street into the city!

GETTING AROUND

Chennai has one of the most convenient city rail systems in India. You'll also find the usual mix of taxis and auto-rickshaws prowling the streets. However, most drivers do not want to use their meters; they prefer quoting you a flat rate which is often high (be sure to negotiate the rate before getting in). Drivers at taxi stands tend to be more expensive than those you flag down along the street. Like in most other Indian cities, our preference is to rent a car with driver by the day or half-day. Cars with drivers are very convenient and relatively inexpensive—US$25 per day for an air-conditioned vehicle. You can easily arrange for a car with driver through your hotel tour desk.

TOURIST OFFICE AND TOURS

Most major hotels have a tour desk through which you can arrange tours or rent a car with driver. Also, look for a listing of tour agencies and car rental firms in the local monthly tourist guide, *Hallo! Madras*. Major tour companies and travel agencies include **American Express Travel Service** (Tel. 852-3628), **All India Travel Agency** (826-9753), **Champion Travel and Tours** (Tel. 825-3419), **Guru Travels** (Tel. 483-049), **Ind Travels** (Tel. 825-3103), **Pegasus Travels and Tours** (Tel. 825-0265), and **Sugir Tours and Travels** (Tel. 499-0645). Government tourist offices are well represented in Chennai: **Government of India Tourist Office** (154, Anna Salai, Tel. 852-4295, open 9:15 - 5:45pm, Monday - Friday; also has a desk at the domestic airport counter); **India Tourism Development Corporation** (29, Victoria Crescent, Commander-in-Chief Road, Tel. 827-8884, 6am - 8pm daily except Sunday until 2pm); and the state (Tamil Nadu) **Tourist Information Centre** (Kamaraj Domestic Terminal, 6am to 9:30pm; Anna International Terminal, 10pm to 6am and all morning flights; Central Railway Station, 7am - 7pm; Egmore Railway Station, 7am - 9pm on working days and 2pm - 9pm on holidays).

USEFUL RESOURCES

You will find lots of useful resources on Chennai to help you organize your stay here. Your hotel and tourist offices, as well as bookstores, should have copies of these tourist materials:

Hallo! Madras (200-page monthly tourist guide)
Chennai This Month (60-page monthly tourist guide)
Madras Shopper's Digest (150-page guide)
At Home in Madras: A Handbook (400-page expat handbook)

You also may want to visit this useful Web site before arriving in Chennai:

www.allindia.com/cities/chennai/default.asp

ORIENTATION

While this is a sprawling city, it's also relatively easy to get around in compared to other large cities in India. The city feels more familiar, comfortable, friendly, and less intimidating than other cities. With a car and driver, you should be able to get around Chennai with relative ease. Most of your activities within the city will be confined to an area that forms a triangle of roads. **Fort St. George** lies at the northern point of this triangle, **San Thome Cathedral Basilica** lies at the southern point, and **Panagal Park** lies at the southwest point of the triangle. The city's main street, which runs at a 45 degree angle southwest of Fort St. George, is **Anna Salai**. Still popularly referred to by its old name, **Mount Road**, this long street includes some of the city's major shopping plazas, handicraft emporiums, and bookstores, such as Spencer Plaza, Victoria Technical Institute, Higgenbothams, and Poompuhar. Most of the major shopping is found just northeast of the intersection of Wood Road and Anna Salai. **Kamarajr Salai**, or **South Beach Road**, runs immediately south of Fort St. George and continues the length of the beautiful broad beachfront called The Marina. However, avoid swimming here since these waters are polluted. The southern boundary of this triangle runs from Panagal Park in the West to San Thome Cathedral Basilica in the East along a road that tends to change its name at each major intersection: **Theagaraya Road, Eldam's Road, Church Road, Kulchery Road**, and **Rosary Church Road**. A few major hotels and sites, such as the Taj Coromandel Hotel on **Nungambakkam High Road**, the Welcome Group Park

Sheraton on **T. T. K. Road**, and the Sri Kapaleeswarar Temple on **Sannadhi Street** are all just outside this triangle.

As you navigate this city, expect to encounter lots of traffic and air pollution, especially along the main street, Anna Salai or Mount Road. You'll also encounter the ubiquitous urban beggar but fewer touts than you find in India's more heavily touristed cities.

SHOPPING CHENNAI

Chennai offers lots of good shopping for textiles, art, jewelry, handicrafts, and furniture. Most of the best shops are found either in or nearby the major hotels, adjacent to temple complexes, and along Anna Salai (Mount Road). A few other worthwhile shops are scattered throughout the city.

WHAT TO BUY

❑ **Textiles:** Chennai is well known for its Kanchipuram silks, sarees, and ready-made clothes. One of the most popular shops offering a wide range of excellent quality silks, sarees, and ready-made garments is **Rasi** (also known as the "Radha Silk Emporium," No. 1, Sannadhi Street, Mylapore, just before the entrance to the Kapaleeswarar Temple, Tel. 494-1906). For excellent quality Kanchipuram silks and sarees, see the hugely popular **Nalli's** (Nalli Chinnasami Chetty, 9 Nageswaram Road, opposite Panagal Park, Tel. 434-4115), Other shops worth visiting include **Alison's Fabrics** (43, College Road, Tel. 726-3358), **Kalpa Druma** (61, Cathedral Road, Tel. 826-7652), **Shilpi** (29 Sir C. P. Rsamaswamy Road, Alwarpet, Tel. 449-0918), **Shreenivas Silks and Saris** (77 Sri Thyagaraya Road, Pondy Bazaar, T. Nagar, Tel. 828-4758), **Handloom House** (Rattan Bazaar), and **Khazana** (Taj Coromandel Hotel, No. 17, Nungambakkam High Road, Tel. 827-2827, Ext. 2012).

❑ **Jewelry:** Several shops offer a good selection of gold and silver jewelry as well as precious stones. In fact, more and more stone cutting, polishing, and manufacturing takes place in Chennai these days, even rivaling the work and prices in Jaipur and Agra. Look for unique pink sapphires from Chennai. For an excellent selection of jewelry, especially pink sapphires, visit the **Cottage Industries Exposition** (opposite Taj Coromandel Hotel, 118,

Nungambakkam High Road, Tel. 827-3438); this is the only CIE emporium out of 47 in India that offers the beautiful pink sapphire. Also, visit **Vummidi** (Spencer Plaza, 769, Anna Salai, Tel. 852-3040) and **G. R. Thanga Maligai** (104 Usman Road, T. Nagar) for gold and silver jewelry.

❑ **Furniture:** Look for lots of old furniture, from doors and chests to tables and chairs, from South India and Sri Lanka in a few shops in Chennai. One of the best selections of restored Portuguese, South Indian, and Sri Lankan furniture is found at **Alison's** (43, College Road, Tel. 826-3358). Also, check out the nice selections at **Habitat** (12, Kader Nawaz Khan Road, Tel. 827-9095, just around the corner from the Taj Coromandel Hotel and C.I.E., its parent company). For something different, try **Murray & Co** (101, Anna Salai, Tel. 534-1748) which holds antique furniture auctions every Sunday at 10:30am; inspection is on Saturday, from 10am to 5:30pm, in their furniture showroom (auction hall is located next door). If you're real lucky, you may find a "diamond in the rough" at Murrays. **Khazana** (Taj Coromandel, No. 17, Nungambakkam High Road, Tel. 827-2827, Ext. 2012) has one of the best sections of old furniture pieces, especially doors, tables, and chests, that we encountered in any of the Khazana shops in India. **Chettinad Handicrafts** ("Bay View", 10 Vaantha Avenue, M. R. C. Nagar, Tel. 493-8789) includes an eclectic mix of furniture and accessories from South India and Burma. **Victoria Technical Institute** (765, Anna Salai Road, Tel. 852-3141) has a large collection of new furniture on second floor.

❑ **Art:** Chennai has a small but vibrant art community whose paintings, sculptures, and other art forms are represented in a few excellent galleries which regularly hold exhibitions. Two of the best are **Apparao Gallery** (7, Wallace Garden, IIIrd Street, Tel. 827-2226) and **Art World** (12 Geneshpuram 3rd Street, off Cenotaph Road, Tel. 433-8691). Also, consider visiting the **Cholamandal Artists Village** (23 kilometers south of city center, Injambakkam, Tel. 492-6092) and **Lalit Kala Akademi** (The National Academy of Art, 170, Greams Road, Tel. 827-7692). **Kalpa Druma** (61, Cathedral Road, Tel. 826-7652) has a small but good quality art gallery on second floor.

❏ **Leather goods:** Chennai is a major center for India's leather industry. Several tanneries and factories in the area produce a wide range of leather products (shoes, purses, wallets, backpacks, briefcases, luggage, belts) for export. The only retail outlets for these products are found in a few shops in the Tower Arcade of the Welcomegroup Park Sheraton Hotel and Towers. Try **Gaitonne** and **Gem Palace** in the arcade.

❏ **Books:** If you're looking for a good selection of books on India, be sure to stop at Chennai's oldest bookstore, **Higginbothams** (814, Anna Salai, Tel. 831-841). For one of the most unusual, chaotic, but personable bookstores in all of India, visit the tiny hole in the wall **Giggles** at the Taj Hotel Connemara shopping arcade.

❏ **Other discoveries:** Chennai is also famous for its beautiful sculptured bronze figures, attractive metalwork, stone sculptures, wood carvings, terracotta, and decorative clay pots. You'll see some of this work in the various handicraft emporiums.

WHERE TO SHOP

The best quality shops in Chennai will be found in and around the major hotels and in a few street shops, handicraft emporiums, and bazaars.

❏ **Handicraft emporiums:** Chennai has three handicraft emporiums worth visiting. The largest are **Cottage Industries Exposition (CIE)** (Opposite Taj Coromandel Hotel, 118, Nungambakkam High Road, Tel. 827-3438); **Victoria Technical Institute** (765, Anna Salai Road, Tel. 852-3141); and **Kalpa Druma** (Across from Welcomgroup Chola Sheraton Hotel and Towers, 61, Cathedral Road, Tel. 826-7652).

❏ **Street shops:** Many good quality shops are located near major temples (**Rasi** on Sannadhi Street), near hotels (**Le Accessory** and **Apparao Gallery** at Wallace Garden and **Habitat** on Kader Nawaz Khan Road), and adjacent to Panagal Park (**Nallis**).

❏ **Shopping centers:** Chennai's largest shopping center is the three-storey enclosed **Spencer Plaza** at 769, Anna

Salai. Here you'll find everything from an American Express office to handicraft shops, leather stores, jewelry shops, clothing stores, a pharmacy, and a small grocery store.

❑ **Hotel shopping arcades:** The largest hotel shopping arcade in Chennai is the Tower Arcade in the **Welcomgroup Park Sheraton Hotel and Towers** with its more than 20 shops many of which offer leather goods, handicrafts, and apparel. The Welcomgroup Chola Sheraton includes a shopping arcade of nearly 10 shops offering everything from carpets to handicrafts, gems, silk, and leather goods. The **Taj Hotel Connemara** also has a very small shopping arcade which has been under renovation. The **Taj Coromandel Hotel** is home to one of the best Khazana shops.

❑ **Bazaars:** Chennai has several popular bazaars which primarily appeal to local shoppers. They offer everything from fresh fruit and vegetables to silk sarees and jewelry: **Pondy Bazaar** (T. Nagar), **Luz Bazaar** (R. K. Mutt Road, Mylapore), **Burma Bazaar** (North Beach Road), **Mylapore Temple Bazaar** (North Mado Street and Church Road), and **Parry's Corner**. Some people also classify the modern shopping center of **Spencer Plaza** as a "bazaar." We don't.

BEST OF THE BEST

We found the following shops to be some of the best in Chennai for both selections and quality:

TEXTILES

❑ **Rasi:** *Also known as the "Radha Silk Emporium." No. 1, Sannadhi Street, Mylapore, just before the entrance to the Kapaleeswarar Temple, Tel. 494-1906.* For excellent quality Kanchipuram silks, sarees, and ready-made clothes, see the hugely popular three-storey shop (basement, main, and first floors). Includes beautiful silk sarees from all over India. Will do both men's and women's tailoring in one day. Look for ready-made clothes on the top level. Expect lots of crowds.

❑ **Nalli's:** *Also known as "Nalli Chinnasami Chetty." 9 Nageswaram Road, opposite Panagal Park, Tel. 434-4115).* If you're interested in Kanchipuram silks and sarees, this is a "must visit" shop. Operating in Chennai for over 75 years, the three floors of this old shop are jam-packed with gorgeous silks and sarees for all price ranges (silk fabric starts around Rs 225, or US$5.50, per meter). You'll find every conceivable type of saree here, including designer and embroidered sarees and signed sarees. While it does not provide tailoring services, the shop will bring in a tailor from across the street if you need one. A great place to get educated about silk and sarees. An interesting cultural experience.

❑ **Alison's Fabrics:** *43, College Road, Tel. 726-3358.* Primarily functions as a designer shop for uniquely designed silk and cotton fabrics. Exports both fabrics and furniture abroad.

❑ **Kalpa Druma:** *Across from Welcomgroup Chola Sheraton Hotel, 61, Cathedral Road, Tel. 826-7652.* A wonderful arts, crafts, and textile shop filled with a wide range of tasteful products that appeal to foreign visitors. The lower level of this three-level shop is crammed with textiles, furnishings, linens, carpets, bedspreads, and quilts.

JEWELRY

❑ **Cottage Industries Exposition (CIE):** *Opposite Taj Coromandel Hotel, 118, Nungambakkam High Road, Tel. 827-3438.* This is one of 47 branches of the Kashmiri handicraft empire. But unlike most branches, this one carries the pink sapphire that is unique to Chennai. It also supplies all other CIE shops and Saga Department Stores with jewelry. Offers nice quality gems and jewelry, especially big emerald rings and necklaces.

❑ **Vummidi:** *Spencer Plaza, 769, Anna Salai, Tel. 852-3040.* Nice displays of good quality traditional South India jewelry in this two-level shop.

FURNITURE

❑ **Alison's:** *43, College Road, Tel. 826-3358.* Popular with expats and dealers who come here for excellent quality old South Indian, Portuguese, and Sri Lankan furniture. Includes tables, chairs, chests, cabinets, and doors. Nicely restored. Also offers an interesting collection of old clocks.

❑ **Habitat:** *12, Kader Nawaz Khan Road, Tel. 827-9095, just around the corner from the Taj Coromandel Hotel and CIE, its parent company.* Found on the lower level (Zodiac men's clothing upstairs), this attractive shop includes lots of old furniture from all over India that has been nicely restored: chests, tables, chairs, and cabinets. Also includes numerous home furnishings, such a table covers, napkin sets, stoneware, pillow covers, bronzes, boxes, papier mache window frames, and marble pieces. Includes a carpet gallery. Popular with expats and interior designers.

❑ **Khazana:** *Taj Coromandel, No. 17, Nungambakkam High Road, Tel. 827-2827, Ext. 2012.* One of the best Khazana shops in India for old furniture pieces, especially old doors, chests, and tables.

ARTS AND CRAFTS

❑ **Kalpa Druma:** *Across from Welcome Chola Sheraton Hotel, 61, Cathedral Road, Tel. 826-7652.* Includes one of Chennai's most tasteful selections of quality arts and crafts: bronzes, furniture, wood boxes, sandalwood carvings, metal work, lamps, inlaid wood pictures, paintings, home furnishings, fabrics, sarees, and textiles. A good place to pick up unique gift items.

❑ **Cottage Industries Exposition (CIE):** *Opposite Taj Coromandel Hotel, 118, Nungambakkam High Road, Tel. 827-3438.* This handicraft emporium has it all. While the main floor includes such high ticket items as jewelry, the second level is jam-packed with papier mache boxes, elephants, and balls; nicely designed cotton and silk clothes; wall hangings; brass items; placemats; copper and enamel work; silk sarees and ties; leather goods; cashmere sweaters; embroidered shawls and tablecloths; jackets; and vests.

❑ **Victoria Technical Institute:** *765, Anna Salai Road, Tel. 852-3141.* Established in 1887, this government-run handicraft emporium has just about everything you can conceive of in the handicraft department, from small collectibles to huge pieces of furniture. Its three floors include jewelry, sandalwood carvings, leather goods, bronzes, brass pieces, paintings, clothes, papier mache, inlaid tables, and rugs. Does its own packing and crating.

❑ **Khazana:** *Taj Coromandel Hotel, No. 17, Nungambakkam High Road, Tel. 827-2827, Ext. 2012.* Tasteful selections of handicrafts and related items. Includes carpets, tribal jewelry, carvings, leather bags, bed covers, ready-made clothes, and furniture.

❑ **Le Accessory:** *7, Wallace Garden, IIIrd Street, Tel. 827-2226.* The shop to the left side and the first two floors of this funky three-storey building (top floor is the Apparao Gallery) includes lots of ethnic terracotta jars, stone pieces, brass items, rugs, pillow covers, hand-printed tiles, wall hangings, trays, coasters, bedspreads, and designer silver door knobs.

ART

❑ **Apparao Gallery:** *7, Wallace Garden, IIIrd Street, Tel. 827-2226.* Located on the top floor of the Le Accessory shop (owner's daughter runs this gallery), this important art gallery represents nearly 500 sculptors and painters. The gallery includes a limited selection of water colors, oils, and sculptures on display. Most of the inventory, which is housed in the back of gallery, must first be viewed and selected by reviewing several photo albums. The inventory of paintings is classified into abstract, landscapes, and figurative paintings.

❑ **Art World:** *12 Geneshpuram 3rd Street, off Cenotaph Road, Tel. 433-8691.* Holds major exhibitions of leading sculptors and painters.

❑ **Cholamandal Artists Village:** *Injambakkam, Tel. 492-6092.* Located 23 kilometers south of Chennai city center on the road to Mahabalipurm temple complex. In operation since 1966, this is a village (houses and studios) of 12 to 24 artists who produce contemporary paintings, sculptures, and jewelry. Items for sale are displayed in two galleries. Offers a good opportunity to meet the artists and purchase their works.

❑ **Lalit Kala Akademi:** *The National Academy of Art, 170, Greams Road, Tel. 827-7692.* Holds regular exhibits of paintings of local artists. Exhibitions change every 10 days. Includes sculptures and ceramics at the rear of this aging compound where 10 artists work in a studio. Paintings start at Rs 3,500 and go up.

ACCOMMODATIONS

Hotels in Chennai tend to be clean and deliver good service. Chennai's best hotels include the following which also tend to have some of the best restaurants and shops in the city:

❑ **Welcomgroup Chola Sheraton:** *10 Cathedral Road, Chennai 600 086, Tel. 91-44-828-0101 or Fax 91-44-827-8779, USA & Canada Toll Free 800-325-3535.* The Chola Sheraton, with just 100 rooms has the feel of a luxury boutique hotel. Situated in the heart of the city and just 13 kilometers from the airport, the public areas—reception lobby, Club facilities and restaurants have just been completely renovated. The lobby is bright and welcoming in gleaming marble and as you step inside you note the understated elegance of the decor. Room floors are presently being renovated and should be completed by the time you read this. The staff is friendly and makes guests feel truly looked after. Two levels of room/service upgrades are available. The Executive Club and Club Exclusive rooms offer additional amenities in the rooms as well as special check-in facility, complimentary breakfast, and a complimentary cocktail hour each evening. The Club Exclusive rooms are actually spacious suites with a double sliding door separating the sitting/business area from the sleeping/dressing area. The Peshwari Restaurant offers Northwest Indian Frontier cuisine; Sagari rooftop restaurant offers a buffet at lunch and Chinese cuisine at dinner; and Café Mercara is a 24-hour beverage boutique offering a wide variety of coffees and teas along with light snacks. A shopping arcade offers a bookshop, florist, gem shops and shops selling Kashmir handicrafts and carpets. Conference and business facilities and fitness center.

❑ **Welcomgroup Park Sheraton Hotel & Towers:** *132 T.T.K. Road, Chennai, 600 018, Tel. 91-44-499-4101 or Fax 91-44-499-7201, USA or Canada Toll Free 800-325-*

3535. The Park Sheraton Hotel & Towers, with its 222 rooms and suites, comprises the larger of the Welcomgroup properties in Chennai. The Executive Club rooms offer a valet service, a business center and use of the Executive Club Lounge Bar. The Sheraton Towers at the Park, connected to, but set apart from the main hotel, is comprised of seven floors of tranquil privacy. Complimentary airport transfers, exclusive express sit-down check-in and check-out, a bottle of chilled champagne brought to your room by your butler following check-in, valet service, complimentary breakfast and an evening cocktail hour are some of the upgraded amenities provided to Towers guests. Dakshin serves cuisine from the four southern Indian states. The poolside barbecue, Khyber serves Northwest frontier cuisine under the stars. The Residency serves multi-cuisines and the Gatsby serves a wide variety of cuisines round the clock. Towers' guests also have use of the Beverage Boutique at the atrium. The Gatsby 2000 discotheque is on the ground floor of the Towers. The shopping arcade has leather shops whose only domestic outlet is at the Park Sheraton—the remainder of their goods are for export—as well as shops selling jewelry, handicrafts, textiles, and carpets. Conference facilities, business center, fitness facilities.

❑ **Taj Coromandel:** *17 Nungambakkam High Road, Chennai, 600 034, Tamil Nadu, Tel. 91-44-827-2827 or Fax 91-44-827-0070, USA & Canada Toll Free 800-458-8825.* The Taj Coromandel, a member of The Leading Hotels of the World, has been completely renovated from the Grand Lobby to the exclusive Club Floors. All 200 guestrooms and suites are soothingly decorated and tastefully furnished in muted tones. Try The Golden Dragon 's Sichuan cuisine, or the Patio for Continental dishes, or Southern Spice for Indian cuisine. A Khazana shop to the left of the entrance to the lobby had some very special old wood carved architectural elements for sale. Conference, business and fitness facilities.

❑ **Fisherman's Cove:** *Covelong Beach, Kanchipuram District, Chennai, 603 112, Tel. 91-4224-44-304 or Fax 91-4414-44-303, USA & Canada Toll Free 800-458-8825.* A Taj resort hotel, Fisherman's Cove is located 32 kilometers from the Chennai airport, between Chennai and Mahabalipuram. If you want to get away from the city and loll on the beach, Fisherman's Cove with its 42 rooms and

38 cottages is the place to go. The rooms may seem a bit basic for a luxury resort if you are used to the natural wood finishes and decorative touches of the Aman Resorts or Four Seasons Resorts in Asia. The Tropicana, located on the deck overlooking the swimming pool serves Indian, Continental and Chinese cuisine as well as a buffet at lunch. The Bay View Point is an open air beach restaurant serving grilled and barbecued seafood specialities. Conference facilities for up to 400 people.

Other good hotels to consider include:

❑ **Ambassador Palava:** *53, Montieth Road, Chennai, Tel. 91-44-855-4476 or Fax 91-44-826-8757.* On older property with 103 rooms, 12 suites, multi cuisine restaurant, shopping arcade, and business services.

❑ **Oberoi Trident Hotel:** *1/24 G. S. T. Road, Chennai Tel. 91-44-234-4747 or Fax 91-44-234-6699.* Located near the airport (10 kilometers from the city center), this attractive property includes 162 rooms, 2 restaurants, and a business center.

❑ **Taj Hotel Connemara:** *Binny's Road, Off Anna Salai, Tel. 91-44-852-0123 or Fax 91-44-852-3361.* 148 rooms. A Taj Group hotel that was once a mansion with old world charm. Recently renovated.

❑ **Quality Inn Aruna:** *144, Sterling Road, Tel. 91-44-825-9090 or Fax 91-44-825-8282.* 88 rooms and 6 suites. Includes multi cuisine restaurant, business center, and shopping arcade.

RESTAURANTS

Compared to Mumbai or Delhi, Chennai is not known for its great restaurants. Nonetheless, you will find many excellent vegetarian restaurants as well as many seafood specialties, such as bay prawns, lobster, and curried softshell crab. Tamil Nadu is especially noted for its spicy dishes and the more generous use of rice and coconut in cooking. Since this is an orthodox Hindu area, expect to find more vegetarian restaurants in Chennai than in most other cities. Like in so many other cities of India, the best restaurants in Chennai tend to be found in the major hotels. Some of Chennai's best restaurants include:

- **Peshwari:** *Welcomgroup Chola Sheraton, 10 Cathedral Road, Tel. 828-0101.* Serves excellent Indian tandoori cuisine in an attractive theme setting. Includes lots of grilled, braised, and roasted meats and breads of India's Northwest Frontier. Be prepared to eat with your fingers and with a large bib tied around your neck. Excellent service.

- **Daksin:** *Welcomgroup Park Sheraton Hotel and Towers, T. T. K. Road, Tel. 499-4101.* Elegant South Indian restaurant where numerous dishes are served on banana leaves in silver *thali* trays and patrons eat with their hands. Musical entertainment provided by two drummers, a flutist, and a violinist.

- **Golden Dragon:** *Taj Coromandel Hotel, 17 Nungambakkam High Road, Tel. 827-2827.* Elegant dining in one of Chennai's finest Chinese restaurants. Cantonese. Probably the best Chinese restaurant in all of South India!

- **Other Room:** *Ambassador Pallava Hotel, 53, Monteith Road, Tel. 826-8584.* Continental and North Indian (tandoori) cuisine. Live band and dancing in the evening (except Wednesday). Lunch buffet.

- **Raintree:** *Taj Hotel Connemara, Binnys Road, Tel. 826-0123.* Serves the famous cuisine of South India's Chettiar community (the bankers of South and Southeast Asia) in a lovely outdoor courtyard setting with classical music and dance on selected nights.

- **Cascade:** *Kakani Towers, K. N. K. Road, near Taj Coromandel Hotel, Tel. 462-2514.* Serves a mixture of Chinese, Japanese, Malaysian, and Thai cuisine. Pleasant surroundings and good service.

- **Dahlia:** *Kaveri Complex, Nungambakkam High Road.* Serves excellent Japanese cuisine in a beauty parlor atmosphere. Very popular with the resident Japanese community.

- **Residency:** *Welcomgroup Park Sheraton Hotel and Towers, T. T. K. Road, Tel. 449-4101.* Serves excellent Chinese, Indian, and Continental cuisine. Offers terrific luncheon buffets.

- ❑ **Annalakshmi:** *804 Anna Salai, Tel. 855-0296.* Probably Chennai's best and most special vegetarian restaurant. Offers numerous dishes from all over India. All food cooked at home and served by volunteers of guru Swami Shantanand.

- ❑ **Shanghai:** *Oberoi Trident Hotel, 1/24 G. S. T. Road, Tel. 234-4747.* Located near the airport, this attractive restaurant offers Chinese and Thai dishes with emphasis on seafood specialties.

SEEING THE SITES

Most of Chennai's major sightseeing centers around its colonial history, Hindu temples, and Christian churches. You can easily cover most of the sites within one day. While Chennai has several interesting museums, temples, and churches, the major sites include:

- ❑ **Fort St. George and Museum:** This landmark structure literally marks the area from where the city of Chennai originally developed. Once the center of British power in India, it now houses the Tamil Nadu Legislative Assembly and Council as well as the offices of the states' Secretariat. Originally built in 1654, the six-foot high walls have withstood many sieges and was even surrendered to the French in 1746 for a two-year period. Of special interest is the worn fort museum which houses a very interesting collection of memorabilia, such as coins, prints, arms, porcelain, and an imposing marble statue of Lord Corwallis that stands at the entry to the museum. Its three floors of galleries include a portrait gallery and the history of the French in India.

- ❑ **Kapaleeswarar Temple:** *Between Chitrukullan North Street and Kutchery Road, Mylapore. Open 4am - noon and 4pm - 8pm daily.* Originally constructed in the 13th century, this is the largest Hindu temple complex in Chennai, a "must see" for any visit to the city. Dedicated to Siva, the 37 meter tall intricately carved *gorpuram* is a masterpiece of Dravidian architecture. A busy temple with hundreds of worshipers. A self-proclaimed guide will probably attach himself to you and then demand an exorbitant fee for his services. Tip him a nominal amount—probably half of what he asks.

❑ **Parthasarathi Temple:** *Peter's Road, Triplicane. Open 6:30 - noon and 4-8pm.* Originally built in the 8th century by the Pallavas, this Vishnu temple is dedicated to Krishna. Considered to be the oldest temple in Chennai.

❑ **San Thome Church (Santhome Cathedral Basilica):** *End of Kutchery Road, Mylapore.* Built near the beach during the 14th and 15th centuries, this church is famous for is historical figures and tombs. St. Thomas, one of the 12 apostles, is said to be buried here (martyred at St. Thomas Mount in 72AD). Several archbishops are buried in the floor of the church. St. Francis Xavier lived here for four months in 1545. Pope Paul IV visited here in 1986.

❑ **St. Mary's Church:** *Fort St. George.* Consecrated in 1679, this is the oldest Anglican church in India. Governor Elihu Yale (of Yale University fame) was married here.

❑ **Church of Our Lady of Expectation:** *Saint Thomas' Mount, Alandur.* Located near the Meenambakkam airport, this is the place where St. Thomas the Apostle was supposedly martyred. Climb the 130+ granite steps to the church on top of the hill for a panoramic view of Chennai and the Bay of Bengal.

❑ **National Art Gallery** and the **Government Museum**: *Pantheon Road. Open 8am to 5pm. Closed Friday.* Located next to each other in Egmore, both were built in 1857. Built in classical Jaina-Jaipuri style. Include interesting sections on geology, archaeology, anthropology, numismatics, and sculpture. The museum includes an excellent collection on bronzes.

❑ **High Court:** *North of Fort St. George at the intersection of N. S. C. Bose Road and Rajaji Salai. Open 10am - 5pm, Monday - Saturday.* An excellent example of Indo-Saracenic architecture. Highly ornamented building constructed of red sandstone. Visitors can tour the corridors and courts.

❑ **Marina Beach:** Locals like to boast that this is either the world's largest or second largest beach. Adjacent to the city, the beach runs for over 12 kilometers. It's big and inviting, but don't swim in its polluted waters. The promenade is used for early morning joggers and evening strollers. Lots of interesting activities along the way.

South Of Chennai

Many visitors to Chennai also include trips to two important temple sites south of the city: Kanchipuram and Mamallapuram. You can visit both places in the same day. However, be sure to leave enough time for the horrendous traffic jam that forms south of Chennai as well as possible stops along the way at the Cholamandal Artists' Village (Injambakkam), Dakshina Chitra (Heritage Centre), Fisherman's Cove Resort, and crocodile farm. **Cholamandal Artists' Village** includes two galleries as well as studios from which in-resident artists produce paintings and sculptures. An interesting place to stop but much more interesting art can be found in Chennai's major art galleries. **Dakshina Chitra**, which is located 20 kilometers south of Chennai and next to Dizzy World, is a 10-acre site designed to preserve, present, and promote the cultural heritage of the diverse people of South India. It includes reconstructed buildings and craft demonstrations as well as discriminatory admission fees (Rs 50 for Indians and Rs 175 for foreigners). Interesting but a much over-hyped and somewhat disappointing venture.

Kanchipuram, the Golden City of 1,000 Temples, is the former capital of the powerful Pallavas. It's located 76 kilometers southwest of Chennai. One of Hindu's seven holy pilgrimage sites, it's an important site for pilgrims who visit the temples to Shiva and Vishnu (temples close between 12:30pm and 4pm). You'll find some shopping opportunities here, especially for Kanchipuram silk and sarees. However, prices are often higher here than in shops in Chennai.

Mamallapuram is located 59 kilometers south of Chennai and 64 kilometers southeast of Kanchipuram. This is a popular site for tourists. It includes four major areas. It's an especially impressive site for its large base reliefs, carved monoliths, and stone temple (only one remains out of seven—the rest have been claimed by the sea). The small town here includes numerous shops that offer a wide range of arts and crafts, especially lots of brass figures. Be careful in acquiring a guide. You can pick up a guide at the town entrance. However, the guides are notorious for ripping off tourists by demanding exorbitant fees at the end of the tour. Agree to a price before he gets into your car. The guide should get about one-fourth to one-third of what he demands. Be firm with these extortionists who envision themselves making US$20 an hour from naive tourists who cave in to their demands!

ENTERTAINMENT

Don't expect a lot of nightlife in this conservative religious community. Most entertainment centers are classical dance and music or is confined to discos, nightclubs, and bars at the major hotels.

Since Chennai is known as a major cultural center in India, much of its entertainment centers around classical dance and Carnatic music. Check with your hotel or the Government of India Tourist Office (154, Anna Salai, Tel. 852-4295) for current performance dates and times. Many of the classical music and dance performances take place at the Music Academy (corner of T. T. K. Road and Dr. Radhakrishnan Salai, Tel. 827-5619) and at Kalakshetra (Temple of Art). Numerous music concerts take place during the annual music festival which occurs between mid-December and January. February is Chennai's dance festival month.

Discos and nightclubs can be found at several major hotels, such as the Welcomgroup Park Sheraton Hotel and Towers (**Gatsby 2000**), Taj Coramandel (**Friday Fundance**), Ambassador Pallava Hotel (**Socko**), and Sindoori Hotel (**After Dark**). **Bars** are also found in the major hotels: Welcomgroup Park Sheraton Hotel and Towers (**Bolan Bar**), Taj Hotel Connemara (**The Bar**), Taj Coramandel (**Fort St. George**), Chola Sheraton (**Durrant's Bar**), The Trident (**Arcot**), and The Sindoori Hotel (**Sakaba**).

Index

MUMBAI (BOMBAY)

DELHI

VARANASI

AGRA

CHENNAI
(MADRAS)

The Authors

Winston Churchill put it best—*"My needs are very simple—I simply want the best of everything."* Indeed, his attitude on life is well and alive amongst many of today's sophisticated travelers. With limited time and careful budgeting, many travelers seek both quality and value as they search for the best of the best.

Ron and Caryl Krannich, Ph.Ds, discovered this fact of travel life 15 years ago when they were living and working in Thailand as consultants with the Office of Prime Minister. Former university professors and specialists on Southeast Asia, they discovered what they really loved to do—shop for quality arts, antiques, and home decorative items—was not well represented in most travel guides that primarily focused on sightseeing, hotels, and restaurants. While some travel guides included a small section on shopping, they only listed types of products and names and addresses of shops, many of which were of questionable quality. And budget guides simply avoided quality shopping altogether.

The Krannichs knew there was much more to travel than what was represented in most travel guides. Avid collectors of Thai, Burmese, Indonesian, and South Pacific arts, antiques, and home decorative items, the Krannichs learned long ago that one of the best ways to experience another culture and meet its talented artists and craftspeople was by shopping for local products. Not only would they learn a great deal about the culture and society, they also acquired some wonderful products, met many interesting and talented individuals, and helped support local arts and crafts.

But they quickly learned shopping in Asia was very different from shopping in North America and Europe. In the West, merchants nicely display items, identify prices, and periodically run sales. At the same time, shoppers in the West can easily do comparative shopping, watch for sales, and trust quality and delivery; they even have consumer protection! Americans and Europeans in Asia face a shopping culture based on different principles. Like a fish out of water, they make many mistakes: don't know how to bargain, fail to communicate effectively with tailors, avoid purchasing large items because they don't understand shipping, and are frequent victims of scams and rip-offs. To shop a country right, travelers need to know how to find quality products, bargain for the best prices, avoid scams, and ship their purchases with ease. What they most need is a combination travel and how-to book that focuses on the best of the best.

In 1987 the Krannichs inaugurated their first shopping guide to Asia—*Shopping in Exotic Places*—which covered Hong Kong, South Korea, Thailand, Indonesia, and Singapore. Receiving rave reviews from leading travel publications and professionals, the book quickly found an enthusiastic audience amongst other avid travelers and shoppers. It broke new ground as a combination travel and how-to book. No longer would shopping be confined to just naming products and identifying names and addresses of shops. It also included advice on how to pack for a shopping trip (take two suitcases, one filled with bubble-wrap), comparative shopping, bargaining skills, and communicating with tailors. Shopping was serious stuff requiring serious treatment of the subject by individuals who understood what they were doing. The Krannichs subsequently expanded the series to include separate volumes on Hong Kong, Thailand, Indonesia, Singapore and Malaysia, Australia and Papua New Guinea, the South Pacific, and the Caribbean.

Beginning in 1996, the series took on a new look as well as an expanded focus. Known as the Impact Guides and appropriately titled *The Treasures and Pleasures . . . Best of the Best*, new editions covered Hong Kong, Thailand, Indonesia, Singapore, Malaysia, Paris and the French Riviera, and the Caribbean. In 1997 and 1999 new volumes appeared on Italy, Hong Kong, and China. New volumes for 2000 will cover India, Australia, Thailand, Hong Kong, Singapore and Bali, Egypt and Jordan, Israel, Vietnam, and the Philippines. While the primary focus remains shopping for quality products, the books also include useful information on the best hotels, restaurants, and sightseeing. As the authors note, *"Our readers are discerning travelers who seek the best of the best. They are looking for a very special travel experience which is not well represented in other travel guides."*

The Krannichs passion for traveling and shopping is well represented in their home which is uniquely designed around their Asian and South Pacific art collections. *"We're fortunate in being able to create a living environment which pulls together so many wonderful travel memories and quality products,"* say the Krannichs. *"We learned long ago to seek out quality products and buy the best we could afford at the time. Quality lasts and is appreciated for years to come. Many of our readers share our passion for quality shopping abroad."* Their books also are popular with designers, antique dealers, and importers who use them for sourcing products and suppliers.

While the Impact Guides keep the Krannichs busy traveling to exotic places, their travel series is an avocation rather than a vocation. The Krannichs also are noted authors of more than 30 career books, some of which deal with how to find international and travel jobs. The Krannichs also operate one of the world's largest career resource centers. Their works are available in most bookstores or through the publisher's online bookstore: *www.impactpublications.com*

If you have any questions or comments for the authors, please direct them to the publisher:

Drs. Ron and Caryl Krannich
IMPACT PUBLICATIONS
9104-N Manassas Drive
Manassas Park, VA 20111-5211
Fax 703-335-9486
E-mail: *krannich@impactpublications.com*

More Treasures
and Pleasures

The following "Impact Guides" can be ordered directly from the publisher. Complete the following form (or list the titles), include your name and address, enclose payment, and send your order to:

IMPACT PUBLICATIONS
9104-N Manassas Drive
Manassas Park, VA 20111-5211 (USA)
Tel. 1-800-361-1055 (orders only)
703/361-7300 (information) Fax 703/335-9486
E-mail: *india@impactpublications.com*
Online bookstore: ***www.impactpublications.com***

All prices are in U.S. dollars. Orders from individuals should be prepaid by check, moneyorder, or Visa, MasterCard, or American Express number. If your order must be shipped outside the U.S., please include an additional US$1.50 per title for surface mail or the appropriate air mail rate for books weighting 24 ounces each. We accept credit card orders by telephone, fax, email, and online (see Impact Publication's travel bookstore on the World Wide Web. Orders are usually shipped within 48 hours. For information on the authors and on our travel resources, please visit our site on the Internet's World Wide Web: ***www.impactpublications.com***

Qty.	TITLES	Price	TOTAL
__	Treasures and Pleasures of Australia	$16.95	_____
__	Treasures and Pleasures of the Caribbean	$16.95	_____
__	Treasures and Pleasures of China	$14.95	_____
__	Treasures and Pleasures of Hong Kong	$16.95	_____
__	Treasures and Pleasures of India	$16.95	_____

__ Treasures and Pleasures of Indonesia $14.95 _____
__ Treasures and Pleasures of Italy $14.95 _____
__ Treasures and Pleasures of Paris
    and the French Riviera $14.95 _____
__ Treasures and Pleasures of Singapore
    and Bali $16.95 _____
__ Treasures and Pleasures of Singapore
    and Malaysia $14.95 _____
__ Treasures and Pleasures of Thailand $16.95 _____

SUBTOTAL ------------- $ _____

- Virginia residents add 4.5% sales tax $ _____

- Shipping/handling ($5.00 for the first
  title and $1.50 for each additional book) $ _____

- Additional amount if shipping outside U.S. $ _____

TOTAL ENCLOSED ---------- $ _____

SHIP TO:

Name _____

Address _____

_____

_____

PAYMENT METHOD:

❑ I enclose check/moneyorder for $ _____
  made payable to IMPACT PUBLICATIONS.

❑ Please charge $ _____ to my credit card:

❑ Visa ❑ MasterCard ❑ American Express ❑ Discover

Card # _____

Expiration date: _____/_____

Signature _____

Experience the "best of the best" in travel Treasures and Pleasures!

Emphasizing the "best of the best" in travel and shopping, the unique Impact Guides take today's discerning travelers into the fascinating worlds of artists, craftspeople, and shopkeepers where they can have a wonderful time discovering quality products and meeting talented, interesting, and friendly people. Each guide is jam-packed with practical travel tips, bargaining strategies, key shopping rules, and recommended shops, hotels, restaurants, and sightseeing. The only guides that show how to have a five-star travel and shopping adventure on a less than stellar budget!

New for 2000!

▶ *The Treasures and Pleasures of Australia: Best of the Best.* April 2000. ISBN 1-57023-060-9

▶ *The Treasures and Pleasures of Hong Kong: Best of the Best.* April 2000. ISBN 1-57023-115-X

▶ *The Treasures and Pleasures of Singapore and Bali: Best of the Best.* April 2000. ISBN 1-57023-133-8

▶ *The Treasures and Pleasures of Thailand: Best of the Best.* April 2000. ISBN 1-57023-076-5

▶ *The Treasures and Pleasures of India: Best of the Best.* January 2000. ISBN 1-57023-056-0

Rave Reviews About The Impact Guides:

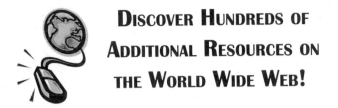

DISCOVER HUNDREDS OF ADDITIONAL RESOURCES ON THE WORLD WIDE WEB!

Looking for the newest and best books, videos, computer software, and kits to help you travel, land a job, negotiate a higher salary, or start your own business? Want to learn the most effective way to shop the world, find a job in Asia or relocate to San Francisco? Curious about how to find a job 24 hours a day using the Internet or about what you'll be doing five years from now? Trying to keep up-to-date on the latest travel and career resources, but are not able to find the latest catalogs, brochures, or newsletters on today's "best of the best" resources?

Now you're only a click away with Impact Publications' electronic solution to the resource challenge. Visit this rich site to quickly discover everything you ever wanted to know about traveling, shopping, finding jobs, changing careers, and starting your own business—including many useful resources that are difficult to find in local bookstores and libraries. The site also includes what's new and hot, helpful tips, and monthly specials. Check it out today!

www.impactpublications.com